£3.50
16/8

A PI[illegible]L GUI[illegible]K AND IRISH GAAP

A PRACTICAL GUIDE TO UK AND IRISH GAAP

Robert Kirk, FCA and
Stephen McNamee, FCA

CHARTERED ACCOUNTANTS IRELAND

Published in 2020 by
Chartered Accountants Ireland
Chartered Accountants House
47–49 Pearse Street
Dublin 2
www.charteredaccountants.ie

ISBN 978-1-910374-46-7

Typeset by Datapage
Printed and bound by CPI Group (UK) Ltd, Croydon, CR0 4YY

MIX
Paper from responsible sources
FSC www.fsc.org FSC® C013604

Contents

Introduction

Prior to 1 January 2015, in the UK and Republic of Ireland the form and content of company financial statements had been driven by a combination of company law (via the EU 4th and 7th Directives) and the application of standard statements of accounting practice (SSAPs) and financial reporting standards (FRSs). In addition, a number of Statements of Recommended Practice (SORPs) were introduced by both private and not-for-profit associations that addressed issues specific to those entities. Although SORPs were not mandatory they were expected to be applied. Underlying this approach was the requirement to show a true and fair view of a company's financial statements.

The FRSs and SSAPs were supplemented by a series of Urgent Issues Task Abstracts or Consensus Pronouncements, in effect mini standards, the objective of which was to close any loopholes in the main standards and to deal quickly with accounting issues that emerged suddenly in financial reporting, e.g. the 'Year 2K' problem. From 1 January 2015 all of these documents ceased to apply and were replaced by a single FRS – FRS 102 *The Financial Reporting Standard applicable in the UK and Republic of Ireland*.

Subsequently, due to changes in EU legislation, a special section for smaller entities was incorporated into FRS 102 (Section 1A *Small Entities*) and a new standard for micro-entities introduced, FRS 105 *The Financial Reporting Standard applicable to the Micro-entities Regime*.

To understand the purpose and rationale of these standards, it is worthwhile to consider their origin and evolution.

A BRIEF HISTORY OF THE DEVELOPMENT OF FRS 102 AND FRS 105

The EU's IAS Regulation (Regulation (EC) 1606/2002) requires that companies governed by the law of a Member State, whose securities are admitted to trading on a regulated market in the EU (publicly traded companies), are required to prepare their consolidated accounts on the basis of EU-adopted IFRS. Article 5 of the IAS Regulation gives Member States the ability to extend the use of EU-adopted IFRS to:

(a) the individual accounts of publicly traded companies; and
(b) the consolidated and/or individual accounts of companies other than publicly traded companies.

In August 2002, the then Department for Trade and Industry (DTI) in the UK issued a consultation document on the possible extension of the

IAS Regulation. Following that consultation, the Government decided that companies would be permitted to choose whether or not to switch the basis of preparation of their accounts to EU-adopted IFRS. Following a further consultation document, 'Modernisation of Accounting Directives/IAS Infrastructure,' issued by the DTI and HM Treasury in March 2004, the UK Government maintained the option for companies to switch to EU-adopted IFRS and extended the option to building societies, limited liability partnerships (LLPs) and certain banking and insurance entities.

In the March 2004 document, the UK Government stated that ultimately it would be preferable for all companies to use the same accounting framework and that, after 2008, it would review the impact of the IAS Regulation to establish if it would be appropriate to mandate wider use of EU-adopted IFRS. The timing of this review would depend, in part, on the development by the Accounting Standards Board (ASB) of a financial reporting regime for smaller companies.

In August 2009 the ASB published a Consultation Paper, 'The Future of UK GAAP', outlining its proposals on how a specialised standard for small and medium-sized enterprises would be implemented in these islands. It was clear that the ASB was committed to work within the International Accounting Standards Board (IASB) framework and to converge UK and Irish GAAP with the framework to the fullest extent possible consistent with the needs of UK and Irish entities. As a consequence of this approach, it was always anticipated that UK and Irish GAAP would cease to exist.

The IASB had proposed a differential, three-tier reporting regime based on public accountability. The ASB envisaged that the UK/Irish framework would follow a similar three-tiered structure.

The ASB's Proposed Reporting Framework[1]

Tier	Accounting Regime	Nature of entity	Reduced disclosures for:
1	EU-adopted IFRS	Publicly accountable	Qualifying subsidiaries
2	FRSME	Entities without public accountability	Qualifying subsidiaries
3	FRSSE	Smaller entities without public accountability	

Under these proposals all entities would have the option to voluntarily adopt a higher tier. For example, Tier 3 entities applying the FRSSE

1 ASB, 'The Future of Financial Reporting in the United Kingdom and Republic of Ireland: The Key Facts', October 2010.

(the Financial Reporting Standard for Smaller Entities) could instead opt to apply either the Tier 2 FRSME (which was based on the IASB's *IFRS for SMEs*) or EU-adopted IFRS under Tier 1; while Tier 2 entities had the option to apply EU-adopted IFRS.

The ASB believed that its proposals would improve financial reporting in the following ways:

(a) reporting arrangements would be simplified by having more targeted and proportionate reporting requirements based on the nature of an entity's accountability obligations and its size;
(b) basing UK and Irish GAAP on IFRS would provide a consistent basis for preparing financial reports and reduce the burden associated with understanding and compliance with different reporting requirements and interpretations of accounting principles. There would also be advantages in terms of accounting education and the professional development of accountants and auditors;
(c) improved comparability and understandability of financial reports would also assist in accessing capital markets and in building investor and creditor confidence by strengthening transparency; and
(d) it would enable the UK and the Republic of Ireland to devote their standard-setting resources to influencing the IASB and ensuring that IFRS satisfied the needs of constituents in the region.

In developing these proposals, the ASB worked with what had become the UK government's Department for Business, Innovation & Skills in considering issues arising from the interaction between accounting standards and company law, including the definition of public accountability to be used. In its 2009 Consultation Paper, the ASB took the view that using IFRS as the basis of future UK and Irish GAAP for certain categories of entity was compatible with the requirements of the EU Accounting Directives. It saw no conflict that would present an insuperable legal barrier to its proposal.

However, mainly due to French and German objections, the European Union were not prepared to give companies derogation from the 4th and 7th Directives. The result was a difficult 'marriage' between complying with the standards and European law.

As we have noted, UK and Irish entities had been given the option to prepare their accounts under EU-adopted IFRS – however, the majority continued, instead, to be subject to companies legislation, which implements into national law the provisions of the EU Accounting Directives. In other words, they continued to prepare their accounts in compliance with the ASB's accounting standards.

Financial Reporting Exposure Drafts 43, 44 and 45

FRED 43 *Application of Financial Reporting Standards* and FRED 44 *Financial Reporting Standard for Medium-sized Entities* (FRSME) were published in

October 2010 for both the UK and the Republic of Ireland and proposed the three-tier system as per the 2009 Consultation Paper but with some exemptions for prudentially regulated small entities that met the small size criteria under the FRSSE. In Ireland, the small size criteria were: less than 50 employees, turnover below €8.8 million and assets less than €4.4 million; in the UK the criteria were: less than 50 employees, turnover below £6.5 million and assets less than £3.26 million. This amendment was intended to help smaller credit unions to adopt the FRSME. The ASB presented the proposed reporting framework as a flowchart, reproduced below.[2]

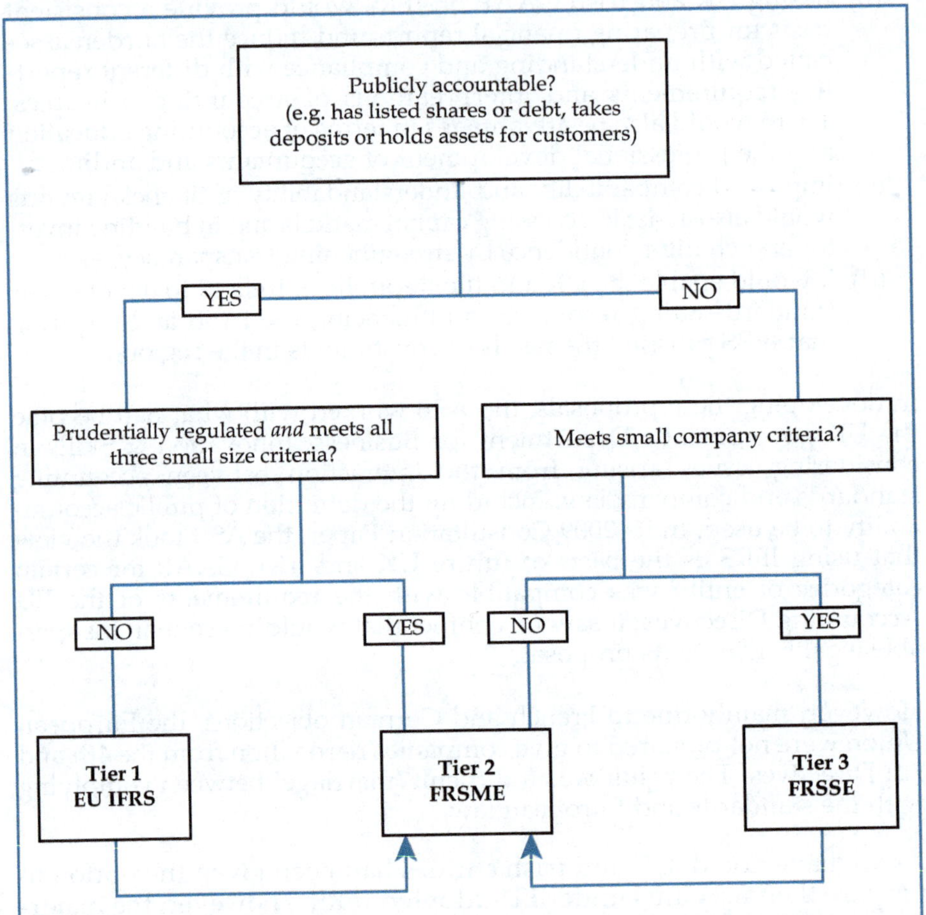

Notes: An entity may "opt up" to a higher tier. Qualifying subsidiaries using Tier 1 or Tier 2 may take disclosure exemptions.

2 ASB, 'The Future of Financial Reporting in the United Kingdom and Republic of Ireland: The Key Facts', October 2010.

In addition, qualifying subsidiaries of parents (whose financial statements were publicly available and where no shareholder objected) could opt for reduced disclosures.

The FRSME was based on the IASB's *IFRS for SMEs*, with the necessary amendments for application in the UK and Republic of Ireland to avoid conflict with EU Directives. The most significant changes were:

- exemption from consolidation if permitted by companies legislation;
- removing certain options not permitted by the Directives;
- inserting some disclosure regarding fair value of certain financial liabilities;
- providing transitional relief for dormant companies; and
- introducing a parent company cash flow statement exemption.

In addition, a further exposure draft, FRED 45 *Financial Reporting Standard for Public Benefit Entities*, was published in March 2011 to introduce a specialised standard for not-for-profit entities. This covered subjects such as concessionary loans, legacies and donations, and the adoption of merger accounting in certain circumstances.

Financial Reporting Exposure Drafts 46–48

After the ASB received the comment letters on FREDs 43–45, it issued revised exposure drafts, FREDs 46–48, in January 2012.

FRED 46 *Application of Financial Reporting Requirements* proposed a revised financial reporting structure whereby:

(i) entities required by law to apply EU-adopted IFRS must do so;
(ii) certain qualifying entities may apply the EU-adopted IFRS with reduced disclosures as set out in FRED 47;
(iii) all other entities apply the draft standard set out in FRED 48; and
(iv) entities eligible to apply the FRSSE may continue to apply it.

FRED 47 *Reduced Disclosure Framework* proposed a reduced disclosure framework, consistent with previous proposals. The ASB recommended that certain entities (mainly subsidiaries and ultimate parents) may apply the recognition and measurement requirements of EU-adopted IFRS with reduced disclosures.

FRED 48 *The Financial Reporting Standard applicable in the UK and Republic of Ireland* proposed replacing all current accounting standards with a single FRS. The ASB adapted the *IFRS for SMEs*, as issued by IASB, as the basis for FRED 48.

FREDs 46–48 were largely actioned with the publication, respectively, of FRS 100 *Application of Financial Reporting Requirements* and FRS 101

Reduced Disclosure Framework in October 2012, and FRS 102 in March 2013. The issuing of these standards was one of the first major actions of the Financial Reporting Council, which had replaced the ASB in July 2012. The FRC also made a commitment that it would review FRS 102 every three years.

The introduction of these new FRSs applied to accounting periods commencing on or after 1 January 2015, with all previous standards withdrawn for accounting periods commencing on or after 1 January 2015. The Statement of Principles was also withdrawn. Early application of the new standards was permitted for accounting periods ending on or after 31 December 2012, subject to certain conditions.

FRS 100 also confirmed that on early adoption, all previous standards were withdrawn earlier.

FRSSE Retained

In view of the European Commission's proposals to change the financial reporting requirements for small and micro-sized entities, the ASB considered that the FRSSE needed to be retained. It agreed to consult further on this standard once the Commission's proposals were clarified.

FRS 100 *Application of Financial Reporting Requirements*

FRS 100 sets the framework under which an entity decides which accounting standard to apply. It also includes key definitions and imposes requirements in relation to SORPs.

FRS 100 was, and in most part still is (apart from the subsequent deletion of the FRSSE and its replacement by FRS 105 and the implementation of Section 1A of FRS 102), applied as follows:

Listed companies for consolidated financial statements	– full EU-adopted IFRS
Listed company subsidiaries and parent companies	– may avail of FRS 101
Non-listed companies	– FRS 102 or full EU-adopted IFRS
Small companies	– FRSSE or FRS 102

FRS 100 requires a 'statement of compliance' in the notes to the financial statements in accordance with the relevant standard.

FRS 101 Reduced Disclosures for Subsidiaries and Ultimate Parents

FRS 101 sets out an optional reduced disclosure framework for certain qualifying entities, allowing them to ignore the disclosure requirements in FRS 102. Non-financial institution qualifying entities (i.e. subsidiaries and parents whose financial statements are included in the consolidated accounts of an entity that prepares publically available financial statements) can avail of the following disclosure exemptions:

- Section 3 *Financial Statement Presentation* (statement of cash flows);
- Section 7 *Statement of Cash Flows* (in full);
- Section 11 *Basic Financial Instruments* (all disclosure) and Section 12 *Other Financial Instruments Issues* (all disclosure provided equivalent disclosures are provided in the consolidated accounts);
- Section 17 *Property, Plant and Equipment* and Section 18 *Intangible Assets other than Goodwill* (disclosure of capital or contractual commitments);
- Section 26 *Share-based Payment* (details of fair value, movement in options during the year, how cash settled liability is determined and any modifications) provided it is included in consolidated accounts and that it does not relate to a group arrangement involving the equity of another entity other than the parent; and
- Section 33 *Related Party Disclosures* (key management compensation).

Financial institutions that are qualifying entities can avail of the same exemptions except for disclosures relating to Sections 11 and 12.

There are no exemptions for qualifying entities that have to prepare, or who voluntarily prepare, consolidated accounts.

If a qualifying entity has financial liabilities that are not part of a trading portfolio or are not derivatives, it must also provide additional disclosure to comply with EU law. These are covered in **Chapter 12**.

A qualifying entity can only take advantage of the disclosure exemptions if:

(a) its shareholders have been notified in writing and do not object;
(b) it applies all other recognition, measurement and disclosure requirements in the FRS; and
(c) it states, in its notes to the financial statements, what sections and paragraphs it is taking exemption from and the name of the parent whose consolidated accounts include those of the entity.

FRS 102 The FRS Applicable in the UK and Republic of Ireland

FRS 102 is intended to apply to reporting entities providing a true and fair view of their financial statements for a reporting period. However, those entities preparing consolidated financial statements under full EU-adopted IFRS, i.e. listed companies, are not eligible.

FRS 102 could, however, apply to individual parents or subsidiaries of listed companies. These entities could also, as 'qualifying entities', have the option of taking advantage of the disclosure exemptions in FRS 101.

All listed companies, and any entity that voluntarily chooses to disclose earnings per share, that prepares interim reports described as "applied in accordance with IAS 34", or that provides segment reporting, must fully comply with IAS 33, IAS 34 and IFRS 8 respectively.

In addition, FRS 103 *Insurance Contracts* must be applied to all insurance contracts.

Statements of Recommended Practice (SORPs) have been published in the UK and Ireland for many years. They are not mandatory but are expected to be adopted in order to provide a true and fair view. Under the new regime all private sector SORPs were withdrawn, while a number of public sector SORPs were revised in line with FRS 102.

These public sector SORPs have been developed separately from FRS 102 by organisations such as the Charities Commission and the UK Vice Chancellors' Committee. They are based on FRS 102 and were updated for the triennial review of FRS 102 published in March 2018.

As noted previously, the new FRSs had to be applied for accounting periods beginning on or after 1 January 2015, with early application permitted for accounting periods ending on or after 31 December 2012 on the proviso that entities that were within the scope of a SORP could only adopt early if that did not conflict with the requirements of a current SORP or legal requirements. The fact of early adoption had to be disclosed.

SORPs are not covered in this publication and readers should refer to those documents in addition to following the rules in FRS 102.

Derivation Table

FRS 102 was developed by following a dual methodology:

(a) extracting the fundamental concepts from the IASB's *Conceptual Framework for Financial Reporting* and the principles and related mandatory guidance from IFRSs (including Interpretations); and

(b) considering the modifications that would be appropriate on the basis of users' needs and cost–benefit considerations.

The table below identifies the primary sources in full IFRSs from which the principles in each section of FRS 102 were derived.

Section in FRS 102	**Source(s)**
Preface	Preface to International Financial Reporting Standards
1 Scope	–
2 Concepts and Pervasive Principles	IASB Framework, IAS 1 *Presentation of Financial Statements* (2007)
3 Financial Statement Presentation	IAS 1
4 Statement of Financial Position	IAS 1
5 Statement of Comprehensive Income and Income Statement	IAS 1
6 Statement of Changes in Equity and Statement of Comprehensive Income and Retained Earnings	IAS 1
7 Statement of Cash Flows	IAS 7 *Statement of Cash Flows*
8 Notes to the Financial Statements	IAS 1
9 Consolidated and Separate Financial Statements	IAS 27 *Consolidated and Separate Financial Statements* (2008)
10 Accounting Policies, Estimates and Errors	IAS 8 *Accounting Policies, Changes in Accounting Estimates and Errors*
11 Basic Financial Instruments 12 Other Financial Instruments Issues	IAS 32 *Financial Instruments: Presentation* IAS 39 *Financial Instruments: Recognition and Measurement* IFRS 7 *Financial Instruments: Disclosures*
13 Inventories	IAS 2 *Inventories*
14 Investments in Associates	IAS 28 *Investments in Associates*
15 Investments in Joint Ventures	IAS 31 *Interests in Joint Ventures*
16 Investment Property	IAS 40 *Investment Property*
17 Property, Plant and Equipment	IAS 16 *Property, Plant and Equipment*
18 Intangible Assets other than Goodwill	IAS 38 *Intangible Assets*
19 Business Combinations and Goodwill	IFRS 3 *Business Combinations* (2008)
20 Leases	IAS 17 *Leases*
21 Provisions and Contingencies	IAS 37 *Provisions, Contingent Liabilities and Contingent Assets*
22 Liabilities and Equity	IAS 1 and IAS 32
23 Revenue	IAS 11 *Construction Contracts* IAS 18 *Revenue*
24 Grants	IAS 20 *Accounting for Government Grants and Disclosure of Government Assistance*
25 Borrowing Costs	IAS 23 *Borrowing Costs*

26 Share-based Payment	IFRS 2 *Share-based Payment*
27 Impairment of assets	IAS 2 *Inventories* and IAS 36 *Impairment of Assets*
28 Employee Benefits	IAS 19 *Employee Benefits*
29 Income Tax	IAS 12 *Income Taxes*
30 Foreign Currency Translation	IAS 21 *The Effects of Changes in Foreign Exchange Rates*
31 Hyperinflation	IAS 29 *Financial Reporting in Hyperinflationary Economies*
32 Events after the End of the Reporting Period Date	IAS 10 *Events after the Reporting Date*
33 Related Party Disclosures	IAS 24 *Related Party Disclosures*
34 Specialised Industries	IAS 41 *Agriculture* IFRS 6 *Exploration for and Evaluation of Mineral Resources*
35 Transition to the FRS	IFRS 1 *First-time Adoption of International Financial Reporting Standards*

Later Developments

Since the initial implementation of FRS 102 in March 2013, two significant changes have been implemented that impact on financial reporting in the UK and the Republic of Ireland.

First, a new EU Directive was issued, which combined the 4th and 7th Directives for company and group reporting respectively. This Directive had a twofold effect: it introduced a new accounting regime for micro-entities; and it introduced substantial reductions in disclosure requirements for small entities. EU Member States were required to adopt the Directive by 2015.

Secondly, in 2017 the FRC carried out its first triennial review of FRS 102 (which was incorporated into the standard and published in March 2018) and made over 160 changes. Most of the changes were editorial, but a number of important amendments were made, particularly with regard to accounting for investment properties, intangible assets and financial instruments.

A New Regime for Micro-entities – FRS 105

FRS 102 was designed with the large private company in mind, and it was realised that it did not make sense to enforce the same rules on micro-entities – the local coffee shop, hairdresser or corner shop – and for such businesses to incur significant costs to comply with a standard that for the most part did not apply to their situation. The local coffee shop did not need to make up to 300 disclosures in its annual accounts, nor introduce complicated rules on fair value reporting, capitalisation of interest and so on.

The new accounting regime for micro-entities, FRS 105 in the UK and Republic of Ireland, introduces a simplified and more appropriate accounting framework, and can result in considerable cost savings for those qualifying businesses that choose to adopt it.

The basic structure of FRS 102 is retained in FRS 105 to enable companies to switch to a higher level of reporting if at some point they exceed the micro-entity criteria. In the Republic of Ireland, micro-entities are defined as meeting two of the following three criteria: entities with 10 employees or less; turnover of €700,000 or less; and balance sheet assets of €350,000 or less. In the UK, two of the following must be met: entities with 10 employees or less; turnover of £632,000 or less; and balance sheet assets of £316,000 or less.

The UK implemented the required legislation in December 2013 for accounting periods commencing on or after 1 December 2013; in the Republic of Ireland the legislation was passed in May 2017, but qualifying micro-entities were able to backdate its implementation to financial statements commencing on or after 1 January 2015.

In both jurisdictions, compliance with FRS 105 also complies with the legal requirement to provide a true and fair view, thus no additional disclosures are required (although additional disclosures may be provided if they wish). The key differences in recognition, measurement and disclosure for FRS 105 are outlined at the end of each chapter of this book.

A New Regime for Small Entities – Section 1A, FRS 102

At the same time as the new micro-entity regime was introduced, a similar significant development also occurred for small entities: the insertion of a new Section 1A into FRS 102 and the insertion of new Schedules specifically designed for smaller entities to create a simpler financial reporting regime.

The rationale for this development was the same as for micro-entities, i.e. the realisation that FRS 102 was too costly and cumbersome for smaller entities. However, unlike micro-entities, the recognition and measurement rules were felt to be important and were retained. Small companies, therefore, must deal with fair value reporting and the amortised cost rules for basic financial instruments, which can be quite complicated.

The main, and only, benefit of Section 1A, therefore, is to significantly reduce the amount of disclosure required by identifying what must be mandated to be disclosed under company law. To achieve that purpose, an additional 22 paragraphs were incorporated as Section 1A, detailing the disclosures that would be mandatory (but that do not necessarily provide a true and fair view) for small entities.

In the Republic of Ireland, small entities are those meeting two of the following three criteria: entities with 50 employees or less; turnover of €12 million or less; and balance sheet assets of €6 million or less. In the UK, two of the following must be met: less than 50 employees; turnover of £10.2 million or less; and £5.1 million or less in balance sheet assets.

In both jurisdictions, compliance with the mandatory disclosures will, unfortunately, not necessarily provide a true and fair view. Thus the entity will have to decide what additional information must be provided to achieve that aim. It is left up to the directors of the small entity to decide what disclosures (from the 300+ disclosures in FRS 102) are required.

The mandatory disclosures required under Section 1A have been included at the end of each chapter of this book.

FRS 102 Triennial Review

When FRS 102 was first published in March 2013, it was promised that after three years adoption in practice it should be reviewed and updated, and subsequently reviewed every three years. The first triennial review was completed in 2017, resulting in an amended FRS 102 published in March 2018. The amendments were to be applied for accounting periods commencing 1 January 2019, although, if all applied together, they could be adopted earlier.

The review entailed looking at a number of sources:

- reviewing changes in the *IFRS for SMEs* on which FRS 102 is largely based;
- reviewing recent developments in the full IFRSs; and
- receiving feedback from preparers and users of FRS 102 on its application to date.

As a result, 162 amendments were incorporated into FRS 102, most of which were minor changes in wording and 'crossing Ts and dotting Is'. However, a number of important changes in recognition and measurement have been made to areas such as financial instruments, intangible assets and investment properties, amongst others. Major changes to the full IFRSs on revenue recognition, financial instruments and leases have not yet been incorporated into FRS 102, but it is envisaged that these will be included in the next triennial review.

THE STRUCTURE OF THIS BOOK

This book provides an in-depth review of the content of the main standard, FRS 102 (including Section 1A, Small Entities), but also considers the new micro-entities regime (FRS 105) and how it differs from the main standard. To help readers follow a more logical progression when preparing their financial statements, the book is structured around the key components of financial statements, bringing together the relevant Sections of the standards as they apply to that component. Numerous examples are used throughout to support a better understanding of how to apply the Standard. In this new edition, the inclusion of extracts from the annual accounts of many different types and size of business in Ireland and Northern Ireland have been used to highlight good practice in the application of FRS 102.

This edition is updated to FRS 102 as published in March 2018, and as such includes the major amendments implemented in the FRC's first triennial review. Where these are considered significant, they are specifically mentioned as recent so that readers can identify where the changes have taken place.

At the end of each chapter, the a checklist of the reduced mandatory disclosures adopted by the small entities regime under FRS 102 Section 1A are listed (see above), as are the differences in accounting treatment and disclosure for micro-entities under FRS 105 when compared to FRS 102.

The chapters are broken down as follows:

- Chapter 1 – Presentation of Financial Statements: dealing with the preparation of the primary financial statements of a reporting entity under FRS 102, it covers six Sections of the Standard.
- Chapter 2 – Concepts and Persuasive Principles: a short chapter covering only one Section, but one of vital importance as it must be referred to if a solution to an unusual accounting problem cannot be found elsewhere in the Standard.
- Chapter 3 – Asset Valuation – Non-current Assets: this chapter covers five Sections of the Standard, including how to account for: property, plant and equipment; investment properties; government grants; the impairment of assets; and the possibility of capitalising borrowing costs.
- Chapter 4 – Asset Valuation – Intangible Assets: covers intangible assets other than goodwill and leases. (Leases is included within this chapter, rather than in Chapter 6, Liabilities, on the basis that they give rise to right-of-use assets.)
- Chapter 5 – Asset Valuation – Inventories: a short chapter covering the topic of inventories.
- Chapter 6 – Liabilities: this chapter covers provisions and contingencies, income tax and the Section that distinguishes liabilities from equity.
- Chapter 7 – Performance Measurement: concentrating on performance measurement, this chapter covers revenue recognition and how to distinguish between a change in policy and a change in estimate as well as accounting for errors.
- Chapter 8 – Employee Costs: this chapter covers all types of employee benefits, including share-based payments.

- Chapter 9 – Foreign Currency Translation: this chapter covers the three issues of foreign currency transaction accounting, translation accounting and how to deal with hyperinflationary situations.
- Chapter 10 – Disclosure Sections: this chapter mainly covers the disclosures required for post-balance sheets events and related party transactions.
- Chapter 11 – Group Accounting: chapter covering the process of preparing consolidated financial statements, and how to account for associate and joint arrangement relationships.
- Chapter 12 – Financial Instruments: this chapter breaks financial instruments into basic and complex issues and how to account for both financial assets and liabilities in the financial statements.
- Chapter 13 – Specialised Activities: Section 34 *Specialised Activities* is one of the longest sections of FRS 102 and so has been split into two chapters. This chapter deals with specialised activities such as agriculture, heritage assets, pension scheme accounts and additional disclosures for financial institutions.
- Chapter 14 – Public Benefit Entities: the second part of Section 34 covers the unusual situations that emerge in public benefit entity accounting, such as legacies and donations, concessionary loans and the possible use of merger accounting.
- Chapter 15 – Transition to FRS 102: the final chapter covers the procedures that an entity has to apply when applying FRS 102 for the first time and the reconciliations required to be disclosed as part of that process.

Acknowledgements

We would like to thank the following companies for their kind permission to publish extracts from their company accounts: Bibby Line Group Limited; Brett Martin Limited; Carbery Food Ingredients Limited; Dairygold Co-Operative Limited; Eakin Brothers Limited; Eason & Son Limited; Fyffes Limited; GP Wood Limited; McEniff's Grand Canal Hotel Limited, Musgrave Group plc; Ornua Co-operative Limited; Randox Holdings Limited; and Ulster Carpet Mills (Holdings) Limited.

We would also like to thank Michael Diviney and Liam Boyle at Chartered Accountants Ireland for their help in drafting, editing and producing this book. Thanks is due also to Brian Murphy for his review of an early proof.

Chapter 1

PRESENTATION OF FINANCIAL STATEMENTS

FRS 102 ('the FRS') includes a number of sections at its start (Sections 3 to 9) explaining what primary statements should be included in an annual report together with some detail on their presentation. The headings are virtually the same as the full IFRS (IAS 1 *Presentation of Financial Statements*).

1.1 FINANCIAL STATEMENT PRESENTATION (SECTION 3)

Section 3 of FRS 102 covers the broad aspects that reporting entities must bear in mind when deciding the format and content of their financial statements. Most of this has already been adopted by local accounting standards and company law.

Fair Presentation

The FRS requires entities to publish financial statements that fairly present the financial position, financial performance and cash flows of an entity. This obviously requires directors to faithfully represent transactions in accordance with the definitions and recognition criteria for assets, liabilities, income and expenses.

The Financial Reporting Council (FRC) takes the view that applying the FRS (with additional disclosure) is presumed to result in a fair presentation.

Additional disclosures are necessary when compliance with the specific requirements in the FRS is insufficient to enable users to understand the effect of particular transactions. In practice, this should be fairly rare.

Compliance with the FRS

Every entity, when preparing its financial statements under the FRS, must make an explicit and unreserved statement of compliance with the FRS in the notes. However, that statement cannot be adopted unless the entity is sure that the financial statements comply with all the requirements of the FRS.

Example 1.1: Statement of Compliance Note to the Financial Statements

2. Basis of preparation and accounting policies
These consolidated financial statements have been prepared in accordance with FRS 102, the Financial Reporting Standard applicable in the UK and Republic of Ireland issued by the Financial Reporting Council. They are presented in the currency units (€) of the Republic of Ireland.

Where a **public benefit entity** (PBE) is applying the special sections of the FRS with the prefix PBE attached, it must make an explicit statement that it is a PBE.

In extremely rare circumstances, it may be possible that compliance with the FRS could be so misleading that it would conflict with the objective of the financial statements. This is sometimes known as the 'fair presentation override'. The use of this override has been attempted by Plcs using full IFRS. However, the Financial Reporting Review Panel (FRRP) in the UK has taken a hard line and refused a listed company's attempt to override IAS 32 *Financial Instruments: Presentation* by placing participating preference shares (PPS) in equity when their substance was in fact debt[1]. Presentation in accordance with IAS 32 would have resulted in substantially all of the carrying value of the PPS being allocated to the liability component and the fixed net cash dividend being treated as an expense in the profit and loss account. The FRRP considered that this treatment would not fairly present the substance of the PPS as permanent capital in the company with participation in the future income and gains arising, as such, it would be so misleading that it would conflict with the objective of financial statements set out in the *Conceptual Framework for Financial Reporting*.

The FRRP found that the circumstances did not constitute an extremely rare case where compliance with a standard would be so misleading as to require departure from the requirements of IAS 32. A fair presentation could have been achieved through full recognition of the liability component in compliance with the standard, supplemented by disclosures explaining the characteristics and permanent nature of the instruments.

The fair presentation override is, therefore, unlikely to be seen in practice.

---

1 Financial Reporting Review Panel, Press Notice 113, 'Findings of the Financial Reporting Review Panel in respect of the accounts of The Investment Company PLC for the years ended 31 March 2007 and 31 March 2006', 8 August 2008.

Disclosure if Able to Exercise Fair Presentation Override

If an entity is able to exercise the fair presentation override, it must disclose the following:

(a) that management has concluded that the financial statements fairly present the financial position, the performance and the cash flows of the entity;
(b) it has complied with the FRS except for a particular requirement; and
(c) the nature of departure, including details of the normal accounting treatment, the reason for its non-adoption and the actual accounting treatment adopted.

In addition, if an entity has departed from the FRS in a prior period and that has affected the financial statements of the current period, the disclosures should also be provided, as above, for the current period.

Going Concern

Each year, all reporting entities need to assess their ability to continue as a going concern. If they discover material uncertainties that cast significant doubt about their ability to carry on as a going concern, those uncertainties must be disclosed.

If the financial statements are not prepared under the going concern concept (probably using the break-up basis of accounting, where assets and liabilities are valued as if being sold off or paid off immediately), that fact should be disclosed together with the basis on which the financial statements **have** been prepared, and the reason why the reporting entity is no longer regarded as a going concern.

Frequency of Reporting

All reporting entities should report at least annually. If the reporting period chosen is longer or shorter than a year, there is a need to disclose:

(a) that fact;
(b) the reason for using a longer or shorter period; and
(c) the fact that comparatives are not entirely comparable.

Consistency of Presentation

In order to achieve comparability, it is important that entities retain both the same presentation and classification from one period to the next, unless:

(a) there is a significant change in the nature of operations; or
(b) the FRS requires a change in presentation.

If a reporting entity decides to change its presentation or classification, the previous year's comparatives need to be restated in order to ensure comparability from year to year. For example, Readymix Plc decided a number of years ago to move haulage costs from distribution expenses to cost of sales, but in doing so it also had to restate the previous year's classification to ensure comparability and consistency in presentation. However, if that is impracticable in terms of cost or effort, it does not have to take place.

When the comparatives are reclassified, the following needs to be disclosed:
(a) the nature of the reclassification;
(b) the amount of each item (or class of items) that is reclassified; and
(c) the reason for the reclassification.

If it is impracticable to reclassify, an entity should disclose why that is the case. An example of a reclassification can be seen in full IFRS in the financial statements of C & C Group Plc.

C & C Group Plc

Annual Report and Accounts 2011

NOTES, FORMING PART OF THE FINANCIAL STATEMENTS (EXTRACT)

1. Prior year reclassification

To enhance the transparency and understanding of the underlying net revenue performance of the Group and to mirror reporting practice within the drinks industry, the Directors considered it appropriate to highlight separately the value of Revenue net of excise duties (Net revenue) and consequently amended the classification of excise duty in the income statement. Excise duties represent a significant proportion of Revenue, are set by external regulators over which the Group has no control and are generally passed on to the consumer. On this basis, the Directors consider that the disclosure of Net revenue provides a more meaningful analysis of underlying performance. In the previous financial years, the Group classified excise duty costs within operating costs.

This classification amendment has no impact on the profit for the financial year or the previous financial year or on the financial position (net assets) of the Group as reported. The impact of the classification change on operating costs for continuing operations in both year's is shown below:

	2011		2010	
	Operating costs €m	Operating profit €m	Operating costs €m	Operating profit €m
Previous classification	**701.2**	**88.5**	419.5	71.3
Impact of change	**(260.1)**	**–**	(128.1)	–
Current classification	**441.1**	**88.5**	291.4	71.3

Comparative Information

Comparatives for the previous reporting period for all amounts in the financial statements should be disclosed, including notes. This includes both narrative and descriptive information, if relevant. Occasionally, the FRS may permit non-disclosure. For instance, reconciliations of items of fixed assets, in accordance with the Companies Act 2014 (in the ROI) and the Companies Act 2006 (in the UK), need not have comparatives presented.

Materiality and Aggregation

Each material class of similar items should be disclosed separately. However, dissimilar items should be disclosed separately unless they are immaterial. To get around that problem, aggregation of similar items may make the item itself material. For example, while the purchase of 20 laptops at €500 each is material, the purchase of one on its own is not.

Omissions or misstatements are material if they could affect user decisions – that really depends on the size and nature of the omission/misstatement.

Specific disclosures are not required if the information is not material. This is true even if disclosure is a specific requirement, or described as 'minimum requirements' in the FRS.

Complete Set of Financial Statements

FRS 102 describes the primary statements that form the heart of an entity's financial statements. A complete set of financial statements should include:

(a) a statement of financial position at the reporting date;
(b) either:
   (i) a single statement of comprehensive income for the reporting period displaying all items of income and expenses and items of other comprehensive income, or
   (ii) an income statement and separate statement of comprehensive income for the reporting period;
(c) a statement of changes in equity;
(d) a statement of cash flows; and
(e) notes, including a summary of the significant accounting policies adopted and any other explanatory information for the reporting period.

If the only changes to equity arise from profit or loss, payments of dividends, corrections of prior period errors or changes in accounting policy, then the entity may present a single statement of income and retained earnings instead of the statement of comprehensive income and the statement of changes in equity.

If an entity has no items of comprehensive income, it may present only an income statement; or present a statement of comprehensive income clearly labelled at the bottom 'profit or loss'.

There is a requirement for a minimum of two sets of financial statements and notes, including comparatives, and each financial statement should be displayed with equal prominence. An entity may use titles other than those used in the FRS as long as these are not misleading (e.g. 'balance sheet' may be used instead of 'statement of financial position').

Identification of the Financial Statements

Each of the financial statements should be clearly identified and, in addition, the following should be displayed:

(a) the name of the reporting entity;
(b) whether the financial statements cover an individual entity or a group of entities;
(c) the date of the end of the reporting period or the period covered by the financial statements;
(d) the presentation currency; and
(e) the level of rounding, if any.

In addition, the following must be disclosed in the notes:

(a) the legal form of the entity, its country of incorporation and the address of its registered office or principal place of business, if different; and
(b) a description of the nature of the entity's operations and of its principal activities.

Presentation of Information not required by FRS 102

The FRS does not specifically address segment reporting, earnings per share (EPS) or interim reporting. However, under the FRS, if companies wish to make such disclosures they must apply the full relevant EU-adopted IFRS (i.e. IAS 33 *Earnings Per Share*, IAS 34 *Interim Financial Reporting* and IFRS 8 *Operating Segments*) which describe the basis for preparing and presenting that information. The FRC has published FRS 104 *Interim Financial Reporting* as a simplified version of IAS 34, but it is not obligatory to adopt if a company wishes to publish interim accounts.

1.2 STATEMENT OF FINANCIAL POSITION (SECTION 4)

The statement of financial position (or balance sheet) presents an entity's assets, liabilities and equity at a specific date, i.e. at the end of the reporting period.

Information to be Presented in the Statement of Financial Position

Non-banking/non-insurance entities must prepare a balance sheet in accordance with company law, but they can include additional line items, headings and sub-totals if such are relevant in understanding the entity's financial position.

Debtors and Creditors: Amounts Falling Due within One Year

Assets and liabilities must be classified separately between current and non-current items on the face of the statement of financial position and must comply with the headings under company law.

A liability must be classified as due within one year if the entity does not have an unconditional right to defer settlement of the liability for at least 12 months after the reporting date.

Where debtors of more than one year's duration are **material** (and in the absence of their disclosure on the face of the statement of financial position), they must be disclosed within current assets on the face of the balance sheet; if not material, they can be disclosed in the notes instead.

Information to be Presented either on the Face of the Statement of Financial Position or in the Notes

An entity with share capital should disclose the following on the statement of financial position or in the notes:

(a) for each class of share capital: the number issued, fully paid, par value per share, rights and restrictions, shares held by subsidiaries, associates or joint ventures and shares received under options; and
(b) a description of each reserve within equity.

An entity without share capital, e.g. a partnership or trust, should disclose equivalent information.

Information to be Presented in the Notes

If, at the reporting date, an entity has a binding sale agreement for a major disposal of assets or a group of assets and liabilities, it must disclose the following information:

- a description of the assets or group of assets and liabilities;
- a description of the facts and circumstances of the sale or plan; and
- the carrying amount of assets or group of assets/liabilities.

The following example illustrates what a balance sheet should look like according to FRS 102. It is based on a set of illustrative financial statements published by the Accounting Standards Board (the predecessor to the FRC) in October 2010. The suggested layout is designed to ensure compliance with both the FRS and existing company legislation.

Example 1.2: Illustrative Balance Sheet

Balance Sheet
at 31 December 20X1

	Note	**20X1**	20X0
		£000	£000
Non-current assets			
Investment property		345	345
Property, plant and equipment		3,466	3,751

Tangible assets	**3,811**	4,096
Intangible assets	**1,245**	1,412
Investments	**360**	360
	5,416	5,868
Deferred tax assets	100	90
Debtors due after more than one year	175	175
Total other non-current assets	**275**	265
Total non-current assets	**5,691**	6,133
Current assets		
Stocks	**831**	706
Debtors – due within one year	**1,202**	1,318
– due after more than one year	**175**	175
Cash at bank and in hand	**212**	186
Total current assets	**2,420**	2,385
Creditors: amounts falling due within one year		
Trade creditors	**1,296**	1,800
Bank loans and overdrafts	18	
Current tax liability	100	120
Other financial liabilities	212	255
Other creditors, including tax and social security	**330**	375
Accruals and deferred income	**198**	180
Total current liabilities	**1,824**	2,355
Net current assets	**596**	30
Total assets less current liabilities	**6,112**	5,988
Creditors: amounts falling due after more than one year	**2,840**	2,900
Deferred tax liabilities	112	97
Other provisions	353	313
Provisions for liabilities	**465**	410
Total non-current liabilities	**3,305**	3,310
Net assets	**2,807**	2,678
Capital and reserves		
Called up share capital	100	100
Share premium account	1,400	1,400
Profit and loss account	1,307	1,178
Equity attributable to owners of the company	**2,807**	2,678

The Irish group, Musgrave Group Plc, provides a good real-life example of a balance sheet (statement of financial position) in accordance with FRS 102.

Musgrave Group Plc
CONSOLIDATED BALANCE SHEET
as at 29 December 2018

	Notes	2018 €m	2017 €m
Fixed assets			
Intangible assets	11	103.1	55.6
Tangible assets	12	400.2	366.2
Investment properties	12	37.3	37.4
		540.6	459.2
Current assets			
Stocks	14	146.2	144.0
Debtors – Amounts falling due within one year	15	486.6	478.3
Debtors – Amounts falling due after more than one year	16	29.3	28.2
Cash at bank and in hand	20	54.3	145.7
		716.4	796.2
Creditors – Amounts falling due within one year	18	(704.7)	(748.1)
Net current assets		11.7	48.1
Total assets less current liabilities		552.3	507.3
Creditors – Amounts falling due after more than one year	19	(33.8)	(7.3)
Provisions for liabilities	21	(42.3)	(48.6)
		476.2	451.4
Pension liability	30	(66.4)	(121.0)
Net assets		409.8	330.4
Capital and reserves			
Called-up share capital presented as equity	23/24	28.8	28.8
Share premium account	24	2.7	2.7
Capital redemption reserve	24	2.5	2.5
Revaluation reserve	24	20.6	21.0
Other reserves	24	2.0	4.7
Profit and loss account	24/25	353.2	270.7
Equity shareholders' funds		409.8	330.4

The notes on pages 31 to 56 form an integral part of these financial statements.

1.3 STATEMENT OF COMPREHENSIVE INCOME AND INCOME STATEMENT (SECTION 5)

FRS 102 requires reporting entities to disclose either a single statement of comprehensive income or two statements and the content therein.

Presentation of Total Comprehensive Income

Entities must present total comprehensive income for a period either:

(a) in a single statement of comprehensive income; or
(b) in two statements – an income statement (i.e. a profit and loss account under company law) and a statement of comprehensive income.

A change from a single-statement to a two-statement approach is regarded as a change in accounting policy under Section 10 of the FRS.

Single-statement Approach

All items of income and expense are included for the period unless FRS 102 requires otherwise. A different treatment is required for:

(a) correction of material errors or changes in accounting policies are presented as retrospective adjustments of prior periods rather than as part of the profit and loss for the period;
(b) the five types of other comprehensive income recognised outside profit but included in comprehensive income:
    (i) gains and losses on translation (Section 30 – see **Chapter 9**),
    (ii) actuarial gains and losses (Section 28 – see **Chapter 8**),
    (iii) changes in fair values of hedging instruments (Section 12 – see **Chapter 12**),
    (iv) changes in fair values of investments in subsidiaries, associates and joint ventures (Sections 9, 14 and 15 – see **Chapter 11**), and
    (v) gains and losses on revaluation of property, intangible assets and heritage assets (Sections 17, 18 and 34 – see **Chapters 3, 4** and **13**).

A non-banking/non-insurance entity or group must present items in the profit and loss account under company law. Banking/insurance entities and groups must present under various Schedules to the Companies Acts (in the Republic of Ireland, the Companies Act 2014 (CA 2014); in the UK, the Companies Act 2006 (CA 2006)).

In addition, reporting entities must include the following line items:

(a) each item of other comprehensive income (OCI) by nature. These can be disclosed net of tax or gross, with total tax on all items deducted separately;
(b) share of OCI of associates and jointly controlled entities under the equity method; and
(c) total comprehensive income.

An entity should also disclose the following, as allocations, separately:

(a) profit or loss for the period attributable to:
   (i) non-controlling interests and
   (ii) owners of the parent; and
(b) total comprehensive income for the period attributable to:
   (i) non-controlling interests and
   (ii) owners of the parent.

Two-statement Approach

Non-banking/non-insurance entities must prepare a profit and loss account in accordance with the Companies Acts (ROI and UK) and banking/insurance entities and groups must prepare under separate Schedules to the Companies Acts. The statement of comprehensive income will commence with profit/loss as the first line and have the same line items as (a) to (c) above under the single-statement approach.

Requirements Applicable to Both Approaches

Turnover must be presented on the face of the income statement or statement of comprehensive income (the profit and loss account), which must also present the total of any:

(a) post-tax profit or loss of a discontinued operation; and
(b) post-tax gain or loss on impairment or on disposal of net assets of a discontinued operation.

This must be presented on a line-by-line basis (i.e. multi-column approach) as shown in the Appendix to Section 5 of FRS 102, as reproduced below.

Statement of comprehensive income [or profit and loss account]
for the year ended 31 December 20X1

	20X1			20X0		
	Continuing operations	**Discontinued operations**	**Total**	Continuing operations (as restated)	Discontinued operations (as restated)	Total (as restated)
	CU	CU	CU	CU	CU	CU
Turnover	**4,200**	**1,232**	**5,432**	3,201	1,500	4,701
Cost of Sales	**(2,591)**	**(1,104)**	**(3,695)**	(2,281)	(1,430)	(3,711)
Gross profit	**1,609**	**128**	**1,737**	920	70	990
Administrative expenses	**(452)**	**(110)**	**(562)**	(418)	(120)	(538)
Other operating income	**212**	**–**	**212**	198	–	198

	20X1			20X0		
	Continuing operations	Discontinued operations	Total	Continuing operations (as restated)	Discontinued operations (as restated)	Total (as restated)
	CU	CU	CU	CU	CU	CU
Operating profit	**1,369**	**18**	**1,387**	700	(50)	650
Profit on disposal of operations	**–**	**301**	**301**	–	–	–
Interest receivable and similar income	**14**	**–**	**14**	16	–	16
Interest payable and similar charges	**(208)**	**–**	**(208)**	(208)	–	(208)
Profit before tax	**1,175**	**319**	**1,494**	508	(50)	458
Tax on profit or loss	**(390)**	**(4)**	**(394)**	(261)	3	(258)
Profit/(loss) after tax and profit/(loss) for the financial year	**785**	**315**	**1,100**	247	(47)	200
Other comprehensive income						
Actuarial losses on defined benefit pension plans			**(108)**			(68)
Deferred tax movement relating to actuarial losses			**28**			18
Total comprehensive income for the year			**1,020**			150

Although IFRS 5 *Non-current Assets Held for Sale and Discontinued Operations* has not been implemented in full by FRS 102, it is still necessary to isolate the impact of discontinued operations in the statement of comprehensive income or income statement. A discontinued operation is one that is defined as a component of an entity that has either been disposed of or is held for sale, and:

(a) represents a major line of business or geographical area of operations; or
(b) is part of a single co-ordinated plan to dispose of a separate major line of business or geographical area of operations; or
(c) is a subsidiary acquired exclusively with a view to resale.

Corrections of material errors and changes in accounting policies are retrospective adjustments of prior periods and **not** part of profit or loss for the period.

Additional line items, headings, sub-totals, etc. are included only if they are relevant to an understanding of financial performance. Exceptional items should be disclosed separately in the profit and loss account or in the statement of comprehensive income.

If an entity decides to disclose operating activities, it must only include activities that are normally regarded as operating. Examples include exceptional write-offs of inventory, profits or losses on the sale of property, plant and equipment, investment property and intangible assets, and restructuring costs, etc.

An example of the correction of a material error using the two-statement approach is given overleaf. It assumes that during 2020 an error was found in the valuation of inventories which resulted in an overstatement in the cost of sales of €8,000 and subsequent effect on income tax expense of €3,000.

Example 1.3: Correction of Material Error

XYZ Ltd
Profit and Loss Account
for the year ended 31 December 2020

	2020	2019 Restated
	€	€
Revenue	80,000	75,000
Cost of sales (2019: previously stated €66,000)	(60,000)	(58,000)
Gross profit	20,000	17,000
Distribution costs	(6,000)	(4,000)
Administrative expenses	(3,000)	(2,000)
Finance costs	(2,000)	(1,000)

Profit before tax		9,000	10,000
Income tax expense	(2019: previously stated €5,000)	(6,000)	(2,000)
Profit for the year		3,000	8,000

XYZ Ltd
STATEMENT OF COMPREHENSIVE INCOME
for the year ended 31 December 2020

	2020	2019
	€	€
Profit for the year (2019: previously stated €3,000)	**3,000**	**8,000**
Other comprehensive income		
Exchange differences on translating foreign operations net of tax	5,000	(3,000)
Actuarial gains/(losses) on defined benefit pension obligations net of tax	2,000	(1,000)
Other comprehensive income for the year	7,000	(4,000)
Total comprehensive income for the year (2019: previously stated €9,000)	**10,000**	**4,000**

Ordinary Activities and Extraordinary Items

Ordinary activities are defined as any activities undertaken as part of an entity's business, including incidental activities. They include any effects on the entity of changes in the political, regulatory, economic and geographical environments regardless of their frequency or nature. FRS 102 has had to retain the term 'extraordinary items' (required by company law), but these possess a high degree of abnormality that fall outside the ordinary activities of the business and are not expected to recur. In practice, these will rarely be disclosed due to the very broad definition of ordinary activities.

Analysis of Expenses

FRS 102 no longer requires a specific classification to be adopted for analysing expenses but traditionally the following two classifications have been adopted:

- analysis by **nature** of the expense – depreciation, purchases, transport, advertising costs, etc.;
- analysis by **function** of the expense – cost of sales, distribution, administration costs, etc.

Both of these classifications are illustrated below, although classification by **function** is probably the more popular in practice of the two approaches.

Illustrative Financial Statements (Two-statement Approach)[2]

Alternative 1 – Illustrating the Classification of Expenses by Function

XYZ Group
CONSOLIDATED PROFIT AND LOSS ACCOUNT
for the year ended 31 December 20X2

	Notes	20X2	20X1
		€	€
Turnover	5	6,863,545	5,808,653
Cost of sales		(5,178,530)	(4,422,575)
Gross profit		1,685,015	1,386,078
Other operating income	6	88,850	25,000
Distribution costs		(175,550)	(156,800)
Administrative expenses		(810,230)	(660,389)
Other expenses		(106,763)	(100,030)
Interest payable and similar charge	7	(26,366)	(36,712)
Profit on ordinary activities before tax	8	654,956	457,147
Taxation	9	(270,250)	(189,559)
Profit on ordinary activities after taxation and profit for the financial year		384,706	267,588

Alternative 2 – Illustrating the Classification of Expenses by Nature

XYZ Group
CONSOLIDATED PROFIT AND LOSS ACCOUNT
for the year ended 31 December 20X2

	Notes	20X2	20X1
		€	€
Turnover	5	6,863,545	5,808,653
Other operating income	6	88,850	25,000
Changes in inventories of finished goods and work in progress		3,310	(1,360)
Raw material and consumables used		(4,786,699)	(4,092,185)
Employee salaries and benefits		(936,142)	(879,900)
Depreciation and amortisation expense		(272,060)	(221,247)
Impairment of property, plant and equipment		(30,000)	–

[2] These illustrative examples are taken from the IASB's *IFRS for SMEs 2009 Illustrative Financial Statements Presentation and Disclosure Checklist.*

Other expenses		(249,482)	(145,102)
Interest payable and similar charges	7	(26,366)	(36,712)
Profit on ordinary activities before tax	8	654,956	457,147
Taxation	9	(270,250)	(189,559)
Profit on ordinary activities after taxation for the financial year		384,706	267,588

Under Both Classifications (by Nature and by Function)

XYZ Group
CONSOLIDATED STATEMENT OF COMPREHENSIVE INCOME
for the year ended 31 December 20X2

	20X2	20X1
Profit for the year	384,706	267,588
Actuarial deficit on defined benefit pension scheme	(95,678)	(76,543)
Foreign exchange gains on translation of foreign subsidiaries	23,112	34,112
Total comprehensive income for the year	312,140	225,157

The following is an Irish example of classification by function. Note that as there are no items to be included in other comprehensive income that statement has not been completed. The company could have opted instead for a statement of profit and retained earnings.

GP Wood Limited
STATEMENT OF COMPREHENSIVE INCOME
for the Financial year Ended 31 December 2018

	Note	2018 €	2017 €
Turnover – continuing operations	4	**49,336,477**	45,121,482
Cost of sales		**(45,591,777)**	(40,327,942)
Gross profit		**6,744,700**	4,793,540
Distribution costs		**(1,887,580)**	(2,095,327)
Administrative expenses		**(2,503,862)**	(2,525,476)
Operating profit	5	**2,353,258**	172,737
Interest receivable and similar income	9	**-**	265
Interest payable and expenses	10	**(365,812)**	(403,013)

Profit/(loss) before tax		**1,987,446**	(230,011)
Tax on profit/(loss)	11	**(185,465)**	-
Profit/(loss) for the financial year		**1,801,981**	(230,011)

There were no recognised gains and losses for 2018 or 2017 other than those included in the statement of comprehensive income.

There was no other comprehensive income for 2018 (2017: €NIL).

The next example, from Dairygold Co-Operative Society Ltd, partially illustrates the nature of expense approach with grant and intangible asset amortisation and depreciation being included as individual expenses. Note also the separate presentation of restructuring costs as an exceptional item in the previous year's comparatives.

Dairygold Co-Operative Society Ltd
CONSOLIDATED INCOME STATEMENT
for the year ended 31 December 2018

	Notes	**2018 €'000**	2017 €'000
TURNOVER	2	**992,887**	965,525
Cost of sales		**(790,934)**	(762,753)
Gross Profit		**201,953**	202,772
Operating costs		**(158,703)**	(153,725)
Grant amortisation		**1,198**	1,796
Intangible asset amortisation		**(1,250)**	(2,104)
Depreciation		**(19,335)**	(19,920)
Change in fair value of investment properties		**4,993**	3,583
Operating Profit before Restructuring Costs	3	**28,856**	32,402
Restructuring costs	4	**-**	(957)
Operating Profit after Restructuring Costs		**28,856**	31,445
Share of gains of joint ventures		**488**	341
Share of gains of associates		**34**	25
PROFIT on ordinary activities before investment income, interest and taxation		**29,378**	31,811
Net (loss)/profit in financial assets at fair value through profit and loss	5	**(14,982)**	492
Interest payable and similar charges	6	**(5,926)**	(6,096)
Interest receivable and similar income	6	**327**	220

PROFIT on ordinary activities before taxation		**8,797**	26,427
Taxation credit/(charge) on profit on ordinary activities	8	**430**	(4,933)
PROFIT after taxation		**9,227**	21,494
Attributable to:			
Non-controlling interests	27	**421**	490
Owners of the parent entity		**8,806**	21,004
PROFIT for the financial year		**9,227**	21,494

The above results are derived from continuing operations.

1.4 STATEMENT OF CHANGES IN EQUITY AND STATEMENT OF INCOME AND RETAINED EARNINGS (SECTION 6)

Statement of Changes in Equity

The statement of changes in equity presents the profit or loss for a period, any incomes and expenses directly recognised in equity, changes in accounting policies, corrections of material errors, and new capital invested and dividends paid out during the period.

Information to be Presented in the Statement of Changes in Equity

The information to be presented in the statement of changes in equity is as follows:

(a) total comprehensive income for the period, separating non-controlling and parent interests;
(b) for each component of equity, the effects of retrospective application or restatement regarding Section 10 (correction of errors and changes in accounting policies – see **Chapter 7**);
(c) for each component of equity, a reconciliation between opening and closing balances separating:
    (i) profit or loss,
    (ii) each item of comprehensive income,
    (iii) investments by, dividends paid out, etc. and changes in ownership interest that do not result in a loss of control (can be disclosed in the notes or on the statement itself).

Though the FRS does not provide a sample statement of changes in equity, a good example can be seen in the financial statements of Ornua Co-operative Ltd.

Ornua Co-operative Ltd
GROUP STATEMENT OF CHANGES IN EQUITY
for the period ended 29 December 2018

	Share Capital	Share Premium	Cash Flow Hedging Reserve	Capital Levy Account	Revenue Reserves	Annual Bonus Fund	Redeemable Loan Stock	Members Equity Interests	Non-controlling Interests	Total
	€'000	€'000	€'000	€'000	€'000	€'000	€'000	€'000	€'000	€'000
At 31 December 2016	19,607	32	(4,372)	256	466,414	–	20,502	502,439	1,083	503,522
Profit for the period	–	–	–	–	18,759	–	–	18,759	(343)	18,416
Other comprehensive income/ (expense) for the period:										
Remeasurement of net defined benefit obligation	–	–	–	–	4,183	–	–	4,183	–	4,183
Cash flow hedges										
– Change in value of hedging instruments	–	–	4,416	–	–	–	–	4,416	–	4,416
– Reclassification to profit and loss	–	–	5,258	–	–	–	–	5,258	–	5,258
Currency translation differences	–	–	–	–	(24,075)	–	–	(24,075)	(49)	(24,124)
Total tax on component of other comprehensive income	–	–	(1,572)	–	(562)	–	–	(2,134)	–	(2,134)
Transfer on exercise of call option	–	–	–	–	928	–	–	928	(928)	–
Redemption of loan stock (note 7)	–	–	–	–	–	–	(3,960)	(3,960)	–	(3,960)

	Share Capital	Share Premium	Cash Flow Hedging Reserve	Capital Levy Account	Revenue Reserves	Annual Bonus Fund	Redeemable Loan Stock	Members Equity Interests	Non-controlling Interests	Total
	€'000	€'000	€'000	€'000	€'000	€'000	€'000	€'000	€'000	€'000
At 30 December 2017	**19,607**	**32**	**3,730**	**256**	**465,647**	**–**	**16,542**	**505,814**	**(237)**	**505,577**
Profit for the period	–	–	–	–	25,865	–	–	25,865	(782)	25,083
Other comprehensive income/(expense) for the period:										
Remeasurement of net defined benefit obligation	–	–	–	–	(2,394)	–	–	(2,394)	–	(2,394)
Cash flow hedges										
– Change in value of hedging instruments	–	–	(3,748)	–	–	–	–	(3,748)	–	(3,748)
– Reclassification to profit and loss	–	–	(4,416)	–	–	–	–	(4,416)	–	(4,416)
Currency translation differences	–	–	–	–	3,302	–	–	3,302	(48)	3,254
Total tax on component of other comprehensive income	–	–	1,166	–	226	–	–	1,392	–	1,392
Transfer to annual bonus fund	–	–	–	–	(2,000)	2,000	–	–	–	–
Redemption of loan stock (note 7)	–	–	–	–	–	–	(4,455)	(4,455)	–	(4,455)
At 29 December 2018	**19,607**	**32**	**(3,268)**	**256**	**490,646**	**2,000**	**12,087**	**521,360**	**(1,067)**	**520,293**

A description of each reserve account is included in note 19.

The layout of a simple SME group having only some foreign currency hedges and perhaps a trade investment classified as 'available for sale' might look like the following:

GROUP CONSOLIDATED STATEMENT OF CHANGES IN EQUITY
for the year ended 31 December 20X2

	Share capital	**Retained earnings**	**Hedges foreign currency**	**Available for sale asset**	**Attributable to owners of parent**	**Non-controlling interests**	**Total equity**
	€000	**€000**	**€000**	**€000**	**€000**	**€000**	**€000**
Balance at 1 Jan 20X1	**400**	**150**	**(40)**	**20**	**530**	**50**	**580**
Prior year adjustment							
Correction of error		5			5	1	6
Change in accounting policy		10			10	2	12
Restated balance at 1 Jan 20X1	**400**	**165**	**(40)**	**20**	**545**	**53**	**598**
Total comprehensive income							
Profit or loss		40			40	8	48
Translation of foreign operations		4			4	1	5
Actuarial losses		(3)			(3)	(1)	(4)
Changes in fair value of hedges			2		2	–	2
Revaluation of available-for-sale asset				(4)	(4)	–	(4)
Disposal		1	(1)				
Dividends paid		(12)			(12)	(3)	(15)
Restated 31 Dec 20X1	**400**	**195**	**(39)**	**16**	**572**	**58**	**630**
Total comprehensive income							
Profit or loss		60			60	12	72
Issue of share capital	150				150		150
Translation of foreign operations		6			6	2	8
Actuarial gains		4			4	1	5
Changes in fair value of hedges			(4)		(4)		(4)
Dividends paid		(15)			(15)	(3)	(18)
Balance at 31 Dec 20X2	**550**	**250**	**(43)**	**16**	**773**	**70**	**843**

Statement of Income and Retained Earnings

As stated above, it is likely that many private companies will not have any of the items that would be recorded in a single **statement of comprehensive income**. In that case, if the only changes to equity arise from profit or loss, payments of dividends, corrections of prior period errors and changes in accounting policy, the entity may present a single **statement of income and retained earnings** instead of a statement of comprehensive income (single statement or two statements) and a statement of changes in equity. An illustrative example, based on the IASB's *IFRS for SMEs 2009 Illustrative Financial Statements Presentation and Disclosure Checklist*, is shown below.

Alternative 1 – Illustrating the Classification of Expenses by Function

XYZ Group

CONSOLIDATED STATEMENT OF INCOME AND RETAINED EARNINGS

for the year ended 31 December 2020

	Notes	**2020**	**2019**
		€	**€**
Turnover	5	6,863,545	5,808,653
Cost of sales		(5,178,530)	(4,422,575)
Gross profit		1,685,015	1,386,078
Other operating income	6	88,850	25,000
Distribution costs		(175,550)	(156,800)
Administrative expenses		(810,230)	(660,389)
Other expenses		(106,763)	(100,030)
Interest payable and other charges	7	(26,366)	(36,712)
Profit on ordinary activities before tax	8	654,956	457,147
Taxation	9	(270,250)	(189,559)
Profit for the year on ordinary activities after tax		**384,706**	**267,588**
Retained earnings at start of year		**2,171,353**	**2,003,765**
Dividends		(150,000)	(100,000)
Retained earnings at end of year		**2,406,059**	**2,171,353**

Note: The format illustrated above aggregates expenses according to their function (cost of sales, distribution, administrative, etc.). As the only changes to XYZ Group's equity during the year arose from profit or loss and payment of dividends, it has elected to present a single statement of income and retained earnings instead of separate statements of comprehensive income and changes in equity.

Information to be Presented on the Face of the Statement of Income and Retained Earnings

The information to be presented on the face of the statement of income and retained earnings is as follows:

(a) retained earnings at the start of the period;
(b) dividends declared and paid or payable during the period;
(c) restatements of retained earnings for corrections of prior period errors;
(d) restatements of retained earnings for changes in accounting policy; and
(e) retained earnings at the end of the period.

EXAMPLE 1.4: STATEMENT OF INCOME AND RETAINED EARNINGS

Gartandee Ltd have prepared a trial balance as at 31 March 2019 as follows:

	€000	€000
Sales		50,332
Purchases	29,778	
Property, plant and equipment – cost	59,088	
Property, plant and equipment – accumulated depreciation		25,486
Inventories as at 1 April 2018	7,865	
Interest	200	
Accruals		426
Distribution costs	8,985	
Administrative expenses	7,039	
Retained earnings		23,707
Trade receivables	9,045	
Cash at bank	182	
Dividends paid	250	
8% bank loan repayable 2022		5,000
Share capital		10,000
Share premium		5,000
Trade payables		2,481
	122,432	122,432

The following additional information is available:

1. The share capital of the company consists of ordinary shares with a nominal value of €1 each.
2. Dividends of €250,000 were paid during the current year.
3. The sales figure in the trial balance includes the sales made on credit for April 2019, amounting to €3,147,000.

4. The inventories at 31 March 2019 cost €8,407,000. Included in this figure are inventories that cost €480,000 but which can be sold for only €180,000.
5. Transport costs of €157,000 relating to March 2019 are not included in the trial balance as the invoice was received after the year end.
6. The company discovered a material error in its 2018 financial statements and the effect of the error was an overstatement of €600,000 of profit for the year ended 31 March 2018 and an equivalent understatement of a loan.
7. The corporation tax charge for the year has been calculated as €235,000.

The statement of income and retained earnings and the balance sheet would be presented as follows:

STATEMENT OF INCOME AND RETAINED EARNINGS
for the year ended 31 March 2019

	€000	€000
Revenue (€50,332,000 – €3,147,000)		47,185
Cost of sales (€7,865,000 + €29,778,000 – €8,107,000)		(29,536)
Gross Profit		17,649
Distribution costs (€8,985,000 + €157,000)	9,142	
Administrative expenses	7,039	(16,181)
Profit from operations		1,468
Finance costs (€200,000 + €200,000)		(400)
Profit before tax		1,068
Income tax expense		(235)
Profit after taxation		833
Retained earnings at start of the year		23,707
Correction of prior period error		(600)
Dividends paid for the year		(250)
Retained earnings at end of the year		23,690

BALANCE SHEET
as at 31 March 2019

	€000	€000
Non-current assets		
Property, plant and equipment (€59,088,000 – €25,486,000)		33,602
Current assets		
Inventories (€8,407,000 – €300,000)	8,107	
Trade receivables (€9,045,000 – €3,147,000)	5,898	
Cash at bank	182	14,187
		47,789

Equity		
Ordinary share capital		10,000
Share premium	5,000	
Retained earnings	23,690	28,690
		38,690
Non-current liabilities		
Bank loans		5,000
Loan		600
Current liabilities		
Trade payables and accruals (€2,481,000 + €157,000 + €426,000 + €200,000)	3,264	
Taxation	235	3,499
		47,789

A good example of a statement of profit and loss and retained earnings is included in the 2017 financial statements of Northern Ireland company, Brett Martin Ltd.

Brett Martin Limited
STATEMENT OF INCOME AND RETAINED EARNINGS
for the year ended 31 December 2017

	Note	**2017 £**	2016 £
Turnover	5	**132,932,494**	124,418,605
Cost of sales		**(106,055,382)**	(96,211,411)
Gross profit		**26,877,112**	28,207,194
Distribution costs		**(11,449,769)**	(10,449,486)
Administrative expenses		**(10,030,837)**	(9,225,776)
Operating profit	6	**5,396,506**	8,531,932
Interest payable and similar expenses	9	**(716,050)**	(789,807)
Profit before tax		**4,680,456**	7,742,125
Tax on profit	10	**(1,155,213)**	(1,738,929)
Profit for the financial year		**3,525,243**	6,003,196
Retained earnings at the beginning of the year		**39,399,317**	38,496,121
Profit for the financial year		**3,525,243**	6,003,196
Dividends declared and paid		**(2,750,000)**	(5,100,000)
Retained earnings at the end of the year		**40,174,560**	39,399,317

1.5 STATEMENT OF CASH FLOWS (SECTION 7)

The statement of cash flows shows the historical changes in cash and cash equivalents – separating operating, investing and financing activities.

In general, all financial statements prepared in accordance with FRS 102 must include a statement of cash flows. However, FRS 102 does permit a parent entity that presents its separate financial statements with its consolidated financial statements to elect not to include a statement of cash flows in its separate financial statements.

A number of specific exclusions from Section 7 are incorporated into FRS 102 as follows:

- mutual life assurance companies;
- pension funds;
- investment funds, as long as substantially all of the investments are highly liquid, they are carried at market value and the entity prepares a statement of changes in net assets. A small entity, under Section 1A, is not required to comply with Section 7 (see **Section 1.8** below).

Cash Equivalents

Cash equivalents have short maturities (less than three months). Bank overdrafts are normally treated as financing cash flows unless they are payable on demand, in which case they are treated as cash equivalents. The statement reconciles the movement in cash and cash equivalents rather than the previous local standard, which treated most cash equivalents as short-term financing.

Information to be Presented in the Statement of Cash Flows

Cash flows must be presented under three main headings: operating activities, investing activities and financing activities.

Operating Activities

These are the principal revenue-producing activities of the entity. Examples include:

(a) cash receipts from the sale of goods and the rendering of services;
(b) cash receipts from royalties, fees, commissions and other revenue;
(c) cash payments to suppliers;
(d) cash payments to employees;
(e) cash payments or refunds of tax unless these are specifically identified with financing and investing activities;
(f) cash receipts and payments from investments, loans and other trading contracts; and
(g) cash advances and loans made to other parties by financial institutions.

Investing Activities

These are cash flows to acquire and dispose of long-term assets and investments other than cash equivalents. Examples include:

(a) cash payments to acquire property, plant and equipment, intangible assets and other long-term assets;
(b) cash receipts from the sale of property, plant and equipment, intangible assets and other long-term assets;
(c) cash payments to acquire debt or equity instruments of another entity;
(d) cash receipts from the sale of equity or debt instruments of another entity;
(e) cash advances and loans made to other parties;
(f) cash receipts from the repayment of advances and loans to other parties;
(g) cash payments for futures contracts, forward contracts, option contracts, etc. except if held for trading;
(h) cash receipts from futures contracts, forward contracts, option contracts, etc. except if held for trading.

When a contract is accounted for as a hedge, an entity should classify the cash flows in the same manner as the cash flows that are being hedged.

Financing Activities

These are cash flows that result in changes in the size and composition of contributed equity and borrowings of an entity. Examples include:

(a) cash proceeds from issuing shares;
(b) cash payments to redeem equity;
(c) cash proceeds from issuing debentures, loans; notes, bonds, mortgages and other short- and long-term borrowing;
(d) cash repayments of amounts borrowed; and
(e) cash payments by a lessee for the reduction of the outstanding finance lease liability.

Reporting Cash Flows from Operating Activities

Two methods are permitted:

(a) the **direct method,** by disclosing gross cash receipts and payments, either taken directly from the accounting records or by adjusting sales, cost of sales, etc. for changes in working capital and other non-cash items; or
(b) the **indirect method,** where a measure of profit is adjusted for changes in working capital, non-cash items (such as depreciation) and all other items which relate to financing or investing.

The latter has always been compulsory under local GAAP and because of the difficulties in isolating VAT at the cash points, it is likely that most reporting entities will continue to adopt the indirect method. However, the IASB is likely to make the direct method compulsory in the long term as it is regarded as being more user-friendly than the indirect method, being easier for a non-accountant to understand and interpret.

Reporting Cash Flows from Investing and Financing Activities

Major classes of gross cash receipts and payments must be reported separately. However, the aggregate cash flows of acquisitions and disposals should be presented separately and classified as investing activities.

Netting off cash flows is only permitted if the cash flows represent those of the customer not the entity itself (e.g. rent collected by an agent on behalf of client), and where the cash turnover is quick, the amounts large and maturities short (e.g. principal amounts related to credit card customers).

There are special netting rules for financial institutions (see **Chapter 13**).

Foreign Currency Cash Flows

Cash flows should be recorded in the entity's functional currency by applying the exchange rate between the functional currency and the foreign currency at the date of the cash flow or using an average rate that approximates actual (usually a weighted average rate).

Cash flows of the foreign subsidiary must be translated at the dates of the cash flows, or an exchange rate that approximates the actual rate (e.g. a weighted average exchange rate for the period).

Unrealised gains and losses arising on changes in foreign currency rates are not cash flows. To reconcile opening and closing cash, the effect of exchange rate changes on cash must be reported in the cash flow statement separately from the three headings of operating, investing and financing activities. This can normally be achieved by a single reconciling line at the bottom of the statement (see later extracts from published accounts).

Interest and Dividends

Interest and dividends received and paid should be reported separately and classified consistently from period to period as operating, investing or financing activities.

Interest paid and interest and dividends received can be treated as operating, financing or investing cash flows; dividends paid can be treated as either financing or operating cash flows.

Income Tax

Normally tax is an operating cash flow unless it can be specifically identified with financing and investing activities.

Non-cash Transactions

These must be excluded from the statement of cash flows but should be disclosed elsewhere in the notes so that the reporting entity provides relevant information on their impact on investing or financing activities. Examples include:

(a) the acquisition of assets via finance leases;
(b) the acquisition of an entity by means of an equity issue; and
(c) the conversion of debt into equity.

Components of Cash and Cash Equivalents

The components of cash and cash equivalents should be disclosed and a reconciliation made to equivalent items in the balance sheet. However, an entity is not required to present the reconciliation if the amount of cash and cash equivalents presented in the statement of cash flows is identical to the amount similarly described in the balance sheet.

Other Disclosures

Entities should comment on any significant cash and cash equivalents not available for use by the entity, e.g. under foreign exchange control or legal restrictions.

Entities should disclose an analysis of changes in net debt, showing changes resulting from:

(a) cash flows from the entity;
(b) acquisition and disposal of subsidiaries;
(c) new finance leases;
(d) other non-cash changes; and
(e) recognition of changes in market value and exchange rate movements.

A good example of disclosure of a reconciliation of net cash flow to movement in net debt is provided by the Irish company, Carbery Food Ingredients Ltd.

Carbery Food Ingredients Ltd

ANNUAL REPORT AND ACCOUNTS 2018 (EXTRACT)

Analysis of Net Debt

(i)	Reconciliation of net cash flow to movement in net debt	**(€'000)**
	Decrease in cash and increase in demand debt in year	(10,220)
	Increase in term debt	(2,848)
	Change in net debt resulting from cash flows	(13,068)
	Increase in term and demand debt from acquisitions	(3,285)
	Translation adjustment	(966)
	Movement in net debt in year	(17,319)
	Net debt at 1 January 2018	(12,740)
	Net debt at 31 December 2018	(30,059)

(ii) Analysis of changes in net funds

	At 1/1/2018 (€'000)	Cash flow (€'000)	Acquisitions (€'000)	Exchange Movement (€'000)	31/12/2018 (€'000)
Cash at bank and in hand	16,859	(5,912)	–	186	11,133
Bank overdrafts	(1,668)	(4,308)	(222)	–	(6,198)
Total cash and demand debt	15,191	(10,220)	(222)	186	4,935
Loans repayable	(27,896)	(2,854)	(3,063)	(1,152)	(34,965)
Finance leases and hire purchases	(35)	6	–	–	(29)
	(27,931)	(2,848)	(3,063)	(1,152)	(34,994)
Net debt	(12,740)	(13,068)	(3,285)	(966)	(30,059)

Acquisition and Disposal of a Subsidiary

The acquisition of a subsidiary requires the computation of goodwill. Under FRS 102, the only method permitted to compute goodwill is the 'partial method'. This is illustrated in the example below.

Example 1.5: Goodwill Computation on Acquisition

Wallander Ltd acquired 80% of Lewis Ltd on 1 January 2020 for €500,000 in cash, when the fair value of the identifiable net assets of Lewis Ltd was €300,000. The goodwill arising on the acquisition is computed using the partial method as follows:

Parent	**€000**
Consideration paid	500,000
Less fair value of identifiable net assets acquired (80% × 300,000)	(240,000)
Goodwill arising on acquisition	260,000

The goodwill of €260,000 relates only to the parent company, Wallander Ltd, and no goodwill arises in respect of a non-controlling interest (NCI). The date of acquisition journal entry will be as follows:

		€000	**€000**
Dr	Net assets	300	
	Cr Bank		500
	Cr NCI (20% × €300,000)		60
Dr	Goodwill	260	

Any subsequent impairment of goodwill will be charged wholly against consolidated retained earnings (i.e. against the parent). So, assuming goodwill suffers an impairment of 50% during 2021, the journal entry would be:

	€000	€000
Dr Consolidated retained earnings	130	
Cr Goodwill		130

When a subsidiary is disposed of there is a loss of control and thus the net assets, including goodwill, of the subsidiary should be removed and compared with proceeds on sale. A profit or loss on disposal will then result. An example is provided below.

Example 1.6: Loss of Control

Vera Ltd purchased 80% of the shares of Morse Ltd for €800,000 cash on 1 January 2020. At that date Morse Ltd had the following identifiable net assets, stated at fair value:

- non-current assets of €180,000
- current assets of €280,000
- liabilities of €110,000.

Vera Ltd had retained profits of €260,000 for the year ended 31 December 2020. Therefore, net assets also increased by €260,000 to €610,000 at 31 December 2020.

Non-controlling interests are measured at their proportionate share of the identifiable net assets of Morse Ltd. On 31 December 2020, Vera Ltd sells its entire 80% stake in Morse Ltd for €1,300,000.

How would these transactions be recorded in the consolidated financial statements of the Vera group?

The **purchase** of shares by Vera Ltd on 1 January 2020 is recorded in the consolidated financial statements as follows:

	€000	€000
Dr Non-current assets	180	
Dr Current assets	280	
Cr Liabilities		110
Cr Bank		800
Cr Non-controlling interest*		114
Dr Goodwill (balance figure)	564	
Being acquisition of Morse Ltd.		

Dr	Net assets	208	
	Cr Consolidated retained earnings		260
Dr	Non-controlling interest	52	

Being retained profit of Morse Ltd for 2020.

* NCI at 1 January 2020 is computed as (€180,000 + €280,000 – €110,000) × 20% = €114,000.

The **disposal** of Vera Ltd's entire 80% stake in Morse Ltd represents a loss of control and is recorded as follows in the consolidated financial statements:

		€000	€000
Dr	Bank	1,300	
	Cr Goodwill		564
	Cr Net assets		610
Dr	Non-controlling interest	166	
	Cr Profit on disposal – P/L (balance figure)		292

Illustrative Statement of Cash Flows

An example of a statement of cash flows, using the indirect method, is given in the FRC's 'FRS 102 Factsheet 3: Illustrative Statement of Cash Flows', from which the below is extracted.

STATEMENT OF CASH FLOWS
for the year ended 31 December 20X1

	20X1 €000
Cash flows from operating activities	
Operating profit for the financial year	6,022
Adjustments for :	
Depreciation of property, plant and equipment	869
Amortisation of intangible assets	50
Profit on disposal of property, plant and equipment	(20)
Decrease/(increase) in trade and other receivables	(72)
Decrease/(increase) in inventories	(194)
Increase/(decrease) in trade payables	234
Cash from operations	6,889
Income taxes paid	(2,992)
Net cash from operating activities	**3,967**

In the illustrative statement above, although the indirect method has been incorporated into the face of the statement of cash flows, it is possible to move that reconciliation into the notes. This would therefore ensure that only genuine cash movements are included in the statement.

Examples of both the direct and indirect methods are provided below.

Example 1.7: The Direct and Indirect Methods of Reporting Operating Cash Flows

A company's profit and loss account for the year ended 31 March 2019 is shown below, together with its balance sheet as at 31 March 2019.

PROFIT AND LOSS ACCOUNT
for the year ended 31 March 2019

	€000
Sales	1,504
Cost of sales	(774)
Gross profit	730
Administrative and selling expenses	(450)
Interest payable	(36)
Dividends received	44
Profit before tax	288
Taxation	(66)
Profits after tax	222

BALANCE SHEET
as at 31 March 2019

	2019		2018	
	€000	€000	€000	€000
Assets				
Non-current assets				
Tangible assets				
Property, plant and equipment		976		940
Investments		500		500
		1,476		1,440
Current assets				
Inventories	462		424	
Trade receivables	280		314	
Cash at bank	30		Nil	
	772		738	

Creditors: amounts falling due within one year				
Trade payables	364		352	
Accrued interest payable	6		–	
Taxation	66		110	
Bank overdraft	–		46	
Current liabilities	436		508	
Net current assets		336		230
		1,812		1,670
Creditors: amounts falling due after more than one year				
Long-term loans	180		260	
Non-current liabilities		180		260
		1,632		1,410
Equity				
Share capital		440		400
Share premium		140		120
Retained earnings		1,052		890
		1,632		1,410

Assume the following information is also available:

(a) administrative and selling expenses include employee salaries of €296,000 and equipment depreciation of €140,000.

(b) There were no non-current asset disposals during the year ended 31 March 2019.

(c) A dividend of €60,000 was paid in June 2018.

Direct Method

STATEMENT OF CASH FLOWS
for the year ended 31 March 2019

		€000	€000
Cash flows from operating activities			
Cash receipts from customers	*W1*	1,538	
Cash paid to suppliers of goods and services	*W3*	(814)	
Cash paid to employees		(296)	
Cash generated from operations			428
Interest paid	*W4*	(30)	
Taxation paid	*W5*	(110)	(140)
Net cash inflow from operating activities			288
Cash flows from investing activities			
Payments to acquire property, plant and equipment	*W6*	(176)	
Dividends received		44	
			(132)

Cash flows from financing activities			
Proceeds on the issue of share capital	*W7*	60	
Repayment of long-term borrowings	*W8*	(80)	
Dividends paid		(60)	
			(80)
Net increase/(decrease) in cash and cash equivalents			76
Cash and cash equivalents at 1 April 2018			(46)
Cash and cash equivalents at 31 March 2019			30

Note: interest paid could have been classified under investing or financing activities. Dividends paid could be classified as operating or investing activities.

W1 Cash receipts from customers: €314,000 + €1,504,000 – €280,000 = €1,538,000 (opening trade receivables + sales – closing trade receivables)

W2 Purchases: €462,000 + €774,000 – €424,000 = €812,000 (closing inventories + cost of sales – opening inventories)

W3 Cash paid to suppliers: €352,000 + €812,000 + €450,000 – €296,000 – €140,000 – €364,000 = €814,000 (opening trade payables + purchases + (administrative and selling expense less employee salaries and depreciation) – closing trade payables)

W4 Interest paid: €36,000 – €6,000 = €30,000 (interest payable – closing interest accrued)

W5 Taxation paid: €110,000 + €66,000 – €66,000 = €110,000

W6 Payments to acquire property, etc.: €940,000 – €140,000 – €976,000 = €176,000

W7 Proceeds on the issue of shares: €440,000 + €140,000 – €400,000 – €120,000 = €60,000 (movement in share capital and share premium account)

W8 Repayment of long-term loans: €260,000 – €180,000 = €80,000 (movement, i.e. a decrease in long-term borrowings)

Indirect method

The indirect method only changes the presentation of the cash flows from operating activities. It can be included within the statement of cash flows or in the notes:

	€000
Cash flows from operating activities	
Profit before interest and taxation (€288,000 + €36,000)	324
Depreciation	140
Dividends received	(44)
Increase in inventories (€462,000 – €424,000)	(38)
Decrease in trade receivables (€280,000 – €314,000)	34
Increase in trade payables (€364,000 – €352,000)	12
	428

Currently, all Irish companies have opted for the indirect method, probably because it reconciles profit before interest and tax to operating cash flows and does not require changes to the company's accounting systems to identify actual operating cash flows.

Note: the new note requiring a reconciliation of cash flow to net debt is only required for accounting periods commencing from the 1 January 2019 (see the extract from Carbery Food Ingredients Ltd above).

1.6 NOTES TO THE FINANCIAL STATEMENTS (SECTION 8)

Purpose of the Notes

Section 8 of FRS 102 sets out the principles underlying information that is to be presented in the notes to the financial statements. The notes provide narrative descriptions or disaggregations of items in the financial statements as well as information about items not qualifying for recognition in the financial statements.

Structure of the Notes

The notes shall present information:

(a) on the basis of preparation and on specific accounting policies adopted;
(b) disclosures required by the FRS not presented on the face of the statements; and
(c) additional notes that are relevant to an understanding of the financial statements.

The notes should be presented in a systematic manner and cross-referenced to the financial statements. Normally they are presented in the following order:

(a) a statement of compliance with the FRS;
(b) a summary of the significant accounting policies applied;
(c) supporting information for items presented on the face of the financial statements in the order in which each statement and line item is presented; and
(d) other disclosures, including: contingent liabilities and assets, non-financial disclosures, the amount of dividends proposed or declared and the amount of any cumulative preference dividends not recognised.

It is common to include some brief information about the reporting entity (usually before the statement of compliance), such as:

1. information on the legal form of the entity and its domicile, country of incorporation and registered office;
2. a description of the nature of the entity's operations and principal activities; and
3. the date when the financial statements were authorised and the persons giving that authorisation.

An example is given in the IASB's *IFRS for SMEs 2009 Illustrative Financial Statements Presentation and Disclosure Checklist*, and is reproduced below.

Example 1.8: Illustrative Accounting Policies and Notes

XYZ Group
ACCOUNTING POLICIES AND EXPLANATORY NOTES
TO THE FINANCIAL STATEMENTS (EXTRACT)
for the year ended 31 December 20X2

1. General information

XYZ (Holdings) Limited ('the Company') is a limited company incorporated in A Land. The address of its registered office and principal place of business is ____________. XYZ Group consists of the Company and its wholly-owned subsidiary XYZ (Trading) Limited. Its principal activities are the manufacture and sale of candles.

The accounting policies note for the Irish bookshop and stationers chain, Easons, illustrates this well.

Eason & Son Ltd
ANNUAL REPORT – NOTES TO THE FINANCIAL STATEMENTS (EXTRACT)
for the year ended 28 January 2018

1. General information

These financial statements comprising the Profit and Loss Account, the Statement of Comprehensive Income, the Balance Sheet, the Statement of Changes in Equity and the related notes constitute the individual financial statements of Eason & Son Limited for the financial year ended 28 January 2018.

Eason and Son Limited is a private company incorporated in the Republic of Ireland and the Company's registered number is 1279. The Registered Office is Unit 1, Elm Road, Dublin Airport Logistics Park, Swords, Co. Dublin, which is also the principal place of business of the Company. The nature of the Company's operations and principal activities are the retailing of newspapers, magazines, books, stationery and greeting cards.

Most companies in the Republic of Ireland and Northern Ireland would disclose the date and names of the directors authorising the financial statements at the foot of the balance sheet.

Disclosure of Accounting Policies

The disclosure of accounting policies should include:

(a) details of measurement bases used; and
(b) other accounting policies used that are relevant to an understanding of the financial statements.

Information about Judgements

Any judgements that management has made in applying the accounting policies that have the most significant effect on the amounts recognised in the financial statements should be disclosed.

Some examples where disclosure might be required where there is considerable judgment could include:

- whether a lease transferring substantially all the risks and rewards incidental to the ownership of an asset should be treated as a finance or an operating lease;
- determining whether or not goods have been sold if they were sold on consignment;
- whether or not the existence of a special purpose entity (SPE) indicates that the entity controls the SPE and therefore should be consolidated (see **Section 1.7** below);
- whether or not it is more likely than not that economic benefits will flow out of the entity due to a present obligation, i.e. is it a contingent liability or a full provision?

Information about Key Sources of Estimation Uncertainty

Information on key sources of estimation uncertainty at the end of the period that have a significant risk of causing material adjustment to the carrying amounts of assets and liabilities should be provided, including their nature and carrying amount at the end of the reporting period.

Determining the carrying amount of assets and liabilities requires the estimation of the effects of uncertain future events on those assets and liabilities. Often these estimates involve assumptions about how to adjust cash flows for risk, what discount rates to adopt or what future salary increases are likely. The disclosure of these major sources of estimation uncertainty at the end of the reporting period should enhance the relevance and understandability of the information in the financial statements.

Again, this can be illustrated with an example taken from the IASB's *IFRS for SMEs 2009 Illustrative Financial Statements Presentation and Disclosure Checklist*.

Example 1.9: Illustrative Financial Statements

Notes to the Financial Statements (Extract)

3. Key sources of estimation uncertainty

Long-service payments

In determining the liability for long-service payments (explained in note 19), management must make an estimate of salary increases over the following five years, the discount rate for the next five years to use in the present value calculation, and the number of employees expected to leave before they receive the benefits.

A good example, which combines both the use of judgement and estimation uncertainty, is provided by GP Wood Ltd in its financial statements for the year ended 31 December 2016.

GP Wood Limited

Notes to the Financial Statements (Extract)

for the year ended 31 January 2016

2. Judgements in applying accounting policies and key sources of estimation uncertainty

When preparing the financial statements, management makes a number of judgements, estimates and assumptions about the recognition and measurement of assets, liabilities, income and expenses.

Significant management judgements

The following are significant management judgements in applying the accounting policies of the company that have the most significant effect on the financial statements.

Allowances for impairment of trade receivables

The company estimates the allowance for doubtful receivables based on assessment of specific accounts where the company has objective evidence comprising default in payment terms or significant financial difficulty that certain customers are unable to meet their financial obligations.

Estimation uncertainty

Information about estimates and assumptions that have the most significant effect on recognition and measurement of assets, liabilities, income and expenses is provided below. Actual results may be substantially different.

Useful lives of depreciable assets

The annual depreciation charge depends primarily on the estimated lives of each type of asset and, in certain circumstances, estimates of fair values and residual values. The directors annually review these asset lives and adjust them as necessary to reflect current thinking on remaining lives in light of technological change, prospective economic utilisation and physical condition of the assets concerned. Changes in asset lives can have significant impact on depreciation charges for the period. It is not practical to quantify the impact of changes in asset lives on an overall basis, as asset lives are individually determined, and there are a significant number of asset lives in use. The impact of any change would vary significantly depending on the individual changes in assets and the classes of assets impacted.

An even better example is from Ulster Carpet (Holdings) Mills Ltd, which separates the use of judgement and disclosure of critical estimates in its accounting policy note in accordance with paragraphs 8.6 and 8.7 of FRS 102.

Ulster Carpet Mills (Holdings) Ltd
NOTES TO THE FINANCIAL STATEMENTS (EXTRACT)
for the year ended 31 March 2018

3. Accounting policies *(continued)*

Judgements and key sources of estimation uncertainty

The preparation of the financial statements requires management to make judgements, estimates and assumptions that affect the amounts reported. These estimates and judgements are continually reviewed and are based on experience and other factors, including expectations of future events that are believed to be reasonable under the circumstances.

Significant judgements

The judgements (apart from those involving estimations) that management has made in the process of applying the entity's accounting policies and that have the most significant effect on the amounts recognised in the financial statements are as follows:

- To determine whether there are indicators of impairment of the group's tangible assets. Factors taken into consideration in reaching such a decision include the economic viability and expected future financial performance of the asset.
- To determine whether leases entered into by the group as lessee are operating or finance leases. These decisions depend on an assessment of whether the risks and rewards of ownership have been transferred from the lessor to the lessee on a lease by lease basis.

Key sources of estimation uncertainty

Accounting estimates and assumptions are made concerning the future and, by their nature, will rarely equal the related actual outcome. The key assumptions and other sources of estimation uncertainty that have a significant risk of causing a material adjustment to the carrying amounts of assets and liabilities within the next financial year are as follows:

- Tangible fixed assets are depreciated over their useful lives taking into account residual values where appropriate. The actual lives of the assets and residual values are assessed annually and may vary depending on a number of factors. In re-assessing asset lives, factors such as technological innovation, product life cycles and maintenance programs are taken into account. Residual value assessments consider issues such as future market conditions, the remaining life of the asset and projected disposal values.
- Stocks are stated at the lower of cost and estimated selling price less costs to complete and sell. At each reporting date, stocks are assessed for impairment and this value may vary depending on a number of factors.
- Impairment of trade debtors is reviewed on an ongoing basis. The company trades with a large and varied number of customers on credit terms. Some debts due will not be paid through the default of a small number of customers. The company uses estimates based on historical experience and current information in determining the level of debts for which an impairment charge is required.

1.7 CONSOLIDATED AND SEPARATE FINANCIAL STATEMENTS (SECTION 9)

Requirement to Present Consolidated Financial Statements

Section 9 of the FRS requires most groups to be consolidated under the FRS. Nonetheless, a major exemption that only calls for consolidation if required by companies legislation has been included in the FRS for legal reasons. As such, the present exemption for small and medium-sized groups will remain.

Thus, a parent entity must prepare consolidated financial statements **only if** it is required to do so by companies legislation.

A subsidiary is an entity that is controlled by a parent. Control is the power to govern the financial and operating policies of an entity so as to obtain economic benefits from its activities. In addition, a special purpose entity (SPE) must be consolidated when the substance of the relationship indicates that it is controlled by a parent.

Control is presumed to exist when the parent owns, directly or indirectly, more than 50% of the voting power, unless it can be demonstrated that ownership does not constitute control. Control can also exist when the parent owns half or less of the voting power of an entity but it has:

(a) power over more than 50% of voting rights via an agreement with other investors; or
(b) power to govern the financial and operating policies under statute or agreement; or
(c) power to appoint or remove the majority of the members of the board of directors; or
(d) power to cast the majority of votes at meetings of the board of directors.

A parent can also achieve control via the use of options or convertibles currently exercisable; or by having an agent with the ability to direct the activities for the benefit of the controlling entity.

A subsidiary is **not excluded** from consolidation simply because the investor is a venture capital entity; nor if its activities are dissimilar from those other entities in the group; nor because it operates in a jurisdiction that imposes restrictions on transferring cash out of the jurisdiction. Additional disclosures about the different activities should remedy the lack of relevant information. Exclusion on the grounds of disproportionate expense is only permitted if a subsidiary is immaterial.

However, a subsidiary should be **excluded** if there are long-term restrictions hindering the exercise of a parent's rights or if the subsidiary is held exclusively with a view to subsequent resale. In the latter case, if held as part of an investment portfolio, it should be measured at fair value with any changes being reported in profit and loss. If that is not the case, then an entity can elect for either a fair value or cost approach. A subsidiary may also be excluded if its inclusion is not material for the purpose of giving a true and fair view. Two or more subsidiaries may only be excluded if they are not material when taken together.

Special Purpose Entities

An entity, be it a trust, partnership or unincorporated entity, may be established to accomplish a narrow objective (e.g. to effect a lease or to facilitate an employee share ownership plan (ESOP)), usually by imposing strict requirements on its operations.

All SPEs must be included in the consolidated financial statements. In addition to (a)–(d) above, the following circumstances may indicate that an entity controls an SPE:

1. the activities of the SPE are conducted according to the specific business needs of the entity;

2. the entity has ultimate decision-making powers over the SPE;
3. the entity has rights to obtain a majority of the benefits of the SPE and is exposed to its risks; and
4. the entity retains a majority of residual or ownership risks related to the SPE or its assets.

However, post-employment schemes are excluded from being SPEs as they are covered in Section 28 Employee Benefits.

Consolidation Procedures

The group is presented as a single economic entity and should:

(a) combine the financial statements of its parent and subsidiaries on a line-by-line basis;
(b) eliminate the parent company's investment in each subsidiary and the parent's portion of equity of each subsidiary;
(c) measure and present any non-controlling interest in profit or loss separately from the owner's interest; and
(d) measure and present any non-controlling interest in the net assets separately from the parent entity's equity to include its share of identifiable net assets at acquisition as well as its share of changes in equity since the date of combination.

The split of profit or loss between the owner's interest and the non-controlling interests is determined on the basis of existing ownership interests and must ignore the possible exercise of options/convertibles.

Intragroup Balances and Transactions

Intragroup balances and transfers are eliminated in full. However, intragroup losses may indicate an impairment that requires recognition in the consolidated accounts.

Uniform Reporting Date and Reporting Period

The parent and its subsidiaries should adopt the same reporting date. Where that is impracticable and the dates differ, the consolidated financial statements must be made up:

(a) from the financial statements of subsidiaries from the last reporting date prior to the parent's year end, **but** no more than three months earlier; or
(b) from interim financial statements prepared at the same date as the parent.

Uniform Accounting Policies

Consolidated accounts should be prepared using uniform accounting policies and appropriate adjustments need to be made in preparing those accounts.

Acquisition and Disposal of Subsidiaries

The income and expenses of a subsidiary are consolidated from the date of acquisition until the parent ceases to control the subsidiary.

The difference between the proceeds and the carrying amount of the subsidiary at the date of disposal, excluding exchange differences originally recorded in reserves, is recorded as a gain or loss in the consolidated statement of comprehensive income (or in the profit and loss account, if presented), i.e. they are not recycled. (See **Example 1.6** earlier in this chapter.)

Disposal – Where Control is Lost Where a parent ceases to control a subsidiary, a gain or loss should be recognised in the consolidated statement of comprehensive income or in the profit and loss account as the difference between:

(a) the proceeds from the disposal (or the event that resulted in the loss of control); and
(b) the proportion of the carrying amount of the subsidiary's net assets, including any related goodwill, disposed of (or lost) as at the date of disposal or date control is lost.

The cumulative amount of any exchange differences recognised in equity are not recognised in profit or loss as part of the gain or loss on disposal of the subsidiary and instead are transferred directly to retained earnings. (See **Example 1.6**.)

Disposal – Where Control is Retained Where a parent reduces its holding in a subsidiary and control is retained, it is accounted for as a transaction between equity holders. No gain or loss shall be recognised at the date of disposal.

Acquisition – Control Achieved in Stages Where a parent acquires control of a subsidiary in stages, the transaction must be accounted as the cost of the business combination, being the aggregate of the fair values of the assets given, liabilities assumed and equity instruments issued by the acquirer at the date of each transaction in the series.

Acquisition – Increasing a Controlling Interest in a Subsidiary Where a parent increases its controlling interest in a subsidiary, the identifiable assets and liabilities and a provision for contingent liabilities of the subsidiary are not revalued to fair value and no additional goodwill shall be recognised at the date the controlling interest is increased. The transaction is therefore accounted for as a transaction between equity holders.

If an entity ceases to be a subsidiary but the parent still has an investment holding, it should be accounted for as a financial asset in accordance with Sections 11 or 12 of the FRS (see **Chapter 12**) provided it is neither an associate nor a jointly controlled entity. The fair value of the retained investment is taken as the cost on initial measurement of the financial asset.

Non-controlling Interests (NCIs) in Subsidiaries

NCIs should be disclosed within equity separately from the parent shareholders' equity; likewise, in the profit and loss account their share should be shown separately. NCIs should also be disclosed separately in the statement of comprehensive income, if applicable.

The profit or loss and each component of other comprehensive income must be attributed to the owners and to the NCI, even if this results in a deficit in the NCI. This is demonstrated in the example below.

Example 1.10: Illustration of Non-controlling Interest in Consolidated Profit and Loss Account

Consolidated Profit and Loss Account (Extract)
for the year ended 31 March 2019

	2019	2018
	€000	€000
Profit before tax	xx	xx
Income tax expense	xx	xx
Profit for the year	xx	xx
Other comprehensive income		
Available-for-sale financial assets	xx	xx
Exchange difference on closing rate method	xx	xx
Income tax relating to components of other comprehensive income	(xx)	(xx)
Other comprehensive income for the year	xx	xx
Total comprehensive income for the year	xx	xx
Profit attributable to:		
Owners of the parent	xx	xx
Non-controlling interests	xx	xx
	xx	xx
Total comprehensive income attributable to:		
Owners of the parent	xx	xx
Non-controlling interests	xx	xx
	xx	xx

The following is an example of an Irish company, Ornua Co-operative Ltd, applying the required layout.

Ornua Co-operative Ltd
GROUP INCOME STATEMENT
for the period ended 29 December 2018

	Notes	2018 €'000	2017 €'000
Turnover		**2,082,059**	2,069,219
Cost of sales		**(1,824,823)**	(1,816,837)
Gross profit		**257,236**	252,382
Selling and distribution expenses		**(143,827)**	(154,459)
Administration expenses – excluding amortisation		**(65,961)**	(56,050)
Administration expenses – amortisation		**(7,029)**	(6,628)
Operating profit before exceptional items		**40,419**	35,245
Exceptional items	4	**(2,728)**	(2,081)
Operating profit after exceptional items		**37,691**	33,164
Share of results of associates & joint ventures	10	**(500)**	(62)
Interest payable (net)	5	**(3,654)**	(3,058)
Net interest expense on defined benefit pension schemes	24	**(910)**	(955)
Profit on ordinary activities before taxation	2	**32,627**	29,089
Tax on profit on ordinary activities	6	**(7,544)**	(10,673)
Profit for the financial period		**25,083**	18,416
Profit attributable to:			
Owners of the parent		**25,865**	18,759
Non-controlling interest		**(782)**	(343)
		25,083	18,416

The notes on pages 47 to 78 form part of these financial statements.

Disclosures in the Consolidated Financial Statements

The following must be disclosed:

(a) the fact that the financial statements are consolidated;
(b) the basis for concluding that control exists when less than 50% of the votes are held;
(c) any difference in the reporting date between the parent and its subsidiaries;

(d) the nature and extent of any significant restrictions to transfer funds;
(e) the name of any subsidiary excluded from consolidation and the reason for its exclusion; and
(f) the nature and extent of its interest in unconsolidated special purpose entities and the risks associated with those interests.

Individual and Separate Financial Statements

Preparation of Individual and Separate Financial Statements

The FRS does not require a parent to produce separate financial statements for itself or its subsidiaries. Separate financial statements are those prepared by a parent in which its investments in subsidiaries, associates and jointly controlled entities are accounted for at either cost or fair value.

Accounting Policy Election

When a parent prepares separate financial statements and describes that it is following the FRS, it must account for its investments in subsidiaries, associates and jointly controlled entities at:
(a) cost less impairment;
(b) fair value with changes recognised in OCI (or profit or loss); **or**
(c) fair value with changes recognised in profit or loss.

While the same accounting policy for all investments in a single class must be applied, entities can elect to employ different policies for different classes of investments.

Disclosures in Separate Financial Statements

Where a parent prepares separate financial statements, the parent must:
(a) disclose that the statements are separate financial statements; and
(b) describe the methods used to account for investments in subsidiaries, jointly controlled entities and associates, and identify the consolidated financial statements or other primary financial statements to which they relate.

If a parent adopts one of the exemptions from presenting consolidated financial statements, it must disclose the grounds for that exemption. There is also additional disclosure required by company law if it adopts the fair value through profit or loss model (outlined in **Chapter 12** (regarding Section 11)).

Exchanges of Business or Other Non-monetary Assets for an Interest in a Subsidiary, Joint Venture or Associate

When an entity exchanges a business for an interest in another entity and this latter entity becomes a subsidiary, associate or jointly controlled entity, the following accounting treatment is required:

(a) To the extent an entity retains an ownership interest, assume that it is owned throughout the transaction and held at carrying amount.
(b) Goodwill – is the difference between the fair value of consideration given less the fair value of the pre-transaction net assets of the other entity (which can include cash for equalisation of values).
(c) If the fair value of consideration received is greater than the carrying value of net assets given up, a gain is reported.
(d) If the fair value of consideration received is less than the carrying amount of net assets given up, a loss is reported.

However, to the extent that the transaction is artificial, then no gain or loss should be reported.

Intermediate Payment Arrangements

Intermediate payment arrangements can take a variety of forms:
(a) Usually, they are established by a sponsoring entity and constituted as a trust.
(b) The relationship between the sponsoring entity and the intermediary may take different forms. For example, if the relationship is a constituted trust then the sponsoring entity will not have a right to direct the intermediary's activities, although it may give advice to the intermediary or provide the information the intermediary needs to carry out its activities.
(c) The arrangements are most commonly used to pay employees or compensate suppliers, but could also benefit past employees and their dependants, and the intermediary may be entitled to make charitable donations.
(d) The precise identities of the beneficiaries are not usually agreed at the outset.
(e) The sponsoring entity often has the right to appoint or veto the appointment of the intermediary's trustees (or its directors or the equivalent).
(f) The payments made to the intermediary and the payments made by the intermediary are often cash payments, but may involve other transfers of value.

Examples include employee share ownership plans (ESOPs) used to facilitate employee remuneration schemes. An entity makes payments to a trust and the trust uses its funds to accumulate assets to pay the entity's employees for services the employees have rendered to the entity.

Although the trustees of an intermediary must act at all times in accordance with the interests of the beneficiaries, most intermediaries are specifically designed to serve the purposes of the sponsoring entity, and to ensure that there will be minimal risk of any conflict arising between the duties of the trustees of the intermediary and the interest of the sponsoring entity, such that there is nothing to encumber the implementation of the wishes of the sponsoring entity in practice. Where this is the case, the sponsoring entity has *de facto* control.

Accounting for Intermediate Payment Arrangements

When a sponsoring entity makes payments to an intermediary, there is a rebuttable presumption that the entity has exchanged one asset for another and that the payment itself does not represent an immediate expense. To rebut this presumption, at the time the payment is made to the intermediary, the entity must demonstrate that:

(a) it will not obtain future economic benefit from the amounts transferred; or
(b) it does not have control of the right or other access to the future economic benefit it is expected to receive.

Where a payment to an intermediary is an exchange by the sponsoring entity of one asset for another, any assets that the intermediary acquires in a subsequent exchange transaction will also be under the control of the entity. Accordingly, assets and liabilities of the intermediary shall be accounted for by the sponsoring entity as an extension of its own business and recognised in its own individual financial statements. An asset will cease to be recognised as an asset of the sponsoring entity when the asset of the intermediary vests unconditionally with the identified beneficiaries.

A sponsoring entity may distribute its own equity to an intermediary in order to facilitate employee shareholdings under a remuneration scheme. Where this is the case and the sponsoring entity has control, or *de facto* control, of the assets and liabilities of the intermediary, the commercial effect is that the sponsoring entity is, for all practical purposes, in the same position as if it had purchased the shares directly.

Where an intermediary holds the sponsoring entity's equity instruments, the sponsoring entity must account for the equity instruments as if it had purchased them directly. The sponsoring entity must account for the assets and liabilities of the intermediary in its individual financial statements as follows:

(a) Consideration paid for the equity investments is deducted from equity until the equity instruments vest unconditionally with employees.
(b) Consideration paid or received for the purchase or sale of the sponsoring entity's own equity investments are shown as separate amounts in the statement of changes in equity.
(c) Other assets and liabilities of the intermediary are recognised as assets and liabilities of the sponsoring entity.
(d) No gain or loss shall be recognised in profit or loss or OCI on the purchase, sale, issue or cancellation of the entity's own equity instruments.
(e) Finance costs and any administration expenses must be recognised on an accruals basis.
(f) Any dividend income arising on the sponsoring entity's own equity instruments is excluded from profit or loss and deducted from the aggregate of dividends paid.

Disclosures in Individual and Separate Financial Statements

Sufficient information must be disclosed in the notes to enable users to understand the significance of the intermediary and the arrangement in the context of the sponsoring entity's financial statements. This information should include:

(a) a description of the main features of the intermediary, including the arrangements for making payments and for distributing equity instruments;
(b) any restrictions relating to the assets and liabilities of the intermediary;
(c) the amount and nature of the assets and liabilities held by the intermediary that have not yet vested unconditionally with the beneficiaries of the arrangement;
(d) the amount that has been deducted from equity and the number of equity instruments held by the intermediary that have not yet vested unconditionally with the beneficiaries;
(e) for entities that have their equity instruments listed or publicly traded on a stock exchange or market, the market value of the equity instruments held by the intermediary that have not yet vested unconditionally with employees;
(f) the extent to which the equity instruments are under option to employees, or have been conditionally gifted to them; and
(g) the amount that has been deducted from the aggregate dividends paid by the sponsoring entity.

1.8 SMALL ENTITIES – FRS 102 SECTION 1A

Small entities have three options on how their financial statements can be prepared:

- follow FRS 102 formats as per the Companies Acts (ROI and UK);
- use the abridged balance sheet and profit and loss account; or
- use the adapted balance sheet and profit and loss account.

Abridged Balance Sheet

If a small entity applies an abridged balance sheet it must still provide a true and fair view. In doing so, it must therefore consider any necessary additional disclosures in the notes to the financial statements, for example in relation to disaggregating the information in the balance sheet.

Irish law does not provide for the preparation of abridged statutory financial statements. Consequently, this option to prepare an abridged balance sheet and profit and loss account is not available to Irish small entities. This is not, however, the same as abridgement for filing purposes.

Adapted Balance Sheet

A small entity can adapt one of the balance sheet formats but must, as a minimum, include in its statement of financial position line items that present the following, distinguishing between those items that are current and those that are non-current:

(a) property, plant and equipment;
(b) investment property carried at fair value through profit or loss;
(c) intangible assets;
(d) financial assets (excluding amounts shown under (e), (f), (j) and (k));
(e) investments in associates;
(f) investments in jointly controlled entities;
(g) biological assets carried at cost less accumulated depreciation and impairment;
(h) biological assets carried at fair value through profit or loss;
(i) inventories;
(j) trade and other receivables;
(k) cash and cash equivalents;
(l) trade and other payables;
(m) provisions;
(n) financial liabilities (excluding amounts shown under (l) and (m));
(o) liabilities and assets for current tax;
(p) deferred tax liabilities and deferred tax assets (classified as non-current);
(q) non-controlling interest, presented within equity separately from the equity attributable to the owners of the parent; and
(r) equity attributable to the owners of the parent.

A small entity must also disclose, either in the statement of financial position or in the notes, the following sub-classifications of the line items presented:

(a) property, plant and equipment in classifications appropriate to the small entity;
(b) goodwill and other intangible assets;
(c) investments, showing separately shares and loans;
(d) trade and other receivables, showing separately amounts due from related parties and amounts due from other parties;
(e) trade and other payables, showing separately amounts payable to trade suppliers and amounts payable to related parties; and
(f) classes of equity, such as called up share capital, share premium, retained earnings, revaluation reserve, fair value reserve and other reserves.

The descriptions above and the ordering of items or aggregation of similar items, may be amended according to the nature of the small entity and its transactions, to provide information that is relevant to an understanding of the small entity's financial position, providing the information given is at least equivalent to that required by the balance sheet format had it not been adapted.

A small entity must present current assets separately from non-current assets, and similarly current liabilities from non-current liabilities.

Abridged Profit and Loss Account

Again, a small entity choosing to prepare an abridged profit and loss account must still give a true and fair view. A small entity therefore must also consider and provide additional disclosure that is necessary in the notes to the financial statements, for example in relation to disaggregating gross profit or loss and disclosing turnover.

Irish law does not provide for the preparation of abridged statutory financial statements. Consequently, this option to prepare an abridged profit and loss account is not available to Irish small entities. This is not, however, the same as abridgement for filing purposes.

Adapted Profit and Loss Account

A small entity choosing to adapt one of the profit and loss account formats must, as a minimum, include in its income statement line items that present the following amounts for the period:

(a) revenue;
(b) finance costs;
(c) share of the profit or loss of investments in associate and jointly controlled entities accounted for using the equity method;
(d) profit or loss before taxation;
(e) tax expense excluding tax allocated to other comprehensive income or equity; and
(f) profit or loss.

A small entity may include additional line items and it can amend the descriptions used above, and their order, when this is necessary to explain the elements of financial performance, providing the information given is at least equivalent to that required by the profit and loss account format had it not been adapted.

The following is an example of an Irish company presenting its balance sheet in accordance with Section 1A of FRS 102.

McEniff's Grand Canal Hotel Ltd
BALANCE SHEET
as at 31 December 2017

		2017		2016	
	Notes	**€**	**€**	**€**	**€**
Fixed assets					
Tangible assets	4		4,050,394		12,459
Current assets					
Stocks	5	66,295		65,901	
Debtors	6	295,626		179,742	
Cash at bank and in hand		1,003,704		1,567,403	
		1,365,625		1,813,046	

Creditors: amounts falling due within one year	**7**	(1,512,512)		(861,237)	
Net current (liabilities)/ assets			(146,887)		951,809
Total assets less current liabilities			3,903,507		964,268
Creditors: amounts falling due after more than one year	**9**		(1,528,297)		(283,009)
Provisions for liabilities	**10**		(10,903)		0
Net assets			2,364,307		681,259
Capital and reserves					
Called up share capital presented as equity			161		161
Share premium account			134,966		134,966
Profit and loss reserves	**11**		2,229,180		546,132
Total equity			2,364,307		681,529

1.9 MICRO-ENTITIES

Micro-entities are exempt from the presentation requirements outlined in this chapter. There is no requirement for micro-entities to present a statement of cash flows or a statement of changes in equity, but they must present a statement of financial position in one of the formats shown below.[3]

Format 1	**CU**	**CU**
Called up share capital not paid	X	
Fixed assets	X	
Current assets	X	
Prepayments and accrued income	X	
Creditors: amounts falling due within one year	(X)	
Net current assets / (liabilities)		X/(X)
Total assets less current liabilities		X
Creditors: amounts falling due after more than one year		(X)
Provisions for liabilities		(X)
Accruals and deferred income		(X)
		X
Capital and reserves		X

[3] FRS 105 *The Financial Reporting Standard applicable to the Micro-entities Regime*, para. 4.3.

Format 2	**CU**	**CU**
Assets		
Called up share capital not paid		X
Fixed assets		X
Current assets		X
Prepayments and accrued income		X
		X
Capital, Reserves and Liabilities		
Capital and reserves		X
Provisions for liabilities		X
Creditors		
Amounts falling due within one year	X	
Amounts falling due after one year	X	
		X
Accruals and deferred income		X
		X

Micro-entities must also present their profit or loss for a period or their income statement in the format below.[4]

	CU	**CU**
Turnover		X
Other income		X
Cost of raw materials and consumables		(X)
Staff costs		(X)
Depreciation and other amounts written off assets		(X)
Other charges		(X)
Tax		(X)
Profit or loss		X/(X)

A sample statement of financial position from an Irish hardware retailing micro-entity is provided below. This company chose not to file its income statement.

STATEMENT OF FINANCIAL POSITION
for the year ended 31 March 2017

	2018 **€**	2017 €
Fixed assets	**3,074**	3,968
Current assets	**331,919**	320,635
Creditors: amounts falling due within one year	**(40,934)**	(32,666)
Net Current Assets	**290,985**	287,969
Total Assets less Current Liabilities	**294,059**	291,937
Accruals and deferred income	**(2,000)**	(2,951)
Net Assets	**292,059**	288,986
Capital and Reserves	**292,059**	288,986

[4] FRS 105 *The Financial Reporting Standard applicable to the Micro-entities Regime*, para. 5.3.

DISCLOSURE CHECKLIST: PRESENTATION OF FINANCIAL STATEMENTS – FRS 102

(References are to the relevant Section of FRS 102)

	PARA.
Compliance with FRS 102	
An entity whose financial statements comply with this FRS shall make an explicit and unreserved statement of such compliance in the notes. Financial statements shall not be described as complying with this FRS unless they comply with all the requirements of this FRS.	3.3
When an entity departs from a requirement of this FRS in accordance with paragraph 3.4, it shall disclose the following: (a) that management has concluded that the financial statements fairly present the entity's financial position, financial performance and cash flows; (b) that it has complied with the FRS, except that it has departed from a particular requirement to achieve a fair presentation; and (c) the nature of the departure, including the treatment that the FRS would require, the reason why that treatment would be so misleading in the circumstances that it would conflict with the objective of financial statements set out in Section 2, and the treatment adopted.	3.5
When an entity has departed from a requirement of this FRS in a prior period, and that departure affects the amounts recognised in the financial statements for the current period, it shall make the disclosures set out in paragraph 3.5(c).	3.6
Going concern	
When management is aware, in making its assessment, of material uncertainties related to events or conditions that cast significant doubt upon the entity's ability to continue as a going concern, the entity shall disclose those uncertainties. When an entity does not prepare financial statements on a going concern basis, it shall disclose that fact, together with the basis on which it prepared the financial statements and the reason why the entity is not regarded as a going concern.	3.9
Frequency of reporting	
An entity shall present a complete set of financial statements (including comparative information – see paragraph 3.14) at least annually. When the end of an entity's reporting period changes and the annual financial statements are presented for a longer or shorter period than one year, the entity shall disclose the following: (a) that fact; (b) for each period presented, the adjustments to each item in the financial statements that management has concluded would be necessary to achieve a fair presentation; and (c) the fact that comparative amounts presented in the financial statements (including the related notes) are not entirely comparable.	3.10
Consistency of presentation	
When the presentation or classification of items in the financial statements is changed, an entity shall reclassify comparative amounts unless the reclassification is impracticable. When comparative amounts are reclassified, an entity shall disclose the following: (a) the nature of the reclassification; (b) the amount of each item or class of items that is reclassified; and (c) the reason for the reclassification.	3.12
If it is impracticable to reclassify comparative amounts, an entity shall disclose why.	3.13

	PARA.
Comparative information	
Except when this FRS permits or requires otherwise, an entity shall present comparative information in respect of the preceding period for all amounts presented in the current period's financial statements. An entity shall include comparative information for narrative and descriptive information when it is relevant to an understanding of the current period's financial statements.	3.14
Materiality and aggregation	
An entity shall present separately each material class of similar items. An entity shall present separately items of a dissimilar nature or function unless they are immaterial.	3.15
Complete set of financial statements	
A complete set of financial statements of an entity shall include all of the following: (a) a statement of financial position as at the reporting date; (b) either: (i) a single statement of comprehensive income for the reporting period displaying all items of income and expense recognised during the period, including those items recognised in determining profit or loss (which is a subtotal in the statement of comprehensive income) and items of other comprehensive income, or (ii) a separate income statement and a separate statement of comprehensive income. If an entity chooses to present both an income statement and a statement of comprehensive income, the statement of comprehensive income begins with profit or loss and then displays the items of other comprehensive income; (c) a statement of changes in equity for the reporting period; (d) a statement of cash flows for the reporting period; (e) notes, comprising significant accounting policies and other explanatory information.	3.17
If the only changes to equity during the periods for which financial statements are presented arise from profit or loss, payment of dividends, corrections of prior period errors and changes in accounting policy, the entity may present a single statement of income and retained earnings in place of the statement of comprehensive income and statement of changes in equity (see paragraph 6.4).	3.18
If an entity has no items of other comprehensive income in any of the periods for which financial statements are presented, it may present only an income statement, or it may present a statement of comprehensive income in which the 'bottom line' is labelled 'profit or loss'.	3.19
In a complete set of financial statements, an entity shall present each financial statement with equal prominence.	3.21
Identification of the financial statements	
An entity shall clearly identify each of the financial statements and the notes and distinguish them from other information in the same document. In addition, an entity shall display the following information prominently, and repeat it when necessary for an understanding of the information presented: (a) the name of the reporting entity and any change in its name since the end of the preceding reporting period; (b) whether the financial statements cover the individual entity or a group of entities; (c) the date of the end of the reporting period and the period covered by the financial statements; (d) the presentation currency, as defined in Section 30 *Foreign Currency Translation*; and (e) the level of rounding, if any, used in presenting amounts in the financial statements.	3.23

	PARA.
An entity shall disclose the following in the notes: (a) the legal form of the entity, its country of incorporation and the address of its registered office (or principal place of business, if different from the registered office); and (b) a description of the nature of the entity's operations and its principal activities....	3.24
Presentation of information not required by this FRS	
This FRS does not address presentation of interim financial reports. An entity applying this FRS shall describe the basis for preparing and presenting the information....	3.25
Components of cash and cash equivalents	
An entity shall present the components of cash and cash equivalents and shall present a reconciliation of the amounts presented in the statement of cash flows to the equivalent items presented in the statement of financial position. However, an entity is not required to present this reconciliation if the amount of cash and cash equivalents presented in the statement of cash flows is identical to the amount similarly described in the statement of financial position.	7.20
Other disclosures [Statement of Cash Flows]	
An entity shall disclose, together with a commentary by management, the amount of significant cash and cash equivalent balances held by the entity that are not available for use by the entity. Cash and cash equivalents held by an entity may not be available for use by the entity because of, among other reasons, foreign exchange controls or legal restrictions.	7.21
An entity shall disclose an analysis of changes in net debt from the beginning to the end of the reporting period showing changes resulting from: (a) the cash flows of the entity; (b) the acquisition and disposal of subsidiaries; (c) new finance leases entered into; (d) other non-cash changes; and (e) the recognition of changes in market value and exchange rate movements. When several balances (or parts thereof) from the statement of financial position have been combined to form the components of opening and closing net debt, sufficient detail shall be shown to enable users to identify these balances. This analysis need not be presented for prior periods.	7.22
Disclosure of accounting policies	
An entity shall disclose its significant accounting policies comprising: (a) the measurement basis (or bases) used in preparing the financial statements; and (b) the other accounting policies used that are relevant to an understanding of the financial statements.	8.5
Information about judgements	
An entity shall disclose, along with its significant accounting policies or other notes, the judgements, apart from those involving estimations (see paragraph 8.7), that management has made in the process of applying the entity's accounting policies and that have the most significant effect on the amounts recognised in the financial statements.	8.6
Information about key sources of estimation uncertainty	
An entity shall disclose in the notes information about the key assumptions concerning the future, and other key sources of estimation uncertainty at the reporting date, that have a significant risk of causing a material adjustment to the carrying amounts of assets and liabilities within the next financial year. In respect of those assets and liabilities, the notes shall include details of: (a) their nature; and (b) their carrying amount as at the end of the reporting period.	8.7

	Para.
Disclosures in consolidated financial statements	
The following disclosures shall be made in consolidated financial statements: (a) the fact that the statements are consolidated financial statements; (b) the basis for concluding that control exists when the parent does not own, directly or indirectly through subsidiaries, more than half of the voting power; (c) any difference in the reporting date of the financial statements of the parent and its subsidiaries used in the preparation of the consolidated financial statements; (d) the nature and extent of any significant restrictions (e.g. resulting from borrowing arrangements or regulatory requirements) on the ability of subsidiaries to transfer funds to the parent in the form of cash dividends or to repay loans; (e) the name of any subsidiary excluded from consolidation and the reason for with exclusion; and (f) the nature and extent of its interest in unconsolidated special purpose entities, and the risks associated with those interests.	9.23
Disclosures in separate financial statements	
When a parent prepares separate financial statements, those separate financial statements shall disclose: (a) that the statements are separate financial statements; and (b) a description of the methods used to account for the investments in subsidiaries, jointly controlled entities and associates.	9.27
A parent that uses one of the exemptions from presenting consolidated financial statements (described in paragraph 9.3) shall disclose the grounds on which the parent is exempt.	9.27A
When a parent adopts a policy of accounting for its investments in subsidiaries, associates or jointly controlled entities at fair value with changes in fair value recognised in profit or loss, it must comply with the requirements of paragraph 36(4) of Schedule 1 to the Regulations [the Large and Medium-sized Companies and Groups (Accounts and Reports) Regulations 2008 (SI 2008/410)] by applying the disclosure requirements of Section 11 *Basic Financial Instruments* to those investments.	9.27B
Disclosures in individual and separate financial statements	
When a sponsoring entity recognises the assets and liabilities held by an intermediary, it should disclose sufficient information in the notes to its financial statements to enable users to understand the significance of the intermediary and the arrangement in the context of the sponsoring entity's financial statements. This should include: (a) a description of the main features of the intermediary, including the arrangements for making payments and for distributing equity instruments; (b) any restrictions relating to the assets and liabilities of the intermediary; (c) the amount and nature of the assets and liabilities held by the intermediary that have not yet vested unconditionally with the beneficiaries of the arrangement; (d) the amount that has been deducted from equity and the number of equity instruments held by the intermediary that have not yet vested unconditionally with the beneficiaries of the arrangement; (e) for entities that have their equity instruments listed or publicly traded on a stock exchange or market, the market value of the equity instruments held by the intermediary which have not yet vested unconditionally with employees; (f) the extent to which the equity instruments are under option to employees, or have been conditionally gifted to them; and (g) the amount that has been deducted from the aggregate dividends paid by the sponsoring entity.	9.38

DISCLOSURE CHECKLIST: PRESENTATION OF FINANCIAL STATEMENTS – SMALL ENTITIES

(References are to the relevant Appendix of FRS 102 Section 1A)

The mandatory disclosure requirements for small entities required under the Companies Act 2014 (ROI) (CA 2014), the Companies Act 2006 (UK) (CA 2006) and the Small Companies and Groups (Accounts and Directors' Report) Regulations 2008 (UK) (S.I. 409 of 2008) are as follows:

	PARA.
As a minimum, when relevant to its transactions, other events and conditions, a small entity in the Republic of Ireland [and in the UK] shall provide the disclosures set out in this appendix.	1AD.1 (ROI) 1AC.1 (UK)
These notes shall be presented in the order in which, where relevant, the items to which they relate are presented in the statement of financial position and in the income statement. (Schedule 3A, paragraph 43(2) CA 2014 (ROI)) (Schedule 1, paragraph 42(2) S.I. 2008/409 (UK)) Paragraphs 8.3 and 8.4 of FRS 102 address similar requirements.	1AD.2 (ROI) 1AC.2 (UK) (similar)
Basis of preparation	
A small entity shall ensure that its financial statements include a statement as to whether they have been prepared in accordance with Section 1A of FRS 102 and for any material departure from Section 1A of FRS 102, the effect of the departure and the reasons for it are noted in the financial statements. [Section 291(7) CA 2014]	1AD.3 (ROI only)
True and fair override	
If it appears to the small entity that there are special reasons for departing from any of the principles set out in company law in preparing the small entity's financial statements in respect of any reporting period, it may do so, in which case particulars of the departure, the reasons for it, and its effects on the statement of financial position and income statement shall be given in the notes to the financial statements. (Section 291(6) CA 2014 (ROI) and Schedule 3A, paragraph 19) (Schedule 1, paragraph 10(2) S.I. 2008/409 (UK)) This is only expected to occur in special circumstances. Paragraphs 3.4 and 3.5 of FRS 102 address similar requirements.	1AD.11 (ROI) 1AC.10 (UK) (similar)
Notes supporting the statement of financial position	
Where an asset or liability relates to more than one of the items listed in the statement of financial position, its relationship to other items shall be disclosed either under the item where it is shown or in the notes to the financial statements. (Schedule 3A, paragraph 4(7) CA 2014 (ROI)) (Schedule 1, paragraph 9A S.I. 2008/409 (UK))	1AD.12 (ROI) 1AC.11 (UK) (similar)
Other	
The financial statements shall state the following: (a) the name and legal form of the small entity; (b) the place of registration of the small entity and the number under which it is registered; (c) the address of its registered office;	1AD.52 (ROI only) (similar to 1AC.37 (UK))

	PARA.
(d) if relevant, the fact that the small entity is being wound up, and where appropriate, whether a receiver or a provisional liquidator has been appointed and the former name as well as the existing name of the small entity if the winding up of the small entity commences within one year after the date on which it has changed its name. (Section 291(3A) CA 2014) Paragraph 3.24(a) addresses similar requirements to (a), (b) and (c).	1AD.52 (ROI only) (similar to 1AC.37 (UK))
The financial statements must state: (a) the part of the UK in which the small entity is registered; (b) the small entity's registered number; (c) whether the small entity is a public or private company and whether the small entity is limited by shares or by guarantee; (d) the address of the small entity's registered office; and (e) where appropriate, the fact that the entity is being wound up. (Section 396 CA 2006) Paragraph 3.24(a) addresses similar requirements.	1AC.37 (UK only) (similar to 1AD.52 (ROI))
Where items to which Arabic numbers are given in any of the formats have been combined, unless they are not material, the individual amounts of any items which have been combined shall be disclosed in a note to the financial statements. (Schedule 3A, paragraph 4(5) CA 2014 (ROI)) (Schedule 1, paragraph 4(3) S.I. 2008/409 (UK))	1AD.53 (ROI) 1AC.38 (UK) (similar)
Amounts in respect of items representing assets or income may be set off against amounts in respect of items representing liabilities or expenditure or vice versa in accordance with applicable accounting standards, provided that the gross amounts are disclosed in a note to the financial statements. (Schedule 3A, paragraph 7 CA 2014 (ROI))	1AD.55 (ROI only)
Additional disclosures encouraged for small entities	
When relevant to its transactions, other events and conditions, a small entity in the UK is encouraged to provide the following disclosures: (a) a statement of compliance with FRS 102 as set out in paragraph 3.3, adapted to refer to Section 1A; (b) a statement that it is a public benefit entity as set out in paragraph PBE3.3A; (c) the disclosures relating to material uncertainties related to events or conditions that cast significant doubt upon the small entity's ability to continue as a going concern as set out in paragraph 3.9; (d) dividends declared and paid or payable during the period (for example, as set out in paragraph 6.5(b)); and (e) on first-time adoption of this FRS an explanation of how the transition has affected its financial position and financial performance as set out in paragraph 35.13.	1AE.1 (UK only)
When relevant to its transactions, other events and conditions, a small entity in the Republic of Ireland is encouraged to provide the disclosures in paragraph 1AE.1(b), (c) and (e).	1AE.2 (ROI only)

Disclosure Checklist: Presentation of Financial Statements – Micro-entities (Republic of Ireland only)

(References are to the relevant Section of FRS 105)

The mandatory disclosure requirements for micro-entities required under FRS 105 and the Companies Act 2014 (ROI) (CA 2014) are as follows:

	Para.
An Irish micro-entity shall disclose particulars of any departure from the principles set out in company law in preparing the micro-entity's financial statements, the reasons for it and its effects on the statement of financial position and income statement in accordance with Appendix B to Section 6 *Notes to the Financial Statements*.	3.15 (ROI only)
An Irish micro-entity shall disclose information in relation to the following items in accordance with Appendix B to Section 6: (a) a change in the format of the statement of financial position adopted; (b) an asset or liability that relates to more than one of the items listed in the statement of financial position; and (c) any debts included under 'creditors' against which security has been given.	4.5 (ROI only)
Notes	
The notes shall be presented in the order in which, where relevant, the items to which they relate are presented in the statement of financial position and in the income statement. (Schedule 3B, paragraph 31(2) CA 2014)	6B.1 (ROI only)
Basis of preparation	
A micro-entity shall ensure that its financial statements include a statement as to whether they have been prepared in accordance with this FRS and for any material departure from this FRS, the effect of the departure and the reasons for it are noted in the financial statements. (Section 291(7) CA 2014)	6B.2 (ROI only)
Accounting policies	
A micro-entity shall disclose in the notes to its financial statements the accounting policies adopted by the micro-entity in determining: (a) the items and amounts to be included in its statement of financial position; and (b) the items and amounts to be included in its income statement. (Section 321(1) CA 2014)	6B.3 (ROI only)
In any case where any goodwill acquired by a micro-entity is shown or included as an asset in the micro-entity's statement of financial position, the period chosen for writing off the consideration for that goodwill and the reasons for choosing that period shall be disclosed in a note to the financial statements. (Schedule 3B, paragraph 25(4) CA 2014) See paragraph 14.4 [of FRS 105].	6B.4 (ROI only)

	PARA.
Changes in presentation and accounting policies and correcting prior period errors	
Where any change is made in the format adopted in preparing a statement of financial position of a micro-entity, the reasons for the change, together with full particulars of the change, shall be given in a note to the financial statements in which the new format is first adopted. (Schedule 3B, paragraph 3(2) CA 2014) See paragraph 4.5(a) [of FRS 105].	6B.5 (ROI only)
Where a micro-entity changes an accounting policy and has disclosed such change in the notes to the financial statements, the notes to those financial statements shall also disclose: (a) the reason for the change in accounting policy; and (b) to the extent practicable, the impact of the change in accounting policy on the financial statements for the current reporting period and on the financial statements of preceding periods. (Section 321(3) CA 2014) See paragraph 8.10A [of FRS 105].	6B.6 (ROI only)
Where the corresponding amount for the immediately preceding reporting period is not comparable with the amount to be shown for the item in question in respect of the reporting period to which the statement of financial position or income statement relates, the former amount may be adjusted, and particulars of the adjustment and the reasons therefor shall be given in a note to the financial statements. (Schedule 3B, paragraph 5 CA 2014) This is likely to be relevant when there has either been a change in accounting policy or the correction of a material prior period error. See Section 8 *Accounting Policies, Estimates and Errors.*	6B.7 (ROI only)
Departure from principles in company law	
If it appears to the micro-entity that there are special reasons for departing from any of the principles set out in company law in preparing the micro-entity's financial statements in respect of any reporting period, it may do so, in which case particulars of the departure, the reasons for it, and its effects on the statement of financial position and income statement must be given in the notes to the financial statements. (Schedule 3B, paragraph 19 CA 2014) This is only expected to occur in special circumstances. See Section 3 FRS 105, *Financial Statement Presentation.*	6B.8 (ROI only)
Notes supporting the statement of financial position	
Where an asset or liability relates to more than one of the items listed in the statement of financial position, its relationship to other items shall be disclosed either under the item where it is shown or in the notes to the financial statements. (Schedule 3B, paragraph 4(4) CA 2014) See paragraph 4.5(b) [of FRS 105].	6B.9 (ROI only)
Impairment of assets	
Value adjustments for impairment of fixed assets (including fixed asset investments) must be disclosed (either separately or in aggregate) in a note to the financial statements if not shown separately in the income statement. (Schedule 3B, paragraphs 23(1) and (2) CA 2014)	6B.10 (ROI only)

	Para.
Any value adjustments for impairment of fixed assets (including fixed asset investments) that are reversed because the reasons for which they were made have ceased to apply must be disclosed (either separately or in aggregate) in a note to the financial statements if not shown separately in the income statement. (Schedule 3B, paragraph 23(3) CA 2014) See paragraph 22.22 [of FRS 105].	6B.11 (ROI only)
Indebtedness, guarantees and financial commitments	
In respect of 'creditors' shown in the micro-entity's statement of financial position there shall be stated: (a) the aggregate amount of any debts included under that item in respect of which any security has been given; and (b) an indication of the nature of the securities so given. (Schedule 3B, paragraph 34 CA 2014) See paragraph 4.5(c) [of FRS 105].	6B.12 (ROI only)
Particulars shall be given of any charge on the assets of the micro-entity to secure the liabilities of any other person, including, where practicable, the amount secured. (Schedule 3B, paragraph 35(1) CA 2014)	6B.13 (ROI only)
Particulars and the total amount or estimated total amount shall be given with respect to any other financial commitment, guarantee or contingency not provided for in the statement of financial position. (Schedule 3B, paragraph 35(2) CA 2014) See paragraphs 9.28(a), 11.9, 12.128(a), 13.17(a), 14.3, 15.17, 15.33, 16.19 and 27.5(a) [of FRS 105]. The aggregate amount of any such commitments, guarantees or contingencies which are undertaken on behalf of or for the benefit of: (a) any parent or fellow subsidiary of the micro-entity; (b) any subsidiary of the micro-entity; or (c) any undertaking in which the micro-entity has a participating interest, shall be separately stated and those within each of clauses (a), (b) and (c) shall also be stated separately from those within any other of those clauses. (Schedule 3B, paragraph 35(6) CA 2014)	6B.14 (ROI only)
An indication of the nature and form of any valuable security given by the micro-entity in connection with its commitments, guarantees and contingencies not provided for in the statement of financial position must be given. (Schedule 3B, paragraph 35(3) CA 2014) See paragraphs 9.28(b), 10.22, 12.28(b), 13.17(b) and 27.5(b) [of FRS 105].	6B.15 (ROI only)
The total amount of any commitments not provided for in the statement of financial position concerning retirement benefits shall be disclosed separately. (Schedule 3B, paragraph 35(4) CA 2014) See paragraph 23.22 [of FRS 105].	6B.16 (ROI only)
Particulars shall be given of retirement benefit commitments which are included in the statement of financial position. (Schedule 3B, paragraph 35(5) CA 2014) See paragraph 23.23 [of FRS 105].	6B.17 (ROI only)

	Para.
Appropriation of profit or loss	
The income statement, statement of financial position or notes to the financial statements of a micro-entity for a reporting period shall show: (a) the aggregate amount of dividends paid in the reporting period (other than dividends for which a liability existed at the immediately preceding reporting date); (b) the aggregate amount of dividends the micro-entity is liable to pay at the reporting date (other than dividends for which a liability existed at the immediately preceding reporting date); (c) separately, any transfer between the retained earnings and other reserves; (d) any other increase or reduction in the balance on retained earnings since the immediately preceding reporting date; (e) the profit or loss brought forward at the beginning of the reporting period; and (f) the profit or loss carried forward at the end of the reporting period. (Schedule 3B, paragraph 33 CA 2014) See paragraph 17.16 [of FRS 105] in relation to sub-paragraphs (a) and (b).	6B.18 (ROI only)
Related party disclosures	
Transactions with directors (Sections 307 and 308 of the Companies Act 2014)	
The financial statements of a micro-entity shall disclose, both for the current and the preceding reporting period, in the notes to the financial statements the particulars of the following arrangements (see paragraphs 6B.20 to 6B.23).	6B.19 (ROI only)
Loans, quasi-loans and credit transactions	
Exemption: The disclosure requirements in paragraphs 6B.20 to 6B.23 of FRS 105 do not apply in relation to an individual director and persons connected with him or her if the aggregate value of all agreements, transactions and arrangements did not, at any time during the reporting period, exceed €7,500 for that director and those persons. Section 308(6) states that references to 'director' are also to be read as references to an 'officer who is not a director' as applicable. (Sections 308(3), 308(5) and 308(6) CA 2014)	
The particulars required in respect of loans, quasi-loans and credit transactions entered into by the micro-entity with or for persons who at any time during the reporting period, were directors of the company or of its parent or persons connected with such directors, separately for each director or other person, are: (a) the name of the person for whom the arrangements were made and where that person is or was connected with a director of the micro-entity or its parent, the name of the director; (b) the value of the arrangements at the beginning and end of the reporting period; (c) advances made under the arrangements during the reporting period; (d) amounts repaid under the arrangements during the reporting period; (e) the amounts of any allowance made during the reporting period in respect of any failure or anticipated failure by the borrower to repay the whole or part of the outstanding amount; (f) amounts outstanding under the arrangements waived during the reporting period; (g) an indication of the interest rate; and (h) the arrangements' other main conditions. (Section 307(3) CA 2014)	6B.20 (ROI only)

	PARA.
Additionally, a separate total of the amounts stated for the purposes of each of paragraphs (b) to (f) above, and the amounts stated for the purposes of paragraph (b) expressed as a percentage of the net assets of the micro-entity at the beginning and end of the reporting period shall be disclosed. (Section 307(8)(a) and (c) CA 2014) These additional requirements are extended to persons who are officers (but not directors) of the micro-entity or its parent, and separate disclosure in respect of these officers is required on an aggregate basis, as well as the number of officers for whom such arrangements were made. (Section 307(9) CA 2014)	6B.20 (ROI only)
The particulars required in respect of an agreement to enter into loans, quasi-loans or credit transactions by the micro-entity with or for persons who at any time during the reporting period, were directors of the company or directors of its parent or persons connected with such directors, are those of sub-paragraphs (a), (g) and (h) of paragraph 6B.20, and additionally the value of the arrangements agreed to. (Section 307(4) CA 2014) All the above disclosures shall be made separately for each director or other person.	6B.21 (ROI only)
Guarantees and security provided by the micro-entity	
The particulars required for guarantees entered into and security provided by the micro-entity on behalf of persons who at any time during the reporting period were directors of the micro-entity or of its parent or persons connected with such directors in connection with a loan, quasi-loan or credit transaction entered into with or for those directors or other persons, separately for each director or other person, are: (a) the name of the person for whom the arrangements were made and where that person is or was connected with a director of the micro-entity or its parent, the name of the director; (b) the amount of the maximum liability that may be incurred by the micro-entity; (c) any amount paid and any liability incurred by the micro-entity for the purpose of fulfilling the guarantee or on foot of the provision of security (including any loss incurred by reason of enforcement of the guarantee or loss of the security); and (d) the arrangements' main terms. (Section 307(5) CA 2014) Additionally, a separate total of the amounts stated for the purposes of each of items (b) and (c) above is required. (Section 307(8)(b) CA 2014) This requirement is extended to persons who are officers (but not directors) of the micro-entity or its parent, and separate disclosure in respect of these officers is required on an aggregate basis, as well as the number of officers for whom such arrangements were made. (Section 307(9) CA 2014)	6B.22 (ROI only)
The particulars required in respect of agreements by the micro-entity to enter into guarantees or provide security on behalf of persons who at any time during the reporting period were directors of the micro-entity or of its parent or persons connected with such directors in connection with a loan, quasi-loan or credit transaction entered into with or for those directors or other persons, are those of sub-paragraphs (a), (b) and (d) of paragraph 6B.22. (Section 307(6) CA 2014) The disclosures shall be made separately for each director or other person.	6B.23 (ROI only)

	PARA.
Additional requirements	
Where at any time during the reporting period the aggregate of the amounts of: (a) the amount outstanding under arrangements waived comprising loans, quasi loans and credit transactions; and (b) the amount of the maximum liability that may be incurred by the micro-entity in respect of arrangements comprising guarantees entered into or security provided in connection with a loan, quasi-loan or credit transaction amount to more than 10% of the net assets of the micro-entity, the aggregate amount shall be stated and the percentage of net assets that the total represents. (Section 307(10) CA 2014)	6B.24 (ROI only)
A micro-entity that is a parent shall provide the information required by paragraphs 6B.19 to 6B.24 in its financial statements in relation to both the micro-entity and its subsidiaries. (Section 308(4) CA 2014) The micro-entities regime is not available if consolidated financial statements are prepared.	6B.25 (ROI only)
Other related party disclosures	
Where a micro-entity, or a nominee of the micro-entity or a person acting in that person's own name but on behalf of the micro-entity, holds shares in the micro-entity or an interest in such shares, the notes to the financial statements shall give separately: (a) the number and aggregate nominal value of those shares and, where shares of more than one class have been acquired, the number and aggregate nominal value of each class of such shares, at the beginning and end of the reporting period together with the consideration paid for such shares; (b) a reconciliation of the number and nominal value of each class of such shares from the beginning of the reporting period to the end of the reporting period showing all changes during the reporting period, including further acquisitions, disposals and cancellations, in each case showing the value of the consideration paid or received, if any; (c) the reasons for any acquisitions made during the reporting period; (d) the proportion of called-up share capital held at the beginning and end of the reporting period; and (e) particulars of any restriction on profits available for distribution by virtue of the application of Section 320. (Section 320 CA 2014)	6B.26 (ROI only)
Other	
Amounts in respect of items representing assets or income may be set off against amounts in respect of items representing liabilities or expenditure or vice versa in accordance with applicable accounting standards, provided that the gross amounts are disclosed in a note to the financial statements. (Schedule 3B, paragraph 7 CA 2014) See Section 2 [of FRS 105] *Concepts and Pervasive Principles*.	6B.27 (ROI only)
In accordance with Sections 325(1A)(b) and 328 [CA 2014] a micro-entity that chooses not to prepare a directors' report shall provide the information required by Section 328 in respect of acquisitions or disposals of own shares. (Section 325(1A)(b) CA 2014)	6B.28 (ROI only)

DISCLOSURE CHECKLIST: PRESENTATION OF FINANCIAL STATEMENTS – MICRO-ENTITIES (UNITED KINGDOM ONLY)

(References are to the relevant Section of FRS 105)

The mandatory disclosure requirements for micro-entities required under FRS 105, the Companies Act 2006 (UK) (CA 2006) and the Small Companies and Groups (Accounts and Directors' Report) Regulations 2008 (UK) (S.I. 409/2008) are as follows:

	PARA.
If in any reporting period a micro-entity is or has been party to arrangements that are not reflected in its statement of financial position and at the reporting date the risks or benefits arising from those arrangements are material, the nature and business purpose of the arrangements must be given in the notes to the financial statements to the extent necessary for enabling the financial position of the micro-entity to be assessed. (Section 410A CA 2006)	6A.1 (UK only)
The notes to a micro-entity's financial statements must disclose the average number of persons employed by the micro-entity in the financial year. (Section 411 CA 2006)	6A.2 (UK only)
Details of advances and credits granted by a micro-entity to its directors and guarantees of any kind entered into by a micro-entity on behalf of its directors must be shown in the notes to the financial statements. The details required of an advance or credit are: (a) its amount; (b) an indication of the interest rate; (c) its main conditions; (d) any amounts repaid; (e) any amounts written off; and (f) any amounts waived. There must also be stated in the notes to the financial statements the totals of amounts stated under (a), (d), (e) and (f). The details required of a guarantee are: (a) its main terms; (b) the amount of the maximum liability that may be incurred by a micro-entity; (c) any amount paid and any liability incurred by a micro-entity for the purpose of fulfilling the guarantee (including any loss incurred by reason of enforcement of the guarantee). There must also be stated in the notes to the financial statements the totals of amounts stated under (b) and (c). (Section 413 CA 2006)	6A.3 (UK only)
The total amount of any financial commitments, guarantees and contingencies that are not included in the statement of financial position must be stated. (paragraph 57(1) of Schedule 1 to the Small Companies Regulations [S.I. 409/2008] or paragraph 55(1) of Schedule 1 to the Small LLP Regulations [S.I. No. 1912 of 2008]). The total amount of any commitments concerning pensions must be separately disclosed. (paragraph 57(3) of Schedule 1 to the Small Companies Regulations [S.I. 409/2008] or paragraph 55(3) of Schedule 1 to the Small LLP Regulations [S.I. No. 1912 of 2008]).	6A.4 (UK only)

	PARA.
The total amount of any commitments which are undertaken on behalf of or for the benefit of: (a) any parent, fellow subsidiary or any subsidiary of a micro-entity; or (b) any undertaking in which a micro-entity has a participating interest, must be separately stated and those within (a) must also be stated separately from those within (b). (paragraph 57(4) of Schedule 1 to the Small Companies Regulations [S.I. 409/2008] or paragraph 55(4) of Schedule 1 to the Small LLP Regulations [S.I.No. 1912 of 2008]). Paragraphs 9.28(a), 11.9, 12.28(a), 13.17(a), 14.3, 15.17, 15.33, 16.19, 23.22 and 27.5(a) [of FRS 105] address these disclosure requirements within the context of specific transactions.	6A.4 (UK only)
An indication of the nature and form of any valuable security given by the micro-entity in respect of commitments, guarantees and contingencies within paragraph 6A.2 must be given (paragraph 57(2) of Schedule 1 to the Small Companies Regulations [S.I. 409/2008] or paragraph 55(2) of Schedule 1 to the Small LLP Regulations [S.I. No. 1912 of 2008]). Paragraphs 9.28(b), 10.22, 12.28(b), 13.17(b) and 27.5(b) [of FRS 105] address these disclosure requirements within the context of specific transactions.	6A.5 (UK only)

Chapter 2

CONCEPTS AND PERVASIVE PRINCIPLES

FRS 102 has, for the first time, incorporated within the standard the basic concepts and principles that underpin financial reporting. Section 2 of FRS 102 plays a key role for preparers of financial statements in that when they come across an unusual transaction and cannot find the solution in other sections of FRS 102, they must first refer to Section 2 to decide how it should be accounted for, i.e. is it an asset or an expense, an income, a liability or equity? The inclusion of the basic concepts and principles of the subject in a specific section of the FRS represents a new development in financial reporting.

In previous UK and Irish GAAP, basic concepts and principles were included in a Statement of Principles as a guideline to use when interpreting transactions not covered in the specific standards and to aid the standard-setters in devising consistent standards. A similar document was published by the International Accounting Standards Board (IASB), entitled a *Conceptual Framework for Financial Reporting*. In FRS 102 the framework plays a more important role. FRS 102 and FRS 105 are standalone documents and there will certainly be transactions that will not be covered in these standards' other sections. It is important, therefore, that preparers and users can refer to basic principles when deciding the appropriate accounting treatment. It is made clear that there is no need to refer to any other standard-setting body's pronouncements or to the full IFRSs. Section 2 of FRS 102 therefore plays a pivotal role in making decisions on how to treat unusual transactions. However, there is a limit on how this section of FRS 102 can be used – if the principles are in conflict with the specific requirements of another section, the more specific section prevails. The same concepts and principles apply to FRS 105.

2.1 OBJECTIVE OF FINANCIAL STATEMENTS

The objective of financial statements is to provide information about the financial position, performance and cash flows of the reporting entity that is useful for decision-making by a broad range of users. It should also reveal the results of management's stewardship of the entity's resources. The financial statements, therefore, have both a predictive and a confirmatory role.

2.2 QUALITATIVE CHARACTERISTICS OF INFORMATION IN FINANCIAL STATEMENTS

There are a number of qualitative characteristics that must be at the back of a preparer's mind when trying to meet both the decision-making and stewardship objectives of financial statements. These are outlined as follows.

Understandability

The financial statements must be comprehensible to users who have a reasonable knowledge of business and a willingness to study the information diligently. However, FRS 102 does not allow relevant information to be omitted simply on the grounds of it being too difficult to understand.

Relevance

Information must be relevant to decision-making – it must either help to influence future economic decisions by helping to evaluate past, present or future events or by confirming or correcting past evaluations.

Materiality

Information is material if its omission or misstatement could influence economic decisions. This often depends on the size of the item or error judged in the particular circumstances of its omission/misstatement. However, it is inappropriate not to correct immaterial departures from FRS 102 with the intention of achieving a particular presentation.

Reliability

The financial statements must be prepared in a neutral manner and thus be free from any bias and material error. They must try to faithfully represent the reality of the underlying transactions.

Substance over Form

Transactions must always be recorded according to their substance and commercial reality and not their legal form. This becomes important when the legal form of a transaction clearly fails to reflect the commercial reality of what is happening. In that case substance overrules the legal form of the transaction.

Prudence

The uncertainties that surround financial reporting are acknowledged by the exercise of prudence, i.e. a degree of caution. However, it does not allow the deliberate understatement of assets nor the overstatement of liabilities. In general, it applies more to asset recognition and measurement as it is more difficult to recognise liabilities as they must not be mere intentions but genuine obligations of the reporting entity (see **Chapter 6**).

Completeness

Information contained in the financial statements must be complete within the bounds of materiality and cost.

Comparability

Information must be provided to allow comparison of financial information over time, across different entities and within like items within the entity itself. The measurement and display of information, therefore, must be consistent and users must be informed of the accounting policies adopted and any changes therein.

Timeliness

This means providing information within a reasonable timeframe. Undue delay causes loss of relevance and thus a balance is required between timely reporting and reliable information. However, the overriding consideration is how best to satisfy the needs of users.

Balance between Benefit and Cost

The benefits from any information provided in the financial statements should always exceed the costs of creating that information – judgement must be exercised. However, entities must consider that the benefits may be enjoyed by a broad range of external users.

2.3 FINANCIAL POSITION

A statement of financial position contains the following elements:

(a) **Asset** – a resource controlled by the entity as a result of past events and from which future economic benefits are expected to flow to the entity (FRS 102, para 2.15).
(b) **Liability** – a present obligation arising from past events, the settlement of which is expected to result in an outflow from the entity of resources embodying economic benefits (FRS 102, para 2.15).
(c) **Equity** – residual interest in the assets after deducting all its liabilities (FRS 102, para 2.15).

Some items may fail the recognition criteria and, in particular, the probability of future economic benefits flowing to/from the entity. Essentially this means that the balance sheet or statement of financial position is the primary document when preparing the financial statements. The emphasis is clearly on 'getting the balance sheet right' and thus income/gains and expenses/losses can only result in a change in net assets, e.g. income is an increase in assets or a decrease in liabilities, and vice versa for expenses.

Asset

An asset's future economic benefit is its potential to contribute to the flow of cash to the entity – either from use or disposal.

Physical form is not essential as some assets are intangible, e.g. broadcasting licences, milk quotas, etc.

A right of ownership is also not essential, e.g. a finance lease is an asset in a lessee's statement of financial position.

Liability

For a liability to exist there must be a present obligation (legal or constructive) to act or perform in a particular way.

A **legal obligation** is a binding contract or statutory requirement.

A **constructive obligation** is an established pattern of past practice, published policies or specific current statement that the entity will accept certain responsibilities and there is a valid expectation that it will discharge those responsibilities. It must be distinguished from a mere intention that can always be reversed in a future reporting period.

Settlement of liabilities is usually made in cash, by the provision of services, by the conversion of debt into equity or by a waiver/forfeiture of rights.

Equity

Equity is the residual of recognised assets after recognised liabilities have been deducted. It may be sub-classified into various reserves (e.g. retained earnings, revaluation reserves, translation reserves).

2.4 PERFORMANCE

Performance is the relationship of the income and expense of an entity during a reporting period – in a single statement of comprehensive income or in two financial statements (a profit and loss account and a statement of comprehensive income). Total comprehensive income and profit or loss are frequently used as measures of performance, or used in the calculation of earnings per share (EPS) and return on capital employed (ROCE).

Income represents either increases in assets or decreases in liabilities, and expenses are decreases in assets or increases in liabilities.

Income

Income incorporates both revenue and gains:

- **Revenue** represents income arising in the ordinary activities of the entity, e.g. fees, sales, rent, interest, dividends;

- **Gains** represent income not defined as revenue – usually displayed separately for decision-making purposes, e.g. actuarial surpluses, foreign exchange gains, etc.

Expenses

'Expenses' encompasses losses as well as expenses:

- **Expenses** arise in the ordinary activities of the entity, e.g. cost of sales, wages, depreciation;
- **Losses** are other items meeting the definition, but displayed separately for decision-making purposes, e.g. actuarial deficits, foreign exchange losses.

2.5 RECOGNITION OF THE ELEMENTS OF FINANCIAL STATEMENTS

'Recognition' is the process of incorporating into the financial statements items that not only pass the definition of an asset, liability, income or expense but also satisfy the following criteria:

(a) it is **probable** that any future economic benefits will flow to/from the entity; and
(b) the item has a cost or value that can be **reliably measured**.

A failure to recognise an item is not rectified merely by disclosure of the **accounting policies** adopted or by disclosure in the **notes**.

Probability of Future Economic Benefit

If there is a degree of uncertainty about future economic benefits, an entity must use evidence at the end of the period, assessed individually or in a group for a large population of insignificant items, to decide the probability of economic benefits being derived.

Reliability of Measurement

The elements of the financial statements must have a cost or value that can be reliably measured. The cost/value may be known, but often it is estimated. If it cannot be reliably measured, then it must not be recognised. However, the asset or liability may subsequently qualify for recognition at a later date if circumstances change.

If transactions fail the above recognition criteria, they may still be disclosed in the notes, e.g. contingent liabilities and capital commitments.

2.6 MEASUREMENT OF THE ELEMENTS OF FINANCIAL STATEMENTS

'Measurement' is the process of determining the monetary amounts at which assets, liabilities, income and expenses should be recorded in the financial statements. It involves selecting a basis of measurement.

Two common bases of measurement are historical cost and fair value.

(a) Historical cost:

- assets are recorded at the consideration given to acquire the asset;
- liabilities are recorded at the amount of proceeds received;
- amortised cost is the historical cost of an asset or liability plus or minus that portion of its historical cost previously expensed or recorded as income (an example of this approach is covered in **Chapter 12**).

(b) Fair value:

- assets are recorded at the amount for which the asset could be exchanged;
- liabilities are recorded at the amount for which they could be settled between willing parties in arms' length transactions.

Guidance on measuring fair value is provided in Section 11 of FRS 102, unless specifically covered in another section of the FRS.

2.7 PERVASIVE RECOGNITION AND MEASUREMENT PRINCIPLES

The recognition and measurement of elements are based on the pervasive principles in the IASB's *Conceptual Framework* and the EU-adopted IFRS. Section 10 of FRS 102 (see **Chapter 7**) provides guidance for making a judgement and sets out a hierarchy to follow when deciding on the most appropriate accounting policy to adopt. The second level of the hierarchy requires entities to look to the definition, recognition criteria and measurement concepts set out in Section 10 of FRS 102.

2.8 ACCRUALS BASIS

The financial statements should be prepared using the accruals basis (i.e. matching income with expenditure for the same period regardless of when cash is received or expended), but only if they satisfy the definition and recognition criteria for assets, liabilities, incomes and expenses. The accruals basis is secondary behind ensuring that assets and liabilities are recognised, i.e. the balance sheet or recognition concept overrides the matching or accruals principle.

2.9 RECOGNITION IN FINANCIAL STATEMENTS

Assets

Assets are only recognised if it is probable that future economic benefits associated with them will flow to the entity and that the assets have a cost or value that can be reliably measured. Contingent assets are not recognised unless this flow is virtually certain, but if probable, they can be disclosed in the notes to the financial statements.

Liabilities

Liabilities are only recognised when an obligation exists, it is probable that an outflow of resources will result from the settlement of present obligations and the settlement amount can be reliably measured. Contingent liabilities, if they fail the probability or reliable measure tests, should be disclosed in the notes. In a business combination, however, they must be recorded on the balance sheet (see **Chapter 11**).

Income

Income results directly from recognising and measuring assets and liabilities – income is an increase in assets or a reduction in liabilities.

Expenses

Expenses result directly from recognising and measuring assets and liabilities – expenses are decreases in assets or increases in liabilities and can be reliably measured.

Total Comprehensive Income and Profit or Loss

Total comprehensive income and profit or loss is simply the arithmetical difference between total income and total expenses, including everything recorded in both the profit and loss account and the statement of comprehensive income.

2.10 MEASUREMENT AT INITIAL RECOGNITION

Initially assets and liabilities are measured at historical cost unless FRS 102 requires another basis, such as fair value.

2.11 SUBSEQUENT MEASUREMENT

Financial Assets and Financial Liabilities

Basic financial assets and liabilities (see Section 11, as discussed in **Chapter 12**) are measured at amortised cost less impairment, except for investments in non-convertible and non-puttable preference shares and non-puttable ordinary shares, which are measured at fair value with changes reported in profit or loss. Also, certain instruments may be designated as at fair value through profit or loss.

All other financial assets and liabilities are reported at fair value with changes recognised in profit or loss, unless FRS 102 permits an alternative such as amortised cost.

Non-financial Assets

Most non-financial assets are initially recorded at historical cost and are subsequently measured on other measurement bases, e.g.:

(a) property, using either the cost or revaluation models; and
(b) inventories, at the lower of cost and selling price less costs to complete and costs to sell.

For some non-financial assets, FRS 102 permits or requires subsequent remeasurement at fair value. Examples include:

(a) investments in associates and joint ventures measured at fair value (Sections 14 and 15 – see **Chapter 11**);
(b) investment property that an entity measures at fair value (Section 16 – see **Chapter 3**);
(c) agricultural assets that an entity measures at fair value less estimated costs to sell (Section 34 – see **Chapter 13**);
(d) property, plant and equipment under the revaluation model (Section 17 – see **Chapter 3**);
(e) intangible assets under the revaluation model (Section 18 – see **Chapter 3**).

Liabilities other than Financial Liabilities

Most non-financial liabilities are measured at the best estimate of the amount required to settle the obligation at the reporting date.

2.12 OFFSETTING

An entity must not offset assets and liabilities or income and expenses unless it is required or permitted to do so by FRS 102. The following are not regarded as offsetting:

(a) measuring assets net of valuation allowances, e.g. doubtful debts; and
(b) profit/loss on disposal of non-current assets, as long as this is not part of normal operating activities.

2.13 CONCLUSION

Undoubtedly, Section 2 is one of the most important sections of the FRS in that it distils the building blocks of financial reporting into nine pages. A builder would never dream of building a house without strong foundations. Similarly, it is vital for financial reporting that the fundamental principles are clearly set out in the standard, thus providing a reference point to find an acceptable solution within the confines of the basic accounting framework when unusual transactions occur. This will allow greater consistency and comparability of reporting.

It should be pointed out, however, that if a reporting entity cannot follow the logic of Section 2, it is permitted, but not required, to view the full EU-adopted IFRS (see paragraph 10.6 of FRS 102). However, in the authors' opinion this should be extremely rare and also would break the standalone nature of the FRS.

The concepts and pervasive principles in Section 2 apply to smaller entities falling under Section 1A. Micro-entities have a simplified and more user-friendly version of the concepts and principles provided by FRS 105 *The Financial Reporting Standard applicable to the Micro-entities Regime.*

The amendments to FRS 102 in March 2018 incorporated an Appendix detailing the methodology to be adopted when measuring fair value. The best evidence is a quoted price for an identical asset in an active market but it also recognises that valuation techniques may have to be adopted where this is not the case.

Disclosure Checklist: Concepts and Pervasive Principles – FRS 102

There are no specific disclosures.

Disclosure Checklist: Concepts And Pervasive Principles – Small Entities

There are no specific disclosures.

Disclosure Checklist: Concepts And Pervasive Principles – Micro-entities (Republic of Ireland only)

(References are to the Relevant Section of FRS 105)

The mandatory disclosure requirements for micro-entities required under FRS 105 and the Companies Act 2014 (ROI) (CA 2014) are as follows:

	Para.
An Irish micro-entity shall disclose information in relation to assets or income set off against amounts in respect of items representing liabilities or expenditure or vice versa in accordance with Appendix B to Section 6 *Notes to the Financial Statements*.	2.38 (ROI only)

Chapter 3

ASSET VALUATION – NON-CURRENT ASSETS

In this chapter we will examine the accounting and disclosure requirements for non-current assets. Typically these are reported at the top of the balance sheet, though this is not a requirement in FRS 102. However, under company law, reporting entities must follow the Schedules to the Companies Acts (in the Republic of Ireland, the Companies Act 2014 (CA 2014); in the UK, the Companies Act 2006 (CA 2006)) and therefore there will **not** be the same flexibility under FRS 102 – they **must** be reported at the top of the balance sheet.

3.1 PROPERTY, PLANT AND EQUIPMENT (SECTION 17)

Scope

Property, plant and equipment are tangible assets that:

(a) are held for use in the production or supply of goods and services, for rental or for administrative purposes; and
(b) are expected to be used during more than one period.

Spare parts for property, plant and equipment are usually carried as inventory, but major spare parts are reported as property if they are expected to be used over more than one accounting period.

Typical examples of property, plant and equipment include:

- factory buildings used to manufacture a company's products;
- motor vehicles used by the sales staff in performance of their duties and vehicles provided for administration staff, including the CEO and directors;
- administration building;
- fixtures and fittings; and
- plant and machinery.

EXAMPLES FROM THE PUBLISHED ACCOUNTS OF LISTED IRISH COMPANIES

Aer Lingus Plc	Property, equipment, aircraft fleet and major spares.
FBD Holdings Plc	Land and buildings, fixtures and fittings, hotels and golf resorts.
Icon Plc	Buildings, computer equipment, office furniture and fixtures, laboratory equipment, motor vehicles.
Irish Continental Group Plc	Passenger ships.
Ryanair Plc	Plant and equipment, fixtures and fittings, motor vehicles, buildings.
Total Produce Plc	Freehold buildings, leasehold improvements, plant and equipment, motor vehicles.
Kenmare Resources Plc	Plant and equipment, buildings and airstrip, mobile equipment, construction in progress.
Origin Enterprises Plc	Land and buildings, plant and machinery, motor vehicles.
Paddy Power Plc	Freehold buildings, leasehold improvements, fixtures and fittings, computer equipment, motor vehicles.

Biological assets (such as herds of cattle), heritage assets and mineral rights and reserves are outside the scope of Section 17 and are covered under Section 34 *Specialised Activities* (see **Chapter 13**).

Recognition

The following recognition criteria must be applied to determine whether or not an asset can be reported:

(a) there must be probable future economic benefits flowing to the entity; and
(b) its cost **must** be reliably measured.

Major spare parts may require replacement at regular intervals and thus the cost of replacement may be capitalised, provided it is expected to provide incremental future benefits to the entity. The carrying amounts of the parts replaced are then derecognised.

Major components must be allocated part of the initial cost and be depreciated separately over their useful lives.

Example 3.1: Component Accounting

Athenry Ltd operates a cruise ship, which was acquired on 1 October 2009. Details of the component costs of the ship and their useful lives are as follows:

Component	Original Cost	Depreciation Method
Ship's fabric, i.e. hull, decks, etc.	€500 million	25 years straight-line
Cabins and entertainment area fittings	€300 million	12 years straight-line
Propulsion system	€130 million	estimate of 50,000 hours

In the year ended 30 September 2017 the ship had experienced a high level of engine trouble, costing the company considerable lost revenue and compensation costs. The measured expired life of the propulsion system at 30 September 2017 was 40,000 hours. Due to the unreliability of the engines, a decision was taken in early October 2017 to replace the whole of the propulsion system at a cost of €180 million. The expected life of the new propulsion system was 60,000 hours and in the year ended 30 September 2018 the ship had used its engines for 6,000 hours.

At the same time as the propulsion system replacement, the company took the opportunity to upgrade the cabins and entertainment facilities at a cost of €80 million and to repaint the ship's fabric at a cost of €25 million. After the upgrade it was estimated that the useful life would be five years.

Solution

The ship should be broken down into its key components. The net book value of these assets at 30 September 2017 is as follows:

	€million
Ship's fabric (€500m × 17/25)	340
Cabins, etc. (€300m × 4/12)	100
Propulsion system (€130m × 10/50)	26
	466

Ship's fabric Depreciation will be unaffected as the painting is not an improvement under FRS 102, so the charge for 2018 should be 1/25 × €500m = €20 million.

Cabins, etc. The upgrade of €80 million has extended their useful life and thus should be capitalised. The revised book value will now be €100 million + €80 million = €180 million and should be depreciated over the remaining five years, i.e. €36 million per annum.

Propulsion system The old system is now obsolete and therefore the full €26 million included in book value should be written off in the income statement. Depreciation of the new system should be €18 million based on 6,000 hours (10% of total expected life of 60,000 hours).

Summary

PROFIT AND LOSS ACCOUNT (EXTRACT)
for the year ended 30 September 2018

	€million
Depreciation of ship's fabric	20
Depreciation of cabins, etc.	36
Depreciation of propulsion system	18
Impairment of old propulsion system	26
Repairs and maintenance	25

BALANCE SHEET (EXTRACT)
as at 30 September 2018

	€million
Ship's fabric (€340m – €20m)	320
Cabins, etc. (€180m – €36m)	144
Propulsion system (€180m – €18m)	162

EXAMPLE 3.2: REPLACEMENT PARTS

Castlebar Ltd manufactures paint but must protect its plant with a specialised inner coating to avoid leakages and possible pollution. Although the plant should last 20 years, experience reveals that the inner coating needs to be replaced every four years. The company separates out the cost of the inner coating at €40,000 and depreciates it over the four years.

At the end of Year 3 it is clear that the inner coating needs replacing earlier than expected and the company does so at a cost of €50,000.

Solution

The net carrying amount of the old inner coating must be written off immediately as an expense of €10,000 and the new coating capitalised at €50,000 and depreciated over four years.

A real example of component accounting, under IFRS, is provided by the Irish Continental Group Plc:

Irish Continental Group Plc

2017 Annual Report and Financial Statements

NOTES TO THE FINANCIAL STATEMENTS (EXTRACT)

2. Summary of accounting policies

...

Property, plant and equipment

Vessels

Vessels are stated at cost, with the exception of the fast ferry *Jonathan Swift* which is stated at deemed cost upon transition to IFRS, less accumulated depreciation and any accumulated impairment losses.

Depreciation on vessels is charged so as to write off the cost or deemed cost less residual value over the estimated economic useful life on a straight-line basis. The amount initially recognised in respect of Ropax ships less estimated residual value, is allocated between hull and machinery and hotel and catering elements for depreciation purposes. In respect of LoLo vessels, all value is attributed to hull and machinery.

In considering residual values of passenger ships, the Directors have taken into account the valuation of the scrap value of the ships per light displacement tonne. Residual values are reviewed annually and updated if required. Estimations of economic life and residual values of ships are a key accounting judgement and estimate in the financial statements.

The estimated economic useful lives of vessels is as follows:

Hull	
• Conventional Ropax Ships	30–35 years
• Fast ferries	15-25 years
• LoLo	25 years
Hotel and Catering	10 years.

For conventional ferries, hull and machinery components are depreciated over an initial estimated useful life of 30 years but this is reviewed on a periodic basis for vessels remaining in service 25 years after original construction.

The carrying values of passenger ships are reviewed for impairment when there is any indication that the carrying values may not be recoverable in which case the assets are written down to their recoverable amount.

Drydocking
Costs incurred in renewing the vessel passenger certificate are capitalised as a separate component within passenger ships and depreciated over the period to expiry of certificate.

Major Inspections

Major inspections may be capitalised as a replacement if the recognition criteria are satisfied. If necessary, the estimated cost of a future similar inspection may be used as an indicator of cost.

Example 3.3: Major Inspection

Model Airlines operates a small executive aviation service for its clients and has a legal requirement to have its one aircraft inspected every three years for airworthiness. The first inspection cost €30,000 and was incurred during the current reporting period.

Solution

An asset of €30,000 can be recognised for the major inspection and expensed to profit and loss at €10,000 per annum over the three years.

An example of this approach is provided by Ryanair for its major overhaul of aircraft.

Ryanair Holdings Plc

Annual Report and Financial Statements 2018

NOTES TO THE FINANCIAL STATEMENTS (EXTRACT)

Property, plant and equipment
Property, plant and equipment is stated at historical cost less accumulated depreciation and provisions for impairments, if any. Cost includes expenditure that is directly attributable to the acquisition of the asset. Cost may also include transfers from other comprehensive income of any gain or loss on qualifying cash-flow hedges of foreign currency purchases of property, plant and equipment. [...]

Depreciation is calculated so as to write off the cost, less estimated residual value, of assets on a straight-line basis over their expected useful lives at the following annual rates:

	Rate of Depreciation
Hangar and buildings	5%
Plant and equipment (excluding aircraft)	20–33.3%
Fixtures and fittings	20%
Motor vehicles	33.3%

Aircraft are depreciated on a straight-line basis over their estimated useful lives to estimated residual values. The estimates of useful lives and residual values at year-end are:

Aircraft Type	Number of Owned Aircraft at March 31, 2018	Useful Life	Residual Value
Boeing 737–800s	400 (a)	23 years from date of manufacture	15% of current market value of new aircraft, determined periodically

(a) The Company operated 431 aircraft as of March 31, 2018, of which 31 were leased.

The Company's estimate of the recoverable amount of aircraft residual values is 15% of current market value of new aircraft, determined periodically, based on independent valuations and actual aircraft disposals during the current and prior periods.

An element of the cost of an acquired aircraft is attributed on acquisition to its service potential, reflecting the maintenance condition of its engines and airframe. This cost, which can equate to a substantial element of the total aircraft cost, is amortised over the shorter of the period to the next maintenance check (usually between 8 and 12 years for Boeing 737–800 aircraft) or the remaining life of the aircraft. The costs of subsequent major airframe and engine maintenance checks are capitalised and amortised over the shorter of the period to the next check or the remaining life of the aircraft.

Advance and option payments made in respect of aircraft purchase commitments and options to acquire aircraft are recorded at cost and separately disclosed within property, plant and equipment. On acquisition of the related aircraft, these payments are included as part of the cost of aircraft and are depreciated from that date.

Rotable spare parts held by the Company are classified as property, plant and equipment if they are expected to be used over more than one period and are accounted for and depreciated in the same manner as the related aircraft.

Gains and losses on disposal of items of property, plant and equipment are determined by comparing the proceeds from disposal with the carrying amount of property, plant and equipment, and are recognised on a net basis within other income in profit and loss.

Aircraft maintenance costs
The accounting for the cost of providing major airframe and certain engine maintenance checks for owned aircraft is described in the accounting policy for property, plant and equipment.

For aircraft held under operating lease agreements, Ryanair is contractually committed to either return the aircraft in a certain condition or to compensate the lessor based on the actual condition of the airframe, engines and life-limited parts upon return. In order to fulfill such conditions of the lease, maintenance, in the form of major airframe overhaul, engine maintenance checks, and restitution of major life-limited parts, is required to be performed during the period of the lease and upon return of the aircraft to the lessor. The estimated airframe and engine maintenance costs and the costs associated with the restitution of major life-limited parts, are accrued and charged to profit or loss over the lease term for this contractual obligation, based on the present value of the estimated future cost of the major airframe overhaul, engine maintenance checks, and restitution of major life-limited parts, calculated by reference to the number of hours flown or cycles operated during the year.

Ryanair's aircraft operating lease agreements typically have a term of seven years, which closely correlates with the timing of heavy maintenance checks. The contractual obligation to maintain and replenish aircraft held under operating lease exists independently of any future actions within the control of Ryanair. While Ryanair may, in very limited circumstances, sub-lease its aircraft, it remains fully liable to perform all of its contractual obligations under the 'head lease' notwithstanding any such sub-leasing.

All other maintenance costs, other than major airframe overhaul, engine maintenance checks, and restitution of major life-limited parts costs associated with leased aircraft, are expensed as incurred.

Land and Buildings

Land and buildings are separable assets and should be accounted for separately even if acquired together.

Measurement at Recognition

Property, plant and equipment should be recognised initially at cost. FRS 102 permits revaluation as an option in the UK and in Ireland and, in addition, it also permits the option of capitalising borrowing costs provided certain criteria are met (see **Section 3.5 'Borrowing Costs'**).

Elements of Cost

The following are examples of costs that should be included in property, plant and equipment on initial recognition:

(a) the purchase price, including legal fees and import duties but after any trade discounts;
(b) any costs directly attributable to bringing the asset to the location and condition necessary for operating in the way intended by management, e.g. costs attributable to site preparation, initial delivery and handling, installation and assembly and testing of functionality;
(c) the initial estimate of the cost of dismantling and restoring the site;
(d) any borrowing costs capitalised as per Section 25 of FRS 102 (see **Borrowing Costs** below).

However, the following are **not** permitted by FRS 102 to be included in the initial cost of property:

(a) the costs of opening a new facility;
(b) the costs of introducing a new product or service (including advertising/promotion);
(c) the costs of conducting business in a new location; and
(d) administration and other general overheads.

Any income and related expenses of incidental operations are recognised in profit or loss.

Example 3.4: Initial Recognition at Cost of Property, Plant and Equipment

Bruff Ltd has recently purchased an item of plant from Garryowen Ltd, the details of which are as follows:

	€	€
Basic list price of plant		240,000
Trade discount applicable to Bruff Ltd – 12.5% on list price		
Ancillary costs:		
Shipping and handling costs		2,750
Estimated pre-production testing		12,500
Maintenance contract for three years		24,000
Site preparation costs:		
Electrical cable installation	14,000	
Concrete reinforcement	4,500	
Own labour costs	7,500	26,000

Bruff Ltd paid for the plant (excluding the ancillary costs) within four weeks of order, thereby obtaining an early settlement discount of 3%.

Bruff Ltd had incorrectly specified the power loading of the original electrical cable to be installed by the contractor. In the above table, the cost of correcting this error of €6,000 is included in the figure of €14,000.

The plant is expected to last for 10 years. At the end of this period there will be compulsory costs of €15,000 to dismantle the plant and €3,000 to restore the site to its original usable condition.

Solution

Example of initial cost of plant purchased

	€	€
Basic list price of plant		240,000
Less: trade discount (12.5%)		(30,000)
		210,000
Shipping and handling costs		2,750
Pre-production testing		12,500
Site preparation costs:		
Electrical cable installation (€14,000 – €6,000 abnormal)	8,000	
Concrete reinforcement	4,500	
Own labour costs	7,500	
		20,000
Dismantling and restoration costs (€15,000 + €3,000)		18,000
Initial cost of plant		263,250

Note: abnormal costs of rectifying the power loading cannot be included as it would not normally be incurred in getting the asset to its intended location and working condition.

Cash discounts should be treated as a reduction in administration or selling costs and may not be included as part of property, plant and equipment. Maintenance costs are a revenue cost.

In some industries there is a legal requirement that old equipment be dismantled – this future cost should also be capitalised, albeit discounted back to present value (see also **Chapter 6**). It is particularly pertinent to mining and oil and gas extraction.

Measurement of Cost

Cost is the cash price equivalent at the recognition date. If payment is deferred beyond normal credit terms, then cost is the present value of all future payments.

EXAMPLE 3.5: PURCHASE OF EQUIPMENT ON DEFERRED SETTLEMENT TERMS

Derrybeg Ltd acquired a major piece of equipment, costing €4 million, on a two-year, interest-free credit agreement. Assuming an appropriate discount rate to be 10%, then both the cost of the equipment and the liability should be recorded at €4m × $1/(1.1)^2$ = €3,305,786. The unwinding of the discount results in an interest charge to be recorded in profit and loss of €330,578 and €363,636, respectively, in the two years after the purchase of the equipment, with the liability increased back up to €4 million over the two years to be settled at that amount.

Exchanges of Assets

If property is exchanged, it should be at fair value unless that exchange lacks commercial substance or the fair value is not reliably measured, in which case the entity should instead use the carrying amount of the asset given up.

Measurement after Initial Recognition

An entity must measure all items of property, after initial recognition, using either the cost or the revaluation model for all classes of property, plant and equipment and must apply the same model to all assets within a particular class.

Cost Model

Entities using the cost model must measure property, plant and equipment at cost less any accumulated depreciation and accumulated **impairment losses**. The costs of day-to-day servicing should be recognised in profit or loss in the period in which the costs are incurred.

EXAMPLE 3.6: COST MODEL

Bunbeg Ltd acquired plant for €800,000 with an expected useful life of four years. After three years the net book value, using the straight-line method for depreciation and assuming a nil residual value, is €200,000. Unfortunately, the plant was damaged and its recoverable amount is now only €50,000.

The company must therefore impair the asset immediately and write it down from €200,000 to €50,000, i.e. by €150,000.

Revaluation Model

As long as a reliable measure is available, property, etc. may be revalued to its fair value at the date of revaluation, less any subsequent depreciation and impairment losses. There is no time limit for revaluations, as long as the values are kept up to date.

Land and buildings are recognised in other comprehensive income and in equity (under the heading of revaluation reserves). However, they are recognised in the profit and loss account if they represent a reversal of a revaluation loss on the same asset previously written off to profit. Decreases in values are written off to profit unless there exists a balance on the revaluation reserve for that asset, in which case the loss is recognised in other comprehensive income.

Example 3.7: Cost and Revaluation Models

Irvine Ltd acquired property costing €2 million in 2018 and this was revalued by Hops & Co, Chartered Surveyors, on 31 December 2019 at €1.9 million and on 31 December 2020 at €1.8 million. The asset has an estimated economic life of 50 years. Subsequently, in 2021, the property was revalued again at €1.9 million.

Solution

Cost Model

€2m ÷ 50 years = €40,000 per annum depreciation
The net book value will be recorded as follows:

31/12/2018	€2m less €40,000 depreciation	= €1.96m
31/12/2019	€2m less €80,000 depreciation	= €1.92m
31/12/2020	€2m less €120,000 depreciation	= €1.88m
31/12/2021	€2m less €160,000 depreciation	= €1.84m

In addition, Irvine Ltd would need to be concerned about any possible impairment, especially if property values were to fall. In 2019 property values fell, but it is possible that the property's value in use through future discounted cash flows could exceed its net book value and no impairment would need to be created.

Revaluation Model

31/12/2018

At 31/12/2018, the net book value would be the same as using the cost model.

31/12/2019

On revaluation of the property to €1.9 million, we would record the revaluation itself as follows:

Dr Profit and loss	€0.02m	
Cr Property, plant and equipment (€1.92m net book value less €1.9m)		€0.02m

Being the revaluation decrease for the year written off to profit and loss for 2019.

31/12/2020

Dr Depreciation (profit and loss) (€1.9m ÷ 48 years)	€0.04m	
Cr Accumulated depreciation		€0.04m

Being the depreciation charge for 2020 based on the revaluation at 31 December 2019 of €1.9m.

On 31 December 2020 the property falls again to €1.8 million and the accounting entries should be:

Dr Profit and loss	€0.06m	
Cr Property, plant and equipment (€1.86m – €1.8m)		€0.06m

Being the revaluation decrease in 2016 being charged to profit and loss.

31/12/2021

On 31 December 2021 the property recovers to €1.9 million, but depreciation still has to be charged for 2021 based on the 2020 valuation:

Dr Depreciation (profit and loss) (€1.8m ÷ 47 years = €0.04m)	€0.04m	
Cr Accumulated depreciation		€0.04m

Being the depreciation charge for the year ended 31 December 2021.

Dr Property, plant and equipment (€1.9m – €1.76m)	€0.14m	
Cr Profit and loss (reversal of impairment)		€0.08m
Cr Revaluation reserve		€0.06m

Being the revaluation of the property as at 31 December 2021.

The asset is now stated at €1.90 million compared to the historical cost net book value of €1.84 million, hence the revaluation reserve of €0.06 million.

Depreciation

Reporting entities should allocate the amount initially recognised to its major components of property, plant and equipment and each component should be recognised separately.

Land, however, usually has an unlimited life and is not depreciated, except for quarries, landfill sites, etc.

The depreciation charge should be recognised in cost of sales unless included in the carrying amount of another asset, e.g. equipment used to manufacture inventories.

Example 3.8: Calculation of Depreciation

Poolbeg Ltd acquired a machine at a cost of €600,000 with an estimated useful life of five years, assuming a nil residual value and adopting straight-line depreciation. The company uses the machine to produce inventory for the first three years and then switches to manufacturing plant that can be used to manufacture other products.

Solution

Depreciation per annum is €600,000 ÷ 5 years = €120,000. For the first three years the depreciation is added to the cost of manufacturing inventories for those years and expenses when the inventory is sold. For the last two years the depreciation is added to plant as it creates new plant meeting the definition of property, plant and equipment.

The journal entries would be as follows:

	€	€
Year 1–3 (per annum)		
Dr Cost of sales (inventory)	120,000	
Cr Accumulated depreciation		120,000
Year 4–5 (per annum)		
Dr Property, plant and equipment	120,000	
Cr Accumulated depreciation		120,000

Depreciable Amount and Depreciation Method

The depreciable amount should be allocated on a systematic basis over the asset's useful life.

The residual value and useful life of assets need not be reviewed every year, but if there is clearly an indication that either the useful life or the estimate of the residual value of an asset has changed since the previous reporting period, then that change should be reflected in the financial statements of the current accounting period. It is therefore a change in accounting estimate and not a change in accounting policy. That change, therefore, must be reported in profit or loss and not recorded as a prior period adjustment. Under the full IFRSs an annual review is required, but this was felt to be too onerous for companies applying the FRS and therefore, on cost–benefit grounds, it was not introduced.

Example 3.9: Change in Useful Life

On 1 April 2018, Moyard Ltd acquired a machine for €400,000. The estimated useful life is 10 years with no residual value. The company operates the straight-line method.

On 31 March 2023 Moyard Ltd reassesses the useful life as a further nine years from 31 March 2023, but no change in the method of depreciation or residual value has been made.

Solution

For the year ended 31 March 2023, the net book value at the start of the year is €240,000 (€400,000 – €160,000 depreciation). The book value must now be spread over the 10 remaining years at €24,000 per annum (i.e. €240,000 ÷ 10 years).

Depreciation begins when the asset is available for use and ceases from the date it is derecognised. It does not cease merely on retirement from active use unless fully depreciated, but the charge can be zero while there is no production. In practice this means that as long as the asset is installed and is capable of being operated it must be depreciated, even if it is not actually being used for production. Depreciation also can only cease when the machine is derecognised (e.g. sold) and not when a decision has been made to sell the asset. Also, depreciation may not be suspended temporarily if the machine is idle, although under the unit-of-production methods it is possible to have a depreciation charge of nil if no production occurs during the period.

The following factors must be considered in determining the useful life of an asset:

(a) the expected usage by reference to the asset's capacity or physical output;
(b) any expected wear and tear;
(c) technical or commercial obsolescence; and
(d) legal or similar limits, e.g. on leases.

Depreciation Method

The depreciation method selected by a reporting entity must reflect the pattern in which an entity expects to consume the asset's future economic benefits, but straight-line, reducing-balance and the unit-of-production methods are the only ones specifically mentioned in the FRS.

If a company has acquired a piece of equipment that is legally obsolete after a certain output and must be decommissioned, then the most appropriate method would be to divide the total cost of the machine by the maximum output and depreciate on a unit-of-production basis. However, most companies should adopt the straight-line method for the majority of their assets and perhaps only adopt the reducing-balance method for vehicles, where the costs of repairs rise over later years to be balanced by lower depreciation in those years.

The method chosen should be changed if there is an indication that the method is not appropriate – the new method should reflect the new pattern of depreciation. Companies are not required to review their methodology each year and it is only if there is an indication that the existing method is no longer appropriate that a change should be made. Any change is a change in accounting estimate and reported as per Section 10 of FRS 102 (see **Chapter 7**).

Example 3.10: Change in Depreciation Method

Buslines Ltd previously adopted the straight-line method of depreciation for its buses but, due to funding problems, it now expects to keep the buses for an additional two years beyond their original estimated useful life. Realising that repairs are likely to rise in the later years of holding the buses, the company has decided to switch to the reducing-balance method. The original cost of the buses was €200,000, with an estimated useful life of 10 years (six years have elapsed to date). The reducing-balance method will be introduced at a rate of 30% per annum.

Solution

	€	
Original cost	200,000	
Depreciation to date	120,000	Straight-line 6 years
Net book value	80,000	
Depreciation charge (30%)	24,000	Reducing-balance for first year of change
Net book value	56,000	

Example 3.11: Three Different Methods of Depreciation

Assume equipment was bought for €20,000 and can be sold for €1,500 for scrap after five years. Usage is expected to be:

	Output (in units)
Year 1	2,000
Year 2	1,000
Year 3	1,000
Year 4	2,000
Year 5	2,000

(a) Straight-line: (€20,000 – €1,500) ÷ 5 years = €18,500 ÷ 5 years = €3,700 per annum

(b) Reducing-balance at 40% per annum:

Year 1	40% ×	€20,000 = €8,000	
Year 2	40% ×	€12,000 = €4,800	
Year 3	40% ×	€7,200 = €2,880	
Year 4	40% ×	€4,320 = €1,728	
Year 5	40% ×	€2,592 = €1,037	Net book value sold €1,500 scrap

Profit on disposal = €1,500 – €1,037 = €463

(c) Machine unit €18,500 ÷ 8,000 units = €2.3125 per unit

Year 1	2,000 units × €2.315 = €4,625	
Year 2	1,000 units × €2.315 = €2,313	
Year 3	1,000 units × €2.315 = €2,313	
Year 4	2,000 units × €2.315 = €4,625	
Year 5	2,000 units × €2.315 = €4,624	(rounded)
	€18,500	

Impairment

Recognition and Measurement of Impairment

At the end of each period an entity should apply Section 27 *Impairment of Assets* of FRS 102 (see **Section 3.4** below) to assess whether or not an asset should be impaired and, if so, how to recognise and measure the impairment loss. Section 27 explains how an entity reviews the carrying amount of its assets, how it determines the recoverable amount and when it must recognise or reverse an impairment loss.

Compensation for Impairment

Any compensation for impairment should be included in profit or loss, but only when it becomes virtually certain that it will be paid to the entity.

Property, Plant and Equipment Held for Sale

A plan to dispose of an asset before its previously expected disposal date is an indicator that the asset is impaired and should trigger a recalculation of its recoverable amount for impairment purposes. However, it does not have to be transferred to current assets, as required by full IFRS, if it meets certain criteria under IFRS 5 *Non-current Assets Held for Sale and Discontinued Operations*.

Derecognition

An asset should be derecognised:

(a) on disposal; or
(b) when no future economic benefits are expected from its use or disposal.

Any gain/loss on derecognition should be included in profit or loss when derecognised. The date of disposal is governed by Section 23 *Revenue* (see **Chapter 7**) on the sale of goods, but Section 20 *Leases* (see **Chapter 4**) applies to sale and leasebacks.

Any gain/loss is the difference between the net disposal proceeds and the carrying amount of the item.

Example 3.12: Disposal of Property

On 1 January 2018 an entity sold a building with a carrying amount of €1 million for €1.5 million. The estate agent's fees were 5% of the proceeds and legal costs were €5,000.

Solution

The profit on disposal of the building is €0.42 million (€1.5 million less book value of €1,000,000, commission of €75,000 and legal costs of €5,000).

Disclosures

For each class of property, plant and equipment the following should be disclosed:

(a) the measurement bases adopted;
(b) the depreciation methods used;

(c) the useful lives or depreciation rates used;
(d) the gross carrying amount and accumulated depreciation at both the start and the end of the period; and
(e) a reconciliation between the carrying amounts at the start and end of the period, showing additions, disposals, acquisitions, revaluations, impairment losses, depreciation and any other changes. This reconciliation is not required for prior periods.

The entity should also disclose:
(a) the existence and the amounts of retentions on title pledged as security; and
(b) the amount of contractual commitments for the acquisition of property.

If the revaluation model has been adopted, the following must also be disclosed:
(a) the effective date of revaluation;
(b) whether an independent valuer was involved;
(c) the methods applied in estimating the fair values; and
(d) for each revalued class of property, plant and equipment the carrying amount that would have been recognised had the assets been carried under the cost model.

The following is an illustration of the accounting policies and property schedules for a reporting entity adopting the cost model (taken from the IASB's *IFRS for SMEs 2009 Illustrative Financial Statements Presentation and Disclosure Checklist*).

Example 3.13: Illustrative Financial Statements – Property, Plant and Equipment

Accounting Policies and Explanatory Notes (Extract)

Property, plant and equipment
Items of property, plant and equipment are measured at cost less accumulated depreciation and any accumulated impairment losses.

Depreciation is charged so as to allocate the cost of assets less their residual values over their estimated useful lives, using the straight-line method. The following rates are used for the depreciation of property, plant and equipment:

Buildings	2%
Fixtures and equipment	10–30%

9. Property, plant and equipment

	Land and Buildings €	Fixtures and equipment €	Total €
Cost			
1 January 20X1	1,960,000	907,045	2,867,045
Additions	—	435,000	435,000
Disposals	—	(240,000)	(240,000)
At 31 December 20X1	1,960,000	1,102,045	3,062,045
Additions	—	485,000	485,000
Disposals	—	(242,550)	(242,550)
At 31 December 20X2	1,960,000	1,344,495	3,304,495
Accumulated depreciation and impairment			
1 January 20X1	360,000	321,043	681,043
Annual depreciation	30,000	189,547	219,547
Less accumulated depreciation on assets disposed of		(240,000)	(240,000)
At 31 December 20X1	390,000	270,590	660,590
Annual depreciation	30,000	240,360	270,360
Impairment	—	30,000	30,000
Less accumulated depreciation on assets disposed of	—	(204,928)	(204,928)
At 31 December 20X2	420,000	336,022	756,022
Carrying amount			
31 December 20X1	1,570,000	831,455	2,401,455
31 December 20X2	1,540,000	1,008,473	2,548,473

During the period, the group noticed a significant decline in the efficiency of two of its vehicles and so carried out a review of their fair values less costs to sell. The review led to the recognition of an impairment loss of €30,000. The carrying amount of the group's fixtures and equipment includes an amount of €40,000 (20X1: €60,000) in respect of assets held under finance leases.

A good example of the disclosure required, which is similar to the full IAS standard, is provided by the Musgrave Group Plc as set out below.

Musgrave Group Plc

ANNUAL REPORT 2017 – NOTES TO THE FINANCIAL STATEMENTS (EXTRACTS)

for the year ending 31 December 2017

Accounting Policies

[...]

Tangible assets

Tangible assets are stated at cost (or deemed cost) less accumulated depreciation and accumulated impairment losses. Cost includes the original purchase price and costs directly attributable to bringing the asset to its working location and condition for its intended use.

(i) Land and buildings (including leasehold improvements) and shop properties

Land and buildings include freehold and leasehold premises (including leasehold improvements) and offices. Land and buildings and shop properties are stated at cost (or deemed cost for land and buildings held at valuation at the date of transition to FRS 102) less accumulated depreciation and accumulated impairment losses.

Shop properties are purchased as individual assets, as a collection of assets, or through the purchase of legal entities, where those entities do not meet the definition of a business.

(ii) Plant and machinery, equipment and motor vehicles

Plant and machinery, equipment and motor vehicles are stated at cost less accumulated depreciation and accumulated impairment losses.

(iii) Construction in progress

Assets in the course of construction are stated at cost and are not depreciated.

(iv) Depreciation and residual values

Land, investment properties and construction in progress are not depreciated. Depreciation on other assets is calculated, using the straight-line method, to allocate the cost less their residual values over their estimated useful lives, as follows:

• Buildings	10 to 50 years
• Shop properties	2 to 25 years
• Plant, machinery and equipment	3 to 20 years
• Motor vehicles	3 to 10 years

The assets' residual values and useful lives are reviewed, and adjusted, if appropriate, at the end of each reporting period. The effect of any change is accounted for prospectively.

(v) Subsequent additions and major components

Subsequent costs are included in the asset's carrying amount or recognised as a separate asset only when it is probable that economic benefits associated with the item will flow to the Group and the cost can be measured reliably.

The carrying amount of any replaced component is derecognised. Major components are treated as a separate asset where they have significantly different patterns of consumption of economic benefits.

Repairs, maintenance and minor inspection costs are expensed as incurred.

(vi) De-recognition
Tangible assets are derecognised on disposal or when no future economic benefit is expected. On disposal, the difference between the net disposal proceeds and the carrying amount is recognised in profit or loss.

[...]

12 Tangible assets

Group Cost/deemed cost	Land and buildings €m	Shop properties €m	Construction in progress €m	Plant machinery & equipment €m	Motor vehicles €m	Total €m
At 1 January 2017	117.7	324.9	0.3	234.3	32.2	709.4
Additions	0.5	48.1	-	15.9	4.5	69.0
Disposals	-	(16.6)	-	-	(2.6)	(19.2)
Reclassification	-	0.1	(0.3)	0.2	-	-
Reclassification to investment properties	1.2	(0.9)	-	-	-	0.3
Translation adjustment	(0.2)	(3.0)	-	(0.7)	-	(3.9)
At 30 December 2017	119.2	352.6	-	249.7	34.1	755.6
Accumulated depreciation						
At 1 January 2017	10.7	136.4	-	200.5	21.5	369.1
Charge for the year (note 5)	3.2	20.9	-	11.1	2.1	37.3
Provision for impairment (note 5)	-	1.9	-	-	-	1.8
Disposals	-	(14.1)	-	-	(2.6)	(16.7)
Translation adjustment	(0.1)	(1.5)	-	(0.6)	-	(2.2)
At 30 December 2017	13.8	143.6	-	211.0	21.0	389.4
Net book amounts						
At 1 January 2017						
Cost	117.7	324.9	0.3	234.3	32.2	709.4
Accumulated depreciation	(10.7)	(136.4)	-	(200.5)	(21.5)	(369.1)
	107.0	188.5	0.3	33.8	10.7	340.3
At 30 December 2017						
Cost	119.2	352.6	-	249.7	34.1	755.6
Accumulated depreciation	(13.8)	(143.6)	-	(211.0)	(21.0)	(389.4)
	105.4	209.0	-	38.7	13.1	366.2

Land and buildings valued at the date of transition to FRS 102 using the deemed cost exemption are analysed as follows:

	2017 €m	2016 €m
Historical cost equivalent	72.7	70.2
Revaluation surplus (note 24)	25.8	25.9
Net book amounts	98.5	96.1

The net book amounts of land and buildings and shop properties are comprised of:

	Land and buildings		Shop properties	
	2017 €m	2018 €m	2017 €m	2018 €m
Freehold properties	101.9	103.3	127.2	119.6
Leasehold properties	3.5	3.7	29.3	25.9
Plant and equipment	-	-	52.5	43.0
	105.4	107.0	209.0	188.5

An impairment of €1.9 million (2016: €6.7 million) has been recorded for tangible assets, whereby certain assets have been written down to their estimated recoverable value. This relates to shop properties.

During the year, tangible assets with a carrying value of €2.5 million (2016: €7.2 million) were sold. These assets had a cost of €19.2 million (2016: €15.2 million) and accumulated depreciation and impairment of €16.7 million (2016: €8.0 million). Profit on the disposal of these assets of €1.3 million (2016: €1.1 million loss) has been recognised in the profit and loss account (note 5), within distribution costs.

3.2 INVESTMENT PROPERTY (SECTION 16)

Definition and Initial Recognition of Investment Property

Investment property is defined as property held by the owner (or by a lessee under a finance lease) to earn rental income, or for capital appreciation, or both, rather than being used in the production or supply of goods, for administrative purposes or for sale in the ordinary course of business.

Judgement will be required to determine whether or not a property qualifies as an investment property. Where a company provides ancillary services that are insignificant to the arrangement as a whole, it should still be treated as an investment property. In March 2018, FRS 102 was amended to permit an option for investment properties rented out to other group entities to use the cost model and thereby alleviate consolidation adjustments, but the fair value model can also be used.

Example 3.14: Investment Property Rented to another Group Entity

Louth Ltd has a year end of 31 December. On 1 January 2015, it purchased an investment property for €1.5 million and rents it to another group entity. Its useful economic life is estimated at 20 years.

Louth Ltd applies FRS 102 for the first time in its 2016 accounts, and measures the property at fair value as follows:

31 Dec 2016 and 1 Jan 2017: €2.4 million

31 Dec 2017 and 1 Jan 2018: €3.3 million

31 Dec 2018 and 1 Jan 2019: €3.6 million

Louth Ltd chooses to adopt the amendments introduced in March 2018 to FRS 102 in its 2019 accounts and to measure the property under the cost model. On transition, it also chooses to treat the fair value of the property at the date of transition as deemed cost.

The date of transition is the start of the comparative period to the period in which the amendments are first applied. In this case, it will be 1 January 2018 and the fair value of €3.3 million will now become the deemed cost.

The fair value gain of €0.3 million (€3.6m – €3.3m) recognised since the transition date will need to be reversed:

DR	Retained earnings		€0.3m	
	CR	Property		€0.3m

However, the deemed cost figure of €3.3 million still includes the fair value gain of €1.8 million (€3.3m – €1.5m) recognised between the date of purchase and the date of transition.

Carrying the property at this value in the accounts will mean that the fair value uplift will need to be recorded in a revaluation reserve within equity and so a further reserve transfer is required:

DR	Retained earnings		€1.8m	
	CR	Revaluation reserve		€1.8m

Note: there is no impact on distributable profits – the gain has always been unrealised and so has always been undistributable. But whereas under fair value accounting it may have been recorded within retained earnings, under the cost method it must be recorded in a separate revaluation reserve.

At 31 December 2018, a year's worth of depreciation will need to be recognised based on the deemed cost of €3.3 million and the remaining useful economic life at the date of transition of 17 years:

DR	Retained earnings		€194,000	
	CR	Property		€194,000

Deferred tax will also need to be adjusted accordingly.

Additional disclosures will be required in the accounts for the year ended 31 December 2019 and subsequent periods until the property is sold. These are in FRS 102, Section 17, paragraph 17.32A and are the same as for any 'revalued' asset, giving details of the last valuation and the historical cost.

Examples of investment properties:

1. The renting of property to independent third parties under operating leases in return for rental payments.
2. The renting of property as per 1. above to a lessee who operates a shopping centre.
3. The renting of property as per 1. above but also providing cleaning, maintenance services, etc. for the lessees that are insignificant to the arrangement as a whole.
4. A mixed-use property where the owner uses a small, insignificant part of a building and rents out the rest of the property to independent third parties.

Examples of properties that would **not** be investment properties:

1. The renting of property to independent third parties under finance leases – because the property would be recorded in the books of the lessee with the legal owner having instead a receivable.
2. The acquisition of land to be sold off in smaller plots at a normal profit margin. This would be classified as a land bank for the developer and recorded as inventory.
3. A mixed-use property where the owner occupies a significant portion of the property for their own use (say, 33.33%) and rents out the other two-thirds. This would be split between normal property (one-third) and investment property (two-thirds).

A property interest held by a lessee under an operating lease may be classified as an investment property if, and only if, it would otherwise meet the definition of an investment property.

However, property held for social benefits provision, e.g. social housing held by a public benefit entity, is **not** an investment property. It must be accounted for under the rules applicable to standard property, plant and equipment.

Mixed-use property must be separated between investment property and property, plant and equipment.

Measurement at Initial Recognition

Investment properties should be measured at cost initially – that includes their purchase price and any directly attributable expenditure, e.g. legal fees, property transfer taxes, etc. If some of the payment is deferred, entities must discount future payments. Any self-constructed investment property is measured at cost per Section 17 (see **Section 3.1, Property, Plant and Equipment** above).

Example 3.15: Capitalisation of Investment Property

On 1 March 2018 Longford Ltd purchases an office building for €3 million. The company incurred professional costs of €20,000 and property tax of €30,000 in acquiring the building. It then redevelops the building and converts it into luxury apartments, which will be rented out to third parties under operating leases. The additional costs include €60,000 planning permission fees and €2 million construction costs.

The costs to be capitalised should be:

	€
Purchase price	3,000,000
Professional costs	20,000
Property tax	30,000
Planning permission fees	60,000
Construction costs	2,000,000
	5,110,000

The initial cost of a property interest held under a lease and classified as an investment property must be as prescribed for a finance lease by Section 20 *Leases* (see **Chapter 4**), even if the lease would otherwise be classified as an operating lease if it was in the scope of Section 20. In other words, the asset is recognised at the lower of the fair value of the property or the present value of the minimum lease payments. An equivalent amount is recognised as a liability in accordance with Section 20. If any premium has been paid for a lease, this is treated as part of the minimum lease payments and is therefore included in the cost of the asset, but excluded from the liability.

Measurement after Recognition

One of the main problems in accounting for investment properties is estimating the fair value of those properties, particularly where there is not a strong valuation profession, e.g. in some developing countries. Despite this, in March 2018 the FRC removed the 'undue cost or effort' excuse to revert to the cost model. Effectively, this means that all investment properties must be fair valued with gains and losses reported in profit and loss.

Example 3.16: Reliable Measure of Fair Value

Meath Ltd has an investment property and on 1 January 2018 the value of this property (as determined by a chartered surveyor) was €600,000. On 31 December 2018, the surveyor confirmed the value had increased to €630,000.

Under the previous accounting standard, the entries to bring the investment property up to fair value on 31 December 2018 would have been:

Dr	Investment property	€30,000	
Cr	Investment property revaluation reserve		€30,000

However, under FRS 102, the accounting entries are:

Dr	Investment property	€30,000	
Cr	Profit and loss account		€30,000

An important point to emphasise is that the €30,000 gain would not be a realised profit that could be distributed to shareholders by way of dividend.

EXAMPLE 3.17: NO RELIABLE MEASURE OF FAIR VALUE

Westmeath Ltd acquired an investment property for €4 million but is now unable to reliably measure the fair value of the property without incurring undue cost or effort. The company estimates the useful life of the building to be 40 years from the date of acquisition. The residual value is presumed to be nil as no reliable fair value can be determined and the company has adopted straight-line depreciation.

Solution

Westmeath Ltd will have to adopt a valuation technique that will result in its best estimate of fair value. From 1 January 2019, it will no longer be acceptable to revert to cost on the grounds of undue cost or effort.

Investment Property Rented to Another Group Entity

If a member of a group rents an investment property to another group member it must account for that property either:

(a) at fair value, recording changes in fair value in profit or loss; or
(b) by transferring them to property, plant and equipment and applying the cost model in accordance with Section 17.

An entity choosing to apply (b) must provide all the disclosures required by Section 17, other than those related to fair value measurement.

When only part of a property is rented to another group entity and the remainder is used for other purposes (such as being rented to an external third party or owner-occupied), paragraph 16.4A of FRS 102 only applies to the component of that property that is rented to the other group entity. That is, investment properties rented out to group members can adopt the cost model.

EXAMPLE 3.18: INVESTMENT PROPERTY RENTED TO ANOTHER GROUP MEMBER

Sligo Ltd acquired an investment property from another group entity for €3 million on 1 January 2014. On 31 December 2016 its fair value on the balance sheet was £4 million. At 31 December 2018 it has opted to adopt the cost model and estimates the recoverable amount is now only €1.5 million, with a revised estimate of useful life of 20 years.

Solution

Sligo Ltd can transfer the property from investment property to property, plant and equipment at 31 December 2018 at its deemed cost of €4 million. However, as it was governed by the rules for property, plant and equipment, it must be impaired by €2.5 million (through profit and loss) to reduce the asset to its recoverable amount of €1.5 million.

An entity should transfer a property to or from investment property only when it first meets or ceases to meet the definition of investment property. In March 2018 a number of additional paragraphs were inserted to clearly identify the appropriate accounting treatment when there is a change in usage as follows:

- When a property **ceases** to meet the definition of an **investment property** (e.g. it becomes owner-occupied or inventory), the **deemed cost** for subsequent accounting as PP&E (per Section 17) or inventory (per Section 13) shall be its fair value at the date of change in use.
- If an **owner-occupied** property becomes an **investment property**, an entity shall apply **Section 17** up to the date of change in use. The entity must treat any difference at that date between the carrying amount of the property per Section 17 and its fair value in the same way as a revaluation in accordance with Section 17.
- For a transfer from **inventories to investment property** that will be carried at fair value, any difference between the fair value amount must be recognised in **profit or loss**.

Disclosures

The following must be disclosed for all investment properties accounted for at fair value through profit or loss:

(a) the methods and significant assumptions applied in determining the fair value of investment properties;
(b) the extent to which the fair value has been based on independent professional qualified valuers having recent experience in the location and class of the property being valued. If there has been no such valuation, that fact must be disclosed;
(c) the existence and amounts of restrictions on the ability to realise the properties or on the receipt of any income and proceeds of disposal;
(d) the existence of any contractual obligations to purchase, construct or develop, repair, maintain or enhance the properties;
(e) a reconciliation between the carrying amounts of investment properties at the beginning and the end of the period, showing separately:
    (i) additions, disclosing separately those arising through business combinations,
    (ii) net gains or losses from fair value adjustments,

(iii) transfers to property, plant and equipment when a reliable measure of fair value is no longer available without undue cost or effort,
(iv) transfers to and from inventories and owner-occupied property,
(v) any other changes.

This reconciliation need not be presented for prior periods.

The Northern Ireland company, Eakin Brothers Ltd, provides a good example of how the disclosure requirements could be applied.

Eakin Brothers Limited

BALANCE SHEET (EXTRACT)
as at 31 December 2018

		2018		2017	
	Notes	£	£	£	£
Fixed assets					
Tangible assets	3		373,371		205,172
Investment properties	4		545,000		466,650
			918,371		671,822

NOTES TO THE FINANCIAL STATEMENTS (EXTRACTS)
for the year ended 31 December 2018

1. Accounting policies

[…]

1.4. Investment properties
Investment property, which is property held to earn rentals and/ or for capital appreciation, is initially recognised at cost, which includes the purchase cost and any directly attributable expenditure. Subsequently it is measured at fair value at the reporting end date. The surplus or deficit on revaluation is recognised in profit or loss.

Where fair value cannot be achieved without undue cost or effort, investment property is accounted for as tangible fixed assets.

[…]

4. Investment property

	2018
	£
Fair value	
At 1 January 2018	466,650
Net gains or losses for fair value adjustments	78,350
At 31 December 2018	545,000

Investment property comprises properties at 79/81 Main Street, Claudy and 9 Maydown Road, Maydown. The fair value of the investment property at Claudy has been arrived at on the basis of a valuation carried out at 31 December 2013 by John V. Arthur, BSc (Est Man), FRICS, IRRV, Chartered Valuation Surveyor, who is not connected with the company. The valuation was made on an open market value basis by reference to market evidence of transaction prices for similar properties. Mr Arthur has confirmed in August 2016 that there has been no significant movement in valuation since this date and that it continues to adequately represent the current fair value. The directors are of the opinion that there has been no further movement at the year end.

The investment property at Maydown was agreed for sale post year end at a value of £145,000 and the directors therefore consider this to be a reasonable estimate of fair value at the year end.

Example from Full IFRS

Under full IFRS, companies are permitted a clear choice between adopting the fair value or the cost model – it is an accounting policy choice unlike FRS 102. A good example of an Irish listed company complying with the cost approach is provided by Greencore Group plc.

Greencore Group plc

Annual Report and Financial Statements 2018

NOTES TO THE GROUP FINANCIAL STATEMENTS (EXTRACT)

1. Group Statement of Accounting Policies

[...]

Investment Property
Investment property is shown at cost less depreciation and any impairment. The cost of investment property comprises its purchase

price and any costs directly attributable to bringing it into working condition for its intended use. Investment property is depreciated so as to write off the cost, less residual value, on a straight-line basis over the expected life of each property. Freehold buildings held as investment property are depreciated over their expected useful life, normally assumed to be 40–50 years. Freehold land is not depreciated.

Rental income arising on investment property is accounted for on a straight-line basis over the lease term of the ongoing leases and is recognised within other income.

In relation to the recognition of income on the disposal of property, income is recognised when there is an unconditional exchange of contracts, or when all necessary terms and conditions have been fulfilled.

[...]

16. Investment Property

	2018	2017
	£m	£m
Opening net book amount	**6.3**	6.2
Currency translation adjustment	**–**	0.1
Closing net book amount	**6.3**	6.3
Analysed as:		
Cost	**6.3**	6.3
Net book amount	**6.3**	6.3

The majority of the Group's Investment Property portfolio is land and therefore is not depreciated.

The fair value of the Group's investment properties at 28 September 2018 was £6.5m (2017: £7.3m). The valuation was carried out by the Group during the current financial year, using external independent advisors, and was arrived at by reference to location, market conditions and status of planning applications. The fair values of investment properties are considered a Level 3 fair value measurement.

An increase or decrease in the price per hectare of 5% would result in a 5% increase or decrease in the fair value of the land.

The alternative fair value model is illustrated by Donegal Investment Group Plc, which includes transfers to investment property from property, plant and equipment.

Donegal Investment Group Plc
Annual Report & Financial Statements 2017
NOTES TO THE CONSOLIDATED FINANCIAL STATEMENTS (EXTRACT)

3. Significant accounting policies (Extract)

(g) Investment property
Investment properties are properties which are held either to earn rental income or for capital appreciation or for both, but not for sale in the ordinary course of business, for use in the production or supply of goods and services or for administrative purposes. Investment properties are measured at fair value with any change therein recognised in profit or loss. An external, independent valuer, having an appropriate recognised professional qualification and recent experience in the location and category of property being valued, values the portfolio every twelve months.

When the use of an investment property changes such that it is reclassified as property, plant and equipment, the fair value at the date of reclassification becomes its deemed cost for subsequent accounting purposes.

[...]

15. Investment property

	2017	2016
	€'000	€'000
Group		
Balance at start of year/period	**19,021**	18,634
Change in fair value	**52**	(13)
Disposal	**(15,509)**	(73)
Reclassification from property plant & equipment	**–**	500
Effect of movement in exchange rates	**(12)**	(27)
Balance at end of year/period	**3,552**	19,021

Investment property includes the Oatfield site in Letterkenny along with other land and property assets.

[...]

The fair values of the investment properties are based on market values, being the estimated amount for which a property could be exchanged on the date of valuation between a willing buyer and a willing seller in an arm's length transaction after proper marketing wherein the parties had each acted knowledgeably, prudently and without compulsion.

Where properties are leased over a long period, the valuations are prepared by considering the aggregate of the net annual rents receivable from the properties and, when relevant, associated costs. A yield which reflects the specific risks inherent in the net cash flows is then applied to the net annual rentals to arrive at the property valuation. Lands yields in 2017 were between 1-2% (2016: 1-2%).

In the absence of current prices in an active market, the valuations are generally prepared by considering the aggregate of the estimated cash flows expected to be received from renting out the property. A yield that reflects the specific risks inherent in the net cash flows is then applied to the annual cash flows to arrive at the property valuation.

Valuations reflect, when appropriate; the type of tenants actually in occupation or responsible for meeting lease commitments or likely to be in occupation after letting of vacant accommodation and the market's general perception of their credit-worthiness; the allocation of maintenance and insurance responsibilities between lessor and lessee; and the remaining economic life of the property.

The property valuations have been prepared in a year which continues to have considerable market uncertainty. As such the fair value of investment properties has been categorised as a level 3 fair value based on the inputs to the valuation techniques used. The table above reflects a reconciliation from the opening balance to the closing balance. As outlined above, the valuation techniques used are based on comparable market transactions and discounted cashflows. The unobservable inputs in the valuations include comparable market prices of land and buildings, and rental yields, whereby an increase or decrease in these inputs would result in a corresponding change in the fair value measurement.

3.3 GOVERNMENT GRANTS (SECTION 24)

A government grant is assistance by government in the form of a transfer of resources to an entity in return for past or future compliance with specified conditions. Government grants include grants received from non-governmental development agencies and could be called by a different name, e.g. subsidies, subventions, premiums, etc., but their overall purpose is to encourage companies to embark on a particular course of action, such as creating jobs, that they might not otherwise have pursued.

FRS 102 excludes those forms of government assistance that cannot reasonably have a value placed upon them and those transactions that cannot be distinguished from normal trading.

Examples of government grants include:

1. A rural development scheme to help farmers set up bed-and-breakfast facilities to help supplement their income and to encourage them to continue farming.
2. Grant-funding for a new type of technology.
3. The offer of interest-free loans to encourage businesses to set up in a development zone.
4. A scheme to encourage a reduction in greenhouse gases by issuing emission rights free of charge to emit a specified level of greenhouse gases.
5. Grants to encourage investment in new, up-to-date plant and equipment.

Government assistance that is **excluded** from FRS 102 includes:

1. The provision of a factory or road network to enable entities to provide a manufacturing facility.
2. The provision of heat, light and power at a lower rate than other countries as long as that rate is available to all entities in that jurisdiction.
3. Taxable benefits, e.g. accelerated capital allowances, investment tax credits, etc.

Recognition and Measurement

No grants may be recognised until there is reasonable assurance that:

(a) the reporting entity will comply with any conditions attached to the grant; and
(b) the grants will be received.

Grants should be measured at the fair value of the asset received or receivable. If a grant is due to be repaid, it should be recognised as a liability when it passes the definition of a liability under FRS 102.

Unlike full IFRS, which requires the adoption of the accruals model, FRS 102 now permits an alternative 'performance model', which recognises grants in the profit and loss as the entity performs under the contract with government. If an entity, however, decides to retain the accruals model it must adopt the deferred income approach. The 'net of cost' option, by which the grant is netted off against a capital asset, is not permitted.

Performance Model

Grants under this model should be recognised in income as follows:

(a) A grant that does not impose specified future performance conditions on the recipient is recognised in income when the grant proceeds are receivable.
(b) A grant that imposes specified future performance conditions on the recipient is recognised in income only when the performance conditions are met.
(c) Grants received before the revenue recognition criteria are satisfied are recognised as liabilities.

EXAMPLE 3.19: GOVERNMENT GRANT UNDER THE PERFORMANCE MODEL

Saturn Ltd received €350,000 from the Irish Government on 1 January 2018 to establish a manufacturing plant in the Shannon Free Enterprise Zone. However, the incentive is conditional on the plant being erected in the Zone, meeting specified safety and environment legislation and starting commercial production on or before 31 December 2018. All of the conditions must be met otherwise the monies will have to be refunded to the Government.

Assume all the conditions were satisfied by 31 October 2018 when commercial production began.

Solution

The €350,000 received on 1 January 2018 is recorded as a liability at that time. On 31 October 2018 the grant of €350,000 must be recognised in income and the liability derecognised, despite the fact that no production has been achieved. All of the criteria set by Government have been met and thus the grant has been earned. It is also not appropriate to offset the grant against the cost of the asset.

If, however, there were other conditions, such as maintaining a level of employment over the next four years, then the grant would be recognised over the four-year period as the employment is maintained. If the whole grant would have to be unpaid unless the four-year period is achieved, then the grant would not be recorded in profit and loss until the end of the four years.

Accruals Model

FRS 102 requires a classification between revenue- and capital-based grants. Revenue-based grants are reported in profit and loss on a systematic basis to match against the related costs unless those costs have already been incurred, in which case the grant is reported immediately in profit.

Capital-based grants are spread over the useful economic life of the related asset. They are recorded initially in deferred income **only** and they may not be netted off against the cost of the assets concerned.

Example 3.20: Capital-based Grant under Both Methods

On 1 April 2018, Telstar Ltd acquired a piece of plant and machinery for €250,000 with a 40% grant attached. The asset has a useful life of four years and the only condition attached to the grant is that it must be used for a particular purpose for two years. Its expected residual value is €60,000.

Solution

Performance Model If the company adopts the deferred income method, the following should be the accounting treatment:

Dr	Plant		€250,000	
	Cr	Bank		€250,000
Dr	Bank (40% × €250,000)		€100,000	
	Cr	Deferred income		€100,000

Being the initial recording of the purchase of the plant and receipt of grant.

Dr	Profit and loss		€47,500	
	Cr	Accumulated depreciation		€47,500
Dr	Deferred income (50%)		€50,000	
	Cr	Profit and loss		€50,000

Being the depreciation charge on the depreciable amount of the asset (€250,000 – €60,000 = €190,000) spread over the useful life of the plant of four years and the release of capital grant **not** over the life of the plant but over the period of potential clawback of two years.

It could be argued that all of the grant should be released only after year two, but it depends on the clawback provision. It is assumed in this example that it can be clawed back proportionately over the two years.

Accruals Model Under the accruals model, the initial double entries would be the same. The depreciation charge would also be the same. However, the capital grant instead of being released to profit and loss over two years, will be spread to profit over a four-year period to match against its related depreciation charge, which is also spread over four years. The release each year would therefore be 25% × €100,000 = €25,000.

In theory, the better method to adopt would be the performance model as it concentrates on getting assets and liabilities reported correctly on the balance sheet, whereas the accruals model concentrates on matching income and related expenditure and could result in an overstatement of liabilities on the balance sheet for deferred income not yet matched against expenditure but also not repayable to the grant-awarding body. The IASB is likely to revisit this topic in the next few years and this could result in the accruals model being withdrawn in due course.

Non-monetary Grants

Non-monetary grants are recognised at fair value, if fair value can be reliably measured.

Example 3.21: Fair Value Measurement of Non-monetary Grant

The Irish Government has awarded a number of commercial radio licences to broadcast in the Gaeltacht. To ensure the maintenance of the cultural identity of the region and to encourage local ownership it has granted a local company in Spiddal a licence free of charge to broadcast in Connemara. The commercial licences were sold for €200,000 each and each licence is transferable.

Solution

The local entity in Spiddal should initially value the licence at a fair value of €200,000, with a similar figure recorded in income.

Disclosure

The following should be disclosed in relation to government grants:

(a) the accounting policy adopted for grants, i.e. the accruals or performance models;
(b) the nature and amounts of government grants recognised in the financial statements;
(c) unfulfilled conditions and other contingencies not recognised in income; and
(d) an indication of other forms of government assistance from which the entity has benefited.

For (d) it represents action by government designed to provide economic benefits specific to the entity. Examples include free technical or marketing advice, provision of guarantees, and loans at nil or low interest rates.

Randox Holdings Limited is a Northern Ireland company that has adopted the accruals option approach.

Randox Holdings Limited
ANNUAL REPORT (EXTRACTS)
for the year ended 31 December 2018

Notes to the financial statements ...

3. Accounting policies

[...]

Government grants
Capital based grants on tangible fixed assets are shown as deferred income and credited to the profit and loss account by instalments on a basis consistent with the depreciation policy of the relevant assets.

Grants relating to revenue expenditure are credited to the profit and loss account on an earned and due for payment basis.

[...]

19. Deferred income

	Group		Company	
	2018	2017	**2018**	2017
Government grants	**£'000**	£'000	£'000	**£'000**
At 1 January	**1,164**	1,226		
Received	**-**	39		
Released to the profit and loss account	**(87)**	(101)		
At 31 December	**1,077**	1,164		

3.4 IMPAIRMENT OF ASSETS (SECTION 27)

Section 27 of FRS 102 applies to the impairment of all assets other than the following:

(a) assets arising under construction contracts (Section 23 – see **Chapter 7**);
(b) deferred tax assets (Section 29 – see **Chapter 6**);
(c) employee benefits (Section 28 – see **Chapter 8**);
(d) financial assets (Section 11 – see **Chapter 12**);
(e) investment property measured at fair value (Section 16 – see **Section 3.2** above, **'Investment Property'**);
(f) biological assets at fair value (Section 34 – see **Chapter 13**);
(g) deferred acquisition costs and intangible assets arising from FRS 103.

Impairment of Inventories

Selling Price Less Costs to Complete and Sell

Reporting entities must assess at each reporting date whether any inventories are impaired. The carrying amounts of each item of inventory should be compared with its selling price less costs to complete and sell. If an item is impaired, a loss should be recognised as the difference between the carrying amount and the selling price less costs to complete and sell.

If it is impracticable to determine the selling price item by item, entities can group together items of similar product lines with similar purposes and marketed in the same geographical areas for the purpose of assessing impairment.

Reversal of Impairment

A new assessment of selling price less costs to complete and sell must be made in each subsequent period. If the circumstances responsible for the impairment no longer exist, the impairnent should be reversed so that the new carrying amount is the lower of the cost and the revised selling price less costs to complete and sell.

A reversal of impairment is illustrated by the C & C Group Plc (see **Chapter 5**).

Impairment of Assets Other than Inventories

General Principles

Only if the recoverable amount is less than the carrying amount should the carrying amount of an asset be reduced to that recoverable amount. The reduction to the recoverable amount is recognised immediately in profit or loss. However, if the asset was previously revalued and there is an existing revaluation reserve for that asset, then the revaluation reserve is reduced by the impairment and this is also recorded in other comprehensive income. In such a case, only the excess over the revaluation reserve should be charged to profit or loss.

Indicators of Impairment

An entity must assess, at each reporting date, whether there is any indication of impairment. If impairment exists, entities must estimate the recoverable amount of the asset. If there is no indication of impairment, then it is not necessary to estimate the recoverable amount.

If it is not possible to estimate impairment for individual items, then entities must assess the recoverable amount at the level of a **cash generating unit (CGU)**, i.e. the smallest identifiable group of assets that generates cash flows largely independent of cash flows from other groups of assets.

In assessing whether or not an impairment exists, the minimum requirement is to consider the following indicators:

External indicators

(a) An asset's market value has declined significantly over time or normal use.
(b) Significant changes, with an adverse effect on the environment in which the entity operates, or in the market to which the asset is dedicated, have occurred during the period.
(c) Market interest rates have increased during the period and these are likely to materially affect the discount rate.
(d) The carrying amount of net assets is more than their market capitalisation.

Internal indicators

(e) There is evidence of obsolescence or physical damage.
(f) Significant changes with an adverse effect on the entity or the manner in which the asset is used or expected to be used have occurred. Examples might be that the asset is idle; that there are plans to discontinue, restructure or dispose of the asset; or a reassessment of the useful life of the asset from being infinite to finite.
(g) There is evidence from internal reporting indicating that economic performance was worse than expected.

If there is an indication of impairment, then the useful life of the asset and the depreciation method should be reviewed and its residual value adjusted, even if no impairment loss has been recognised.

Measuring Recoverable Amount

The recoverable amount of an asset or a CGU is the higher of its **fair value less costs to sell** and its **value in use**.

It is not always necessary to determine both an asset's fair value less costs to sell and its value in use. If either of these amounts exceeds the asset's carrying amount, the asset is not impaired and it is not necessary to estimate the other amount.

If there is no reason to believe that an asset's value in use materially exceeds its fair value less costs to sell, the asset's fair value less costs to sell may be used as its recoverable amount, e.g. an asset held for disposal.

Fair Value Less Costs to Sell

Fair value less costs to sell is the amount receivable from the sale of assets in an arm's length transaction between knowledgeable, willing parties less costs of disposal. The best evidence of the fair value less costs to sell of an asset is a price in a binding sale agreement in an arm's length transaction or a market price in an active market. If there is no binding sale agreement or active market for an asset, the fair value less costs to sell is based on the best information available to reflect the amount that an entity could obtain, at the reporting date, from the disposal of the asset in an arm's length transaction between knowledgeable, willing parties, after deducting the costs of disposal. In determining this amount, entities must consider the outcome of recent transactions for similar assets within the same industry.

However, restrictions imposed on an asset to sell or purchase must be taken into account when assessing fair value and, for assets held for their service potential, cash flows may not be appropriate so depreciated replacement cost (DRC) may be a suitable alternative measurement model.

Value in Use

Value in use is the **present value** of the future cash flows expected to be derived from an asset. This present value calculation involves the following steps:

1. estimating the future cash inflows and outflows from the continuing use of an asset and from its ultimate disposal; and
2. applying the appropriate discount rate.

The following should be included in an asset's value in use:

(a) an estimate of the future cash flows the entity expects to derive from the asset;
(b) expectations about possible variations in the amount or timing of future cash flows;
(c) the time value of money, represented by the current market risk-free rate of interest;
(d) the price for bearing the uncertainty inherent in the asset; and
(e) other factors, such as illiquidity, that market participants would reflect in pricing the future cash flows expected from the asset.

In measuring value in use, estimates of future cash flows must include:

(a) projections of cash inflows from the continuing use of the asset;
(b) projections of cash outflows that are necessarily incurred to generate the cash inflows from the continuing use of the asset and which can be directly attributed, or allocated on a reasonable and consistent basis, to the asset; and
(c) the net cash flows, if any, expected to be received (or paid) for the disposal of the asset in an arm's length transaction.

An entity can use any recent financial budgets or forecasts to estimate the cash flows and may wish to extrapolate the projections based on the budgets or forecasts using a steady or declining growth rate for subsequent years beyond the budgets or forecasts.

Estimates of future cash flows must not include:

(a) cash flows from financing activities; or
(b) income tax receipts or payments.

Future cash flows should be estimated for the asset in its current condition and should not include any estimated future cash inflows or outflows that are expected to arise from:

(a) a future restructuring to which an entity is not yet committed; or
(b) by improving or enhancing the asset's performance.

The discount rate must be pre-tax, reflecting current market assessments of:

(a) the time value of money; and
(b) the risks specific to the asset for which future cash flow estimates have not been adjusted.

To avoid double-counting, the discount rate used should not reflect risks for which the future cash flow estimates have been adjusted.

A couple of simple examples will help to illustrate the calculation of impairment loss.

Example 3.22: Impairment of Plant Calculation

An entity has a single piece of equipment with a carrying value of €800,000. Due to government restrictions being imposed on exports, production is now cut to 60% of its former level. If the plant were to be sold, it would realise €500,000 net of disposal costs. Cash flow forecasts for the next five years are as follows:

Year 1 €200,000 Year 2 €200,000 Year 3 €150,000
Year 4 €100,000 Year 5 €200,000 (includes disposal proceeds).

Assume the pre-tax discount rate specific to plant is 15%.

Solution

				€000
Carrying value				800
Recoverable amount – higher of:				
value in use: Year	1	€200,000 × 0.87	= €174,000	
	2	€200,000 × 0.76	= €152,000	
	3	€150,000 × 0.66	= €100,000	
	4	€100,000 × 0.57	= €57,000	
	5	€200,000 × 0.50	= €100,000	
		Total	€583,000	
or fair value less costs to sell, i.e. €500,000				
Amount recoverable				583
Impairment loss				217

Example 3.23: Impairment of Plant Calculation

Fairhead Ltd has a single asset that it uses to manufacture computer chips. The book value after four years is €5 million (cost €7 million, accumulated depreciation on a straight-line basis of €2 million). There is no expected residual value. Due to a breakthrough in technology, management's best estimate is that the machine will produce 30% less than forecast in revenue terms. The future cash flows after taking into account the 30% reduction are:

	Year				
	1	2	3	4	5
Future cash flows (in €000)	600	660	710	755	790

The expected growth rates for the following years are:

	Year				
	6	7	8	9	10
Future cash flows	2%	(1)%	(7)%	(16)%	(30)%

If the machine was sold now, it would realise €3.2 million, net of selling costs. The discount rate to be applied to the future cash flows is 10%.

Solution

Value in use

Year	Long-term growth rate	Future cash flows	PV factor at 10%	Discounted future cash flows
		€000		**€000**
1		600	0.90909	545
2		660	0.82645	545
3		710	0.75131	533
4		755	0.68301	516
5		790	0.62092	491
6	2%	806	0.56447	455
7	(1)%	798	0.51316	409
8	(7)%	742	0.46651	346
9	(16)%	623	0.42410	264
10	(30)%	436	0.38554	168
Total				4,272

The impairment loss is calculated by comparing the book value of €5 million with the higher of value in use of €4.272 million and net selling price of €3.2 million. The impairment loss is therefore €5m – €4.272m = €728,000. The new book value of the machine is €4.272 million.

Recognising and Measuring an Impairment Loss for a Cash-generating Unit

An impairment loss must be recognised for a CGU if, and only if, the recoverable amount of the CGU is less than the carrying amount of the unit. It must be allocated to reduce the carrying amount of the assets of the CGU in the following order:

(a) first, to reduce any goodwill allocated to the CGU; and
(b) then, to the other assets of the CGU pro rata on the basis of the carrying amount of each asset in the CGU. This does not apply to current assets, however.

Entities must not reduce the carrying amount of any asset in the CGU below the highest of:

(a) its fair value less costs to sell (if determinable);
(b) its value in use (if determinable); or
(c) zero.

Any excess amount of the impairment loss that cannot be allocated, because of the restriction above, must be reallocated to the other assets of the CGU pro rata on the basis of the carrying amount of those other assets.

Example 3.24: Allocation of Impairment Loss in a CGU

On 31 March 2017, Ballyboo Ltd acquired 100% of ordinary shares in Boggy Ltd for €500,000. The fair value of the net assets at that date was €450,000. Unfortunately, Boggy Ltd made a loss in the year ended 31 March 2018, at which time the net assets were as follows (at fair value):

	€000
Property, plant and equipment	200
Brand name	50
Net current assets	100
	350

An impairment review indicated that the recoverable amount at 31 March 2018 was €300,000. The brand name has a market value of €45,000 and property, plant and equipment of €150,000. Assume goodwill has not been amortised in the first year.

Solution

	Asset values at 31 March 2018	Allocation of impairment loss	Carrying value after impairment loss
	€000	**€000**	**€000**
Goodwill (€500,000 – €450,000)	50	(50)	Nil
Property, plant and equipment	200	(45)	155
Brand name	50	(5)	45
Net current assets	100	–	100
	400	(100)	300

Impairment loss is €400,000 – €300,000 = €100,000

Goodwill is first written off to zero as long as that is its individual recoverable amount. The balance of €50,000 must be allocated on a pro rata basis to the property and brand name as follows:

	NBV	Revised	Reallocation	Recoverable amount
	€000	**€000**	**€000**	**€000**
Property, plant and equipment				
(200/250 = 80%, i.e. reduced by €40,000)	200	160	(5)	155
Brand name				
(50/250 = 20%, i.e. reduced by €10,000)	50	40	5	45

The reallocation is necessary as the brand name must not be recorded below its own individual recoverable amount of €45,000. No impairment is allocated to net current assets.

Additional Requirements for Impairment of Goodwill

The fair value of goodwill cannot be measured directly thus it must be derived by measuring the fair value of a larger group of assets that includes the goodwill.

Goodwill acquired in a business combination must, at acquisition date, be allocated to each of the acquirer's CGUs that are expected to benefit from the synergies of the combination, irrespective of whether other assets or liabilities of the acquiree are assigned to those units.

Part of the recoverable amount of a CGU is attributable to the goodwill of non-controlling interests (NCI). For the purpose of impairment testing a non-wholly-owned CGU with goodwill, the carrying amount of the unit is notionally adjusted by grossing up the carrying amount of goodwill allocated to the unit to include the goodwill attributable to the NCI. This notionally adjusted carrying amount is then compared with the recoverable amount of the CGU to determine whether or not the unit is impaired.

EXAMPLE 3.25: IMPAIRMENT TESTING CGUs WITH GOODWILL AND NON-CONTROLLING INTERESTS

Ballybroke Ltd acquired 80% of Doorin Ltd for €32,000 on 1 January 2018. Doorin Ltd's identifiable net assets at that date had a fair value of €30,000. Ballybroke Ltd recognises:
(a) Goodwill: €32,000 – 80% × €30,000 = €8,000.
(b) Doorin Ltd's identifiable net assets at fair value of €30,000.
(c) Non-controlling interest of 20% × €30,000 = €6,000.

The assets of Doorin Ltd are the smallest group of independent assets, thus it is a CGU. At the end of 2018, Ballybroke Ltd determines that the recoverable amount of Doorin Ltd is €20,000. Assume Ballybroke Ltd adopts straight-line depreciation with an expected useful life of 10 years.

Solution

Testing Doorin Ltd for impairment:

	Goodwill		Identifiable net assets		Total
	€		€		€
Beginning of 2018					
Gross carrying amount	8,000		30,000		38,000
Accumulated depreciation	–		(3,000)	10%	(3,000)
Carrying amount	8,000		27,000		35,000
Unrecognised NCI	2,000	(8,000 × 20/80)	–		2,000
Notionally adjusted carrying amount	10,000		27,000		37,000
Recoverable amount					20,000
Impairment loss					17,000
End of 2018					
Carrying amount	8,000		27,000		35,000
Impairment loss	(8,000)		(7,000)		(15,000)
Carrying amount after impairment loss	NIL		20,000		20,000

If goodwill cannot be allocated to individual CGUs (or groups of CGUs) on a non-arbitrary basis, then entities must test the impairment of goodwill by determining the recoverable amount of either:

(a) the acquired entity in its entirety, if the goodwill relates to an acquired entity that has not been integrated (i.e. the acquired business has not been dissolved into the reporting entity); or
(b) the entire group of entities excluding any entities that have not been integrated, if the goodwill relates to an entity that has been integrated.

Entities must separate goodwill into goodwill relating to entities that have been integrated and goodwill relating to entities not integrated. Also, entities must follow the requirements for CGUs in this section when calculating the recoverable amount of, and allocating impairment losses and reversals to, assets belonging to the acquired entity or group of entities.

Reversal of an Impairment Loss

Under FRS 102, goodwill impairment must never be reversed in a subsequent period.

For all other assets, entities should assess at each reporting date if there is an indication that an impairment loss no longer exists – using the same indicators as for the original decision to impair.

The reversal process depends on whether the impairment involved individual assets or CGUs.

Example 3.26: Reversal of Impairment Loss

Clifden Ltd acquired two companies from Mayo Ltd on 1 May 2018 for €3,000,000 when the fair value of its assets was €2.2 million. At 30 April 2019 the carrying values of the net assets of both companies were €2 million and €500,000, respectively. Goodwill is being amortised over a period of 10 years. An impairment review was carried out at that time and an impairment loss recognised in income. Both companies had reported losses for the year ended 30 April 2020. However, the actual cash flows for the years 2019 and 2020 were higher than expected due to a change in economic conditions. The carrying amounts of the net assets in both companies were €2.3 million and €800,000, respectively. Clifden Ltd therefore carried out a revised calculation of the recoverable amount of the segment based on revised cash flows.

The recoverable amounts of the two companies at the respective dates are as shown below:

	Recoverable amount at 30 April 2019 (based on original cash flows)	Recoverable amount at 30 April 2020 (based on revised cash flows)
	€000	**€000**
Clifden Ltd	1,600	2,900
Mayo Ltd	800	1,000

The depreciated historical costs of Clifden Ltd's and Mayo Ltd's net assets at 30 April 2020 were €2.6 million and €800,000, respectively.

Solution

Assuming there is no reasonable manner by which the goodwill could be allocated to the two companies, the impairment review must take place in two stages:

	Clifden Ltd	Mayo Ltd
	€000	**€000**
Carrying amount of net assets 30 April 2019	2,000	500
Recoverable amount	1,600	800
Impairment	400	Nil

The impairment loss on Clifden Ltd is recognised first, before the two subsidiaries are combined in order to carry out the impairment review on the goodwill:

	€000
Clifden Ltd	1,600
Mayo Ltd	500
	2,100
Goodwill	
(€3 million consideration – €2.2 million fair value of net assets = €800,000	
€800,000 – 10% amortisation of €80,000 = €720,000)	720
	2,820
Total recoverable amount	2,400
Additional impairment loss (goodwill)	420

A further impairment review must take place at 30 April 2020 for two reasons:

(a) both companies are making losses; and

(b) it appears that the original impairment review was inaccurate.

	Clifden Ltd	Mayo Ltd	Goodwill	Total
	€000	€000	€000	€000
Carrying amount of net assets	2,300	800	300	3,400
Recoverable amount	2,900	1,000		3,900
Impairment loss	Nil	Nil		Nil

Neither company is impaired at 30 April 2020, nor is goodwill impaired. Because the actual cash flows were better than forecast it is possible that the original impairment loss may have reversed. The carrying value of the assets is compared with depreciated historical cost:

	Clifden Ltd	Mayo Ltd
	€000	€000
Carrying amount of net assets	2,300	800
Depreciated historical cost	2,600	800
Reversal of impairment loss (income)	300	Nil

An impairment loss may be reversed under FRS 102 if there has been a reversal of the indicators causing the loss in the first place – this is assumed to be the case here. The carrying value of the net assets can be increased up to the lower of the recoverable amount (€2.9 million) and depreciated historical cost (€2.6 million). Therefore, a gain of €300,000 is recognised in the income statement. The impairment loss on goodwill cannot be reversed in accordance with FRS 102.

Reversal where Recoverable Amount was Estimated for an Individual Impaired Asset

When the prior impairment loss was based on the recoverable amount of the individual impaired asset, the following requirements apply:

(a) Entities must estimate the recoverable amount of the asset at the current reporting date.

(b) If the estimated recoverable amount of the asset exceeds its carrying amount, entities must increase the carrying amount to its recoverable amount, subject to the limitation in (c) below. That increase is a reversal of an impairment loss. The entity should recognise the reversal immediately in profit or loss, unless it is a reversal of a previous loss through the revaluation reserve.

(c) The reversal of an impairment loss must not increase the carrying amount of the asset above the carrying amount that would have been determined had no impairment loss occurred in prior years.

(d) After a reversal of an impairment loss is recognised, entities must adjust the depreciation charge to allocate the asset's revised carrying amount, less its residual value (if any), on a systematic basis over its remaining useful life.

Reversal when Recoverable Amount was Estimated for a CGU

When the original impairment loss was based on the recoverable amount of the CGU to which the asset belongs, the following requirements apply:

(a) Entities must estimate the recoverable amount of that CGU at the current reporting date.

(b) If the estimated recoverable amount of the CGU exceeds its carrying amount, that excess is a reversal of an impairment loss. Entities must allocate the amount of that reversal to the assets of the unit, except for goodwill, pro rata with the carrying amounts of those assets, subject to the limitation in (c) below. Only then can any be allocated to goodwill.

Those increases in carrying amounts must be treated as reversals of impairment losses for individual assets and recognised immediately in profit or loss, unless they are reversals of previous revaluation losses.

(c) In allocating a reversal of an impairment loss for a CGU, the reversal must not increase the carrying amount of any asset above the lower of
   (i) its recoverable amount, and
   (ii) the carrying amount that would have been determined (net of depreciation) had no impairment loss been recognised for the asset in prior periods.

(d) After a reversal of an impairment loss is recognised, if applicable, entities must then adjust depreciation for each asset in the CGU in future periods to allocate the asset's revised carrying amount, less its residual value (if any), on a systematic basis over its remaining useful life.

EXAMPLE 3.27: REVERSAL OF IMPAIRMENT LOSS ON A CGU

A CGU comprising a factory, plant and equipment and goodwill becomes impaired as a new, more technologically advanced product has been introduced by a competitor. The recoverable amount falls to €60 million. A loss of €80 million was allocated as follows:

	Net book value (pre-impairment)	Net book value (after impairment)
	€ million	**€ million**
Goodwill	40	Nil
Patent (no market value)	20	Nil
Property, plant & equipment	80	60
	140	60

After three years a new technological breakthrough is made and the recoverable amount increases to €90 million. If no impairment had occurred, the carrying value would have been €70 million.

Solution

An impairment can only be reversed up from €60 million to €70 million and in this case the impairment of the original patent cannot be reversed as it had no market value, therefore only property, plant and equipment can be increased by €10 million.

Disclosure

The following should be disclosed for each class of assets:

(a) the amount of impairment losses recognised in profit or loss and line items in the statement of comprehensive income or in the profit and loss account, if presented;
(b) the amount of reversals of impairment losses in profit or loss and in line items in the statement of comprehensive income.

Entities must also disclose the above for each of the following classes of asset:

(a) inventories;
(b) property, plant and equipment (including investment property accounted for by the cost method);
(c) goodwill;
(d) intangible assets other than goodwill;
(e) investments in associates; and
(f) investments in joint ventures.

An entity must disclose a description of the events and circumstances that led to the recognition or reversal of the impairment loss.

Although not specifically required in FRS 102, an example of an accounting policy that addresses the impairment of assets can be found in the IASB's *IFRS for SMEs 2009 Illustrative Financial Statements Presentation and Disclosure Checklist* and is reproduced overleaf.

Example 3.28: Illustrative Financial Statements – Impairment of Assets

XYZ Group

Accounting Policies and Explanatory Notes (Extract)

2. Basis of preparation and accounting policies

Impairment of assets

At each reporting date, property, plant and equipment, intangible assets and investments in associates are reviewed to determine whether there is any indication that those assets have suffered an impairment loss. If there is an indication of possible impairment, the recoverable amount of any affected asset (or group of related assets) is estimated and compared with its carrying amount. If estimated recoverable amount is lower, the carrying amount is reduced to its estimated recoverable amount, and an impairment loss is recognised immediately in profit or loss.

Similarly, at each reporting date, inventories are assessed for impairment by comparing the carrying amount of each item of inventory (or group of similar items) with its selling price less costs to complete and sell. If an item of inventory (or group of similar items) is impaired, its carrying amount is reduced to selling price less costs to complete and sell, and an impairment loss is recognised immediately in profit or loss.

If an impairment loss subsequently reverses, the carrying amount of the asset (or group of related assets) is increased to the revised estimate of its recoverable amount (selling price less costs to complete and sell, in the case of inventories), but not in excess of the amount that would have been determined had no impairment loss been recognised for the asset (group of related assets) in prior years. A reversal of an impairment loss is recognised immediately in profit or loss.

The disclosure in FRS 102 is considerably reduced from that in IAS 36 *Impairment of Assets*, which often results in listed companies having to spend two pages detailing how they have arrived at their calculations, the assumptions used and the sensitivity of those assumptions.

3.5 BORROWING COSTS (SECTION 25)

This includes interest and other costs arising on financial liabilities. They include:

(a) interest expense calculated using the effective interest method per Section 11 (see **Chapter 12**);

(b) finance charges in regard to finance leases per Section 20 (see **Chapter 4**); and
(c) exchange differences arising from foreign currency borrowings to the extent that they are regarded as adjustments to interest costs.

Examples of interest expenses not only include bank interest from a local bank but also premiums and discounts, which are effectively surrogates for interest. An example of the latter is provided below.

Example 3.29: The Effective Rate of Interest

Listowel Ltd issued a debenture of €100,000. The debenture requires Listowel Ltd to repay the lender €134,010 to redeem the debenture in six years' time. It is a zero coupon bond; thus no interest is paid during the six years.

Solution

The effective rate of interest on the debenture is calculated at 5% (i.e. the present value of a single payment of €134,010 at the end of six years at 5% is €100,000).

The premium of €34,010 would be amortised as follows:

Year	Amortisation of premium (5% × liability)	Liability	Premium
	€	€	€
0		100,000	34,010
1	5,000	105,000	29,010
2	5,250	110,250	23,760
3	5,513	115,763	18,247
4	5,788	121,551	12,459
5	6,078	127,629	6,381
6	6,381	134,010	

Example 3.30: Interest Chargeable on a Time Basis

On 1 July 2018 Ardee Ltd borrowed €100,000 from its local bank. The bank charges interest on the loan at a fixed rate of 6% per annum. Interest is payable annually in arrears. The principal is repayable in full on the sixth anniversary of the loan. Ardee Ltd's year-end is 31 December.

Solution

Interest of €3,000 (borrowing cost) is charged as an expense in determining profit for both years ended 31 December 2018 and 2024 (half years) and €6,000 per annum for the intervening years, December 2019–2023.

Recognition

FRS 102 permits reporting entities to capitalise borrowing costs that are directly attributable to the acquisition, construction or production of a "qualifying asset". A qualifying asset is one which takes a substantial period of time to get ready for its intended use or sale. However, the policy must be applied consistently. If borrowing costs are not capitalised, they must be expensed through profit or loss. Capitalisation can apply to such diverse situations as the growing of forests, the maturing of whiskey stocks and the construction of property.

The costs that may be capitalised are only those that could be avoided if the expenditure had not taken place, i.e. they must be incremental costs.

The borrowing costs that can be capitalised are the actual finance costs incurred less any temporary investment income on that borrowing. However, if the asset is funded by general sources, there is a need to adopt a weighted average capitalisation rate, but the interest that is capitalised must not exceed the actual borrowing costs incurred during a particular accounting period.

In order to ensure that capitalisation of borrowing costs only occurs when physical activity and actual borrowing exists, the following additional rules apply to when an entity may commence, suspend and cease capitalisation.

- **Commencement date** From the date that **both** monies have been borrowed and that activities to construct, mature, etc. have commenced.
- **Suspension** No interest may be capitalised during extended periods when activity has been paused.
- **Cessation** No interest may be capitalised once the asset is substantially complete, i.e. ready for use or sale, matured or grown.

Disclosure

Under company law the disclosure of the finance costs incurred during the period is required, and also the total effective interest expense (using the effective interest rate method) for financial liabilities that are not at fair value through profit or loss.

If the reporting entity capitalises interest, it must also disclose:
(a) the amount of borrowing costs capitalised during the period; and
(b) the capitalisation rate adopted.

Where a reporting entity has an accounting policy that writes off interest directly to profit and loss, the following is an example of the disclosure note that would be included.

Irish Company Ltd

EXTRACT FROM FINANCIAL STATEMENTS

Accounting Policies (Extract)

Borrowing costs
All borrowing costs are recognised in profit or loss in the period in which they are incurred.

3.6 SMALL ENTITIES

There are no explicit minimum disclosure requirements for small entities under Section 1A of FRS 102 for either the UK or the Republic of Ireland. However, small entities may need to provide disclosures as required by FRS 102 Section 13 *Inventories* if required to give a true and fair view.

3.7 MICRO-ENTITIES

The differences in accounting treatment for valuing non-current assets under FRS 105 are noted below.

Property, Plant and Equipment and Investment Property

The accounting treatment is very similar to Sections 16 and 17 of FRS 102. The main differences are as follows:
- Under Section 12, paragraph 12.14 of FRS 105, a micro-entity must adopt the cost model after initial recognition and subsequently record these assets at cost less any accumulated depreciation and any accumulated impairment losses.
- A micro-entity must also expense day-to-day servicing in profit or loss in the period in which the costs are incurred.

Borrowing Costs

Unlike Section 25 of FRS 102, micro-entities do not have an option to capitalise borrowing costs. These must all be written off to profit and loss in the period they are incurred.

Government Grants

Unlike under Section 24 of FRS 102, Section 19 of FRS 105 does not permit micro-entities to adopt the performance model when recognising grants in the financial statements. Micro-entities must therefore adopt the accruals model using the deferred income approach.

The minimum disclosure requirements for micro-entities under FRS 105, for either the UK or the Republic of Ireland, and the mandatory disclosure requirements for micro-entities required under the Companies Act 2014 (ROI) are summarised at the end of this chapter.

Disclosure Checklist: Asset Valuation – Non-current Assets – FRS 102

(References are to the relevant Section of FRS 102)

	PARA.
Property, Plant and Equipment – Section 17	
The following disclosures (other than those related to fair value measurement) are relevant to an entity that chooses to measure investment properties rented to another group entity under the cost model in this section as permitted by paragraph 16.4A(b).	17.30A
An entity shall disclose the following for each class of property, plant and equipment: (a) the measurement bases used for determining the gross carrying amount; (b) the depreciation methods used; (c) the useful lives or the depreciation rates used; (d) the gross carrying amount and the accumulated depreciation (aggregated with accumulated impairment losses) at the beginning and end of the reporting period; (e) a reconciliation of the carrying amount at the beginning and end of the reporting period, showing separately: (i) additions; (ii) disposals; (iii) acquisitions through business combinations; (iv) revaluations; (v) transfers to or from investment property (see paragraphs 16.9 to 16.9C); (vi) impairment losses recognised or reversed in profit or loss in accordance with Section 27 *Impairment of Assets;* (vii) depreciation; and (viii) other changes. This reconciliation need not be presented for prior periods.	17.31
An entity shall disclose the carrying amount at the end of the reporting period of investment property rented to another group entity, where the entity has chosen to account for such properties using the cost model in accordance with this section (see paragraph 16.4A)	17.31A
An entity shall also disclose the following: (a) the existence and carrying amounts of property, plant and equipment to which the entity has restricted title or that is pledged as security for liabilities; and (b) the amount of contractual commitments for the acquisition of property, plant and equipment.	17.32
If items of property, plant and equipment are stated at revalued amounts, the following shall be disclosed: (a) the effective date of the revaluation; (b) whether an independent valuer was involved; (c) the methods and significant assumptions applied in estimating the items' fair values; and (d) for each revalued class of property, plant and equipment, the carrying amount that would have been recognised had the assets been carried under the cost model.	17.32A

	PARA.
Investment Property – Section 16	
An entity shall disclose the following: (a) the methods and significant assumptions applied in determining the fair value of investment property; (b) the extent to which the fair value of investment property (as measured or disclosed in the financial statements) is based on a valuation by an independent valuer who holds a recognised and relevant professional qualification and has recent experience in the location and class of the investment property being valued. If there has been no such valuation, that fact shall be disclosed; (c) the existence and amounts of restrictions on the realisability of investment property or the remittance of income and proceeds of disposal; (d) contractual obligations to purchase, construct or develop investment property or for repairs, maintenance or enhancements; and (e) a reconciliation between the carrying amounts of investment property at the beginning and end of the period, showing separately: (i) additions, disclosing separately those additions resulting from acquisitions through business combinations; (ii) net gains or losses from fair value adjustments; (iii) transfers to property, plant and equipment (see paragraphs 16.9 to 16.9B); (iv) transfers to and from inventories [and owner-occupied property]; and (v) other changes. This reconciliation need not be presented for prior periods.	16.10
In accordance with Section 20, an entity shall provide all relevant disclosures required in that section about leases into which it has entered.	16.11
Government Grants – Section 24	
An entity shall disclose the following: (a) the accounting policy adopted for grants in accordance with paragraph 24.4; (b) the nature and amounts of government grants recognised in the financial statements; (c) unfulfilled conditions and other contingencies attaching to government grants that have not been recognised in income; and (d) an indication of other forms of government assistance from which the entity has directly benefited.	24.6
For the purpose of the disclosure required by paragraph 24.6(c), government assistance is action by government designed to provide an economic benefit specific to an entity or range of entities qualifying under specified criteria. Examples include free technical or marketing advice and the provision of guarantees.	24.7

	PARA.
Impairment of Assets – Section 27	
An entity shall disclose the following for each class of assets indicated in paragraph 27.33: (a) the amount of impairment losses recognised in profit or loss during the period and the line item(s) in the statement of comprehensive income (and in the income statement, if presented) in which those impairment losses are included; and (b) the amount of reversals of impairment losses recognised in profit or loss during the period and the line item(s) in the statement of comprehensive income (and in the income statement, if presented) in which those impairment losses are reversed.	27.32
An entity shall disclose the information required by paragraph 27.32 for each of the following classes of asset: (a) inventories; (b) property, plant and equipment (including investment property accounted for by the cost method); (c) goodwill; (d) intangible assets other than goodwill; (e) investments in associates; and (f) investments in joint ventures.	27.33
An entity shall disclose a description of the events and circumstances that led to the recognition or reversal of the impairment loss.	27.33A
Borrowing Costs – Section 25	
Paragraph 5.5 sets out the presentation requirements for items of profit or loss, including interest payable. Paragraph 11.48(b) requires disclosure of total interest expense (using the effective interest method) for financial liabilities that are not at fair value through profit or loss. When a policy of capitalising borrowing costs is not adopted, this section does not require any additional disclosure.	25.3
Where a policy of capitalisation is adopted, an entity shall disclose: (a) the amount of borrowing costs capitalised in the period; and (b) the capitalisation rate used.	25.3A

DISCLOSURE CHECKLIST: ASSET VALUATION – NON-CURRENT ASSETS – SMALL ENTITIES

(References are to the relevant Appendix of FRS 102 Section 1A)

The mandatory disclosure requirements for small entities required under the Companies Act 2014 (ROI) (CA 2014), the Companies Act 2006 (UK) (CA 2006) and the Small Companies and Groups (Accounts and Directors' Report) Regulations 2008 (UK) (S.I. No. 409 of 2008) are as follows:

	PARA.
Fixed assets	
For each item shown under 'fixed assets' in the small entity's statement of financial position the following information shall be given: (a) the aggregate amounts (on the basis of cost or revaluation, or under the fair value accounting rules) in respect of that item as at the date of the beginning of the reporting period and as at the reporting date respectively; (b) the effect on any amount shown in the statement of financial position in respect of that item of: (i) any revision of the amount in respect of any assets included under that item made during the reporting period as a result of revaluation or under the fair value accounting rules; (ii) acquisitions during the reporting period of any assets; (iii) disposals during the reporting period of any assets; and (iv) any transfers of assets of the small entity to and from that item during the reporting period. (Schedule 3A, paragraphs 45(1) and 45(2) CA 2014) (Schedule 1, Paragraph 48(1) and 48(2) S.I. 409/2008)	1AD.13 (ROI) 1AC.12 (UK) (same)
For each item within paragraph 1AD.13 [1AC.12 in the UK] there shall also be stated: (a) the cumulative amount of depreciation and impairment of assets included under that item as at the date of the beginning and as at the end of the reporting period date; (b) the amount of any such adjustments made in respect of the reporting period; (c) the amount of any adjustments made during the reporting period for disposal of any assets; and (d) the amount of any other adjustments during the reporting period. (Schedule 3A, paragraph 45(3) CA 2014) (Schedule 1, paragraph 48(3) S.I. 409/2008) Comparatives are not required for the movements in fixed assets during the reporting period noted in paragraphs 1AD.13 and 1AD.14. (Schedule 3A, paragraph (2) CA 2014)	1AD.14(ROI) 1AC.13 (UK) (same)

	PARA.
Paragraphs 1AD.13 and 1AD.14 apply to all fixed assets, including investment property, property, plant and equipment, intangible assets (including goodwill), fixed asset investments, biological assets and heritage assets recognised in the statement of financial position. Each item refers to a class of fixed assets shown separately either in the statement of financial position, or in the notes to the financial statements. FRS 102 paragraph 16.10(e) addresses similar requirements for investment property. Paragraphs 17.31(d) and (e) address similar requirements for property, plant and equipment. Paragraphs 18.27(c) and (e) address similar requirements for intangible assets other than goodwill. Paragraph 19.26 addresses similar requirements for goodwill. Paragraphs 34.7(c) and 34.10(e) address similar requirements for biological assets. Paragraphs 34.55(e) and (f) address similar requirements for heritage assets recognised in the statement of financial position.	1AD.14(ROI) 1AC.13 (UK) (same)
Fixed assets measured at revalued amounts	
Where fixed assets are measured at revalued amounts, the items affected and the basis of valuation adopted in determining the amounts of the assets for each item shall be disclosed in the note on accounting policies. (Schedule 3A, paragraph 35(2) CA 2014) (Schedule 1, Paragraph 34(2) S.I. 409/2008) These requirements apply when: • Investments in subsidiaries, associates and joint ventures are measured at fair value with changes in fair value recognised in other comprehensive income. Paragraph 9.27(b) addresses a similar disclosure requirement. • Property, plant and equipment are revalued using the revaluation model set out in paragraphs 17.15B to 17.15F. Paragraph 17.31(a) addresses a similar disclosure requirement. • Intangible assets other than goodwill are revalued using the revaluation model set out in paragraphs 18.18B to 18.18H. Paragraph 18.29A(c) addresses a similar disclosure requirement. These requirements do not apply to investment property and biological assets measured at fair value through profit or loss.	1AD.15 (ROI) 1AC.14 (UK) (same)

	PARA.
Where any fixed assets of the small entity (other than listed investments) are included under any item shown in the small entity's statement of financial position at a revalued amount, the following information must be given: • the years (so far as they are known to the directors) in which the assets were severally valued and the several values; • in the case of assets that have been valued during the reporting period, the names of the persons who valued them or particulars of their qualifications for doing so and (whichever is stated) the bases of valuation used by them. (Schedule 1, paragraph 49 S.I. 409/2008) Paragraphs 17.32A(a) and (c), 18.29A(a) and (c) and 34.55(e)(ii) address similar requirements. These paragraphs do not require the names or qualifications of the persons who valued the fixed assets to be disclosed. These requirements apply in the same circumstances as those set out in paragraph 1AC.14.	1AC.15 (UK only)
In the case of each item in the statement of financial position measured at a revalued amount, the comparable amounts determined according to the historical cost accounting rules shall be shown separately in the statement of financial position or in a note to the financial statements. (Schedule 3A, paragraph 35(3) CA 2014) (Schedule 1, Paragraph 34(3) S.I. 409/2008) The comparable amounts refers to the aggregate amount of cost and the aggregate of accumulated depreciation and accumulated impairment losses that would have been required according to the historical cost accounting rules. (Schedule 3A, paragraph 35(4) CA 2014) (Schedule 1, Paragraph 34(4) S.I. 409/2008) Paragraphs 17.32A(d) and 18.29A(d) address similar requirements. These requirements apply in the same circumstances as those set out in paragraph 1AD.15 [1AC.14 in the UK].	1AD.16(ROI) 1AC.16 (UK) (similar)
Where any amount is transferred to or from any revaluation reserves and the revaluation reserves are shown as separate items in the small entity's statement of financial position, the following information shall be set out in tabular form: (a) the amount of the reserves as at the date of the beginning of the reporting period and as at the reporting date respectively; (b) any amount transferred to or from the reserves during that period; and (c) the source and application respectively of any amounts so transferred. (Schedule 3A, paragraph 49 CA 2014) Paragraph 6.3A addresses similar requirements. These requirements apply in the same circumstances as those set out in paragraph 1AD.15.	1AD.17 (ROI only)

	PARA.
Where fixed assets are measured at revalued amounts the following information must be given in tabular form: (a) movements in the revaluation reserve in the reporting period, with an explanation of the tax treatment of items therein; and (b) the carrying amount in the statement of financial position that would have been recognised had the fixed assets not been revalued. (Schedule 1,paragraph 54(2) S.I. 409/2008)	1AC.17 (UK only)
The treatment for taxation purposes of amounts credited or debited to the revaluation reserve shall be disclosed in a note to the financial statements. (Schedule 3A, paragraph 36(6) CA 2014) (Schedule 1, Paragraph 35(6) S.I. 409/2008) Paragraph 29.27(a) addresses similar requirements. These requirements apply in the same circumstances as those set out in paragraph 1AD.15. [1AC.14 in the UK]	1AD.18 (ROI) 1AC.18 (UK) (same)
Capitalisation of borrowing costs	
Where a small entity adopts a policy of capitalising borrowing costs, the inclusion of interest in determining the cost of the asset and the amount of the interest so included is disclosed in a note to the financial statements. (Schedule 3A, paragraph 29(3) CA 2014) (Schedule 1, Paragraph 27(3) S.I. 409/2008) Paragraph 25.3A(a) addresses a similar requirement to the second part of this.	1AD.19 (ROI) 1AC.19 (UK) (same)
Impairment of assets	
Impairment of fixed assets (including fixed asset investments) shall be disclosed (either separately or in aggregate) in a note to the financial statements if not shown separately in the income statement. (Schedule 3A, paragraphs 23(1) and (2) CA 2014) (Schedule 1, Paragraph 19(3) S.I. 409/2008) Paragraph 27.32(a) addresses similar requirements.	1AD.20 (ROI) 1AC.20 (UK) (similar)
Any impairments of fixed assets that are reversed because the reasons for which they were made have ceased to apply shall be disclosed (either separately or in aggregate) in a note to the financial statements if not shown separately in the income statement. (Schedule 3A, paragraph 23(3) CA 2014) (Schedule 1, Paragraph 20(2) S.I. 409/2008) Paragraph 27.32(b) addresses similar requirements.	1AD.21 (ROI) 1AC.21 (UK) (similar)

Disclosure Checklist: Asset Valuation – Non-Current Assets – Micro-entities

(References are to the relevant Section of FRS 105)

The mandatory disclosure requirements for micro-entities required under FRS 105, the Companies Act 2014 (ROI) (CA 2014), the Companies Act 2006 (UK) (CA 2006) and the Small Companies and Groups (Accounts and Directors' Report) Regulations 2008 (UK) (S.I. No. 409 of 2008) are as follows:

	Para.
A micro-entity shall disclose information in relation to the following items in accordance with the relevant appendix to Section 6 *Notes to the Financial Statements*: (a) financial commitments not recognised in the statement of financial position for the acquisition of property, plant and equipment or investment property; and (b) items of property, plant and equipment or investment property given as security in respect of its commitments, guarantees and contingencies.	12.28
An Irish micro-entity shall disclose information in relation to impairment losses recognised and reversed in accordance with Appendix B to Section 6 *Notes to the Financial Statements.*	22.22 (ROI only)
Impairment of assets	
Value adjustments for impairment of fixed assets (including fixed asset investments) must be disclosed (either separately or in aggregate) in a note to the financial statements if not shown separately in the income statement. (Schedule 3B, paragraphs 23(1) and (2) CA 2014)	6B.10 (ROI only)
Any value adjustments for impairment of fixed assets (including fixed asset investments) that are reversed because the reasons for which they were made have ceased to apply must be disclosed (either separately or in aggregate) in a note to the financial statements if not shown separately in the income statement. (Schedule 3B, paragraph 23(3) CA 2014) See paragraph 22.22 [of FRS 105].	6B.11 (ROI only)

Chapter 4

ASSET VALUATION – INTANGIBLE ASSETS

This chapter covers the broad principles that are included in FRS 102 when entities account for intangible assets other than goodwill, which is covered under business combinations (see **Chapter 11**). There are two separate sections, one covering intangibles in general, the other covering leasing arrangements (on the basis that they can give rise to a right-to-use asset and thus fall within intangible assets).

4.1 INTANGIBLE ASSETS OTHER THAN GOODWILL (SECTION 18)

Intangible assets other than goodwill are defined as identifiable non-monetary assets without physical substance. They are identifiable when:

(a) they are separable; or
(b) they arise from contractual or other legal rights regardless of whether they are transferable or separable.

However, financial assets, heritage assets and mineral rights and reserves are explicitly excluded. Nor does it apply to deferred acquisition costs and insurance contracts, which are covered in FRS 103 *Insurance Contracts*.

Recognition

General Principles for Recognising Intangible Assets

An intangible asset may only be recognised if:

(a) it is **probable** that expected future economic benefits will flow to the entity; and
(b) the cost or value can be **measured reliably**.

The probability of expected future benefits must be assessed using reasonable and supportable assumptions that represent management's best estimate of the economic conditions existing over the useful life of the asset.

Entities should use their own judgement to assess the degree of certainty attached to the flow of economic benefits. However, probability is always assumed to be satisfied for intangible assets acquired separately.

FRS 102 permits internally generated assets to be reported, provided they meet the general principles of asset recognition and the more specific criteria for development. Costs can only be capitalised from the date that recognition criteria are met and will include material costs, employee benefits, legal fees, amortisation of patents and even borrowing costs in some cases (see **Chapter 3**).

Acquisition as Part of a Business Combination

Normally an intangible asset acquired as part of a business combination is measured at fair value as this measurement can be made reliably. However, it is not recognised if the asset:

- cannot be separated from goodwill; or
- is separable from goodwill, but there is no history or evidence of exchange transactions for the same or similar assets or else the fair value would be dependent on immeasurable variables.

Internally Generated Intangible Assets

Expenditure on **research** is expensed. However, FRS 102 permits **development** expenditure to be capitalised as long as it can be clearly distinguished from research expenditure.

The following are all expensed and must **not** be recognised as intangible assets:

(a) internally generated brands, mastheads, publishing titles, customer lists, etc.;
(b) expenditure on start-ups;
(c) expenditure on training activities;
(d) expenditure on advertising and promotional activities;
(e) expenditure on relocating or reorganising part of the entity; and
(f) internally generated goodwill.

However, prepayments may be created if the payment is made in advance of delivery of goods or service, e.g. a television advertising campaign where the adverts have yet to be broadcast.

Research All research expenditure must be expensed to profit or loss when incurred, on the basis that there is no probability of future economic benefits being derived from that expenditure. Examples can include:

(a) activities to create new knowledge;
(b) the search for, evaluation and selection of, research applications;
(c) the search for alternative materials, devices, products, processes, systems or services;
(d) the formulation, design, evaluation of and selection of alternative materials, services, etc.

Development FRS 102 offers an option to capitalise development expenditure, but only if **all** of the following criteria are met:

(a) the project is technically feasible and it will result in future sales or use;

(b) there is an intention to complete the project and to use or sell any assets arising;
(c) the ability to either use assets arising or to sell them;
(d) the project must generate probable future economic benefits, i.e. there must be a market or future sales from its use;
(e) there must be adequate technical, financial and other resources to complete the development; and
(f) any expenditure incurred must be reliably measured.

Examples might include:
(a) the design, construction and testing of pre-production prototypes;
(b) the design of tools, jigs, moulds and dies involving new technology;
(c) the design, construction and operation of a pilot plant that by itself would not be commercially feasible for commercial production; and
(d) the design, construction and testing of alternative new materials, devices, products, processes, etc.

If an entity opts for capitalisation, this policy must be applied consistently to all expenditure passing the criteria for development.

EXAMPLE 4.1: DEVELOPMENT COSTS

Greenock Plc manufactures and distributes a wide range of general pharmaceutical products. Selected data for the reporting period to 31 March 2019 are as follows:

	€000
Profit before income tax	3,400
Non-current assets	23,000
Research and development expenditure	9,400

The research and development expenditure is substantially higher than in previous years and has eroded the company's profits. The finance director has asked for your help on whether it is acceptable to carry forward part of the €9.4 million to a future period.

The reason for the significant increase was the introduction of a five-year laboratory programme to attempt to find an antidote for the common cold. Salaries and other costs associated with that programme amount to €4.7 million.

The following additional expenditures were included:
(a) Costs to test a new tamper-proof dispenser pack for sale of antibiotic capsules: €1.52 million. These will be used for the company's best-selling product and the packs will be introduced in 2020.

(b) Experimental costs to convert a powder into a liquid drug: €1.18 million, leading to phasing out of a powder drug.
(c) Quality control on all production for the year: €1.5 million.
(d) Time and motion study to improve productive efficiency: €100,000.
(e) Construction and testing of a prototype machine for producing hypodermic needles: €400,000. Testing has been successful. The needles represent only 1% of sales at present, but this is expected to increase following the introduction of the new machine.

Solution

Under FRS 102, to capitalise the expenditure the development criteria would have to be met. The €4.7 million incurred to find a cure for the common cold would undoubtedly fail the criteria and would be classified as research expenditure and therefore should be written off to profits. As regards the remaining expenditure, the following might be argued:

(a) Dispenser Pack As the dispenser pack was a new product, costs incurred before the pack met the development criteria are expensed. In this case, determining the technical feasibility of the pack and developing a cost-effective product would have been two key issues. There would be opportunities to capitalise some of this expenditure.

(b) Converting Powders to Liquid Form The tests have not yet proven successful, therefore the technical feasibility test would not be met and the €1.18 million must be expensed. This could be argued to be applied research rather than development.

(c) Costs of Quality Control These costs relate to products being produced and hence can be capitalised into the products produced. No separate intangible, such as 'Superior Quality' could be raised as such an asset is not identifiable. Production costs occur after development and as such are outside the remit of FRS 102's definition of development.

(d) Costs of Time and Motion Study As the equipment is being used in current production, the costs could be capitalised into the cost of the equipment. If there is clearly evidence of an improvement in efficiency, then the costs must be capitalised, but it seems to be general time and motion studies and therefore is really a current production cost.

(e) New Prototype Machine This is a difficult one to classify. It is a question of what has yet to be done. Questions relating to the development criteria need to be asked. For example: has technical feasibility been established, and is it only minor adjustments that are being made? Do any minor adjustments have a material effect on the determination of the costs of the machine? Clearly there would be opportunities to capitalise some of these costs.

Initial Measurement

Intangible assets should initially be measured at cost.

Separate Acquisition

The cost of a separate acquisition of an intangible asset comprises:
(a) its purchase price, including any import duties but after deducting any trade discounts; and
(b) any directly attributable costs of preparing the asset for its intended use.

Acquisition as Part of a Business Combination

The cost of the acquisition of an intangible asset that is part of a business combination is the asset's fair value at the acquisition date.

Listed companies in Ireland have introduced a number of new intangibles in their business combinations that were permitted by the original version of the standard to be capitalised. Examples include:

CPL Resources Plc	Brands, customer contracts and databases, software
Datalex Plc	Computer software
DCC Plc	Customer relationships
First Derivatives plc	Customer lists, software, brand name, developed software
Fyffes Plc	Customer relationships, trademark
Glanbia Plc	Brands/knowhow, customer relationships
Grafton Group Plc	Brands, customer relationships
Icon Plc	Computer software, customer relationships, volunteer list
IFG Group Plc	Computer software
Independent News & Media Plc	Mastheads, radio licences, transit and electronic systems and brands

Origin Enterprises Plc	Brand, customer related, supplier agreements, computer related
Paddy Power Plc	Computer software, licences and customer relationships
Thirdforce Plc	Customer relationships, content and platform, trademarks and order backlog
Total Produce Plc	Customer relationships, supplier relationships and brands
Veris Plc	Brand-related intangibles, customer-related intangibles

Example 4.2: Intangibles in a Business Combination

On 1 October 2016, Omeath Ltd acquired a new subsidiary, Greenore Ltd, purchasing all 15,000 shares. The terms of the purchase agreement included the exchange of four shares in Omeath Ltd for every three shares acquired in Greenore Ltd. On 1 October 2016 the fair value of a share in Omeath Ltd was €10 and in Greenore Ltd €12.

The terms of the agreement also include a further payment of 30c per share acquired if the profits of Greenore Ltd for the two years ending 30 September 2018 exceeded a target figure. The current estimate of the fair value of the earn-out clause is €30,000 at the date of acquisition. There have been no changes to this fair value since acquisition.

Legal and professional fees associated with the acquisition of Greenore Ltd's shares were €12,000, including €2,000 relating to the issue of shares. The senior management of Omeath Ltd estimate that the cost of their time that can be fairly allocated to the acquisition is €2,000. This figure is not included in the legal and professional fees of €12,000 above.

The individual balance sheet of Greenore Ltd at 1 October 2016 comprised net assets that had a fair value at that date of €120,000. Additionally, Omeath Ltd considered Greenore Ltd possessed certain intangible assets that were not recognised in its individual balance sheet:

- **Customer Relationships** Reliable estimate of value €10,000. This value has been derived from the sale of customer databases in the past.
- **Development** The fair value of the project is estimated at €5,000.
- **Employees' Expertise** The director's estimate of value is €8,000.

The market value of a share in Omeath Ltd on 30 September 2017 was €11.00.

Solution

Calculation of goodwill	**€**	**€**
Purchase consideration (cost of the investment)		
Market value of shares issued (15,000 shares × 4/3 × €10)		200,000
Fair value of contingent consideration (earn-out clause)		30,000
Acquisition costs (€12,000 – €2,000)		10,000
		240,000
Fair value of identifiable net assets at acquisition		
As per Greenore's statement of financial position	120,000	
Fair value of customer relationships (until 1 Jan 2019 permitted)	Nil	
Development costs	5,000	
		125,000
Goodwill		115,000

Under the FRS, the costs relating to the issue of equity shares are not permitted to be included in the calculation of goodwill and should instead be included as part of the financial instrument section of the standard (see **Chapter 12**). Also, internally generated research must be expensed immediately and employee expertise (often referred to as the assembled workforce) is not permitted as an intangible asset on the balance sheet. Senior management's own time must be expensed as it would be incurred anyway if there was no acquisition.

Under revised Section 18, paragraph 18.8 of FRS 102, an intangible asset acquired in a business combination will only be **recognised separately** from goodwill when all the following **three conditions** are satisfied:

(a) the recognition criteria set out in paragraph 18.4 are met, i.e. probability of future benefits and reliably measured;
(b) the intangible asset arises from contractual or other legal rights; and
(c) the intangible asset is separable (i.e. capable of being separated or divided from the entity and sold, transferred, licensed, rented or exchanged either individually or together with a related contract, asset or liability).

In addition, a reporting entity has an option to choose to recognise intangible assets separately from goodwill for which condition (a) and only one of (b) or (c) above is met. However, when an entity exercises that option, the policy must be applied to all intangible assets in the same class (i.e. having a similar nature, function or use in the business), and must be applied consistently to all business combinations. In their basis of conclusions, the FRC recognise that licences, copyrights, and internet domain names would be examples of categories of intangible asset that may be treated as a separate class. However, further subdivision may be appropriate, e.g. where different types of licence have different functions within the business. The FRC mentions customer lists, customer relationships and secret recipes as examples of intangibles that would probably fail to meet the criteria.

Another change was introduced by paragraph 18.28A when, as part of a business combination, an acquirer chooses to recognise intangible assets separately from goodwill that meet condition (a) and only one of (b) or (c) in paragraph 18.8, the acquirer will need to disclose the nature of those intangible assets and the reason why they have been separated from goodwill.

The following table sets out some examples of how certain intangible assets could be treated after the revision.

Table 4.1: Examples of Changes to Intangible Assets in Business Combinations

Type of intangible asset	Contractual or other legal rights?	Separable?	Recognise separately from goodwill?
Trademark or trade name	Yes	Yes	Must
Customer list	No	Yes	May
Customer contracts	Yes	Depends on whether transferable	Must if transferable, otherwise may
Licensing and royalty agreements, lease agreements, construction permits	Yes	Depends on whether transferable	Must if transferable, otherwise may
Patented technology	Yes	Yes	Must
Unpatented technology	No	Yes	May
Computer software	Yes if patented or copyrighted	Yes	Must if patented or copyrighted, otherwise may

Acquisition by Way of a Grant

Section 24 *Government Grants* prescribes the accounting treatment required for intangible assets acquired by way of grant (see **Chapter 3**).

Exchanges of Assets

Intangible assets could be exchanged for non-monetary assets or a combination of monetary/non-monetary assets. Cost should be an asset's fair value unless the exchange lacks commercial substance or the fair value cannot be reliably measured. In that case cost is measured at the carrying amount of the asset given up.

Past Expenses not to be Recognised as an Asset

If previous expenditure has been incurred in creating the asset and that expenditure has been expensed in previous years, it cannot be later recognised as part of an asset.

Measurement after Initial Recognition

For each class of intangible asset, after initial recognition an entity may choose either the cost or revaluation model.

Cost Model

Assets are measured at cost less any accumulated amortisation and impairment losses. Impairment is covered in Section 27 (see **Chapter 3**).

Revaluation Model

The revaluation model is unlikely to be a popular option for companies other than start-ups and possibly the IT sector. At present very few listed companies have adopted this option under full IFRS. It could also be argued that it is in effect capitalising inherent intangible assets on top of an acquired asset.

If adopted, the assets must be measured at fair value less accumulated amortisation and impairment losses.

However, the revaluation option is not permitted for assets which were not previously recognised as assets or on the initial recognition of an intangible asset (initial recognition must always be at cost).

If an entity adopts a revaluation policy, then the following must apply:

- **Fair Value** Should use an active market or, if not available, use the date of the last revaluation.
- **Frequency** Must be revalued with sufficient regularity to ensure that the net book value was not recorded at a materially different value from the fair value at the end of a reporting period.
- **Gains/Losses** Any increase is recognised in other comprehensive income and accumulated in equity (revaluation reserve):
  - any increase is recognised in profit or loss if it reverses a revaluation reserve of the same asset previously written off against profit;
  - any decrease is recognised in profit or loss or other comprehensive income if it represents a reversal of a previous surplus.

The rules are very similar to those required for property, plant and equipment (see **Chapter 3**).

Amortisation over Useful Life

All intangible assets are considered to have a finite useful life. If they arise from contractual or other legal rights, the useful lives must not exceed the period of the contract but they could be shorter. If there is a renewal option, an entity must consider if there is evidence to support renewal without significant cost. If there is no reliable estimate available, a 10-year life is assumed.

Amortisation Period and Amortisation Method

The depreciable amount should be allocated over the finite useful life of the asset on a systematic basis. Amortisation should begin when the asset is available for use and cease when the asset is derecognised.

The method chosen should reflect the pattern of consumption of economic benefits, but if that is not possible an entity should adopt the straight-line approach.

Residual Value

An entity should assume that the residual value is zero unless:

(a) there is a commitment by a third party to purchase the asset at the end of its useful life; or
(b) there is an active market for the asset and:
  (i) the residual value can be determined by reference to that market; and
  (ii) it is probable that such a market will exist at the end of the asset's useful life.

Review of Amortisation Period and Amortisation Method

Entities should review both the period and the method of amortisation, at least annually. If the expected life is different from that previously estimated, entities should adjust and report any change under Section 10 *Accounting Policies, Estimates and Errors* (see **Chapter 7**) as a change in accounting estimate.

Recoverability of the Carrying Amount – Impairment Losses

Entities should apply Section 27 (see **Chapter 3**), which explains how and why an entity reviews the carrying amount of assets, how it determines the recoverable amount of an asset and when it recognises or reverses an impairment loss.

Retirements and Disposals

Reporting entities should derecognise an intangible asset and recognise a gain/loss in profit or loss:

(a) on disposal; or
(b) when there are no future economic benefits expected to be derived from its use or disposal.

Disclosures

The following should be disclosed for each class of intangible assets:

(a) the useful lives or amortisation rates used;
(b) the amortisation methods adopted;

(c) the gross carrying amount and accumulated depreciation at the start and end of the period;
(d) the line items of the profit and loss account or statement of comprehensive income in which amortisation is included; and
(e) a reconciliation of the carrying amount at the start and end of the period separating additions, disposals, acquisitions, revaluations, amortisation, impairment losses and other changes.

An entity should also disclose:
(a) a description, the carrying amount and the remaining amortisation period of any individual intangible assets that are material to the entity's financial statements;
(b) for those acquired by grant and initially valued at fair value:
  (i) the fair value initially recognised; and
  (ii) their carrying amount;
(c) the existence and carrying amounts of intangible assets whose title is restricted or that are pledged as security; and
(d) the amount of contractual commitments for acquisition of intangibles.

Under the triennial changes, a reporting entity may choose to recognise additional separable intangibles that meet condition (a) and either (b) or (c) (see page 151) but must then disclose the reason for separation.

Entities must also disclose the aggregate amount of research and development expenditure recognised as an expense during the period.

If intangible assets are revalued, the following must be disclosed:
(a) the date of revaluation;
(b) whether an independent valuer was involved;
(c) the methods applied in estimating fair values; and
(d) for each revalued class of asset, the carrying amounts that would have applied under the cost model.

An example of the required disclosure, using the cost model, is given in the IASB's *IFRS for SMEs 2009 Illustrative Financial Statements Presentation and Disclosure Checklist*, as shown below.

Example 4.3: Illustrative Financial Statements – Intangible Assets

Accounting Policies and Explanatory Notes (Extracts)

2. Basis of preparation and accounting policies

Intangible assets

Intangible assets are purchased computer software that is stated at cost less accumulated amortisation and any accumulated impairment losses. It is amortised over its estimated life of 10 years using the straight-line method. If there is an indication that there has been a significant change in amortisation rate, useful life or residual value of an intangible asset, the amortisation is revised prospectively to reflect the new expectations.

[...]

14. Intangible assets

Software:

Cost	**€**
1 January 2019	8,500
Additions	–
Disposals	–
31 December 2019	8,500
Accumulated depreciation and impairment	
1 January 2019	5,950
Annual amortisation (included in administrative expenses*)	1,700
31 December 2019	7,650
Carrying amount	
31 December 2019	850

* If the entity classifies its expenses by nature in its income statement, this would say 'included in depreciation and amortisation expense'.

4.2 LEASES (SECTION 20)

This section should be applied to all leases other than:

(a) leases to explore for or use minerals (Section 34 – see **Chapter 13**);
(b) licensing agreements (Section 18 – see **Chapter 4**);
(c) property held by lessees accounted for as investment property (Section 16 – see **Chapter 3**);
(d) biological assets held by lessees under finance leases (Section 34 – see **Chapter 13**); and
(e) leases that could lead to a loss to the lessor or lessee as a result of non-typical contractual terms (Section 11 – see **Chapter 12**).

It also includes similar arrangements to a lease agreement, e.g. take or pay contracts, outsourcing arrangements, rights to capacity.

Determining whether an arrangement is, or contains, a lease is based on the substance of the arrangement and requires an entity to assess whether:

(a) fulfilment of the arrangement is dependent on the use of a specific asset or assets. An asset is implicitly specified if, for example, the supplier owns or leases only one asset with which to fulfil the obligation and it is not economically feasible or practicable for the supplier to perform its obligation through the use of alternative assets; and
(b) the arrangement conveys a right to use the asset, i.e. the right to control the use of the underlying asset.

Classification of Leases

A lease agreement is classified as a finance lease if it transfers substantially all the risks and rewards incidental to ownership. It is classified as an operating lease if it does not transfer substantially all the risks and rewards.

FRS 102 contains eight scenarios that may be indicative of a finance lease:

(a) a lease transfers ownership of an asset to the lessee by the end of the lease term;
(b) a lessee has the option to purchase the asset at a price lower than its fair value;
(c) the lease term is for a major part of the asset's economic life;
(d) at the inception of the lease the present value of the minimum lease payments (MLPs) amounts to at least substantially all of the fair value of the leased asset; and
(e) the leased assets are of a specialised nature.

Indicators of situations that could also be classified as a finance lease are:

(a) if the lessee can cancel the lease and the lessor's losses with regard to the cancellation are borne by the lessee;
(b) gains/losses from fluctuations in the residual value of a leased asset accrue to the lessee in the form of a rental rebate; and
(c) the lessee has the ability to continue the lease for a secondary period at a rent that is substantially less than market rental.

If it is clear that the risks and rewards are not substantially transferred, the lease must be classified as an operating lease.

The classification is only made at the inception of the lease and is not changed unless the lessee and the lessor agree to changes in the provisions in the contract, in which case the lease classification must be re-evaluated.

Financial Statements of Lessees – Finance Leases

Initial Recognition

Lessees should initially recognise the rights and obligations under finance leases as assets and liabilities respectively at their fair value or at their present value of minimum lease payments (MLPs), if lower, determined at the inception of the lease. Any initial direct costs should be added to the asset.

The present value of the MLPs should be calculated using the interest rate implicit in the lease. If that cannot be calculated, the lessee's incremental borrowing rate should be used instead.

Subsequent Measurement

A lessee should apportion the MLPs between the finance charge and the reduction of the outstanding liability using the effective interest method. That is, the lessee should allocate the finance charge so as to produce a constant periodic rate of interest on the remaining balance of the liability. Any contingent rentals should be charged as expenses if and when incurred.

A lessee should depreciate a finance lease as per Section 17 *Property, Plant and Equipment* (see **Chapter 3**), over the shorter of the total lease term or the asset's useful life and should also assess for any possible impairment at the end of each period.

Example 4.4: Finance Lease (Lessee)

On 1 January 2018, Glendun Ltd leased a motor vehicle under a finance lease. The cash price of the vehicle was €20,000 while the instalments are to be €6,000 per annum over the next four years, commencing on 1 January 2018. The vehicle is expected to have a life of five years and Glendun Ltd can take out a secondary lease for a further two years at a nominal rental of €100 per annum.

Solution

		€
Total payments under the contract	€6,000 × 4	24,000
Cash price of vehicle		20,000
Finance cost		4,000

Initial recording:

			€	€
Dr	Motor vehicles		20,000	
Dr	Finance costs in suspense		4,000	
	Cr	Obligation to finance company		24,000

Apportionment of finance cost
The first instalment is paid in advance so no finance charge can be included. The finance costs must be spread using a constant rate of return over the three remaining payments. Entities could choose either the actuarial method or the sum-of-digits method. The actuarial method is, strictly speaking, the more correct approach and requires the calculation of an implicit rate of interest that the finance company should be able to provide or that can be computed from a sophisticated calculator. However, most entities are likely to adopt the simpler sum-of-digits approach, as shown below:

Sum of digits (excluding first payment) = 3 × (3 + 1) ÷ 2 = 6

	Obligation at start	Rental paid in year	Net obligation for the year		Finance cost for the year	Obligation at end
	€	€	€		€	€
01/01/2018	20,000	6,000	14,000	(3/6)	2,000	16,000
01/01/2019	16,000	6,000	10,000	(2/6)	1,333	11,333
01/01/2020	11,333	6,000	5,333	(1/6)	667	6,000
01/01/2021	6,000	6,000				

Using the actuarial method, with a constant rate of interest of 14%, the calculations would be:

	Obligation at start	Rental paid in year	Net obligation for the year	Finance cost for the year	Obligation at end
	€	€	€	€	€
01/01/2018	20,000	6,000	14,000	1,960	15,960
01/01/2019	15,960	6,000	9,960	1,394	11,354
01/01/2020	11,354	6,000	5,354	646	6,000
01/01/2021	6,000	6,000			

Depreciation of motor vehicle
Depreciation is spread over the shorter of the total lease term (including secondary period) of six years and the useful life of the vehicle of five years. Depreciation should therefore be €20,000 ÷ 5 years = €4,000 per annum using the straight-line basis.

Position of lease agreement at 31 December 2019:

- Finance lease obligation €11,333, which must be split between current and non-current liabilities of €5,333 and €6,000, respectively.
- The motor vehicle should be recorded at its net book value of €20,000 less €8,000 = €12,000 at the end of 2019.

Note: Section 20, paragraph 20.11 of FRS 102 requires the finance charge to be allocated to each period during the lease term so as to produce a constant periodic rate of interest on the outstanding liability. The sum-of-digits method is not specifically mentioned, but it is assumed that as it is a close approximation to the actuarial method it would still be appropriate.

Disclosures

Lessees should make the following disclosures for finance leases:

(a) for each class of asset – the net carrying amount at the end of the reporting period (in **Example 4.4** above, €12,000);

(b) the total of future MLPs at the end of the period for each of the following periods:

  (i) not later than one year,

  (ii) later than one year and not later than five years, and

  (iii) later than five years;

Taking **Example 4.4** above, the future MLPs under finance leases would be:

	2019	**2018**
	€	**€**
Within one year	6,000	6,000
After one year but not later than five years	5,354	9,960
Later than five years	–	–
	11,354	15,960

(c) a general description of the lessee's significant leasing arrangements, including: contingent rentals, renewal options, escalation clauses, subleases and restrictions.

In addition, the requirements for disclosure about assets in accordance with Sections 17, 18, 27 and 34 apply to lessees for assets leased under finance leases.

The disclosure required by the FRS is best illustrated with an example taken from the IASB's *IFRS for SMEs 2009 Illustrative Financial Statements Presentation and Disclosure Checklist*.

EXAMPLE 4.5: ILLUSTRATIVE FINANCIAL STATEMENTS – FINANCE LEASES

ACCOUNTING POLICIES AND EXPLANATORY NOTES (EXTRACTS)

2. Basis of preparation and accounting policies

Leases

Leases are classified as finance leases whenever the terms of the lease transfer substantially all the risks and rewards of ownership of the leased asset to the Group. All other leases are classified as operating leases.

Rights to assets held under finance leases are recognised as assets of the Group at the fair value of the leased property (or, if lower, the present value of minimum lease payments) at the inception of the lease. The corresponding liability to the lessor is included in the balance sheet as a finance lease obligation. Lease payments are apportioned between finance charges and reduction of the lease obligation so as to achieve a constant rate of interest on the remaining balance of the liability. Finance charges are deducted in measuring profit or loss. Assets held under finance leases are included in property, plant and equipment, and depreciated and assessed for impairment losses in the same way as owned assets.

[...]

7. Finance costs

	2019	2018
	€	€
Interest on bank loan and overdraft	(21,250)	(30,135)
Interest on finance leases	(5,116)	(6,577)
	(26,366)	(36,712)

[...]

20. Obligations under finance leases

The Group holds one piece of specialised machinery with an estimated useful life of five years under a five-year finance lease. The future minimum lease payments are as follows:

	2019	2018
	€	€
Within one year	25,000	25,000
Later than one year but within five years	25,000	50,000
Later than five years	–	–
	50,000	75,000

The obligation is classified as:

	2019	2018
	€	€
Current liability	21,461	19,884
Non-current liability	23,163	44,624
	44,624	64,508

Financial Statements of Lessees – Operating Leases

Recognition and Measurement

Payments for operating leases should be expensed on a straight-line basis unless another systematic basis is representative of the time pattern of the user's benefit, even if the payments are not on that basis or the payments are structured to increase in line with expected inflation to compensate for expected cost increases.

Example 4.6: Operating Lease

Arran Ltd leases some office space from Morton Ltd for five years under an operating lease. The lease payments are structured to reflect the expected 5% annual general inflation over the five-year term of the lease, as follows:

	€	
Year 1	240,000	
Year 2	252,000	
Year 3	264,600	Total €1,326,150 ÷ 5 years = €265,230 per annum
Year 4	277,830	
Year 5	291,720	

Arran Ltd recognises annual rent expense equal to the amounts owed to the lessor, as shown above. If the escalating payments are not clearly structured to compensate the lessor for expected inflationary cost increases based on published indices or statistics, then Arran recognises the annual rent expense on a straight-line basis: €265,230 each year (sum of the amounts payable under the lease divided by five years).

The aggregate benefit of lease incentives must be recognised by lessees as a reduction in the expense recognised over the lease term on a straight-line basis, unless another systematic basis is more representative of the time pattern of the lessee's benefit from the use of the leased asset. Any costs incurred by the lessee, e.g. termination costs of a pre-existing lease, relocation or leasehold improvements) must be accounted for in accordance with the applicable section of FRS 102.

In addition, where an operating lease becomes an onerous contract, an entity must also apply Section 21 *Provisions and Contingencies* (see **Chapter 6**).

Disclosures

Lessees should make the following disclosures for operating leases:

(a) the total of future MLPs under non-cancellable operating leases for each of following periods:
   (i) not later than one year,
   (ii) later than one year and not later than five years, and
   (iii) later than five years;
(b) lease payments expensed.

The disclosure required by FRS 102 is illustrated with an example, based on the IASB's *IFRS for SMEs 2009 Illustrative Financial Statements Presentation and Disclosure Checklist*.

Example 4.7: Illustrative Financial Statements – Operating Leases

Accounting Policies and Explanatory Notes (Extracts)

2. Basis of preparation and accounting policies

Leases

Rentals payable under operating leases are charged to profit or loss on a straight-line basis over the term of the relevant lease.

[...]

21. Commitments under operating leases

The Group rents several sales offices under operating leases. The leases are for an average period of three years, with fixed rentals over the same period.

	2019	**2018**
	€	**€**
Minimum lease payments under operating leases recognised as an expense during the year	26,100	26,100

At year end, the Group has outstanding commitments under non-cancellable operating leases that fall due as follows:

	2019	**2018**
	€	**€**
Within one year	13,050	26,100
Later than one year but within five years	–	13,050
Later than five years	–	–
	13,050	39,150

Financial Statements of Lessors – Finance Leases

A lessor must recognise assets held under a finance lease in their balance sheet as a receivable at an amount equal to the **net investment in the lease.**

The net investment in a lease is the lessor's **gross investment in the lease** discounted at the interest rate implicit in the lease.

The gross investment in the lease is the aggregate of:

(a) the minimum lease payments receivable by the lessor under a finance lease; and

(b) any unguaranteed residual value accruing to the lessor.

For finance leases other than manufacturer or dealer lessors, initial direct costs are included in the initial measurement of the finance lease receivable and that reduces the amount of income recognised over the lease term.

Subsequent Measurement

The recognition of finance income must be based on a pattern that reflects a constant periodic rate of return on the lessor's net investment in the finance lease. Lease payments relating to the period, excluding costs for services, are applied against the gross investment in the lease to reduce both the principal and the unearned finance income. If there is an indication that the estimated unguaranteed residual value used in computing the lessor's gross investment in the lease has changed significantly, the income allocation over the lease term is revised, and any reduction in respect of amounts accrued is recognised immediately in profit or loss.

Example 4.8: Lessor Accounting

Derrynane Ltd is an electrical wholesaler and on 1 July 2019 it purchased, on credit, 20 television sets for €3,600. These are offered for sale under a finance lease for a cash deposit of €80 and eight quarterly instalments of €60 each, the first instalment being payable after three months, at the end of which ownership would transfer to the buyer. They could also be sold for cash at €280 each. In July eight sets were sold for which the cash deposits were paid.

Solution

Price structure:

	€	
Cost	180	(€3,600 ÷ 20 sets)
Gross profit	100	
Cash price	280	
Finance cost	280	
Lease selling price	560	(€80 + (8 × €60))

Under the sum-of-digits method: 8(8 + 1) ÷ 2 = 36

Instalment 1:	Interest = 8/36 × €280 = €62 Capital repaid = €80 – €62 = €18
Instalment 2:	Interest = 7/36 × €280 = €54 Capital repaid = €80 – €54 = €26

Lease receivables at 31 December 2019:

Sales = €2,240 less deposits €640 (8 × €80) less two instalments €352 (8 sets × €44) = €1,248

		€
Sales	8 × €280	2,240
Interest receivable	(8 sets × €116)	928

Note: as per the note immediately after **Example 4.4**, the sum of digits is an approximate method to the actuarial approach.

Example 4.9: Finance Lease (Lessor)

Assume that Bruce Ltd leased a machine to Collins Ltd on 1/1/2019 and that the lease requires payment of €10,000 at the end of each year for four years. Assuming the relevant discount rate is 10%, the present value factor of an ordinary annuity for four years discounted at 10% per period equals (from the relevant table) 3.1699. The total present value of the lease payments is €31,699 (€10,000 × 3.1699).

Solution

Bruce Ltd (as lessor) will record its investment at the beginning of the lease (on 1/1/2019):

			€	€
Dr	Lease receivable		40,000	
	Cr	Equipment inventory		31,699
	Cr	Unearned interest revenue		8,301

Notes:

1. €40,000 is the total amount of lease payments to be received by the lessor when the time value of money is ignored.
2. Equipment inventory is credited for €31,699 because this is a finance lease – the control over the asset having transferred from the lessor (to the lessee).
3. The difference between the two amounts represents the total interest expected to be earned over the term of the lease. Since it has not yet been earned, it is unearned revenue (a liability). As interest revenue is earned during the lease period, unearned revenue is reduced each period.

Date	Total cash received	Interest revenue 10%	Unearned revenue balance	Lease receivable balance
	€	€	€	€
01/01/2019			8,301.00	40,000
31/12/2019	10,000	3,169.90	5,131.10	30,000
31/12/2020	10,000	2,486.89	2,644.21	20,000
31/12/2021	10,000	1,735.58	908.63	10,000
31/12/2022	10,000	908.63	0	0
Total	40,000	8,301.00		

Interest is calculated as follows:

	€	€
€31,699 × 10%		= 3,169.90
€31,699 + €3,169.90 – €10,000	= 24,868.90	
€24,868.90 × 10%		= 2,486.89
€24,858.90 + €2,486.89 – €10,000	= 17,355.79	
€17,355.79 × 10%		= 1,735.58
€17,355.79 + €1,735.58 – €10,000	= 9,091.37	
€ 9,091.37 × 10%		= 908.63
€ 9,091.37 + €908.63 – €10,000	= Nil	

The table suggests the journal entries each year for the lessor. The first journal entry is for the receipt of cash and reduction of lease receivable, the second journal entry is for recognising interest revenue earned on the lease and the corresponding decrease in unearned revenue.

For example, on 31 December 2020, the journal entries for the lessor are:

		€	€
Dr	Cash	10,000.00	
	Cr Lease receivable		10,000.00

and

Dr	Unearned revenue	2,486.89	
	Cr Interest revenue		2,486.89

EXAMPLE 4.10: FINANCE LEASE (LESSOR)

Thomas Ltd leased a machine from Glenn Ltd on 1 January 2019. The lease terms are as follows:

Lease term	3 years
Annual rental payments	€8,000 (beginning of each period)
Economic life of asset	4 years
Guaranteed residual value	€10,000
Historical cost of machine	€23,000
Incremental borrowing rate	10%

Solution

Minimum lease payments include the periodic rental payments of €8,000 and the guaranteed residual value of €10,000 at the end of the lease.

Present value of rental payments = €8,000 × 2.7355	=	€21,884
Present value of guaranteed residual value = €10,000 × 0.7513	=	€7,513
Total present value of minimum lease payments = €21,884 + €7,513	=	€29,397

Historical cost of machine	€23,000, so this is a sales-type lease for the lessor
Manufacturer's profit to lessor at inception of lease	€29,397 – €23,000 = €6,397

Total lease receivable	(€8,000 × 3) + €10,000 = €34,000
Hence, unearned revenue at the beginning of lease	€34,000 – €29,397 = €4,603

Date	Total cash received	Interest revenue	Unearned revenue balance	Remaining principal balance	Lease receivable balance
	€	€	€	€	€
01/01/2019			4,603	29,397	34,000
01/01/2019	8,000		4,603	21,397	26,000
31/12/2019	8,000	2,140	2,463	15,537	18,000
31/12/2020	8,000	1,554	909	9,091	10,000
31/12/2021	0	909	0	0	0

Interest is calculated as follows:

€29,397 – €8,000 = €21,397 ⟶ €21,397 × 10% = €2,140
€21,397 + €2,140 – €8,000 = €15,537 ⟶ €15,537 × 10% = €1,554
€15,357 + €1,554 – €8,000 = €9,091 ⟶ €9,091 × 10% = €909

€9,091 + (10% × €9,091) = €10,000 guaranteed residual value

Journal entries:

At the beginning of the lease:

			€	€
01/01/2019	Dr	Lease receivable	34,000	
	Dr	Cost of goods sold	23,000	
		Cr Machine inventory		23,000
		Cr Sales		29,397
		Cr Unearned interest revenue		4,603

At the end of the first year:

31/12/2019	Dr	Unearned revenue	2,140	
		Cr Interest revenue		2,140

Journal entries during the last year of the lease:

01/01/2021	Dr	Cash		8,000	
		Cr	Lease receivable		8,000

and

				€	€
31/12/2021	Dr	Unearned revenue		909	
		Cr	Interest revenue		909

and

31/12/2021	Dr	Machine inventory		10,000	
		Cr	Lease receivable		10,000

Manufacturer or Dealer Lessors

Manufacturers or dealers often offer customers the choice of either buying or leasing an asset. A finance lease of an asset by a manufacturer or dealer lessor gives rise to two types of income:

(a) profit or loss equivalent to the profit or loss resulting from an outright sale of the asset being leased at normal selling prices, reflecting any applicable volume or trade discounts; and
(b) finance income over the lease term.

The sales revenue recognised at the commencement of the lease term by a manufacturer or dealer lessor is the fair value of the asset or, if lower, the present value of the MLPs accruing to the lessor, computed at a market rate of interest. The cost of sales recognised at the commencement of the lease term is the cost, or carrying amount if different, of the leased asset less the present value of the unguaranteed residual value. The difference between the sales revenue and the cost of sales is the selling profit, which is recognised in accordance with the entity's policy for outright sales.

If artificially low rates of interest are quoted, then the selling profit must be restricted to that which would apply if a market rate of interest were charged. Any costs incurred by manufacturer or dealer lessors in connection with negotiating and arranging a lease are expensed when the selling profit is recognised.

Example 4.11: Manufacturer or Dealer Lessor

Gowrie Ltd manufactures specialised machinery for bakeries for both sale and lease. On 1 July 2019, it leased a machine to Ayr Ltd incurring €1,000 direct costs in agreeing and executing the lease agreement. The machine cost Gowrie Ltd €195,000 to make and its fair value at the inception of the lease was €212,515. The interest rate implicit in the lease is 10%, which is in line with current market rates. Under the terms of the lease, Ayr Ltd has guaranteed €25,000 of the asset's expected residual value of €37,000 at the end of the five-year lease term.

Solution

After classifying the lease as a finance lease, Gowrie Ltd should make the following journal entries on 1 July 2019:

			€	€
Dr	Lease receivable (net investment in lease, equal to the fair value of leased machine)		212,515	
	Cr	Sales (the present value of the minimum lease payments, which is less than the fair value of the asset due to unguaranteed residual value) (€212,515 – €7,452)		205,063
Dr	Cost of sales (€195,000 less present value of unguaranteed residual value €12,000 × 0.620921 = €7,452)		187,548	
	Cr	Inventory		195,000
Dr	Lease costs (income)		1,000	
	Cr	Cash		1,000

Disclosures

A lessor must provide the following disclosures for finance leases:

(a) a reconciliation between the gross investment in the lease at the end of the reporting period, and the present value of MLPs receivable at the end of the reporting period. In addition, a lessor must disclose the gross investment in the lease and the present value of MLPs receivable at the end of the reporting period, for each of the following periods:
   (i) not later than one year,
   (ii) later than one year and not later than five years, and
   (iii) later than five years;

(b) unearned finance income;

(c) the unguaranteed residual values accruing to the benefit of the lessor;
(d) the accumulated allowance for uncollectible MLPs receivable;
(e) contingent rents recognised as income in the period;
(f) a general description of the lessor's significant leasing arrangements, including, for example, information about contingent rentals, renewal or purchase options and escalation clauses, subleases and restrictions imposed by lease arrangements.

Financial Statements of Lessors – Operating Leases

Recognition and Measurement

A lessor should present assets according to their nature.

A lessor should recognise lease income in profit or loss on a straight-line basis over the lease term unless another systematic basis is more representative or the payments are structured in line with expected inflation to compensate for any expected inflationary cost increases.

A lessor should expense costs, including depreciation, incurred in earning the lease income. Depreciation should be consistent with normal depreciation policy.

A lessor should add to the carrying amount of the leased asset any initial direct costs and recognise these over the lease term on the same basis as the lease income.

If an asset has become impaired, a lessor should apply Section 27 (see **Chapter 3**).

A manufacturer or dealer lessor does not recognise any selling profit on entering the operating lease as it is not the equivalent of a sale.

Disclosures

Lessors should disclose the following for operating leases:

(a) the future MLPs under non-cancellable operating leases in aggregate and for each of the following periods: not later than one year, between two and five years, and later than five years;
(b) the total contingent rentals recognised as income; and
(c) a general description of the lessor's leasing arrangements, including, for example, information about contingent rentals, renewal or purchase options and escalation clauses, and restrictions imposed by lease arrangements.

In addition, entities must comply with the disclosures in Sections 17 and 27 (see **Chapter 3**).

Sale and Leaseback Transactions

The accounting treatment of sale and leaseback transactions depends on the type of lease.

Sale and Leaseback Transaction Resulting in a Finance Lease

A seller-lessee should not recognise immediately as income any excess of sales proceeds over their carrying amount. Entities must instead defer such excess and amortise it over the lease term.

EXAMPLE 4.12: SALE AND LEASEBACK – FINANCE LEASE (LESSEE)

An asset with a carrying value of €300,000 was sold for €400,000 and then leased back at €500,000 under a finance lease for a period of three years. Assume the effective interest rate is 25% and the present value of the asset is €500,000. Minimum lease payments are €614,754.

The annual rental payment (assuming in advance) is €204,918.

In the books of the lessee, entries for the first year would be as follows.

At the time of sale:

			€	€
Dr	Cash		400,000	
	Cr	Asset		300,000
	Cr	Deferred income		100,000

Asset acquired on finance lease:

Dr	Asset under finance lease		500,000	
	Cr	Liability under finance lease		500,000

First lease payment:

Dr	Liability under finance lease		204,918	
	Cr	Cash		204,918

At the end of the year:

Dr	Interest expense		73,770	
	Cr	Interest payable		73,770

(€500,000 – €204,918) × 25%

Second annual rental payment:

Dr	Interest payable	73,770	
Dr	Liability under finance lease	131,148	
	Cr Cash		204,918

At the end of each of the three years, the following entry should be made:

Dr	Deferred finance income	33,333	
	Cr Profit on sale and leaseback		33,333

If the sale of the asset is for €400,000 and the leaseback is at €500,000 and they are not related transactions in substance and have not taken place simultaneously with an outright intent of leasing it back, then there could be some argument for immediately booking €100,000 as a gain on sale and deferring the remaining €100,000 over the lease term. However, it appears that the intent of the transaction was to lease the asset back, therefore it creates a financing arrangement instead of a genuine sales transaction. Accordingly, the entire €100,000 will be deferred and amortised over the lease term.

Sale and Leaseback Transaction Resulting in an Operating Lease

If it is clear that the transaction is established at fair value, the seller-lessee should recognise any profit or loss immediately. If the sales price is below fair value, the seller-lessee should recognise any profit/loss immediately unless the loss is compensated by future lease payments at below market price. In that case the seller-lessee should defer and amortise such loss over the period the asset is expected to be used. If the sales price is above fair value, the excess should be deferred and amortised over the period for which the asset is expected to be used.

Example 4.13: Sale and Leaseback – Operating Lease (Lessee)

Barna Ltd has an asset with a net book value of €70,000. The fair value is €100,000. It can enter into a sale and leaseback agreement, but it has been offered a choice of four different types of agreement, as follows:

	Sale price	Annual rental for five years
(a)	€100,000	€28,000
(b)	€120,000	€28,000
(c)	€80,000	€20,000 (i.e. below market value)
(d)	As per (c) but assuming that the net book value was €95,000.	

Solution

(a) Sale at fair value

			€	€
Journal entries				
Dr	Bank		100,000	
	Cr	Asset		70,000
	Cr	Income		30,000

Income statement (extract)

	€
Profit on sale	30,000
Rental cost	(28,000)

(b) Sale more than fair value

Journal entries

Dr	Bank		120,000	
	Cr	Asset		70,000
	Cr	Income		30,000
	Cr	Deferred income		20,000

Income statement (extract)

Profit on sale	30,000
Deferred income (€20,000 ÷ 5 years)	4,000
Rental cost	(28,000)

(c) Sale at less than fair value

Journal entries

Dr	Bank		80,000	
	Cr	Asset		70,000
	Cr	Income		10,000

Income statement (extract)

Profit on sale	10,000
Rental cost	(20,000)

(d) Sales at less than fair value with loss on sale and future rentals at less than market price

Journal entries

Dr	Bank		80,000	
Dr	Deferred asset		15,000	
	Cr	Asset		95,000

Income statement (extract)

Deferred loss (€15,000 ÷ 5 years)	(3,000)
Rental cost	(20,000)

Disclosure

Disclosure requirements for lessees and lessors apply equally to sale and leaseback transactions. They include a description of significant arrangements and any unique or unusual provisions of the agreement or terms of the sale and leaseback transactions.

4.3 SMALL ENTITIES

There are no explicit minimum disclosure requirements for small entities under FRS 102 Section 1A for either the UK or the Republic of Ireland. However, small entities may need to provide disclosures as required by Sections 18 and 20 if required to give a true and fair view.

4.4 MICRO-ENTITIES

Micro-entities follow the same principles as the full version of FRS 102 in that purchased intangibles should be capitalised but not those that are internally generated. However, one major difference is the requirement in FRS 105 to write off all development expenditure to profit and loss.

Under FRS 105, micro-entities, as per FRS 102, still distinguish between operating and finance leases and the accounting principles are identical. Similarly for lessees, micro-entities must disclose information in relation to financial commitments, guarantees and contingencies not recognised in the statement of financial position arising from operating leases in the notes to the financial statements. In addition, micro-entities must disclose similar information in relation to financial commitments, etc., arising from a sale and leaseback.

Disclosure Checklist: Asset Valuation – Intangible Assets – FRS 102

(References are to the relevant Section of FRS 102)

	Para.
Intangible Assets other than Goodwill – Section 18	
An entity shall disclose the following for each class of intangible assets: (a) the useful lives or the amortisation rates used; (b) the amortisation methods used; (c) the gross carrying amount and any accumulated amortisation (aggregated with accumulated impairment losses) at the beginning and end of the reporting period; (d) the line item(s) in the statement of comprehensive income (and in the income statement, if presented) in which any amortisation of intangible assets is included; (e) a reconciliation of the carrying amount at the beginning and end of the reporting period, showing separately: (i) additions, (ii) disposals, (iii) acquisitions through business combinations, (iv) revaluations, (v) amortisation, (vi) impairment losses, (vii) other changes. This reconciliation need not be presented for prior periods.	18.27
An entity shall also disclose: (a) a description, the carrying amount and remaining amortisation period of any individual intangible asset that is material to the entity's financial statements; (b) for intangible assets acquired by way of a grant and initially recognised at fair value (see paragraph 18.12): (i) the fair value initially recognised for these assets, and (ii) their carrying amounts; (c) the existence and carrying amounts of intangible assets to which the entity has restricted title or that are pledged as security for liabilities; (d) the amount of contractual commitments for the acquisition of intangible assets.	18.28
An entity shall disclose the aggregate amount of research and development expenditure recognised as an expense during the period (i.e. the amount of expenditure incurred internally on intangible items that has not been capitalised as part of the cost of another asset that meets the recognition criteria in this FRS).	18.29
If intangible assets are accounted for at revalued amounts, an entity shall disclose the following: (a) the effective date of the revaluation; (b) whether an independent valuer was involved; (c) the methods and significant assumptions applied in estimating the assets' fair values; and (d) for each revalued class of intangible assets, the carrying amount that would have been recognised had the assets been carried under the cost model.	18.29A

	PARA.
Leases – Section 20	
Financial statements of lessees – finance leases	
A lessee shall make the following disclosures for finance leases: (a) for each class of asset, the net carrying amount at the end of the reporting period; (b) the total of future minimum lease payments at the end of the reporting period, for each of the following periods: (i) not later than one year, (ii) later than one year and not later than five years, and (iii) later than five years; (c) a general description of the lessee's significant leasing arrangements, including, for example, information about contingent rent, renewal or purchase options and escalation clauses, subleases and restrictions imposed by lease arrangements.	20.13
In addition, the requirements for disclosure about assets in accordance with Sections 17, 18 and 27 apply to lessees for assets leased under finance leases.	20.14
Financial statements of lessees – operating leases	
A lessee shall make the following disclosures for operating leases: (a) the total of future minimum lease payments under non-cancellable operating leases for each of the following periods: (i) not later than one year, (ii) later than one year and not later than five years, and (iii) later than five years; (b) lease payments recognised as an expense.	20.16
Financial statements of lessors – finance leases	
A lessor shall make the following disclosures for finance leases: (a) a reconciliation between the gross investment in the lease at the end of the reporting period, and the present value of minimum lease payments receivable at the end of the reporting period. In addition, a lessor shall disclose the gross investment in the lease and the present value of minimum lease payments receivable at the end of the reporting period, for each of the following periods: (i) not later than one year, (ii) later than one year and not later than five years, and (iii) later than five years; (b) unearned finance income; (c) the unguaranteed residual values accruing to the benefit of the lessor; (d) the accumulated allowance for uncollectible minimum lease payments receivable; (e) contingent rents recognised as income in the period; (f) a general description of the lessor's significant leasing arrangements, including, for example, information about contingent rent, renewal or purchase options and escalation clauses, subleases and restrictions imposed by lease arrangements.	20.23

	PARA.
Financial statements of lessors – operating leases	
A lessor shall disclose the following for operating leases: (a) the future minimum lease payments under non-cancellable operating leases for each of the following periods: (i) not later than one year, (ii) later than one year and not later than five years, and (iii) later than five years; (b) total contingent rents recognised as income; (c) a general description of the lessor's significant leasing arrangements, including, for example, information about contingent rent, renewal or purchase options and escalation clauses, and restrictions imposed by lease arrangements.	20.30
In addition, the requirements for disclosure about assets in accordance with Sections 17, 18 and 27 apply to lessors for assets provided under operating leases.	20.31
Sale and leaseback transactions	
Disclosure requirements for lessees and lessors apply equally to sale and leaseback transactions. The required description of significant leasing arrangements includes description of unique or unusual provisions of the agreement or terms of the sale and leaseback transactions.	20.35

Disclosure Checklist: Asset Valuation – Intangible Assets – Small Entities

There are no mandatory disclosures.

Disclosure Checklist: Asset Valuation – Intangible Assets – Micro-entities

(References are to the relevant Section of FRS 105)

The mandatory disclosure requirements for micro-entities required under FRS 105, the Companies Act 2014 (ROI) (CA 2014), the Companies Act 2006 (UK) (CA 2006) and the Small Companies and Groups (Accounts and Directors' Report) Regulations 2008 (UK) (S.I. No. 409 of 2008) are as follows:

	Para.
Intangible assets and goodwill	
A micro-entity shall disclose information in relation to the following items in accordance with the relevant appendix to Section 6 *Notes to the Financial Statements*: (a) financial commitments, guarantees and contingencies not recognised in the statement of financial position for the acquisition of separately acquired intangible assets; and (b) intangible assets given as security in respect of its commitments, guarantees and contingencies.	13.17

Chapter 5

ASSET VALUATION – INVENTORIES

5.1 SCOPE

Section 13 *Inventories* does not apply to:

(a) work in progress under construction contracts (Section 23 – see **Chapter 7**);
(b) financial instruments (Sections 11 and 12 – see **Chapter 12**);
(c) biological assets and agricultural produce at harvest (Section 34 – see **Chapter 13**).

It also does not apply to the measurement of inventories measured at fair value less costs to sell through profit or loss at each reporting date.

Examples of items that would be classified as inventories include:

(a) motor vehicles in the showrooms of motor car dealers as they trade in those vehicles in their ordinary course of business;
(b) a distiller holding manufactured whiskey in barrels to permit the process of maturation to take place; and
(c) oil supplies used in manufacturing company as they are consumed in the production process.

5.2 MEASUREMENT OF INVENTORIES

Inventories should be measured at the lower of their cost or their estimated selling price less any costs to complete and sell. Inventories held for distribution should be measured at their current replacement cost adjusted for any potential service loss.

5.3 COST OF INVENTORIES

Cost of inventories should include:

(a) all costs of purchase;
(b) costs of conversion; and
(c) other costs that have been incurred in bringing the inventories to their present location and condition.

If inventories are acquired in a non-exchange transaction, cost should be measured at their fair value at the date of acquisition (but see Section 34 for public benefit entities – **Chapter 13**).

Costs of Purchase

Costs of purchase comprise the purchase price, import duties, transport costs, handling and other costs directly attributable to the acquisition of finished goods, materials and services. Trade discounts must, however, be deducted. If the inventories are purchased on deferred settlement terms, it is necessary to take the difference between the amount paid and the normal purchase price and recognise that as an interest expense. For example, if a company acquires inventory for €100,000 on a two-year interest-free credit, and assuming an appropriate discount rate is 10%, the cost of the inventory is €82,645 (i.e. €100,000 discounted at 10% = €100,000 × 0.8265. (The year 2 present value factor is 0.8265)). In certain cases, where borrowing costs are capitalised and the inventory is a qualifying asset (e.g. maturing whiskey), the interest is added to the asset of inventory.

Costs of Conversion

This includes direct labour and a systematic allocation of fixed and variable production overheads incurred in converting the raw materials into finished goods. It should also include the indirect costs of production, such as depreciation and the maintenance of factory buildings and equipment.

In certain circumstances production costs can include costs for dismantling, removing or restoring a site on which an item of property, plant and equipment is located. The costs must have been incurred during the period as a consequence of having used that item of property, plant and equipment to produce inventory during that period.

Allocation of Fixed Production Overheads

Fixed production overheads should be allocated on the basis of the normal capacity of its production facilities. Normal capacity is that which is expected to be achieved on average over a number of periods under normal circumstances. The actual level of production may be used if that approximates normal capacity. Unallocated overheads should be expensed in the period incurred. Variable production overheads are allocated to each unit of production on the basis of the actual use of the production facilities.

Joint Products and By-products

When conversion costs are not separately identifiable, an entity should allocate them between products on a rational and consistent basis, e.g. by using the relative sales value method. Most by-products are immaterial and thus should be valued at net selling price less costs to complete and then deducted from the cost of the main product.

EXAMPLE 5.1: BY-PRODUCTS

Dunleer Ltd manufactures a chemical for use in the car industry. The production process requires a mixture of base chemicals followed by a period of maturation. At that point a main product, XYZ, is produced together with a by-product, ABC. The total cost of a production run is €50,000. The output is 500 litres of XYZ and 50 litres of ABC. The sales values are €80,000 and €1,000 (after selling costs), respectively.

Solution

The by-product ABC must be valued at fair value less costs to sell of €1,000 and deducted from the €50,000, to leave €49,000 to be allocated to the main product, XYZ. Thus the cost per litre of XYZ will be €49,000 ÷ 500 litres = €98 per litre.

EXAMPLE 5.2: JOINT PRODUCTS

Dunleer Ltd, instead of producing a by-product and a main product, manufactures joint products as follows:

500 litres XYZ valued at €60,000
400 litres ABC valued at €40,000

Solution

As both are substantial, the costs must be split on some rational basis, e.g. according to their relative sales values, i.e. 6/10ths to XYZ and 4/10ths to ABC. The cost per unit of XYZ will be €30,000 ÷ 500 litres = €60 per litre; and for ABC it will be €20,000 ÷ 400 litres = €50 per litre.

Other Costs Included in Inventories

Any other costs are only brought into the valuation of inventories to the extent that they are incurred in bringing the inventories to their present location and condition. Examples of this might include specific requests from a client to incorporate their logo on to the product and costs attached thereto or specific design costs to make the product client-specific. One cost that is specifically permitted as an option to be incorporated in inventory (although compulsory in the full IFRSs), is the cost of borrowing (see **Chapter 3**).

In some circumstances, a change in the fair value of a commodity in a hedging instrument for the hedge of fixed interest rate risk or commodity price risk may require an adjustment to the carrying amount (Section 12 of FRS 102 – see **Chapter 12**).

Costs Excluded from Inventories

Some examples of costs that should be excluded from inventories include:

(a) abnormal amounts of wasted materials, labour or other production costs;

(b) storage costs, unless they are incurred prior to further production. Thus the cost of storage of finished goods in a warehouse would not be permitted to be included in the cost of inventory;

(c) administration overheads, e.g. salaries of accounting staff would not normally be included unless they are working on the management accounting aspects of the business. Costs of statutory or financial accounting staff would be expensed to profit or loss; and

(d) selling costs, including marketing, depreciation of distribution vehicles, etc.

EXAMPLE 5.3: INVENTORY VALUATION

Dunluce Ltd's inventory at the end of an accounting period to be included in its financial statements includes a finished product with the following costs to date:

	€
Purchase price of materials	9,000
Less: 5% trade discount	(450)
	8,550
Import duty at 10%	855
Direct labour costs	5,850
Allocation of fixed production overheads	2,840
Storage costs of completed units	225
Advertising costs	317
Total cost	18,637

Notes:

1. All of these costs exclude VAT. The company can recover VAT from its suppliers, but it cannot recover import duty.
2. Due to an abnormal production malfunction, one-third of the materials was wasted.
3. Fixed production overheads are allocated on the basis of normal capacity. During the year, however, production was unusually low and a further allocation of €820 would be required if the overheads were allocated on the basis of actual production.

Solution

To comply with FRS 102, Dunluce Ltd should record its inventory as follows:

	€	
Purchase price of materials less trade discount	5,700	(2/3rds × €8,550 to exclude abnormal wasted material)
Import duty at 10%	570	
Direct labour costs	5,850	
Allocation of fixed production overheads	2,840	(must be based on normal, not actual, capacity)
	14,960	

Example 5.4: Valuation of Raw Materials, Work in Progress and Finished Goods

Dunseverick Ltd manufactures window frames from components manufactured by its suppliers. The company does not operate a standard costing system. Materials and work in progress have been valued as follows:

- material costs at the acquisition cost of various components purchased;
- employee costs based on the actual hours worked in assembling the frames; and
- overheads are added in accordance with the requirements in FRS 102.

The draft accounts reveal that the following material and labour costs are included in inventory:

	Raw materials	Work in progress	Finished goods
	€	€	€
Materials	150,000	170,000	300,000
Labour costs		30,000	100,000

The costs incurred in December were as follows:

	€
Direct labour	120,000
Selling costs	80,000
Depreciation of production machinery	10,000
Distribution expenses	15,000
Factory manager's salary	35,000
Other production overheads	60,000
Other administration overheads	70,000

Assume that all work in progress and finished goods were produced in December and the company is operating at a normal level of capacity.

Solution

Calculation of Overheads for Inclusion in Inventory

	€
Depreciation of production machinery	10,000
Factory manager's salary	35,000
Other production overheads	60,000
	105,000

Assume absorption of overheads is on the basis of direct labour costs.
Production absorption rate = €105,000 ÷ €120,000 = 87.5%

Inventory Valuation

	Raw materials	Work in progress	Finished goods	Total
	€	€	€	€
Materials	150,000	170,000	300,000	620,000
Direct labour costs		30,000	100,000	130,000
Production overhead (87.5% of labour cost)		26,250	87,500	113,750
	150,000	226,250	487,500	863,750

Costs of Inventories of a Service Provider

These mainly consist of only labour and personnel costs. Such costs should not be included if they relate to sales or general administration costs, nor can entities include any profit margins.

Costs of Agricultural Produce Harvested from Biological Assets

Such costs should be recognised at their fair value less estimated costs to sell at the point of harvest (see **Chapter 13**).

Example 5.5: Agricultural Produce

Dairy Lakeland Ltd has dairy cows whose milk is largely used in the manufacture of creamy yoghurts. Its dairy cows are classified as biological assets and are accounted for under Section 34 of FRS 102 (see **Chapter 13**). However, up to the point of harvest (milking), the milk is not inventory – it is still part of the biological assets.

At harvest, the milk becomes inventory and is accounted for under Section 13 of FRS 102. Initially it is recorded at fair value less estimated costs to sell because it is not being sold as milk and thus the prices in the local milk market are not relevant.

5.4 TECHNIQUES FOR MEASURING COST

Entities may adopt **standard costing** or the retail method provided they represent a close approximate to cost. Standard costs, however, must be regularly reviewed. If the variances are material and caused by poor standards, then the variances should be apportioned pro rata between the goods sold and those still in inventories. However, if the variances are caused by poor production, they should all be written off as expenses.

Similarly, care must be taken when the **retail (gross profit)** method is used – where the prices of goods have already been reduced for annual sales purposes, there would be a danger of double counting so reducing the goods below their cost price.

5.5 COST FORMULAS

Where possible, if specific costs can be identified, reporting entities should apply them. Otherwise the formulas of first in, first out (FIFO) or weighted average may be adopted. Reporting entities must use the same cost formula for all inventories of a similar nature. The last in, first out (LIFO) method is not permitted.

Example 5.6: FIFO and Weighted Average Cost Formulas

The inventory of Gorey Ltd as at 31 March 2019 includes 11,000 kg of a chemical that is used in the company's manufacturing activities. Purchases of the chemical and its issues into manufacturing during the year ended 31 March 2019 were as follows:

		Number of kg	Cost per kg
		kg	**€**
1 April 2018	Opening inventory	32,000	7.50
May 2018	Issued to production	25,000	
July 2018	Purchased	15,000	8.75
August 2018	Issued to production	12,000	
September 2018	Issued to production	5,000	
December 2018	Purchased	10,000	9.50
January 2019	Issued to production	4,000	

Solution

FIFO

	No. of kg				Cost	
	kg	**kg**		**€ per kg**	**€**	**€**
Issued May 2018	25,000		@	7.50		187,500
Issued August 2018	12,000	7,000	@	7.50	52,500	
		5,000	@	8.75	43,750	96,250
Issued September 2018	5,000		@	8.75		43,750
Issued January 2019	4,000		@	8.75		35,000
Inventory at 31 March 2019	11,000	1,000	@	8.75	8,750	
		10,000	@	9.50	95,000	103,750

Weighted Average (AVCO)

	No. of kg		€ per kg	Total cost	Weighted	Cost
	kg		**€**	**€**	**€**	**€**
Inventory at 1 April 2018	32,000	@	7.50	240,000	7.50	
Issued May 2018	25,000	@	7.50	187,500		187,500
	7,000			52,500		
Purchased July 2018	15,000	@	8.75	131,250		
	22,000			183,750	8.35	

Issued August 2018	12,000	@	8.35	100,200		100,200
	10,000			83,550		
Issued September 2018	5,000	@	8.35	41,750		41,750
	5,000			41,800		
Purchased December 2018	10,000	@	9.50	95,000		
	15,000			136,800	9.12	
Issued January 2019	4,000	@	9.12	36,480		
Inventory 31 March 2019	11,000	@	9.12	100,320		

5.6 IMPAIRMENT OF INVENTORIES

Entities must assess, at each reporting date, whether inventories are impaired and, if so, should be written down to their net selling price less costs to complete and sell. The impairment should be charged to the income statement as an expense. A reversal of a write-down can also occur in some circumstances although it is likely to be rare in practice.

EXAMPLE 5.7: IMPAIRMENT OF INVENTORIES

The inventory of Dunville Ltd at the end of an accounting period reveals the following for four of its finished manufactured goods:

	Costs incurred to date	Expected further costs	Expected selling price
	€	€	€
Machine 1	14,200	1,250	18,000
Machine 2	17,500	1,000	20,000
Machine 3	11,900	1,240	14,000
Machine 4	13,000	2,760	15,000

Sales staff are provided with a 5% commission of the selling price, on sale of a machine.

Solution

	Cost	NRV	Lower of cost or NRV
	€	€	€
Machine A	14,200	(18,000 × 95%) – 1,250 = 15,850	14,200
Machine B	17,500	(20,000 × 95%) – 1,000 = 18,000	17,500
Machine C	11,900	(14,000 × 95%) – 1,240 = 12,060	11,900
Machine D	13,000	(15,000 × 95%) – 2,760 = 11,490	11,490
	56,600	57,400	55,090

5.7 RECOGNITION AS AN EXPENSE

When inventories are sold, their carrying amount should be expensed as part of the cost of goods sold unless they can be utilised as a component of a self-constructed property and thus capitalised.

A detailed example of the valuation of inventory is provided below, including the calculation of net realisable value and whether or not it needs to be applied.

EXAMPLE 5.8: VALUATION OF INVENTORY

The following information relates to Dunville Ltd for the year to 31 December 2019, its first year of trading:

Costs	**€000**	**€000**
Wages and Salaries		
Factory	90	
Administration	48	
Selling	28	
		166
Overheads		
Rent and rates	10	
Heat and power	6	
Depreciation		
Factory buildings and machinery	6	
Salesmen's motor vehicles	2	
Office building and furniture	2	
Sundry Overheads		
Factory	12	
Administration	4	
Selling	6	
		48
Direct material cost of goods sold (80,000 kg)		160
Closing stocks at cost – material value		
Raw materials (20,000 kg)		40
Work in progress (8,000 kg, half completed)		16
Finished goods (16,000 kg)		32

The factory occupies 75% of the total area. Working a 40-hour week, it was operational for 48 weeks of the year with a four-week allowance for holidays. This will be the normal operating level for the company. Turnover for the period was €331,000.

Solution

Inventory Valuations

Raw materials inventories

20,000 kg at €2 per kg = €40,000

Assume that this is lower than the net realisable value (NRV). Even if NRV is lower, as long as the raw material can be incorporated into a finished product that will recover the €2 per kg, the actual cost is the correct value to adopt under FRS 102.

Work-in-progress inventories

	€
Material 8,000 kg × €2 per kg	16,000
Conversion costs 8,000 kg × 1/2 = 4,000 kg	
4,000 kg × €1.21 per kg (*W2*)	4,840
	20,840

Assume that cost is lower than the NRV.

Finished goods inventories

Total cost of production (*W2*)	€3.21 per kg
Net realisable value (*W3*)	€3.69 per kg

This inventory must be valued at the lower of cost or NRV, i.e. 16,000 kg × €3.21 per kg = €51,360.

Workings

(W1) Production

	Kg
Sales	80,000
Closing stocks – finished goods	16,000
Closing stocks – work in progress	4,000
	100,000

(W2) Factory cost of production

	€000	€ per kg	
Direct materials (€160,000 ÷ 80,000)		2.0	
Wages and salaries – factory	90		
Rent and rates (75%)	7.5		
Heat and power (say, 90%)	5.4		
Depreciation – factory	6		
Sundry overheads – factory	12		
	120.9	1.21	(120,900 ÷ 100,000 kg)
		3.21	

(W3) Determination of NRV

	€000	€ per kg
Sales (80,000 kg)	331	4.14
Less: selling expenses (80,000 kg)		
Wages and salaries	28	(0.35)
Depreciation – salesmen's motor vehicles	2	(0.03)
Sundry overheads	6	(0.07)
	36	(0.45)
	295	3.69

The NRV of €3.69 per kg is greater than the cost of €3.21 per kg, therefore stocks of finished goods should be valued at the lower cost figure.

5.8 DISCLOSURES

Entities must disclose the following:

(a) the accounting policies adopted, including the specific cost formula adopted;
(b) the total carrying amount of inventories in appropriate classifications;
(c) the amount of any impairment expensed or reversed during the period in profit or loss; and
(d) the carrying amount of any inventories pledged as security for liabilities.

An example, based on the IASB's *IFRS for SMEs 2009 Illustrative Financial Statements Presentation and Disclosure Checklist*, shows the disclosures required by FRS 102.

Example 5.9: Illustrative Financial Statements – Inventories

Accounting Policies and Explanatory Notes (Extracts)

2. Basis of preparation and accounting policies

Inventories
Inventories are stated at the lower of cost and selling price less costs to complete and sell. Cost is calculated using the first in, first out (FIFO) method.

8. Profit before tax

The following items have been recognised as expenses (income) in determining profit before tax:

	20X2	20X1
	€	€
Research and development cost (included in other expenses)	31,620	22,778
Foreign exchange loss on trade payables (included in other expenses)	1,000	–
Warranty expense (included in cost of sales)	5,260	7,340

11. Inventories

	20X2	20X1
	€	€
Raw materials	42,601	36,450
Work in progress	1,140	900
Finished goods	13,640	10,570
	57,381	47,920

A good example of a listed company whose disclosure is very similar to the FRS has been provided by the C & C Group in its 2009 final accounts. It also includes the disclosure of an impairment loss on its apple juice inventory. This was subsequently reversed in its 2011 financial statements.

C & C Group Plc

Annual Report and Accounts 2009

STATEMENT OF ACCOUNTING POLICIES (EXTRACT)

Inventories

Inventories are stated at the lower of cost and net realisable value. Cost includes all expenditure incurred in acquiring the inventories and bringing them to their present location and condition and is based on the first-in first-out principle.

In the case of finished goods and work in progress, cost includes direct production costs and the appropriate share of production overheads plus excise duties where appropriate. Net realisable value is the estimated selling price in the ordinary course of business, less estimated costs of completion and estimated costs necessary to complete the sale.

Provision is made for slow-moving or obsolete stock where appropriate.

[...]

NOTES FORMING PART OF THE FINANCIAL STATEMENTS (EXTRACT)

15. Inventories

	2009	2008
	€m	€m
Group		
Raw materials & consumables	**32.1**	55.1
Finished goods & goods for resale	**12.4**	23.7
Total inventories at lower of cost and net realisable value	**44.5**	78.8

Inventory write-down recognised as an expense within operating costs amounted to €12.4 million (2008: €2.4 million). This predominantly represents an apple juice stock impairment charge of €11.1 million that arose as a result of the Group's surplus apple juice stocks. At 28 February 2009, the Group's stock holding of apple juice at circa 36 months was deemed excessive in light of anticipated future needs, forward purchase commitments and useful life of stock on hand. The prior year write-down of €2.4 million principally related to finished goods damaged in a third party warehouse.

C & C Group Plc

Annual Report and Accounts 2011

NOTES FORMING PART OF THE FINANCIAL STATEMENTS (EXTRACTS)

6. Exceptional Items

	2011			2010		
	Continuing operations	**Discontinued operations**	**Total**	**Continuing operations**	**Discontinued operations**	**Total**
	€m	**€m**	**€m**	**€m**	**€m**	**€m**
Restructuring costs	4.9	–	**4.9**	3.8	–	3.8
Retirement benefit obligations	(1.1)	(0.9)	**(2.0)**	(2.2)	(0.9)	(3.1)
Recovery of previously impaired inventory	(0.2)	–	**(0.2)**	–	–	–

Costs associated with integrating acquired businesses	8.4	–	**8.4**	1.9	–	1.9
Profit from discontinued operations	–	(224.7)	**(224.7)**	–	(1.8)	(1.8)
Total before tax	**12.0**	**(225.6)**	**(213.6)**	3.5	(2.7)	0.8
Income tax expense	(2.9)	0.1	**(2.8)**	(0.9)	–	(0.9)
Total after tax	**9.1**	**(225.5)**	**(216.4)**	2.6	(2.7)	(0.1)

[...]

(c) Recovery of previously impaired inventory

During the financial year ended 28 February 2009, the Group's stock holding of apple juice at circa 36 months of forecasted future sales was deemed excessive in light of anticipated future needs, forward purchase commitments and useful life of the stock on hand, accordingly the Group recorded an impairment charge in relation to excess apple juice stocks. During the current financial year, some of the previously impaired juice stocks were recovered and used by the Group's acquired Gaymers cider business. As a result this stock was written back to operating profit at its recoverable value.

[...]

16. Inventories

	2011	2010
	€m	€m
Group		
Raw materials & consumables	**26.7**	36.7
Finished goods & goods for resale	**14.0**	18.0
Total inventories at lower of cost and net realisable value	**40.7**	54.7

Inventory write-downs recognised as an expense within operating costs amounted to €1.1 million (2010: €0.9 million). Previously impaired inventory recovered during the financial year and recognised as exceptional income (note 6) amounted to €0.2 million (2010: €nil).

The financial statements of Irish retailer Easons provides details of its accounting policy on classification of inventories. The company also discloses that no stock has been pledged as security.

Eason & Son Ltd

ANNUAL REPORT – NOTES TO THE FINANCIAL STATEMENTS (EXTRACT)

2. Statement of accounting policies

2.10 Stocks
Stocks are valued at the lower of cost and net realisable value after making due allowance for obsolete and slow moving stocks using the first in first out method. Cost includes all direct costs and an appropriate proportion of fixed and variable overheads.

Where there is objective evidence that recoverable amounts of an asset is less than its carrying value the carrying amount of the asset is reduced to its recoverable amount resulting in the impairment loss, recognised in the profit or loss.

[...]

14 Stocks

	2018 €'000	2017 €'000
Finished goods and goods for resale	1,128	1,403

There is no significant difference between the replacement cost of finished goods and their carrying amounts.

Stock considered obsolete is written down to net realisable value. The amount of the write down is €164k (2017: €189k) and the value of stock at cost is €1,292 (2017: €1,592k). There are no stocks pledged as security.

5.9 SMALL ENTITIES

There are no explicit minimum disclosure requirements for small entities under Section 1A of FRS 102, for either the UK or the Republic of Ireland. However, small entities may need to provide disclosures as required by FRS 102, Section 13 if required to give a true and fair view.

5.10 MICRO-ENTITIES

Under FRS 105 the accounting treatment for inventories is identical to that in FRS 102.

Disclosure Checklist: Asset Valuation – Inventories – FRS 102

(References are to the relevant Section of FRS 102)

	Para.
Inventories – Section 13	
An entity shall disclose the following: (a) the accounting policies adopted in measuring inventories, including the cost formula used; (b) the total carrying amount of inventories and the carrying amount in classifications appropriate to the entity; (c) [deleted] (d) impairment losses recognised or reversed in profit or loss in accordance with Section 27; and (e) the total carrying amount of inventories pledged as security for liabilities.	13.22

Disclosure Checklist: Asset Valuation – Inventories – Small Entities

(References are to the relevant Appendix of Section 1A FRS 102)

The mandatory disclosure requirements for small entities required under the Companies Act 2014 (ROI) (CA 2014), Companies Act 2006 (UK) (CA 2006) and the Small Companies and Groups (Accounts and Directors' Report) Regulations 2008 (UK) (S.I. No. 409 of 2008) are as follows:

	Para.
Indebtedness, guarantees and financial commitments	
Particulars shall be given of any charge on the assets of the small entity to secure the liabilities of any other person, including, where practicable, the amount secured. (Schedule 3A, paragraph 51(1) CA 2014) (Schedule 1, paragraph 57(2) S.I. 409/2008)	1AD.28 (ROI) 1AC.30 (UK) (similar)

Disclosure Checklist: Asset Valuation – Inventories – Micro-entities

(References are to the relevant Section of FRS 105)

The mandatory disclosure requirements for micro-entities required under FRS 105, the Companies Act 2014 (ROI) (CA 2014), the Companies Act 2006 (UK) (CA 2006) and the Small Companies and Groups (Accounts and Directors' Report) Regulations 2008 (UK) (S.I. No. 409 of 2008) are as follows:

	Para.
A micro-entity shall disclose information in relation to any items of inventory given as security in respect of its commitments, guarantees and contingencies in accordance with the relevant appendix to Section 6 *Notes to the Financial Statements*.	10.22

	PARA.
Indebtedness, guarantees and financial commitments	
Particulars shall be given of any charge on the assets of the micro-entity to secure the liabilities of any other person, including, where practicable, the amount secured. (Schedule 3B, paragraph 35(1) CA 2014)	6B.13 (ROI only)

Chapter 6
LIABILITIES

This chapter covers provisions and contingencies, income tax liabilities and the liability and equity of financial instruments. Accounting for leases is covered in **Chapter 4**.

6.1 PROVISIONS AND CONTINGENCIES (SECTION 21)

A provision is a liability of uncertain timing or amount.

Section 21 does not apply to provisions that are covered by other sections of this FRS. These include:

(a) leases (Section 20 – see **Chapter 4**);
(b) construction contracts (Section 23 – see **Chapter 7**);
(c) employee benefit obligations (Section 28 – see **Chapter 8**); and
(d) income taxes (Section 29 – see **Section 6.2** below, '**Income Taxes**').

Section 21 also does not apply to reductions in asset values, e.g. provisions for accumulated depreciation, uncollectible receivables, etc.

Section 21 does apply to financial guarantee contracts unless:

(a) an entity has chosen to apply IAS 39 and/or IFRS 9; or
(b) an entity has elected under FRS 103 *Insurance Contracts* to continue the application of insurance contract accounting.

Section 21 does not apply to financial instruments (including loan commitments) that are within the scope of Sections 11 and 12 of FRS 102; nor does it apply to insurance contracts (including reinsurance contracts) that an entity issues and reinsurance contracts that the entity holds, or financial instruments issued by an entity with a discretionary participation feature that are within the scope of FRS 103.

Section 21 does not apply to executory contracts unless they are onerous. Executory contracts are contracts under which neither party has performed any of its obligations, or both parties have partially performed their obligations to an equal extent.

Initial Recognition

A provision should only be recognised when:

(a) the entity has a **present obligation** as a result of a **past event**; and
(b) it is **probable** that it will be required to transfer economic benefits in settlement; and
(c) its amount can be **reliably estimated**.

If either criteria (b) or (c) are failed, the transaction will be recorded in the notes as a contingent liability unless the probability of it occurring is remote, in which case it would be completely omitted from the financial statements.

A provision is a liability and an expense in profit or loss unless it forms part of the cost of an asset, e.g. inventories, property, etc.

A present obligation means an entity has no realistic alternative to settling the obligation. This can happen when it is enforced by law or when the entity has created a constructive obligation by creating a valid expectation that it will discharge the obligation. Obligations for future actions do not satisfy the condition no matter if contractual or how likely they are to occur as the entity can avoid that expenditure, e.g. a management intention to fit smoke filters on a factory.

Example 6.1: Provision or Contingent Liability

A leakage from BCI's production plant contaminated the River Lee. A lawsuit was brought against the company by the local rowing club to seek damages to health as a result of the contamination. The company has acknowledged its guilt and the court is deciding on the extent of compensation to be awarded. The date of the ruling is still uncertain, but it is expected within the year and that the compensation to be paid will be in the range of €400,000–€500,000.

What would happen if there was no court case but legislation requires a clean-up of the contamination?

Solution

This is a provision as:
(a) the entity has a legal obligation as there is a legal action against the company;
(b) it is probable that it will transfer economic benefits as it has admitted guilt;
(c) the amount can be reliably measured at a range of €400,000–€500,000.

The lack of a court case does not change the situation if there is a legal requirement to clean up the contamination. It is still a provision.

Example 6.2: Obligation or Mere Intention

A local dairy farmer has a limited liability company and wishes to smooth out his profits by creating a provision for future losses in a good year to compensate for expected losses in the following year.

Solution

This is known as 'big bath accounting' and is specifically prohibited by the FRS as there is no obligation to pay anyone for the losses and the company could just as easily be wound up before the losses are incurred. It is therefore a mere intention.

Example 6.3: Obligation or Mere Intention

A local business has promised to contribute major funding to the building of a new Business and Management Institute at the New Ireland University in Tullamore. This has been announced both in the press and on television by the Chief Executive of the company.

Solution

This is a constructive obligation as there is now a valid expectation that the company will go ahead with the contribution. It is not a mere intention and thus should be provided as a liability.

Example 6.4: Obligation or Mere Intention

The Green Elastic Company Ltd has contaminated the groundwater at its plant but there is no legal obligation to clean it up. However, the company has always had a deep green policy and in the past it has traditionally cleaned up any contamination it has caused.

Solution

The company has a constructive obligation because of its past policy of cleaning up contamination, which means the public and community has a valid expectation that the damage would be cleaned up.

In practice, a lot of judgement is required in deciding whether or not an obligation has been created.

Initial Measurement

A provision should be measured at the best estimate of the amount required to settle the obligation at the reporting date.

(a) Where there is a large population of items, the estimate of the amounts can reflect the weighting of all possible outcomes by their associated probabilities.

(b) When an obligation arises from a single obligation, the most likely outcome may be the best estimate.

Example 6.5: Probability Analysis

Tullyglass Ltd sells 5,000 honeypots with a warranty attached promising to repair any manufacturing defects that become apparent in the first year after purchase. Major defects are expected to cost €1,000 to repair and minor defects €300.

The company's experience over the last five years would indicate that 50% of sales will not require warranty claims, 30% will require minor repairs and 20% major repairs.

Solution

The expected value of the liability would be calculated as follows:

		€
50% × 5,000 honeypots x €nil	=	Nil
30% × 5,000 honeypots x €300	=	450,000
20% × 5,000 honeypots x €1,000	=	1,000,000
		1,450,000

When the time value of money is material, the provision should be the present value of the amount expected to be required to settle the obligation. The discount rate should be pre-tax, reflecting current market assessments of the time value of money. The specific risks to the liability should be reflected in the discount rate or the amounts required to settle the obligation.

Example 6.6: Impact of the Time Value of Money on Initial Measurement of a Provision

Belvoir Ltd is being sued by a customer for personal injury caused by a severe malfunction in one of its products. The legal advisors estimate from previous court cases that the settlement to be paid could be €500,000 (40% chance) or €800,000 (60% chance). However, the decision will not take place for two more years. Assume the risk-free discount rate for a two-year bond is 5%, but if adjusted for risk the more appropriate rate is 4%.

Solution

Using expected value:

		€	
40% × €500,000	=	200,000	
60% × €800,000	=	480,000	
		680,000	× 1/1.04 × 1/1.04 = €628,698

When some of a provision may be reimbursed by another party, e.g. insurance, the entity should recognise a separate asset, but only if it is virtually certain that the entity will receive the reimbursement. The asset must not be offset against the provision. Under FRS 102, offsetting is permitted in the profit and loss account or the statement of comprehensive income of any reimbursement against its related expenditure.

Subsequent Measurement

A provision can only be discharged by those expenditures for which the provision was originally recognised. No virement across provisions is permitted – each provision must stand on its own two feet!

All provisions should be reviewed at each reporting date and adjusted to reflect current best estimates. Any adjustments are charged in arriving at profit or loss. Any unwinding of discount, however, should be recognised as a finance cost in the profit and loss account.

Example 6.7: Reversal of Provision

Stradbally Ltd recognised a €120,000 provision for restructuring as at 31 December 2018. In April 2019 the restructuring expenses were fully settled for €100,000. In June 2019 the company carried out a major maintenance programme and charged €20,000 to clear off the provision, with the balance of €40,000 being expensed.

Solution

Under FRS 102, a provision can only be utilised for the purpose for which it was created. Thus the following correction needs to be made:

Dr	Maintenance costs	€20,000	
	Cr Profit and loss – reversal of provision		€20,000

Onerous Contracts

Onerous contracts represent the unavoidable costs of meeting an obligation under a contract and which exceed the economic benefits expected to be received under the contract. The costs should be those reflecting the least net cost of exiting from the contract, i.e. the lower of the cost of fulfilling the contract or any compensation or penalties arising from failure to fulfil it, e.g. an onerous lease.

An onerous lease is a present obligation as there is a legal contractual obligation, thus the conclusion in FRS 102 is that an entity must recognise a provision and measure it under the contract's provisions.

Future Operating Losses

Where an entity has determined that it is probable that it will incur future operating losses for several years, the question arises: "Is there a present obligation?" The guidance in Section 21 argues that there is no present obligation as no past event has occurred to create the obligation. Following that decision, the conclusion reached is that no provision should be recognised. However, it may well indicate an impairment and therefore preparers of financial statements would need to investigate Section 27 *Impairment of Assets* (see **Chapter 3**).

Restructuring

Restructuring is a planned programme that materially changes either:

(a) the scope of a business undertaken by an entity; or
(b) the manner in which the business is conducted.

A constructive obligation (and not a mere intention) can only exist when an entity fulfils all of the following:

(a) it has a detailed formal plan for the restructuring identifying at least:
    (i) the part of a business concerned,
    (ii) the principal locations affected,
    (iii) the location, function and approximate number of employees to be compensated for terminating their services,
    (iv) the expenditures to be undertaken,
    (v) when the plan will be implemented; and
(b) it has raised a valid expectation by starting to implement the plan or by announcing its main features to those affected by it.

The conclusion reached is that an entity can only recognise a provision if it has a legal or constructive obligation to carry out the restructuring at the reporting date and has therefore passed all of the above criteria.

EXAMPLE 6.8: CLOSURE OF A DIVISION BUT NO IMPLEMENTATION BEFORE THE FINANCIAL YEAR END

On 9 December 2019 the board of a reporting entity decided to close down its overseas division. This decision was not communicated to any of those affected and no other steps were taken to implement the decision before the financial year end of 31 December 2019.

Solution

There is no present obligation at the year end as no obligating event has occurred and thus no provision should be made.

Example 6.9: Closure of a Division Communicated or Implemented before the Financial Year End

On 9 December 2019 the board of a reporting entity decided to close down its overseas division. On 22 December 2019 a detailed plan for closing down the division was agreed by the board and letters were sent to customers advising them to seek alternative sources of supply, and redundancy notices were sent to the division's staff.

Solution

There is an obligating event here as the decision has been communicated to those affected by the closure, i.e. the customers and the employees, before the year end. There is, therefore, a constructive obligation and thus a provision should be recognised at the year end of 31 December 2019 for the best estimate of the cost of closing down the division.

Contingent Liabilities

Contingent liabilities are either possible but uncertain obligations, or present obligations that fail either (or both) initial recognition conditions (b) or (c) for a provision, i.e. it is not probable that the provision will transfer economic benefits and/or the amount of the provision cannot be reliably estimated. In these situations liabilities should not be recognised in the financial statements but disclosure is required, unless the chances of the contingencies occurring are remote.

Example 6.10: Provision or Contingent Liability

During 2019, Rockabilly Independent Clinic Ltd was sued for clinical negligence for an operation that resulted in the unfortunate death of one of its patients. Lawyers acting on behalf of the company are confident that the death was due to natural causes and not due to any error on behalf of the clinic. However, the patient's family's solicitors are of the opposite view.

Solution

There is a legal obligation as there is a case being taken against the company, but it is only a possible (but more than remote) liability and thus it should be disclosed as a contingent liability in the notes but no provision should be made.

Contingent Assets

An entity should not recognise a contingent asset as an asset. Disclosure is only required in the notes where an inflow of benefits is probable. However, if it is virtually certain that it should not be regarded as contingent, then it should be recorded on the balance sheet as a genuine asset – making contingent assets rare in practice.

Disclosures

Disclosures about Provisions

For each class of provision an entity should disclose a reconciliation showing:

(a) the carrying amount at the beginning and end of the period;
(b) additional provisions made during the period including adjustments;
(c) amounts used during the period;
(d) unused amounts reversed during the period.

} By reconciliation

Comparative information is not required.

Ornua Co-operative Ltd provides a good example of the disclosure of a single provision in the accounting policies and notes to its financial statements.

Ornua Co-operative Ltd
NOTES TO THE FINANCIAL STATEMENTS (EXTRACT)
for year ending 29 December 2018

1. Statement of accounting policies

[...]

p) Provisions and contingent liabilities

Provisions are recognised when the Group has a present obligation (legal or constructive) as a result of a past event, it is probable that the Group will be required to settle the obligation, and a reliable estimate can be made of the obligation. The amount recognised as a provision is the best estimate of the consideration required to settle the present obligation at the end of the reporting period, taking into account the risks and uncertainties surrounding the obligation.

Where the effect of the time value of money is material, the amount expected to be required to settle the obligation is recognised at present value using the pre-tax discount rate.

The unwinding of the discount is recognised as a finance cost in the Income Statement in the period it arises.

A provision for restructuring is recognised when the Group has a detailed, formal plan for the restructuring and has raised a valid expectation in those affected by either starting to implement the plan or announcing its main features to those affected and therefore has a legal or constructive obligation to carry out the restructuring. Insurance provisions are recognised to cover claims including claims which are known to be incurred but not reported at period end. Provision for onerous contracts are made when the unavoidable costs of meeting the obligations under the contract exceed the economic benefits expected to be received under it.

Contingent liabilities are not recognised, except those acquired in a business combination. Contingent liabilities arise as a result of past events when (i) it is not probable that there will be an outflow of resources or that the amount cannot be reliably measured at the reporting date or (ii) when the existence will be confirmed by the occurrence on non-occurrence of uncertain future events not wholly within the Group's control. Contingent liabilities are disclosed in the financial statements unless the probability of an outflow of resources is remote.

[...]

GROUP BALANCE SHEET (EXTRACT)
as at 29 December 2018

Total assets less current liabilities		**780,441**	628,312
Creditors: amounts falling due after one year	16	**(208,908)**	(68,054)
Post employment benefits	24	**(41,572)**	(40,860)
Provision for liabilities	18	**(9,668)**	(13,821)
Net assets		**520,293**	505,577

[...]

18. Provision for liabilities

	Onerous Sales Contracts (i) €'000	Disposal Related Provisions (ii) €'000	Other Provisions (iii) €'000	Total Provisions €'000
At beginning of period	9,150	2,379	2,292	13,821

Provided during the period	5,842	–	1,057	6,899
Utilised during the period	(9,150)	(1,547)	(416)	(11,113)
Translation adjustment	–	61	–	61
At end of period	**5,842**	**893**	**2,933**	**9,668**

(i) The onerous sales contracts provision relates to contracted sales whose revenues do not cover the cost of completing the contract.
(ii) Relates to provisions made in 2015 on disposal of the DPI business for certain costs that will be incurred by the Group subsequent to the disposal.
(iii) Other provisions includes the Group's insurance provision and the Group's Long Term Incentive Plan provision.

The majority of the above provisions will be utilised in one year.

A more detailed example showing the movement for the year, the analysis between current and non-current liabilities and a brief description of the different provisions and their timing and uncertainties, is provided by DCC Plc.

DCC Plc

Annual Report and Accounts 2018

NOTES TO THE FINANCIAL STATEMENTS (EXTRACTS)

5.9 Summary of Significant Accounting Policies

[...]

Provisions

A provision is recognised in the Balance Sheet when the Group has a present obligation (either legal or constructive) as a result of a past event, and it is probable that a transfer of economic benefits will be required to settle the obligation. Provisions are measured at the Directors' best estimate of the expenditure required to settle the obligation at the balance sheet date and are discounted to present value where the effect is material.

A provision for restructuring is recognised when the Group has approved a detailed and formal restructuring plan and announced its main provisions.

Provisions arising on business combinations are only recognised to the extent that they would have qualified for recognition in the financial statements of the acquiree prior to the acquisition.

A contingent liability is not recognised but is disclosed where the existence of the obligation will only be confirmed by future events or where it is not probable that an outflow of resources will be required to settle the obligation or where the amount of the obligation cannot be measured with reasonable reliability. Contingent assets are not recognised but are disclosed where an inflow of economic benefits is probable.

Environmental Provisions
The Group's waste management and recycling activities are subject to various laws and regulations governing the protection of the environment. Full provision is made for the net present value of the Group's estimated costs in relation to restoration liabilities at its landfill sites. The net present value of the estimated costs is capitalised as property, plant and equipment and the unwinding of the discount element on the restoration provision is reflected in the Income Statement.

[...]

3.15 Provisions for Liabilities

A provision is recorded when an obligation exists, resulting from a past event and it is probable that cash will be paid to settle it but there is uncertainty over either the amount or timing of the outflow. The main provisions held by the Group are in relation to reorganisation programs, environmental obligations, cylinder and tank deposits and insurance liabilities.

The reconciliation of the movement in provisions for liabilities for the year ended 31 March 2018 is as follows:

	Rationalisation, restructuring and redundancy £'000	Environmental and remediation £'000	Cylinder and tank deposits £'000	Insurance and other £'000	Total £'000
At 1 April 2017	32,752	86,790	149,700	17,430	286,672
Provided during the year	27,612	5,789	8,669	9,623	51,693
Unwinding of discount applicable to provisions for liabilities	-	263	2,114	-	2,377
Utilised during the year	(15,784)	(9,566)	(2,537)	(4,618)	(32,505)
Unutilised/reversed during the year	(477)	-	(4,440)	(172)	(5,089)
Arising on acquisition (note 5.2)	26	2,039	8,128	4,794	14,987
Exchange and other	622	980	3,351	253	5,206
At 31 March 2018	44,751	86,295	164,985	27,310	323,341

Analysed as:					
Non-current liabilities	26,203	82,229	161,996	8,462	278,890
Current liabilities	18,548	4,066	2,989	18,848	44,451
	44,751	86,295	164,985	27,310	323,341

Rationalisation, restructuring and redundancy
This provision relates to various rationalisation and restructuring programs across the Group. The Group expects that the majority of this provision will be utilised within three years.

Environmental and remediation
This provision relates to obligations governing site remediation and improvement costs to be incurred in compliance with environmental regulations together with the costs associated with removing LPG tanks from customer sites. The net present value of the estimated costs is capitalised as property, plant and equipment. The unwinding of the discount element on the provision is reflected in the Income Statement. Ongoing costs incurred during the operating life of the sites are written off directly to the Income Statement and are not charged to the provision. The majority of the obligations will unwind over a 30-year timeframe but the exact timing of settlement of these provisions is not certain.

Cylinder and tank deposits
This provision relates to DCC LPG's operations where an obligation arises from the receipt of deposit fees paid by customers for LPG cylinders and tanks. On receipt of a deposit the Group recognises a liability equal to the deposit received. This deposit will subsequently be refunded at an amount equal to the original deposit on return of the cylinder or tank together with the original deposit receipt. Cylinder and tank deposits acquired through business combinations are measured initially at their fair value at the acquisition date (i.e. net present value) and the unwinding of the discount element is reflected in the Income Statement. The majority of this obligation will unwind over a 25-year timeframe but the exact timing of settlement of this provision is not certain.

Insurance and other
The Group operates a level of self-insurance for motor liability and public and products liability. Under these arrangements the Group retains certain insurance exposure up to pre-determined self-insurance thresholds. This provision reflects an estimation of claims that are classified as incurred but not reported and also the outstanding loss reserve. A significant element of the provision is subject to external assessments. The utilisation of the provision is dependent on the timing of settlement of the outstanding claims. Historically, the average time for settlement of outstanding claims ranges from 3-5 years from the date of the claim.

Disclosures about Contingent Liabilities

Unless the possibility of any outflow is remote, for each class of contingent liability a brief description of the nature of the contingent liability must be disclosed and, when practicable:

(a) an estimate of its **financial effect**;
(b) an indication of the **uncertainties** relating to the timing or the amount of any outflow; and
(c) the possibility of any **reimbursement**.

If it is impracticable to make one or more of these disclosures, that fact should be stated.

An example of a disclosure note for contingent liabilities is provided by Randox Holdings Ltd.

Randox Holdings Limited

ANNUAL REPORT – NOTES TO THE FINANCIAL STATEMENTS (EXTRACT)

for the year ended 31 December 2018

26. Contingent liabilities

The company is a participant in a group banking arrangement under which all surplus cash balances are held as collateral for bank facilities advanced to group members. In addition, the company has issued an unlimited guarantee to the bank to support these group facilities. There exists a contingent liability to repay certain capital and revenue grants received from grant bodies if certain grant conditions are not achieved. The directors do not anticipate any repayment falling due under the terms on which the grants were received.

An example of a contingent liability note under international standards is provided by Ryanair's financial statements and its contingency around litigation in dispute. Although this note would be much longer than that required by FRS 102, it does give an insight into the information to be provided.

Ryanair Holdings Plc

Annual Report & Financial Statements 2018

NOTES TO THE FINANCIAL STATEMENTS (EXTRACT)

22 Commitments and contingencies

[…]

Contingencies

The Company is engaged in litigation arising in the ordinary course of its business. Although no assurance can be given as to the outcome of any current or pending litigation, management does not believe that any such litigation will, individually or in the aggregate, have a material adverse effect on the results of operations or financial condition of the Company, except as described below.

Since 2002, the European Commission has examined the agreements between Ryanair and various airports to establish whether they constituted illegal state aid. In many cases, the European Commission has concluded that the agreements did not constitute state aid. In other cases, Ryanair has successfully challenged the EU commission finding that there was state aid. In July and October 2014, the European Commission announced findings of state aid to Ryanair in its arrangements with Pau, Nimes, Angouleme, Altenburg and Zweibrücken airports, ordering Ryanair to repay a total of approximately €9.9 million of alleged aid. In July and November 2016, the European Commission announced findings of state aid to Ryanair in its arrangements with Cagliari and Klagenfurt respectively, ordering Ryanair to repay approximately €12.6 million of alleged aid. Ryanair has appealed the seven "aid" decisions to the EU General Court. These appeal proceedings are expected to take between two and four years.

Ryanair is facing similar legal challenges with respect to agreements with certain other airports, notably Paris (Beauvais), La Rochelle, Carcassonne, Girona, Reus, Târgu Mureş and Montpellier. These investigations are ongoing and Ryanair currently expects that they will conclude in late 2018, with any European Commission decisions appealable to the EU General Court.

Ryanair is also facing an allegation that it has benefited from unlawful state aid in a German court case in relation to its arrangements with Frankfurt (Hahn).

Adverse rulings in the above or similar cases could be used as precedents by competitors to challenge Ryanair's agreements with other publicly-owned airports and could cause Ryanair to strongly reconsider its growth strategy in relation to public or state-owned airports across Europe. This could in turn lead to a scaling back of Ryanair's growth strategy due to the smaller number of privately owned airports available for development. No assurance can be given as to the outcome of these proceedings, nor as to whether any unfavourable outcomes may, individually or in the aggregate, have a material adverse effect on the results of operations or financial condition of the Company.

Disclosures about Contingent Assets

If an inflow of benefits is probable but not virtually certain, an entity should disclose a description of the nature of the contingent assets at the end of the period and, when practicable, their financial effect. If it is impracticable, that fact should be stated.

Prejudicial Disclosure

In extremely rare cases, disclosure could be expected to seriously prejudice the position of the entity in a dispute with other parties. In such cases an entity need not disclose the information, but should provide details of the general nature of the dispute together with the fact that the information has not been disclosed and the reason why.

EXAMPLES OF PROVISIONS IN IRISH LISTED COMPANIES

Aer Lingus Plc	Business repositioning, aircraft maintenance, maintenance contracts, frequent flyer programme, and post-cessation of employment obligations
CPL Resources Plc	Deferred and contingent consideration
Dragon Oil Plc	Abandonment and decommissioning costs
Kingspan Resources Plc	Guarantees and warranties
Prime Active Capital Plc	Reorganisation and put liability
CRH Plc	Insurance, guarantees and warranties, rationalisation and redundancy, environment and remediation
DCC Plc	Environmental and remediation, insurance and rationalisation, restructuring and redundancy
Glanbia Plc	Restructuring, UK pension legal claims and lease commitments
Independent News & Media Plc	Restructuring and holiday entitlements
Kenmare Resources Plc	Mine closure, mine rehabilitation
Petroneft Resources Plc	Decommissioning costs and onerous contracts
Readymix Plc	Environment and insurance
United Drug Plc	Deferred consideration, onerous lease contracts

Disclosure about Financial Guarantee Contracts

The nature and business purpose of any financial guarantee contracts an entity has issued should be disclosed and, if applicable, the disclosures required for provisions and contingent liabilities.

Guidance on Recognising and Measuring Provisions – Appendix to Section 21

The Appendix to Section 21 is not a part of the Section proper, but provides preparers and users of financial statements with some examples of how the standard might be operated in specific instances. These are discussed below.

EXAMPLE 6.11: WARRANTIES

A manufacturer of goods has, based on past experience, estimated that it is probable that there will be some claims under warranty agreements that have been sold with the goods.

There is a present obligation as the sale of the product does give rise to a legal obligation and also an outflow of resources is probable for the warranties as a whole.

The conclusion reached is that a provision must be created for the best estimate of the cost of repairing or replacing the goods under the warranty products sold.

EXAMPLE 6.12: WARRANTY PROVISION

In 2019, sales under warranty are €4,000,000. Experience indicates that 80% of the goods sold require no warranty repairs, 10% minor repairs costing 50% of the sale price, and 10% major repairs costing 80% of the sale price. The estimated warranty costs are therefore €520,000, calculated as follows:

		€
€4,000,000 × 80% × 0	=	nil
€4,000,000 × 10% × 50%	=	200,000
€4,000,000 × 10% × 80%	=	320,000
		520,000

Warranty expenditure for 40% of products sold in 2019 is expected to be made in 2020, 40% in 2021 and 20% in 2022. Cash flows already incorporate risk, therefore the discount rate should be a 4% risk-free rate based on government bonds.

Solution

The obligation, at the end of 2019, for products sold in 2019 will be:

	4% discount factor	€
Year 1: 40% × €520,000 = €208,000	0.962	200,096
Year 2: 40% × €520,000 = €208,000	0.925	192,400
Year 3: 20% × €520,000 = €104,000	0.889	92,456
		484,952

Example 6.13: Refunds Policy

A retail store has a policy of refunding purchases to dissatisfied customers even if there is no legal obligation to do so. This is argued to be a present obligation. There is a constructive obligation as there is a valid expectation by customers that the store will refund any purchases.

An outflow of resources is probable and thus the conclusion reached is that an entity should recognise its best estimate of the amount required to settle the refunds.

Example 6.14: Staff Retraining as a Result of Changes in the Income Tax System

The government introduces a number of changes to the income tax system and an entity needs to retrain a large proportion of its workforce.

There is no present obligation as there is no legal or constructive obligation to retrain the staff and thus no obligating event has taken place. In theory, new staff could be brought in already trained. The conclusion reached is that no provision should be recognised.

Example 6.15: A Court Case

A customer is suing Oban Ltd for damages for an injury sustained while using a product sold by Oban. Oban disputes this on the grounds that the customer did not follow the instructions provided. Up to 31 December 2019, lawyers had advised the entity that it would be probable that the entity would not be found liable. However, next year that view changes and by 31 December 2020 it is now probable that the entity will be found liable.

(a) At 31 December 2019
There is a present legal obligation, but no probable obligation exists. The conclusion reached is that no provision should be recognised, but because it is still a possible liability it must be disclosed as a contingent liability unless the probability is remote.

(b) At 31 December 2020
There is still a present obligation, but on the basis of new evidence a clear present obligation exists as there is now a probability that

the entity will have to provide an outflow of benefits to the other party. The conclusion reached is that a provision must be recognised for the best estimate of the amount to settle the obligation at the reporting date.

Decommissioning Costs

In certain industries, particularly extractive/mining industries, expenditure has to be incurred to remove facilities and to restore the production area to its original condition. These are commonly called restoration or decommissioning costs. A provision should be recognised as soon as an obligating event occurs, which can often be at the start of a contract, e.g. a contract with government to develop an oilfield or extract minerals. In these cases both an asset and a liability for the present value of the best estimate of future cash flows to settle the obligation should be created. The asset is recognised as it represents a negative residual value, i.e. the true cost of developing an oilfield or a mine is not just the cost of construction but also the cost of restoring the site as far as possible to its original condition.

Example 6.16: Decommissioning Costs

Troon Ltd purchased an asset on 1 January 2019. The entity is committed to restoration expenditure of €10 million in 10 years' time. Assume an appropriate discount rate is 8%.

1 January 2019 – initial measurement of the provision:

$€10\text{m} \times 1/(1 + 0.08)^{10} = €4,631,935$

Dr	Asset	€4,631,935	
Cr	Provision for decommissioning		€4,631,935

31 December 2019 – measurement of the provision showing the unwinding of the discount and assuming no need to change the best estimate of the cost of carrying out the decommissioning:

$€10\text{m} \times 1/(1 + 0.08)^{9} = €5,002,490$

Dr	Income statement	€370,455	
Cr	Provision for decommissioning		€370,455

(8% × €4,631,935 = €370,455)

The final example is a detailed warranty provision.

Example 6.17: Detailed Warranty Provision

Darkley Ltd provides warranties to its customers at the time of sale of its products. Darkley Ltd has agreed to repair any defects that become apparent in the first 12 months. From previous experience the company knows that there will be claims under the warranties.

At 31 December 2019 Darkley Ltd recognised €80,000 as its warranty provision. Darkley Ltd charged €160,000 against the provision in 2020 on repairs incurred under the warranties, of which €60,000 related to 2020 sales. The liability was discounted in 2019 and €1,000 of discount has unwound during the year.

At 31 December 2020 Darkley Ltd estimated that the following expenditures were likely to be incurred in 2017 to meet its obligations for 2020 sales:

	€
10%	80,000
20%	60,000
50%	50,000
20%	10,000

Assume the cash flows for warranty repairs occur evenly throughout the year and the appropriate discount rate is 6% with a risk adjusted incremental factor of 3%.

In addition, the company is in breach of a licence agreement and its lawyers believe there is an 80% chance that the company will successfully defend its case. However, if it loses its case, there is a 70% chance of paying damages of €500,000 and 30% chance of €600,000, based on similar cases over the past few years. The court case will not occur for another 12 months.

Prepare journal entries for the year ended 31 December 2020.

Solution

		€	€
Dr	Income statement	1,000	
	Cr Provision for warranties		1,000

Being the recognition of the unwinding of discount on discounted opening provision.

		€	€
Dr	Provision for warranties	81,000	
Dr	Income statement (2019 sales: (€80,000 – €61,000))	19,000	
Dr	Income statement (2020 sales)	60,000	
Dr	Income statement (2020 sales)	47,000	
	Cr Bank		160,000
	Cr Provision for warranties		47,000

Probability weighted expected cash flows:

	€
10% × €80,000 =	8,000
20% × €60,000 =	12,000
50% × €50,000 =	25,000
20% × €10,000 =	2,000
	47,000
Risk adjustment: 3% of €47,000	1,410
	48,410

€48,410 × discount rate (3% for half year) 0.97087 = €47,000 present value 2021.

Disclosure

A provision is recognised when the company has a present legal or constructive obligation at the reporting date as a result of a past event and it is probable that the company will have to transfer economic benefits and the amount of the obligation can be estimated reliably. A provision is measured at the best estimate of the amount required to settle the obligation at the reporting date.

Note 28 Provisions
Warranties

	€
Balance as at 31 December	80,000
Unwinding of discount	1,000
Amounts provided during the year	126,000
Amounts utilised during the year	(160,000)
Amounts reversed during the year	–
Balance as at 31 December	47,000
Current liabilities	47,000

A provision is recognised for expected claims on products sold under warranty. These are expected to be realised within one year as the products are under a one-year warranty.

Note 30 Contingent liabilities
In June 2020, legal proceedings were instigated against the company for breach of a licence agreement. The solicitors have advised us that the claim is unlikely to succeed and thus no damages will be awarded to the claimant. The company is confident that even if the claim succeeds, it will not have a material impact on the company's financial statements.

6.2 INCOME TAXES (SECTION 29)

Scope

Section 29 of FRS 102 applies in accounting for income taxes and this includes all domestic and foreign taxes based on taxable profits. VAT and other similar taxes are also covered in this Section.

Section 29 of FRS 102 also applies in accounting for both current and deferred tax – unlike previous UK/Irish GAAP, which split the two into separate standards.

It does not apply to government grants, which are covered by Section 24 (see **Chapter 3**).

Recognition and Measurement of Current Tax

Current tax for current and prior periods should be recognised immediately as a liability. If the amount paid exceeds the amount due, then the excess should be recognised as an asset.

The benefit relating to a tax loss that can be carried back to recover current tax of a previous period should be recognised as an asset.

Current tax is measured at the amount an entity expects to pay or recover using tax rates that have been enacted or substantially enacted by the reporting date.

Recognition of Deferred Tax

Taxable Timing Differences

A deferred tax liability should be recognised for all timing differences at the reporting date. Timing differences are differences between taxable profits and income/expenses as reported in the financial statements because gains/losses are included for tax purposes in a different period than in the financial statements.

EXAMPLE 6.18: TIMING DIFFERENCES

Asset:

		€000
Cost		150
Book value		100
Tax written down value		90
Tax rate	25%	

Tax base = Cost – Cumulative tax allowances

= €150,000 – €90,000

= €60,000

Taxable timing difference = Tax base – NBV

= €60,000 – €100,000

= €40,000

Deferred tax liability = Taxable timing difference × Tax rate

= €40,000 × 25% = €10,000

Examples of similar timing differences:

(a) interest revenue and interest received;
(b) depreciation and capital allowances;
(c) development costs capitalised and amortised but deducted for tax when incurred;
(d) cost of business acquisition is allocated to identifiable assets and liabilities re fair values, but no equivalent adjustment made for tax purposes;
(e) assets revalued but no adjustment for tax;
(f) goodwill or negative goodwill on consolidation but no adjustment for tax;

(g) non-taxable government grants; and
(h) carrying amount of investments in subsidiaries, associates, etc. that become different from the tax bases of the investments.

Deferred tax assets are only recognised on the balance sheet to the extent that they are **probable** and will be recovered against the reversal of deferred tax liabilities or other future taxable profits.

One typically important timing difference is when deferred tax liabilities should be recognised for excess capital allowances over depreciation and subsequently reversed.

Deferred tax should be recognised when income from subsidiaries, associates, branches and joint ventures is recognised in the financial statements yet taxed in the future, except if:
(a) the entity can control the reversal of timing differences; and
(b) it is probable that it will not reverse in the future.

In line with full IFRS, deferred tax is recognised on the fair value exercise that occurs in a business combination and goodwill is thereby adjusted. If certain income/expenses are not taxable or are disallowed for tax, these are classified as permanent differences and no deferred tax should be provided.

An amendment was added to the March 2018 version of FRS 102 requiring business combinations to consider the manner in which the reporting entity expects at the end of the reporting period to recover or settle the book value in order to determine the correct tax rate to apply.

Measurement of Deferred Tax

When measuring deferred tax, reporting entities must use tax rates that have been enacted or substantially enacted by the reporting date and that are expected to apply when timing differences reverse.

If different tax rates exist, entities must apply the average enacted rate or substantially enacted rates expected to apply when the timing differences reverse.

If a reporting entity pays a higher or lower rate tax on dividends, the reporting entity should apply the undistributed rate until the liability to pay a dividend occurs.

Deferred tax on non-depreciable assets that are measured using the revaluation model (Section 17 – see **Chapter 3**) are measured using tax rates that apply to the sale of an asset.

Deferred tax on investment properties measured at fair value (Section 16 – see **Chapter 3**), must adopt tax rates that apply to the sale of assets, except for depreciated investment properties within a business model the objective of which is to measure substantially all of the economic benefits embodied in the property over time.

EXAMPLE 6.19: MEASUREMENT OF DEFERRED TAX LIABILITY

An asset has a carrying value of €100,000 and a tax base of €60,000. A tax rate of 20% applies if the asset is sold and 30% is applied to other income.

Solution

In this scenario, a deferred tax liability of €8,000 (€40,000 × 20%) is recognised if the company expects to sell the asset; while there is a liability of €12,000 (€40,000 × 30%) if the company expects to retain the asset and recover economic benefit from its use.

EXAMPLE 6.20: MEASUREMENT OF DEFERRED TAX LIABILITY

An asset has the following net book and write down values:

	NBV	WDV
	€000	**€000**
Cost	100	100
Depreciation	20	30
Book value	80	70
Revalued	150	150
Capital gain	70	80

Assume capital gains are not taxable until the asset is sold.

Solution

Deferred tax should be provided for on the assumption that a capital gain will be earned. The deferred tax would be:

€70,000 × 30% = €21,000

EXAMPLE 6.21: MEASUREMENT OF DEFERRED TAX LIABILITY

Using the same details from Example 6.19 except assume capital gains are taxable at 40% after deducting an inflation-adjusted cost of €110,000.

By retaining and using the asset:
the tax base is €70,000 but €150,000 is taxable, thus the timing difference is €80,000 and there is a tax liability of €80,000 × 30% = €24,000.

By selling the asset:
the capital gain is €150,000 proceeds less adjusted cost of €110,000 = €40,000

		€
Tax on capital gain	€40,000 × 40% =	16,000
The cumulative tax depreciation of	€30,000 × 30% =	9,000
Total liability		25,000

In the UK only, a new insertion in the March 2018 version of FRS 102 responded to the significant differences in accounting treatment arising in practice in relation to the accounting for gift aid payments made by a subsidiary to its charitable parent. Such payments are made during the nine months following the relevant reporting date and are a distribution to owners but are treated as donations for tax purposes. The amendments require the tax effects of such a gift aid payment, when it is probable that it will be made in the nine months following the reporting date, to be taken into account at the reporting date. This should improve the consistency of reporting between entities and the relevance of the information provided to users. Thus, as an exception, when:

"(a) an entity is wholly-owned by one or more charitable entities;
(b) it is probable that a gift aid payment will be made to a member of the same charitable group, or a charitable venturer, within nine months of the reporting date; and
(c) that payment will qualify to be set against profits for tax purposes, the income tax effects of that gift aid payment must be recognised at the reporting date."

The income tax effects must be measured consistently with the tax treatment planned to be used in the entity's income tax filings. A deferred tax liability must not be recognised in relation to such a gift aid payment.

Normally,the tax expense is recorded in the same component of comprehensive income as the related transaction. However, another amendment has introduced an exception when distributions go to equity but their related tax effects are recorded in profit and loss. In that case the tax expense (income) effects of distributions to owners will be reported in profit or loss.

Measurement of both Current and Deferred Tax

Despite its adoption for other liabilities, the IASB and FRC have both agreed to ban the discounting of any taxation under FRS 102 on cost–benefit grounds.

Withholding Tax on Dividends

Under FRS 102, any dividend that is subject to withholding tax must recognise the dividend inclusive of that tax but exclusive of other taxes, e.g. tax credits.

Similarly, any incoming dividends must include withholding tax but exclude other taxes. Any withholding tax suffered is shown as part of the overall tax charge.

Value-added Tax (VAT)

Turnover and expenses shown in the profit and loss account must be reported exclusive of VAT (i.e. recoverable VAT).

However, companies suffering irrecoverable VAT on their fixed assets must include that VAT in the cost of those assets where that is both practicable and material.

Presentation

Allocation in Comprehensive Income and Equity

All changes in both current and deferred tax assets/liabilities are reported as an increase or reduction in the tax expense. That expense must be allocated or apportioned to the same component of total comprehensive income as the underlying transaction to which it relates, e.g. continuing operations, discontinued operations, revaluation of property, etc. (but see exception above).

Presentation in the Statement of Financial Position

Deferred tax liabilities are reported within provisions and deferred tax assets within debtors.

Offsetting

Current tax may only be offset if there is a legal right of set off and the entity intends to settle on a net basis or realise both an asset and liability at the same time.

Deferred tax assets and liabilities may only be offset if, and only if:

(a) the entity has a legally enforceable right to set off current tax assets against current tax liabilities; and
(b) the deferred tax assets and deferred tax liabilities relate to income taxes levied by the same tax authority on either the same taxable entity or different taxable entities which intend either to settle current tax liabilities and assets on a net basis, or to realise the assets and settle the liabilities simultaneously, in each future period in which significant amounts of deferred tax liabilities or assets are expected to be settled or recovered.

Disclosures

FRS 102 requires reporting entities to disclose sufficient information so that users can evaluate the nature and the financial impact of both current and deferred tax consequences.

The major components of the tax expense must be disclosed. These may include:

(a) the current tax expense/income;
(b) the current tax adjustments from previous periods;
(c) the deferred tax expense/income relating to the origination and reversal of timing differences;
(d) the deferred tax expense/income caused by changes in tax rates;
(e) any deferred tax adjustments arising from a change in status of either the entity or its shareholders; and
(f) the tax expense relating to change in accounting policies and errors (Section 10 – see **Chapter 1**).

The following should also be disclosed separately, where it is material:

(a) the aggregate deferred and current tax recognised in other comprehensive income;
(b) an explanation of significant differences between the tax charge in other comprehensive income and the amount reported to the tax authorities;
(c) the amount of the net reversal of deferred tax assets and deferred tax liabilities expected to occur during the year beginning after the reporting period together with a brief explanation for the expected reversal;
(d) an explanation for any changes in tax rates from the previous period;
(e) the amount of deferred tax assets and liabilities at the end of a reporting period for each type of timing difference and for each type of unused tax losses and credits;
(f) the expiry date of timing differences, unused losses and credits; and
(g) an explanation of the potential tax consequences of paying a dividend if paying at a higher or lower rate of tax.

Carbery Food Ingredients Ltd provides a good example of the disclosures required, as shown below.

Carbery Food Ingredients Ltd

ANNUAL REPORT AND ACCOUNTS 2017 (EXTRACTS)

Taxation

The Group establishes provisions based on reasonable estimates, for possible consequences of audits by the tax authorities of the respective countries in which it operates. The amount of such provisions is based on various factors, such as experience with previous tax audits and differing interpretations of tax regulations by the taxable entity and the responsible tax authority. Management estimation is required to determine the amount of deferred tax assets that can be recognised, based upon likely timing and level of future taxable profits together with an assessment of the effect of future tax planning strategies. Further details are contained in note 7.

[...]

7. TAXATION

	2017 €'000	**2016 €'000**
(a) Tax on profit on ordinary activities	5,575	3,129
Current tax:		
Corporation tax on profit for the year	6,728	1,456
Adjustments in respect of prior years'	(405)	406
Utilisation of tax assets/(losses)	11	(302)
Group current tax	6,334	1,560
Share of joint ventures' current tax	19	(86)
Total current tax	6,353	1,474
Deferred tax:		
Origination and reversal of timing differences	(888)	1,575
Adjustments in respect of prior years	121	(222)
Utilisation of tax (assets)/losses	(11)	302
Total deferred tax	(778)	1,655
Tax on profit on ordinary activities	5,575	3,129

(b) Tax included in statement of other comprehensive income	**2017 €'000**	**2016 €'000**
Actuarial (loss)/gain on pension scheme	(245)	78
Total tax (charge/credit in OCI	(245)	78

(c) Factors affecting the total tax charge

The tax assessed for the year is different from the standard rates of corporation tax.

The differences are explained below:

	2017 €'000	2016 €'000
Profit on ordinary activities before tax	24,235	20,926
Profit on ordinary activities multiplied by the Irish standard rate of tax 12.5% (2016: 12.5%)	3,029	2,616
Effects of:		
Tax depreciation in year in excess of depreciation	(1,125)	1,082
Intangibles amortisation in excess of tax deduction	318	184
Tax exempt earnings and credits	(1,749)	(1,642)
Effect of rate change	(734)	–
Differences in effective tax rates on overseas earnings	4,101	371
Expenses not deductible for tax purposes	1,318	350
Adjustments in respcct of prior years	(284)	184
Others	701	(16)
Total Group tax	5,575	3,129

(d) Factors that may affect future tax charges

The Group has tax losses and credits arising in Ireland of €2.3m that are available indefinitely for offset against future taxable profits of those companies in which losses and credits arose and are recognised as part of current assets either falling due within one year or after more than one year based on management's estimation on timing of recoverability.

Current or deferred tax assets are not recognised in respect of losses that arise in certain subsidiaries if there is insufficient certainty as to the timing of the ultimate utilisation of such tax losses.

The Group's overseas tax rates are higher than those in the Republic of Ireland primarily because the profits earned by the Synergy division are taxed at headline rates of 39.22% in the US and 19.25% in the UK. For 2018 these headline rates are projected to be 26.13% and 19% respectively.

No deferred tax is recognised on the unremitted earnings of overseas subsidiaries and joint venture as the Group has no commitment to repatriate funds that will be subject to taxation in Ireland in the foreseeable future.

6.3 LIABILITIES AND EQUITY (SECTION 22)

Scope

Section 22 of FRS 102 establishes the principles for classifying financial instruments as either liabilities or equity and addresses the accounting treatment required for equity instruments issued to individuals as **owners**.

The section is applied when classifying all types of financial instrument except:

(a) interests in subsidiaries, associates and joint ventures (Sections 9, 14 and 15 – see **Chapter 11**);
(b) employers' rights and obligations under employee benefit plans (Section 28 – see **Chapter 8**);
(c) contracts for contingent consideration in a business combination (Section 19 – see **Chapter 11**);
(d) financial instruments, contracts and obligations under share-based payment transactions to which Section 26 applies, except treasury shares purchased, sold, issued or cancelled in connection with employee share option plans, etc. (see **Chapters 12** and **8**);
(e) insurance contracts (see FRS 103 *Insurance Contracts*);
(f) financial instruments with a discretionary participation feature (see FRS 103 *Insurance Contracts*); and
(g) financial guarantee contracts (Section 21 – see above **Section 6.1** 'Provisions and Contingencies').

Classification of an Instrument as a Liability or Equity

Equity is the residual interest in the assets of an entity after deducting all its liabilities. Equity includes share capital and reserves.

A liability is a present obligation arising from past events, the settlement of which is expected to result in an outflow from the entity of resources embodying economic benefits.

A financial liability is any liability that is:

(a) a contractual obligation:
   (i) to deliver cash or another financial assets to another entity, or
   (ii) to exchange financial assets/financial liabilities under conditions that are potentially unfavourable to the entity; or
(b) a contract that will, or may be, settled in the entity's own equity instruments and:
   (i) a non-derivative under which the entity is, or may be, obliged to deliver a variable number of the entity's own equity instruments, or
   (ii) a derivative which will, or may, be settled other than by the exchange of a fixed amount of cash or another financial asset for a fixed number of the entity's own equity instruments. For this purpose the entity's own equity instruments do not include instruments that are themselves contracts for the future receipt or delivery of the entity's own equity instruments.

An additional paragraph, introduced in the March 2018 version of FRS 102, requires that a financial instrument, where the issuer does not have an unconditional right to avoid settling in cash or by delivery of another financial asset and where settlement is dependent on the occurrence or non-occurrence of uncertain future events beyond the control of the issuer and the holder, is classified as a financial liability unless:

"(a) the part of the contingent settlement provision that could require settlement in cash or another financial asset is not genuine;
(b) the issuer can be required to settle in cash or another financial asset only in the event of liquidation; or
(c) the instrument has all the features and meets the conditions in the previous paragraph."

Some financial instruments that meet the definition of a **liability** are classified as equity because they represent the residual interest in the net assets of the entity:

(a) a puttable instrument is a financial instrument that gives the holder the right to sell that instrument back to the issuer for cash or another financial asset, or one that is automatically redeemed or repurchased by the issuer on the occurrence of an uncertain future event or the death or retirement of the instrument holder. A puttable instrument that has all of the following features is classified as an equity instrument:
   (i) it entitles the holder to a pro rata share of the entity's net assets in the event of the entity's liquidation,
   (ii) the instrument is subordinate to all other classes of instruments,
   (iii) all financial instruments in the class that is subordinate to all other classes of instruments have identical features,
   (iv) apart from the contractual obligation for the issuer to repurchase or redeem the instrument for cash or another financial asset, the instrument does not include any contractual obligation to deliver cash or another financial asset to another entity, or to exchange financial assets or financial liabilities with another entity under conditions that are potentially unfavourable to the entity, and it is not a contract that will or may be settled in the entity's own equity instruments,
   (v) the total expected cash flows attributable to the instrument over the life of the instrument are based substantially on the profit or loss, the change in the recognised net assets or the change in the fair value of the recognised and unrecognised net assets of the entity over the life of the instrument (excluding any effects of the instrument);
(b) instruments, or components of instruments, that are subordinate to all other classes of instruments are classified as equity if they impose on the entity an obligation to deliver to another party a pro-rata share of the net assets of the entity only on liquidation.

Examples of instruments classified as liabilities rather than equity include the following:

(a) An instrument is classified as a liability if the distribution of net assets on liquidation is subject to a ceiling, e.g. a pro rata share of the net assets, but this amount is limited to a ceiling and the excess distributed to a charity organisation or the government. The instrument is not classified as equity.

(b) A puttable instrument is classified as equity if, when the put option is exercised, the holder receives a pro rata share of the net assets of the entity measured in accordance with FRS 102. However, if the holder is entitled to an amount measured on some other basis (such as local GAAP), the instrument is classified as a liability.
(c) An instrument is classified as a liability if it obliges the entity to make payments to the holder before liquidation, such as a mandatory dividend.
(d) A puttable instrument that is classified as equity in a subsidiary's financial statements is classified as a liability in the consolidated group financial statements.
(e) A preference share that provides for mandatory redemption by the issuer for a fixed or determinable amount at a fixed or determinable future date, or that gives the holder the right to require the issuer to redeem the instrument at or after a particular date for a fixed or determinable amount, is a financial liability.

Members' shares in co-operative entities are equity if:
(a) the entity has an unconditional right to refuse redemption of the members' shares; or
(b) redemption is unconditionally prohibited by local law, regulation or the entity's governing charter.

Original Issue of Shares or Other Equity Instruments

An entity should recognise the issue of shares when it issues those instruments and another party is obliged to provide cash or other resources to the entity in exchange for the instruments:
(a) if the cash is received before the instruments are issued, there should be a corresponding increase in equity to the extent of any consideration received;
(b) to the extent that instruments have been subscribed to but no cash has been provided, no increase in equity should be recognised.

Equity should be measured at the fair value of the cash or other resources received or receivable net of direct costs of issue. If payment is deferred and the time value of money is significant, then it should be measured on a present value basis.

However, that does not apply to transactions where a financial liability has been extinguished (partially or in full) by the issue of equity instruments if:

"(a) the creditor is also a direct or indirect shareholder and is acting in its capacity as a direct or indirect existing shareholder;
(b) the creditor and the entity are controlled by the same party or parties before and after the transaction and the substance of the transaction includes an equity distribution by, or contribution to, the entity; or
(c) it is extinguished in accordance with the original terms of the financial liability."

In these circumstances no gain or loss is recognised in profit or loss as the result of such a transaction.

Transaction costs should be treated as a deduction from equity net of any income tax benefit.

The presentation of equity depends on applicable laws, e.g. par value of shares separate from the excess of the amount paid (share premium).

Exercise of Options, Rights and Warrants

The principles on original issue of shares should be applied to equity issued by means of the sale of options, rights, warrants and similar equity instruments.

Bonus Issues of Shares and Share Splits

Bonus issues of shares and share splits do not change total equity, but an entity should reclassify within equity as required by applicable laws.

Convertible Debt or Similar Compound Financial Instruments

A compound financial instrument has elements of both equity and debt and thus the proceeds should be allocated between both the liability and equity components. The liability component should first be determined based on the fair value of a similar liability that does not have an associated equity component. The residual amount is therefore the equity component.

The allocation between liability and equity should not be revised in a subsequent period.

In the periods after issuance, the entity should account for the liability component in accordance with Sections 11 and 12 of FRS 102 (see **Chapter 11**), as appropriate.

The Appendix to Section 22 provides an example of an issuer accounting for convertible debt, which is reproduced below.

Example 6.24: Issuer's Accounting for Convertible Debt

On 1 January 20X5 an entity issues 500 convertible bonds. The bonds are issued at par with a face value of €100 per bond and are for a five-year term, with no transaction costs. The total proceeds from the issue are €50,000. Interest is payable annually in arrears at an annual interest rate of 4%. Each bond is convertible, at the holder's discretion, into 25 ordinary shares at any time up to maturity. At the time the bonds are issued, the market interest rate for similar debt that does not have the conversion option is 6%.

When the instrument is issued, the liability component must be valued first, and the difference between the total proceeds on issue (which is the fair value of the instrument in its entirety) and the fair value of the liability component is assigned to the equity component. The fair value of the liability component is calculated by determining its present value using the discount rate of 6% [i.e. the normal loan rate]. The calculations and journal entries are illustrated below:

	€
Proceeds from the bond issue (A)	50,000
Present value of principal at the end of five years (see calculations below)	37,363
Present value of interest payable annually in arrears for five years	8,425
Present value of liability, which is the fair value of liability component (B)	45,788
Residual, which is the fair value of the equity component (A) – (B)	4,212

The issuer of the bonds makes the following journal entry at issue on 1 January 20X5:

Dr	Cash	€50,000	
	Cr Financial Liability – Convertible bond		€45,788
	Cr Equity		€4,212

The CU4,212 represents a discount on issue of the bonds, so the entry could also be shown 'gross':

Dr Cash	€50,000	
Dr Financial Liability – Convertible bond discount	€4,212	
Cr Financial Liability – Convertible bond		€50,000
Cr Equity		€4,212

After issue, the issuer will amortise the bond discount according to the following table:

	(a) Interest payment	(b) Total interest expense 6% × (e)	(c) Amortisation of bond discount (b) – (a)	(d) Bond discount (d) – (c)	(e) Net liability €50,000 – (d)
	€	€	€	€	€
01/01/2019				4,212	45,788
31/12/2019	2,000	2,747	747	3,465	46,535
31/12/2020	2,000	2,792	792	2,673	47,327
31/12/2021	2,000	2,840	840	1,833	48,167
31/12/2022	2,000	2,890	890	943	49,057
31/12/2023	2,000	2,943	943	0	50,000
Totals	10,000	14,212	4,212		

At the end of 20X5, the issuer would make the following journal entry:

Dr	Interest expense		€2,747	
	Cr	Bond discount		€747
	Cr	Cash		€2,000

Calculations

The present value of principal of €50,000 at 6%

€50,000/(1.06)^5 = €37,363

The present value of the interest annuity of €2,000 (= €50,000 × 4%) payable at the end of each of five years

The €2,000 annual interest payments are an annuity – a cash flow stream with a limited number (n) of periodic payments (C), receivable at dates 1 to n. To calculate the present value (PV) of this annuity, future payments are discounted by the periodic rate of interest (i) using the following formula:

$PV = C/i\ (1 - 1/(1+i)^n)$

Therefore, the present value of the €2,000 interest payments is (€2,000/0.06) × (1 – ((1/1.06)^5)) = €8,425

This is equivalent to the sum of the present values of the five individual €2,000 payments, as follows:

	€
Present value of interest payment at 31 December 20X5 = 2,000/1.06	1,887
Present value of interest payment at 31 December 20X6 = 2,000/1.06^2	1,780
Present value of interest payment at 31 December 20X7 = 2,000/1.06^3	1,679
Present value of interest payment at 31 December 20X8 = 2,000/1.06^4	1,584
Present value of interest payment at 31 December 20X9 = 2,000/1.06^5	1,495
Total	8,425

Yet another way to calculate this is to use a table of present value of an ordinary annuity in arrears, five periods, interest rate of 6% per period. (Such tables are easily found on the Internet.) The present value factor is 4.2124. Multiplying this by the annuity payment of €2,000 determines the present value of €8,425.

An Irish example of how a convertible loan must be split between its equity and liability components was provided by Providence Resources Plc in its *Annual Report 2010*.

Providence Resources Plc

Annual Report 2010

CONSOLIDATED STATEMENT OF FINANCIAL POSITION (EXTRACT)
at 31 December 2010

Equity	Note	2010	2009
		€'000	€'000
Share capital	19	15,058	14,609
Capital conversion reserve fund		623	623
Share premium	19	86,918	71,836
Singleton revaluation reserve		2,919	3,066
Convertible bond – equity portion		2,944	2,944
Foreign currency translation reserve		(2,122)	(1,906)
Share-based payment reserve		3,537	2,519
Loan warrant reserve		5,641	5,641
Cashflow hedge reserve		(3,255)	(588)
Retained deficit		(136,001)	(94,547)
Total equity attributable to equity holders of the Company		(23,738)	4,197

[…]

NOTES TO THE CONSOLIDATED FINANCIAL STATEMENTS (EXTRACT)

1. Statement of accounting policies (Extract)

Financial instruments

[…]

(ii) Compound financial instruments

Compound financial instruments issued by the Group comprise convertible bonds that can be converted to share capital at the option of the holder, and where the number of shares to be issued does not vary with changes in their fair value.

The liability component of a compound financial instrument is recognised initially at the fair value of a similar liability that does not have an equity conversion option. The equity component is recognised initially as the difference between the fair value of the compound financial instrument as a whole and the fair value of the liability component. Any directly attributable transaction costs are allocated to the liability and equity components in proportion to their initial carrying amounts.

Subsequent to initial recognition, the liability component of a compound financial instrument is measured at amortised cost using the effective interest method. The equity component of a compound financial instrument is not remeasured subsequent to initial recognition.

21. Loans and borrowings

	BNP revolving credit facility (a) €'000	BNP loan fees €'000	Convertible bond (b) €'000	Former revolving credit facility €'000	Related revolving credit facility fees €'000	Bridging loan €'000	Deferred financing costs €'000	Total €'000
At 1 January 2009	–	–	37,654	40,858	(98)	11,497	(571)	89,340
Drawn down during year	43,910	(2,535)	–	5,868	–	–	–	47,243
Repaid during year	–	–	–	(44,499)	–	(11,819)	–	(56,318)
Written off to income statement	–	127	990	–	98	–	571	1,786
Foreign exchange	640	–	–	(2,227)	–	322	–	(1,265)
At 31 December 2009	44,550	(2,408)	38,644	–	–	–	–	80,786
Refund during year	(406)	406	–	–	–	–	–	–
Written off to income statement	–	405	1,158	–	–	–	–	1,563
Foreign exchange differences	3,438	–	–	–	–	–	–	3,438
At 31 December 2010	**47,582**	**(1,597)**	**39,802**	**–**	**–**	**–**	**–**	**85,787**

[...]

(b) In July 2008, the Group placed convertible bonds with institutional investors to raise €42 million. The bonds, denominated in units of €100,000 each, carry interest of 12% per annum, payable semi-annually in arrears, and mature on 29 July 2012. On maturity, all outstanding bonds are redeemed at par plus all accrued and unpaid interest. At the election of the holder, the bonds are convertible into ordinary shares of nominal value (€0.001) at a conversion price of €0.10 per ordinary share at any time after 29 September 2008. The bonds are secured on the Group's exploration asset located in Africa. The Group has applied IAS 32 in its accounting treatment of these instruments and has classified these as compound instruments. The directors determined that a market interest rate of 15% would apply to a similar instrument without the convertibility element and used this rate to arrive at the debt component of the instrument which is classified within loans and borrowings in the amount of €39.8 million. The proceeds less the debt component determine the equity portion of the instrument amounting to €2.9 million.

Treasury Shares

Treasury shares are shares issued by the reporting entity but subsequently reacquired by the entity. The fair value of the consideration given for the treasury shares should be deducted from equity and no gain or loss should be recorded in profit or loss.

Distributions to Owners

An entity should reduce equity for the amount of distributions to its owners net of any related income tax benefits. If non-cash assets are distributed, these should be recognised at fair value.

Non-controlling Interest (NCI) and Transactions in the Shares of a Consolidated Subsidiary

NCI is included in equity. Any changes in a parent's controlling interest that do not result in a loss of control should be treated as transactions with equity holders in their capacity as equity holders. No gain or loss should be recognised on these changes in consolidated profit or loss. Also an entity must not recognise any change in the carrying amounts of assets or liabilities as a result of such transactions. In effect, piecemeal acquisition is no longer acceptable under either the FRS or full IFRS.

Any difference between the adjusted NCI and fair value of consideration paid/received is recognised directly in equity. No change in the carrying amount of net assets should be made.

6.4 SMALL ENTITIES

There are no explicit minimum disclosure requirements for small entities under FRS 102 Section 1A, for either the UK or the Republic of Ireland. However, small entities may need to provide disclosures as required by FRS 102, Sections 31, 29 and 22 if required to give a true and fair view. There are disclosures required regarding financial liabilities (these are covered in **Chapter 12**).

6.5 MICRO-ENTITIES

Under FRS 105 the accounting treatment for provisions, contingent liabilities and contingent assets is identical to that in FRS 102. Similarly, no material differences exist in accounting for equity and liabilities.

Micro-entities are not permitted to recognise deferred tax nor to discount current tax assets and liabilities.

In addition, the sections in FRS 105 on withholding tax on dividends and accounting for VAT are included in line with the provisions in FRS 102.

Disclosure Checklist: Liabilities – FRS 102

(References are to the relevant Section of FRS 102)

	Para.
Provisions and Contingencies – Section 21	
Disclosures about provisions	
For each class of provision, an entity shall disclose all of the following: (a) a reconciliation showing: (i) the carrying amounts at the beginning and end of the period, (ii) additions during the period, including adjustments that result from changes in measuring the discounted amount, (iii) amounts charged against the provision during the period, and (iv) unused amounts reversed during the period; (b) a brief description of the nature of the obligation and the expected amount and timing of any resulting payments; (c) an indication of the uncertainties about the amount or timing of those outflows; and (d) the amount of any expected reimbursement, stating the amount of any asset that has been recognised for that expected reimbursement. Comparative information for prior periods is not required.	21.14
Disclosures about contingent liabilities	
Unless the possibility of any outflow of resources in settlement is remote, an entity shall disclose, for each class of contingent liability at the reporting date, a brief description of the nature of the contingent liability and, when practicable: (a) an estimate of its financial effect, measured in accordance with paragraphs 21.7–21.11; (b) an indication of the uncertainties relating to the amount or timing of any outflow; and (c) the possibility of any reimbursement. If it is impracticable to make one or more of these disclosures, that fact shall be stated.	21.15
Disclosures about contingent assets	
If an inflow of economic benefits is probable (more likely than not) but not virtually certain, an entity shall disclose a description of the nature of the contingent assets at the end of the reporting period and, when practicable without undue cost or effort, an estimate of their financial effect, measured using the principles set out in paragraphs 21.7–21.11. If it is impracticable to make this disclosure, that fact shall be stated.	21.16

	PARA.
Prejudicial disclosures	
In extremely rare cases, disclosure of some or all of the information required by paragraphs 21.14 to 21.16 can be expected to prejudice seriously the position of the entity in a dispute with other parties on the subject matter of the provision, contingent liability or contingent asset. In such cases, an entity need not disclose all of the information required by those paragraphs insofar as it relates to the dispute, but shall disclose at least the following. In relation to provisions, the following information shall be given: (a) a table showing the reconciliation required by paragraph 21.14(a) in aggregate, including the source and application of any amounts transferred to or from provisions during the reporting period; (b) particulars of each provision in any case where the amount of the provision is material; and (c) the fact that, and reason why, the information required by paragraph 21.14 has not been disclosed. In relation to contingent liabilities, the following information shall be given: "(a) particulars and the total amount of any contingent liabilities (excluding those which arise out of insurance contracts) that are not included in the statement of financial position; (b) the total amount of contingent liabilities which are undertaken on behalf of or for the benefit of: (i) any parent or fellow subsidiary of the entity; (ii) any subsidiary of the entity; or (iii) any entity in which the reporting entity has a participating interest, shall each be stated separately; and (c) the fact that, and reason why, the information required by paragraph 21.15 has not been disclosed." In relation to contingent assets, the entity shall disclose the general nature of the dispute, together with the fact that, and reason why, the information required by paragraph 21.16 has not been disclosed.	21.17
Disclosure about financial guarantee contracts	
An entity shall disclose the nature and business purpose of the financial guarantee contracts it has issued. If applicable, an entity shall also provide the disclosures required by paragraphs 21.14 and 21.15.	21.17A
Income Tax – Section 29	
An entity shall disclose information that enables users of its financial statements to evaluate the nature and financial effect of the current and deferred tax consequences of recognised transactions and other events.	29.25
An entity shall disclose separately the major components of tax expense (income). Such components of tax expense (income) may include: (a) current tax expense/income; (b) any adjustments recognised in the period for current tax of prior periods; (c) the amount of deferred tax expense/income relating to the origination and reversal of timing differences; (d) the amount of deferred tax expense/income relating to changes in tax rates or the imposition of new taxes; (e) adjustments to deferred tax expense arising from a change in the tax status of the entity or its shareholders; and (f) the amount of tax expense relating to changes in accounting policies and errors (see Section 10, Accounting Policies, Estimates and Errors).	29.26

	PARA.
An entity shall disclose the following separately, where material: (a) the aggregate current and deferred tax relating to items that are recognised as items of other comprehensive income; (b) a reconciliation between: (i) the tax expense/income included in profit or loss, and (ii) the profit or loss on ordinary activities before tax multiplied by the applicable tax rate; (c) the amount of the net reversal of deferred tax assets and deferred tax liabilities expected to occur during the year beginning after the reporting period together with a brief explanation for the expected reversal; (d) an explanation of changes in the applicable tax rate(s) compared with the previous reporting period; (e) the amount of deferred tax liabilities and deferred tax assets at the end of the reporting period for each type of timing difference and for each type of unused tax loss and tax credit; (f) the expiry date, if any, of timing differences, unused tax losses and unused tax credits and (g) in the circumstances described in paragraph 29.14, an explanation of the nature of the potential income tax consequences that would result from the payment of dividends to its shareholders.	29.27
Liabilities and Equity – Section 22	
There are no presentation or disclosure requirements in this Section but see Section 4 *Statement of Financial Position*,paragraph 4.12 dealing with disclosures for share capital – see **Chapter 1.**	

Disclosure Checklist: Liabilities – Small Entities

(References are to the relevant Appendix of Section 1A FRS 102)

The mandatory disclosure requirements for small entities required under the Companies Act 2014 (ROI) (CA 2014), the Companies Act 2006 (UK) (CA 2006) and the Small Companies and Groups (Accounts and Directors' Report) Regulations 2008 (UK) (S.I. No. 409 of 2008) are as follows:

	Para.
Indebtedness, guarantees and financial commitments	
In respect of each item shown under 'creditors' in the small entity's statement of financial position there shall be stated the aggregate amount of any debts included under 'creditors' which fall due for payment or repayment after the end of the period of five years beginning with the day next following the reporting date. (Schedule 3A, paragraph 50(1) CA 2014) (Schedule 1, paragraph 55(1) S.I. 409/2008)	1AD.26 (ROI) 1AC.27 (UK) (similar)
In respect of each item shown under 'creditors' in the small entity's statement of financial position there shall be stated: (a) the aggregate amount of any debts included under that item in respect of which any security has been given; and (b) an indication of the nature of the securities so given. (Schedule 3A, paragraph 50(2) CA 2014) (Schedule 1, paragraph 55(2) S.I. 409/2008) Paragraphs 11.46, 13.22(e), 16.10(c), 17.32(a) and 18.28(c) address similar requirements.	1AD.27 (ROI) 1AC.28 (UK) (similar)
Particulars and the total amount or estimated total amount shall be given with respect to any other financial commitment, guarantee or contingency not provided for in the statement of financial position. (Schedule 3A, paragraph 51(2) CA 2014) (Schedule 1, paragraph 57(1) S.I. 409/2008) The aggregate amount of any such commitments, guarantees or contingencies which are undertaken on behalf of or for the benefit of: (a) any parent or fellow subsidiary of the small entity; (b) any subsidiary of the small entity; or (c) any undertaking in which the small entity has a participating interest, shall be separately stated and those within each of clause (a), (b) and (c) shall also be stated separately from those within any other of those clauses. (Schedule 3A, paragraph 51(7) CA 2014) (Schedule 1, paragraph 57(7) S.I. 409/2008)	1AD.29 (ROI) 1AC.29 (UK) (similar)
An indication of the nature and form of any valuable security given by the small entity in respect of commitments, guarantees and contingencies not provided for in the statement of financial position shall be given. (Schedule 3A, paragraph 51(3) CA 2014) Paragraphs 11.46, 13.22(e), 16.10(c), 17.32(a) and 18.28(c) of Section 1A FRS 102 address similar requirements.	1AD.30 (ROI) 1AC.30 (UK) (similar)

	PARA.
The total amount of any commitments not provided for in the statement of financial position concerning retirement benefits shall be disclosed separately. (Schedule 3A, paragraph 51(4) CA 2014)	1AD.31 (ROI only)
Particulars, including details of significant assumptions underlying the valuation models shall be given of retirement benefit commitments which are included in the statement of financial position. (Schedule 3A, paragraph 51(5) CA 2014)	1AD.32 (ROI only)
Where any commitment referred to in paragraph 1AD.31 or 1AD.32 relates wholly or partly to retirement benefits payable to past directors of the company, separate particulars shall be given of that commitment. (Schedule 3A, paragraph 51(6) CA 2014) Such commitments as referred to in 1AD.29 to 1AD.33 can arise in a variety of situations, including in relation to group entities, investments, property, plant and equipment, leases and retirement benefit obligations. Paragraphs 15.19(d), 16.10(d), 17.32(b), 18.28(d), 20.16, 21.15, 28.40A(a), 28.40A(b), 28.41A(d), 33.9(b)(ii) and 34.62 address similar requirements. Paragraph 28.41(k) addresses similar requirements for the assumptions underlying retirement benefit commitments recognised in the statement of financial position.	1AD.33 (ROI only)
The nature and business purpose of any arrangements of a small entity that are not included in its statement of financial position shall be provided in the notes to the financial statements if the risks or benefits arising from such arrangements are material and in so far as the disclosure of such risks or benefits is necessary for assessing the financial position of the small entity. (Sections 323(1) and 323(1A) CA 2014) (Section 410A CA 2006) Examples of off-balance sheet arrangements include risk and benefit-sharing arrangements or obligations arising from a contract such as debt factoring, combined sale and repurchase arrangements, consignment stock arrangements, take or pay arrangements, securitisation arranged through separate entities, pledged assets, operating lease arrangements, outsourcing and the like. In many cases the disclosures about financial commitments and contingencies required by paragraphs 1AD.28 to 1AD.33 (1AC.29 and 1AC.30) will also address such arrangements.	1AD.34 (ROI) 1AC.31 (UK) (similar)

DISCLOSURE CHECKLIST: LIABILITIES – MICRO-ENTITIES

(References are to the relevant Section of FRS 105)

The mandatory disclosure requirements for micro-entities required under FRS 105, the Companies Act 2014 (ROI) (CA 2014), the Companies Act 2006 (UK) (CA 2006) and the Small Companies and Groups (Accounts and Directors' Report) Regulations 2008 (UK) (S.I. No. 409 of 2008) are as follows:

	PARA.
A micro-entity shall disclose information in relation to financial commitments, guarantees and contingencies not recognised in the statement of financial position in accordance with the relevant appendix to Section 6 *Notes to the Financial Statements*. A micro-entity is not required to disclose the amount of a contingent liability when the possibility of an outflow of resources is remote.	16.19
An Irish micro-entity shall disclose information in relation to dividends paid or payable in accordance with Appendix B to Section 6 *Notes to the Financial Statements*.	17.16 (ROI only)

Chapter 7

PERFORMANCE MEASUREMENT

7.1 REVENUE (SECTION 23)

Section 23 *Revenue* should be applied in accounting for revenue from the following sources:

(a) sale of goods;
(b) rendering of services;
(c) construction contracts; and
(d) interest, royalties and dividends.

Revenues from the following types of transaction are dealt with in other sections of FRS 102:

(a) lease agreements (Section 20 – see **Chapter 4**);
(b) dividends arising from the use of the equity method (Sections 14 and 15 – see **Chapter 11**);
(c) changes in the fair value of financial assets and liabilities or their disposal (Sections 11 and 12 – see **Chapter 12**);
(d) changes in the fair value of investment property (Section 16 – see **Chapter 3**);
(e) the initial recognition and changes in the fair value of biological assets (Section 34 – see **Chapter 13**); and
(f) the initial recognition of agricultural produce (Section 34 – see **Chapter 13**).

FRS 102 also excludes revenue or other income arising from transactions and events dealt with in FRS 103 *Insurance Contracts.*

EXAMPLE 7.1: DIFFERENT TYPES OF REVENUE

Pickwick Ltd sells data projectors but also hires them out over a period of three years. At the end of three years the hired projectors are sold as second-hand models. There are, therefore, three major sources of income – **rental, sale of new projectors** and **sale of second-hand models**. All of these should be treated as revenue under the FRS.

Measurement of Revenue

Revenue should be measured at the fair value of consideration received or receivable. It should, however, exclude any trade discounts and volume rebates.

Only the gross inflows on an entity's own account are permitted to be included in revenue. Any amounts collected on behalf of third parties, such as sales tax and VAT, are excluded.

Example 7.2: Discounts

Browndod Ltd sells one of its products for €1,000 per unit. However, it offers a 25% discount on orders of 500 units or more. On purchases over 5,000 units per annum a further volume discount of 10% is provided on the list price for all units purchased in that financial year.

Assume a customer buys 500 units each month for one annual financial reporting period.

Solution

In this case the revenue must be recorded as follows:

500 units × 12 months	=	6,000 units
6,000 units × € 1,000	=	€6,000,000
€6,000,000 less 35% discount	=	€3,900,000

Example 7.3: Goods Sold on Consignment

Ballintoy Ltd sells goods on consignment to Dunseverick Ltd. Dunseverick can return any goods unsold, but is forced by Ballintoy to sell at a fixed price of €50 per unit. Commission of €5 for each unit sold is deducted by Dunseverick and the balance paid to Ballintoy. Any defective goods are returned to Ballintoy for repair or replacement.

Solution

This is a principal–agent relationship as Ballintoy is exposed to all the major risks associated with the sale of goods. Therefore, Ballintoy Ltd can only record revenue when its agent, Dunseverick Ltd, sells the goods on to the ultimate customer – recording €50 sales on that date as well as €5 commission expenses. A provision for repairs should also be created based on the likely cost of making good any repairs.

Deferred Payment

Where the inflow is deferred and the arrangement, in effect, constitutes a financing transaction, the fair value of the consideration is the present value of all future receipts determined using an imputed rate of interest, e.g. a provision of interest-free credit to the buyer. The imputed rate of interest is the more clearly determinable of either:

(a) the prevailing rate for a similar instrument of an issuer with similar credit rating; or
(b) a rate of interest that discounts the nominal amount of the instrument to the current cash sales price of the goods or services.

The difference between the present value of all future receipts and the nominal value of the consideration should be recognised as interest revenue.

EXAMPLE 7.4: DEFERRED PAYMENT

Ballyvoy Ltd sold goods for €100,000 on a two-years-free credit period. The current cash price would have been €82,645.

Solution

The difference of €17,355 is a finance transaction and **not** a sale. Ballyvoy Ltd should recognise sales of €82,645 on the day the goods are delivered and, after imputing interest at 10%, will record interest received of €8,264 in one year's time and €9,091 in two years' time.

Exchanges of Goods or Services

Revenue should not be recognised when goods or services are exchanged or swapped for similar goods or services. An entity should recognise revenue, however, for dissimilar goods or services. In that case, fair value should be adopted unless (a) the exchange lacks commercial substance or (b) the fair value of neither the asset received nor the asset given up is reliably measured. If these cannot be measured at their fair value, then they should be measured at the carrying amount of the asset given up.

EXAMPLE 7.5: EXCHANGE OF GOODS FOR SERVICES

Basil Ltd has exchanged 50 units of a product for 50 man hours of a solicitor's services. The legal services would normally be charged at €1,000 per hour.

Solution

These are dissimilar activities, so Basil Ltd should record revenue of 50 man hours × €1,000 per hour = €50,000.

On the other hand, if a retailer runs out of milk and borrows milk from another retailer but promises to return a similar quantity the next day, there is no revenue or expense recorded as these are exchanges of similar goods.

Identification of the Revenue Transaction

Usually the revenue recognition criteria are applied separately to each transaction. However, if necessary, the criteria should be applied to separately identifiable components of a single transaction, reflecting their different substance, e.g. when the selling price of a product includes an identifiable amount for subsequent servicing. Conversely, two or more transactions are combined when an entity sells goods and agrees legally to repurchase the goods at a later date, thus negating the substantive effect of the transaction.

Example 7.6: Separate Components of a Contract

A local dealer in PCs sells a new PC to a customer but also promises to maintain the PC for three years from the date of purchase. Normally the dealer is able to charge separately for the two elements of the contract and the customer could purchase either element separately.

Solution

The sale should be split into two separate elements – the sale of a PC and the sale of a maintenance contract. The dealer should recognise the maintenance element at fair value and deduct that from the sale of the PC. The revenue from the maintenance contract must be spread over three years.

Example 7.7: Sale and Repurchase Agreement

Millsbush Ltd is a whiskey distiller. The manufacturing process for its single malt is three years. The whiskey is sold at cost plus 60%.

On the first day of its accounting period Millsbush Ltd sold 100,000 litres of one-year-old whiskey to Irishbank on the following terms:

- Sale price €500,000 (i.e. cost).
- Millsbush has the option to repurchase the whiskey at any time over the next two years at cost plus a mark-up of €120,000.
- The mark-up is based on an annual rate of interest of 12% and will be prorated (i.e. time-apportioned). Irishbank also has the option to sell the whiskey back to Millsbush in two years' time at a price based on a similar formula.

Solution

Initial sale:

Dr	Cash		€500,000	
	Cr	Payables		€500,000

Being the artificial sale recorded under substance as a loan.

At year end:

Dr	Income		€60,000	
	Cr	Payables		€60,000

Being the notional interest incurred of 12% (per annum for two years).

Repurchase:

Dr	Payables		€620,000	
	Cr	Cash		€620,000

Being the repayment of the loan and accumulated notional interest incurred.

Ultimate sale:

Dr	Cash		€800,000	
	Cr	Sales		€800,000

Being the ultimate sale of whiskey to third parties.

For customer loyalty payments, entities should account for the award separately and allocate the fair value of the consideration receivable/received on the initial sale between the award credits and the other components of the sale.

The consideration allocated should be measured by reference to the fair value, i.e. the amount for which the awards could be separately sold.

EXAMPLE 7.8: CUSTOMER LOYALTY CARDS

Café Nous provides its customers with customer loyalty cards and for every 10 cups of coffee a free 11th cup is provided. Assume the cups of coffee are sold, on average, for €2 each, and that at the end of the reporting period 500 customers have cards with approximately 50% completed. It is estimated, from past experience, that 70% of customers use the award system.

Solution

The provision should be calculated as follows and deducted from the total sales for the year:

500 customers × 0.5 free cups (50% completed cards) × 70% take up × €2 = €350.

Sale of Goods

Revenue can only be recognised for the sale of goods when all of the following conditions are satisfied:

(a) the entity has **transferred** to the buyer the **significant risks and rewards** of ownership;
(b) the entity has **retained neither continuing managerial involvement nor effective control** over the goods sold;
(c) the amount of **revenue** can be **measured reliably**;
(d) it is **probable** that the **economic benefits will flow** to the entity; and
(e) the **costs** incurred can be **reliably measured**.

The assessment of whether or not significant risks/rewards are transferred depends on the circumstances of each transaction. That mostly coincides with the transfer of the legal title or the passing of possession, but in other cases it could be at a different time.

Revenue should not be recognised if the entity retains significant risks. Examples of this are:

(a) when the entity retains an obligation for unsatisfactory performance not covered by normal warranties;
(b) when the receipt from revenue is contingent on the buyer selling the goods (e.g. some consignment sales);
(c) when the goods are shipped subject to installation and this represents a significant part of the contract not yet completed; and
(d) when the buyer has the right to rescind the purchase (via contract) and the entity is uncertain about the probability of return.

However, if the entity retains only an insignificant risk of ownership, the transaction is a sale, e.g. when the entity retains legal title solely to protect collectability of the debt due (reservation of title clauses) or if it offers a refund if a customer is not satisfied. However, a provision should separately be considered under Section 21 – see **Chapter 6**.

Examples: Various Types of Sales Contract

1. Sale of goods where the buyer delays delivery

Company A sells goods to Company B. B requests A to hold delivery of the goods while it is preparing its site to be ready for delivery. Company B formally accepts responsibility for the goods on the invoice date on the basis that it would be the usual delivery date.

Assuming the other revenue recognition criteria are met, A recognises revenue on the invoice date because, at that date, it has transferred the significant risks and rewards of ownership to B and it is probable that future economic benefits will flow.

2. Consignment sales

Company A sells goods to Company B. The agreement between the two parties states that B will hold these goods on consignment and will only pay for the goods to the extent that B sells the goods on to third parties.

Assume A has not transferred the significant risks and rewards of ownership to B on delivery, and it is not probable that future economic benefits will flow; nor can the revenue be reliably measured because B will only pay for the goods when it sells them to third parties. In that case, until B sells the goods, it has no requirement to pay A. Accordingly, A does not recognise any revenue until B has sold the goods on to third parties.

3. Payments in advance

Company A sells goods to Company B with the agreement that B pays for the goods in advance of delivery, which will occur in 12 months' time. The risks and rewards of the goods pass to B at the date of delivery.

B pays €20,000 to A on 1 July 2019. A delivers the goods to B on 1 July 2020. Assume an imputed rate of interest of 4%.

Revenue should not be recognised until the date of delivery and thus the advance payment should be treated as a financing transaction with interest at 4% accruing on it.

The following **journal entries** are required:

				€	€
1 July 2019					
	Dr	Cash		20,000	
	Dr	Interest expense (4% × €20,000)		800	
		Cr	Deferred income		20,800
1 July 2020					
	Dr	Deferred income		20,800	
		Cr	Revenue		20,000
		Cr	Interest received		800

Example 7.9: Various Scenarios on Completion of Manufacturing Process

Dark Hedges Ltd manufactures specialist equipment for the oil industry. The equipment is manufactured on the customer's site and legal title passes when final installation and inspection is complete. There is also a two-year warranty to repair any defects.

Scenario 1
On inspection the customer accepts delivery – Dark Hedges Ltd records revenue, but also recognises a provision for its warranty obligation.

Scenario 2
The customer discovers a defect the year after the sale. This has no impact on revenue, but the warranty provision needs to be adjusted.

Scenario 3
On inspection the customer was not satisfied and did not accept delivery – no revenue can be recognised by Dark Hedges Ltd as risks are not transferred; also, no provision should be created for the warranty.

Scenario 4
The customer accepted delivery but went into liquidation before paying for the equipment. Dark Hedges Ltd should still recognise revenue but, in addition, it should also provide for the irrecoverable receivable under Section 11 of the IFRS – see **Chapter 12.**

Rendering of Services

When the outcome can be reliably estimated, an entity should recognise revenue according to the stage of completion of the services. That outcome can only be reliably measured if the following conditions are satisfied:

(a) the amount of **revenue** can be **measured reliably**;
(b) it is **probable** that the **benefits will flow** to the entity;
(c) the **stage of completion** can be **measured reliably**; and
(d) the **costs incurred** and to complete the services can be **measured reliably.**

Example 7.10: Maintenance Contract

Fire Extinguisher Ltd agree to check the fire extinguishers and fire-fighting equipment at a customer's premises every six months over a four-year period. The client paid €8,000 in advance for the full contract.

Solution

Initially the €8,000 should be recorded as a liability (deferred income) as no services have been rendered. As each inspection of the equipment takes place, Fire Extinguisher Ltd should record €1,000 revenue with the balance remaining in deferred income.

When services are performed by an indeterminate number of acts, revenue should be recognised on a straight-line basis over the specified period unless there is evidence to the contrary that an alternative method is better.

Example 7.11: Maintenance of New Boiler

Moneymore Ltd agrees to maintain a new boiler for their customer over a three-year period. On 1 July the customer paid Moneymore Ltd €2,000. From past experience the company believes that the costs will be on average €200 in the first year, €300 in the second year and €500 in the third year.

Solution

Moneymore Ltd should recognise revenue as follows:

Year 1: €400; Year 2: €600; and Year 3: €1,000

The evidence is available that a straight-line method would not be appropriate as the work is more extensive in the final year.

When the outcome cannot be estimated reliably, revenue can only be recognised to the extent of the expenses recognised that are recoverable.

Example 7.12: Uncertain Outcome

A barrister agrees to represent a number of employees for damage to health from asbestosis. The agreement is that no fee will be paid unless the case is won. The barrister will receive 10% of any damages agreed by the courts.

Solution

No revenue can be recorded by the barrister's firm as it may not be recoverable. Only when the case is won can the firm recognise revenue. On the other hand, had the barrister agreed to charge a fixed fee per hour, then the number of hours worked on the case to date multiplied by the rate per hour would be recorded as revenue.

Example 7.13: Sale of Goods and Services

Company B enters into an agreement to buy goods from Company A for €30,000 on 1 February. Company A delivers the goods on 15 February. Company B pays for the goods on 28 February.

The agreement states that from 15 February when A delivers the goods, it must continue to maintain them for a year. B still pays for the goods on 28 February, but is entitled to a refund of 20% of the amount paid if A does not satisfactorily maintain the goods for the year, as required.

A estimates the fair value of the services to be €8,000, so the following should be recorded in the journal entries:

				€	€
February 15					
	Dr	Receivables from B		30,000	
		Cr	Deferred income		8,000
		Cr	Revenue		22,000
February 28					
	Dr	Bank		30,000	
		Cr	Receivable from B		30,000
Future periods as services are provided					
	Dr	Deferred income		8,000	
		Cr	Revenue		8,000

Construction Contracts

When the outcome of a **construction contract** can be estimated reliably, an entity must recognise contract revenue and contract costs as revenue and expenses respectively by reference to the stage of completion of the contract activity at the end of the reporting period (the 'percentage of completion' method). Reliable estimation of the outcome requires not just reliable estimates of the stage of completion but also future costs and collectibility of billings.

FRS 102 should be applied separately to each construction contract. In some circumstances, however, it is necessary to apply this section to the separately identifiable components of a single contract or to a group of contracts together in order to reflect the substance of the contract.

When a contract covers a number of assets, the construction of each asset must be treated as a separate construction contract when:

(a) separate proposals have been submitted for each asset;
(b) each asset has been subject to separate negotiation, and the contractor and the customer are able to accept or reject that part of the contract relating to each asset; and
(c) the costs and revenues of each asset can be identified.

A **group of contracts** must be treated as a **single** construction contract when:

(a) the group of contracts is negotiated as a single package;
(b) the contracts are so closely interrelated that they are, in effect, part of a single project with an overall profit margin; and
(c) the contracts are performed concurrently or in a continuous sequence.

Percentage of Completion Method

The percentage of completion method is used to recognise revenue from rendering services and from construction contracts. An entity must review and, when necessary, revise the estimates of revenue and costs as the service transaction or construction contract progresses.

An entity must determine the stage of completion using the method that measures most reliably the work performed. Possible methods include:
(a) the proportion that costs incurred for work performed to date bear to the estimated total costs;
(b) surveys of work performed; and
(c) the completion of a physical proportion of the service transaction or contract work.

An entity must recognise costs that relate to future activity as an asset if it is probable that the costs will be recovered.

An entity must immediately expense any costs whose recovery is not probable.

When the outcome of a construction contract cannot be estimated reliably:
(a) an entity must recognise revenue only to the extent of contract costs incurred that will probably be recoverable; and
(b) the entity must recognise contract costs as an expense in the period incurred.

When it is probable that total contract costs will exceed total contract revenue on a construction contract, the expected loss should immediately be recognised as an expense, with a corresponding provision for an onerous contract (Section 21 – see **Chapter 6**).

If the collectibility of contract revenue is no longer probable, the entity must recognise the uncollectible amount as an expense rather than as an adjustment of contract revenue.

Example 7.14: Construction Contracts

Ballyduff Ltd has three contracts to build new schools for the Department of Education. The three projects are the Lee, the Liffey and the Lagan. The following information, as at 31 October 2019, is available for each of the three contracts:

	Lee	Liffey	Lagan
	€m	€m	€m
Contract price	19.80	24.83	15.50
Certified value of work completed	10.30	1.25	10.00
Value of work invoiced	8.30	1.00	10.00
Payments received	6.50	1.00	9.00
Costs to date	7.52	1.33	12.93
Estimated future costs to complete	6.56	9.45	5.27
Recognised in previous year:			
Turnover	5.25		
Profit	1.40		

The Liffey and Lagan contracts commenced during the financial year ended 31 October 2019. The Lee contract commenced during the financial year ended 31 October 2018.

Solution

Ballyduff Ltd has adopted the work certified approach to calculate the percentage of work completed.

Overall contract profit or loss

	Lee	Liffey	Lagan
	€m	€m	€m
Contract price	19.80	24.83	15.50
Costs to date	(7.52)	(1.33)	(12.93)
Estimated future costs to complete	(6.56)	(9.45)	(5.27)
Estimated profit	5.72	14.05	(2.70)
Percentage completed:			
€10.30m/€19.80m	= 52%		
€1.25m/€24.83m		= 5%	
€10.0m/€15.50m			= 64.5%
Profit/(loss) to date:			
€5.72m × 52%	= €2.98m		
€14.05m × 5%		= €0.70m	
			(€2.70m)

PROFIT AND LOSS ACCOUNT (EXTRACT)

	Lee	Liffey	Lagan
	€m	€m	€m
Contract revenue recognised (€10.30m – €5.25m) (work certified)	5.05	1.25	10.00
Contract costs (balancing figures)	(3.47)	(0.55)	(12.70)
Recognised profits/(losses) (€2.98m – €1.40m)	1.58	0.70	(2.70)

BALANCE SHEET (EXTRACT)

	Lee	Liffey	Lagan
	€m	€m	€m
Costs to date	7.52	1.33	12.93
Recognised profits/(losses)	2.98	0.70	(2.70)
Progress billings	(8.30)	(1.00)	(10.00)
Due from customers	2.20	1.03	0.23
Progress billings	8.30	1.00	10.00
Amounts received	6.50	1.00	9.00
Trade receivables	1.80	Nil	1.00

Interest, Royalties and Dividends

Revenue is recognised when:

(a) it is **probable** that **economic benefits** associated with the transaction will **flow** to the entity; and

(b) the **amount** can be **measured reliably**.

Revenue should be recognised on the following bases:

(a) **interest** using the **effective interest** method. Related fees, finance charges paid or received as well as transaction costs and other premiums or discounts are included in calculating the effective interest rate;

(b) **royalties** on an **accruals** basis; and

(c) **dividends receivable** when the shareholder's **right to receive payment** is established.

EXAMPLE 7.15: INTEREST RECEIVABLE UNDER THE EFFECTIVE INTEREST METHOD

Icarus Ltd invests €200,000 in a loan to a local company. The local company cannot afford to pay annual interest (i.e. a zero coupon loan), so has agreed that it will redeem the loan at €268,020 in six years' time.

Solution

In substance, the deep discount of €68,020 is the same as if the company had to pay interest at 5% per annum and thus interest received should be recorded as follows over the six years, using that effective interest rate:

Year 1: €10,000; Year 2: €10,500; Year 3: €11,026; Year 4: €11,576; Year 5: €12,156; and Year 6: €12,762.

EXAMPLE 7.16: DIVIDENDS RECEIVABLE

Tiberius Ltd has a 10% shareholding in Omega Ltd and on 30 December 2019 Omega Ltd announced a proposed dividend of €400,000 for the year ended 31 December 2019. The dividend must first be approved by the shareholders at the annual general meeting in February 2020 before Tiberius is entitled to the dividend. The dividend will be paid out on 15 May 2020.

Solution

Assuming both companies have December year ends, Tiberius Ltd cannot recognise dividends receivable until it is ratified by the shareholders in 2020.

However, if Tiberius has a 31 March 2020 year end, then it should recognise the dividend receivable as the dividend was ratified before its year end.

Disclosure

General Disclosures Relating to Revenue

An entity should disclose:

(a) the accounting policies adopted for recognising revenue, including the methods adopted to determine the stage of completion;

(b) the amount of each category of revenue recognised during the period, including revenue from:
  - (i) the sale of goods,
  - (ii) the rendering of services,
  - (iii) interest,
  - (iv) royalties,
  - (v) dividends,
  - (vi) commissions,
  - (vii) grants, and
  - (viii) any other significant types of revenue.

EXAMPLE 7.17: DISCLOSURE

Note 1 – Accounting Policies

Revenue recognition
Revenue is measured at the fair value of the consideration received or receivable net of any trade discounts and value-added tax.

Revenue from the sale of machine parts is recognised when the goods are delivered to the customer and all related ancillary work has been carried out.

Revenue from construction contracts is recognised using the stage of completion method. It is measured by taking the contract costs to date as a percentage of the total estimated costs for each contract. If the outcome of the contract cannot be estimated reliably, then contract revenue is restricted to the extent of contract costs incurred. When the contract costs are probably going to exceed the contract revenue, the expected loss is immediately recognised as an expense.

Note 2 – Revenue

Revenue recognised during the year consists of:

	2020	2019
	€	€
Sale of machine parts	350,000	250,000
Construction contracts	650,000	500,000
Rendering of services	150.000	100.000
	1,150,000	850,000

Disclosures Relating to Revenue from Construction Contracts

An entity should disclose:

(a) the amount of contract revenue recognised as revenue in the period;
(b) the methods used to determine the contract revenue recognised in the period; and
(c) the methods used to determine the stage of completion of contracts in progress.

An entity should present:

(a) the gross amount due from customers for contract work as an asset; and
(b) the gross amount due to customers as a liability.

Example 7.18: Revenue from Construction Contracts

The following is an extract from the Consolidated Balance Sheet as at 31 December 2020:

	Notes	2020
		€000
Assets		
Gross amount due from customers for contract work	3	180
Liabilities		
Advances from customers		500
Gross amount due to customers for contract work	3	200

	€000	€000
Note 3 Amount due from (to) customers		
Costs incurred and recognised profits/(losses)	4,180	740
Progress billings to date	(4,000)	(540)
Amount due from (to) customers	180	(200)

7.2 EXAMPLES OF REVENUE RECOGNITION UNDER THE PRINCIPLES IN SECTION 23 (APPENDIX TO SECTION 23)

Sale of Goods

Example 1 Bill and Hold Sales The seller should recognise revenue when the buyer takes title, provided:

(a) it is probable that delivery will be made;
(b) the item is on hand, identified and ready for delivery to the buyer at the time the sale is recognised;

(c) the buyer specifically acknowledges the deferred delivery instructions; and
(d) the usual payment terms apply.

Revenue is not recognised when there is simply an intention to acquire or manufacture the goods in time for delivery.

Example 2 Installation and Inspection Revenue is recognised immediately upon acceptance of delivery by the buyer when:
(a) the installation process is simple, e.g. only unpacking and connection to power; or
(b) the inspection is performed only for the purposes of the final determination of contract prices, e.g. shipments of iron ore, sugar or soya beans.

Example 3 Goods Sold on Approval when the Buyer has Negotiated a Limited Right of Return If there is uncertainty about the possibility of the return of goods, the seller should recognise revenue when shipment is formally accepted by the buyer or when the goods are delivered and the time period for rejection has elapsed.

Example 4 Consignment Sales under which the Buyer undertakes to Sell the Goods on Behalf of the Seller The seller should recognise revenue when the goods are sold by the buyer to a third party.

Example 5 Cash on Delivery Sales The seller should recognise revenue when delivery is made and the cash is received.

Example 6 Goods are Delivered Only when the Buyer makes the Final Payment in a Series of Instalments Revenue is recognised when the goods are delivered. However, where experience indicates that most sales are consummated, revenue may be recognised when a significant deposit is received, provided the goods are on hand and ready for delivery to the buyer.

Example 7 Payment Received in Advance of Delivery for Goods still to be Manufactured Revenue is recognised when the goods are delivered to the buyer and any monies received are recorded initially in liabilities.

Example 8 Sale and Repurchase Agreements The seller must analyse the terms of a contract to ascertain whether, in substance, the risks and rewards of ownership have been transferred. When the seller retains these, even though the legal title has passed, it is a financing arrangement and does not give rise to revenue.

Example 9 Sales to Intermediate Parties – Dealers, Distributors The seller recognises revenue when the risks and rewards of ownership have passed. However, when the buyer is acting, in substance, as an agent, the sale is treated as a consignment sale.

Example 10 Subscriptions to Publications and Similar Items The seller should normally recognise revenue on a straight-line basis over the period items are dispatched, e.g. monthly subscriptions. However, if the items vary in value, revenue should be recognised on the basis of the sales value of the items dispatched in relation to the total estimated sales value of all items covered by the subscription.

Example 11 Sales Paid by Instalments The seller should recognise revenue at the date of sale. The sales price is the present value of consideration determined by discounting the instalments at the imputed rate of interest. Interest receivable is recognised using the effective interest method.

Example 12 Agreements for the Construction of Real Estate An entity that undertakes the construction of real estate, directly or through subcontractors, and enters into an agreement with one or more buyers before construction is complete must account for the agreement as a sale of services, using the percentage of completion method, but only if:

(a) the buyer is able to specify the major structural elements of the design of the real estate before construction begins and/or specify major structural changes once construction is in progress (whether it actually exercises that ability or not); or
(b) the buyer acquires and supplies construction materials and the entity provides only construction services.

If the entity is required to provide services together with construction materials, it should be accounted for as a sale of goods. In this case, the buyer does not obtain control or the significant risks and rewards of ownership of the work in progress in its current state as construction progresses. Rather, the transfer occurs only on the delivery of the completed real estate to the buyer.

Example 13 Sale with Customer Loyalty Award An entity sells product A for €100. Purchasers of product A get an award credit enabling them to buy product B for €10. The normal selling price of product B is €18. The entity estimates that 40 per cent of the purchasers of product A will use their award to buy product B at €10. The normal selling price of product A, after taking into account discounts that are usually offered but that are not available during this promotion, is €95.

The fair value of the award credit is 40% × (€18 – €10) = €3.20. The entity allocates the total revenue of €100 between product A and the award credit by reference to their relative fair values of €95 and €3.20, respectively.

Therefore:

(a) Revenue for product A is €100 × (€95 ÷ (€95 + €3.20)) = €96.74;
(b) Revenue for product B is €100 × (€3.20 ÷ (€95 + €3.20)) = €3.26.

Rendering of Services

Example 14 Installation Fees The seller should recognise these by reference to the stage of completion of the installation unless incidental to the sale, in which case they are recognised when the goods are sold.

Example 15 Servicing Fees included in the Price of the Product When the selling price of a product includes an identifiable amount for subsequent servicing (e.g. after-sales support), the seller should defer the servicing fee and recognise it as revenue over the period during which the service is performed. The deferral should cover the expected costs together with a reasonable profit on those services.

Example 16 Advertising Commissions These are recognised when the related advertisement or commercial appears before the public.

Example 17 Insurance Agency Commissions These are recognised as revenue on the effective commencement or renewal dates of policies. However, if it is probable that the agent will be required to render further services, the agent should defer part of the commission and recognise it over the period during which the policy is in force.

Example 17A Financial Services Fees Recognition of revenue depends on the purposes for which the fees are assessed and the basis of accounting for any associated financial instrument. The description of fees for financial services may not be indicative of the nature and substance of the services provided. Therefore, it is necessary to distinguish between fees that are an integral part of the effective interest rate of a financial instrument, fees that are earned as services are provided, and fees that are earned on the execution of a significant act.

Example 18 Admission fees These should be recognised when the event takes place. If the subscription relates to a number of events, then the fee should be allocated on a basis that reflects the extent to which the services are performed at each event.

Example 19 Tuition Fees Revenue is recognised over the period of instruction.

Example 20 Initiation, Entrance and Membership Fees If the fee is purely for membership, it should be recognised when there is no significant doubt over its collectability.

If the fee entitles the member to services during the membership period or to purchase goods cheaper than non-members, revenue should be recognised on a basis that reflects the timing, nature and value of the benefits provided.

Franchise Fees

Franchise fees may cover the supply of both initial and subsequent services, equipment and other tangible assets. Revenue should be recognised on a basis that reflects the purpose for which the fees were charged.

Example 21 Franchise Fees: Supplies of Equipment and Other Tangible Assets A franchisor should recognise the fair value of assets sold as revenue when the items are delivered or the title passes.

Example 22 Franchise Fees: Supplies of Initial and Subsequent Services A franchisor should recognise fees as the services are rendered. When a separate fee does not cover the cost of continuing services together with a reasonable profit, part of the initial fee sufficient to cover the costs of continuing services and provide a reasonable profit is deferred and recognised as revenue as services are rendered.

The franchise agreement may provide for the supply of equipment at a price lower than normal. In these cases part of the initial fee to cover costs in excess of that price and provide a reasonable profit should be deferred and recognised over the period that the goods are likely to be sold to the franchisee. The balance of the initial fee is then recognised as revenue when performance of all initial services and other obligations has been substantially achieved.

The initial services and other obligations may depend on the number of individual outlets established in an area. Fees for the initial services should then be apportioned to the number of outlets substantially completed.

If the fee is collectible over an extended period and there is significant uncertainty re the collection of the fee, then revenue should be recognised as the cash instalments are received.

Example 23 Franchise Fees: Continuing Franchise Fees Revenue is recognised as the services are provided or the rights used.

Example 24 Franchise Fees: Agency Transactions Transactions may, in substance, involve the franchisor acting as an agent for the franchisee, e.g. the ordering of supplies or the arrangement of delivery of goods at no profit. No revenue should be reported in these cases.

Example 25 Fees from the Development of Customised Software Software developers recognise revenue by reference to the stage of completion of the development, including the completion of services provided for post-delivery support.

Interest, Royalties and Dividends

Example 26 Licence Fees and Royalties Fees and royalties should be recognised according to their substance. Practically, that may be on a straight-line basis over the life of the agreement.

An assignment of rights for a fixed fee or non-refundable guarantee is in substance a sale, e.g. the licence to use software when the licensor has no obligations after delivery or a granting of rights to exhibit a motion picture film in markets where the licensor has no control over the distributor and no further revenues are expected.

In some cases a licence fee may be contingent on the occurrence of a future event. Revenue, in that case, should only be recognised when it is probable that the fee or royalty will be received – normally when the event has occurred.

EXAMPLE 7.19: MULTIPLE ELEMENT CONTRACT

Mendocino Ltd has signed a four-year deal with Startrek Ltd to use its satellite network for the delivery of its television channels. The deal commenced on 1 April 2018. Mendocino Ltd paid Startrek Ltd €3 million on 1 April 2018. Three further annual instalments of €1.8 million are payable commencing on 1 April 2019. Mendocino Ltd utilises 10% of the operating capacity of Startrek's network with an estimated useful life of eight years. Startrek has agreed a minimum level of service that will be provided.

Mendocino Ltd offers the following customer packages:

- each customer pays €135 per month for television services for a 12-month commitment;
- the contract can be cancelled after 12 months;
- once the contract is signed, each customer receives free receiver equipment and free installation (valued at €270 and €90, respectively, if acquired separately);

or

- a similar package to the above, but with no receiver equipment or installation, at a cost of €120 per month.

Mendocino has signed up 20,000 customers during 2018 and the average unexpired term of a customer contract is eight months.

Solution

There are several components in revenue. The FRS requires recognition criteria to be applied to those separate components. No detailed guidance is provided on how that is achieved.

Fair value of consideration over the 12-month contract is €1,620 (12 × €135) and the fair value of individual components is €1,800 (€270 + €90 + (12 × €120)). The discount of €180 (10%) should be allocated to each component on a reasonable basis, e.g. pro rata.

	Individual fair value	Discount	Bundled fair value
	€	€	€
Receiver equipment	270	27	243
Installation	90	9	81
Monthly subscription	1,440	144	1,296
Total	1,800	180	1,620

On installation, revenue of €324 (€243 + €81) will be recorded. The average elapsed term of a contract is four months, so the total revenue recognised to date will be €756 (€324 + 4/12 × €1,296). For 20,000 contracts, the total revenue is €15.12 million.

The total cash collected will be €10.8 million (20,000 × €135 × 4). The difference from the revenue recognised of €4.32 million will be recognised as a receivable.

A simple example of both the applicable accounting policy adopted and the notes required on revenue recognition is provided below (based on the IASB's *IFRS for SMEs 2009 Illustrative Financial Statements Presentation and Disclosure Checklist*).

Example 7.20: Illustrative Financial Statements – Revenue Recognition

Accounting Policies and Explanatory Notes (Extracts)

2. Basis of preparation and accounting policies

Revenue recognition
Revenue from sales of goods is recognised when the goods are delivered and title has passed. Royalty revenue from licensing candle-making patents for use by others is recognised on a straight-line basis over the licence period. Revenue is measured at the fair value of the consideration received or receivable, net of discounts and sales-related taxes collected on behalf of the government of A Land.

5. Revenue

	20X2	20X1
	€	€
Sale of goods	6,743,545	5,688,653
Royalties – licensing of candle-making patents	120,000	120,000
	6,863,545	5,808,653

A good example of a more complicated revenue recognition model is provided by Datalex Plc for its financial statements ending 31 December 2017.

Datalex Plc

Annual Report 2017

NOTES TO THE FINANCIAL STATEMENTS (EXTRACT)

2. Summary of Significant Accounting Policies (Extract)

2.4 Revenue Recognition

The Group's revenue consists primarily of revenues from the use of software products by the Group's customers and delivery of services. Revenue comprises the fair value of the consideration received or receivable for the sale of products and services in the ordinary course of the Group's activities. Revenue is shown net of value-added-tax and discounts and after eliminating sales within the Group. The Group recognises revenue when the amount of revenue can be reliably measured, it is probable that future economic benefits will flow to the entity and when specific criteria have been met for each of the Group's activities as described below.

(I) Platform Revenue

Platform revenue is earned from the use of the Group's Digital Commerce Platform by our customers. Revenue can also be earned from delivery of an early release platform prior to go-live.

Revenue is earned by charging a fixed or a variable fee as stated within the relevant contractual arrangements.

The use of the platform by our customers can include i) air fare bookings, ii) non-air ancillary bookings such as car, hotel and insurance, iii) air ancillary items such as seat fees or bag fees and iv) hosting fees when the customer's software solution is hosted by us. Contracts for the use of the platform are typically five years in duration.

Platform revenues which are based on variable fees are recognised during the month the bookings take place. Customer contracts may provide for a minimum level of transaction fees. When actual bookings processed are in excess of the minimum level of transaction fees, revenue is earned on a variable basis under the relevant contractual terms. When platform revenue is below the minimum threshold, revenue is recognised based on the contractual minimum level of bookings applicable for the period under the relevant contractual terms, on a straight line basis.

Platform revenues which are based on fixed fees are recognised based on the agreed fee for the applicable period per the relevant contractual terms in place.

Contracts may also include the right to begin charging transaction fees in advance of go-live once the solution is production ready, at which point, revenue recognition commences.

Contracts may also include provision for a termination fee payable by the customer in the event that the contract is terminated by the customer. In situations where a customer terminates a contract before the end of the agreed term, the fair value of any remaining minimum payments, contractually due, is recognised at date of termination.

(II) Professional Services
Professional services revenue is earned from fees charged to deploy the Group's software at new customers, and to deliver new functionality to existing customers. If the professional service is on a contracted time and material basis, then the revenue is recognised as and when the services are performed. If it is a fixed fee, then the services revenue is recognised by reference to the stage of completion accounting method. The Group measures percentage of completion based on labour hours incurred to date as a proportion of total hours allocated to the contract. If circumstances arise that may change the original estimates of revenues, costs or extent of progress toward completion, estimates are revised. These revisions may result in increases or decreases in estimated revenues or costs and are reflected in the period in which the circumstances that give rise to the revision become known by management.

(III) TPF Consulting and Associated Revenue
The Group's consulting and associated revenue primarily consists of revenue generated from the Group's TPF consulting activities. TPF Consulting revenue is derived from fees contracted under service and is recognised on a time and material basis.

7.3 ACCOUNTING POLICIES, ESTIMATES AND ERRORS (SECTION 10)

This section provides guidance for selecting and applying the accounting policies used in preparing financial statements as well as covering how entities should account for changes in accounting estimates and corrections of errors.

Selection and Application of Accounting Policies

Accounting policies are the specific principles, bases, conventions, rules and practices applied by an entity in preparing and presenting its financial statements. They only apply to material items.

Materiality should be judged in the particular circumstances of each case. For example, an entity not capitalising a machine costing €500 on the grounds that the overall cost of plant currently on the balance sheet is €500,000 would be acceptable; but if there were a large number of similar assets each costing €500 adding collectively to €40,000, then they should be capitalised in aggregate.

Management must use judgement in applying its accounting policies. The aim is to provide information that is:

(a) relevant to decision-making;
(b) reliable, in that the financial statements:
    (i) represent faithfully the financial position, performance and cash flows of the entity,
    (ii) reflect economic substance,
    (iii) are neutral and free from bias,
    (iv) are prudent, and
    (v) complete in all material respects.

Management must consider the applicability of the following sources in descending order in making their judgement:

(a) the requirements and guidance in the FRS dealing with similar issues;
(b) if within the scope of a Statement of Recommended Practice (SORP), the rules and guidance in that SORP (e.g. charities);
(c) the definitions, recognition criteria and measurement concepts in Section 2 (see **Chapter 2**).

Management may also consider the guidance in EU-adopted IFRSs dealing with similar issues. However, if an entity wishes to, or has to, prepare earnings per share ratios, exploration and evaluation of mineral resources or operating segment information, it must follow the full international standards, i.e. IAS 33 *Earnings per Share,* IFRS 6 *Exploration for and Evaluation of Mineral Resources* and IFRS 8 *Operating Segments,* respectively.

In Ireland, an example of that issue emerges with the accounting treatment of the research and development (R&D) tax credit – whether it should be accounted for as a form of grant aid rather than as a tax credit. In essence, it could be argued in substance to be a form of grant albeit administered through the tax regime, so perhaps the best analogy is to look to Section 24 *Grants* and to apply the logic therein to the problem. The R&D tax credit was introduced to reduce the economic cost of carrying out R&D activity rather than as a genuine tax relief. However, there is no definitive solution and some companies may still regard it as a reduction in their tax charge.

Consistency of Accounting Policies

Accounting policies must be consistent for similar transactions unless the FRS 102 requires or permits categorisation of items for which different policies might be appropriate.

Changes in Accounting Policies

An entity can only alter an accounting policy if the change:

(a) is required by changes in FRS 102; or
(b) results in more reliable and relevant information.

There are a number of options under FRS 102. For example, if a company switches from the cost to the revaluation model on the grounds that it may be more relevant, this would also be treated as a change in accounting policy.

However, the following are not regarded as changes in accounting policies:

(a) the application of an accounting policy that differs in substance from those previously occurring (e.g. a company with a subsidiary in a country whose economy is now defined as hyperinflationary and having to apply Section 31 (see **Chapter 9**) of FRS 102 for the first time); and
(b) the application of a new policy that did not occur previously or was not material (e.g. the company acquired an intangible asset for the first time and started to amortise it over its useful life).

If FRS 102 allows a choice of accounting treatment and an entity changes its choice, that is a change in accounting policy.

However, the initial application of a policy to revalue property, plant and equipment or intangible assets other than goodwill is a change in accounting policy, to be dealt with as a revaluation in accordance with those specific sections of FRS 102 and not in accordance with Section 10.

Applying Changes in Accounting Policies

On first application of FRS 102, changes in accounting policies should be applied according to the transitional provisions in the Standard. Generally changes are accounted for retrospectively. For example, if a change resulted in an increase to retained earnings of €50,000 on 1 January 2020 but €30,000 was really in relation to years prior to that date, the whole €50,000 can be restated against the retained earnings at 1 January 2020, i.e. there is no need to restate comparative years.

Retrospective Application

When a change in accounting policy is applied retrospectively, the entity should apply the new policy to comparative information as far back as practicable and also adjust the opening balance for each affected component of equity.

EXAMPLE 7.21: CHANGE IN ACCOUNTING POLICY

Dollar Ltd changed its policy of measuring its inventories from FIFO to weighted average. The cumulative effect is a decrease in retained earnings of €50,000 at 1 January 2019, the start of the current reporting period. The company publishes one year's comparative figures and the change affects the last four years by €12,500 per annum. The effect of the change should be reported as follows:

	€
1 January 2018	reduce by 37,500
Profit for the year ended 31 December 2018	reduce by 12,500
Cumulative effect on retained earnings at 1 January 2019	reduce by 50,000

However, if it is not practicable to adjust retrospectively, then simply adjust retained earnings at 1 January 2019 downward by €50,000 with no restatement of prior periods.

Disclosure of a Change in Accounting Policy

An entity should disclose:

(a) the nature of the change in accounting policy;
(b) for the current period and for each prior period, to the extent practicable, the amount of the adjustment for each financial statement line item affected;
(c) the amount of the adjustment relating to periods before those presented, to the extent practicable; and
(d) an explanation if it is impracticable to determine the amounts to be disclosed in (b) or (c).

Example 7.22: Change in Accounting Policy

In 2020 Wexford Ltd changed one of its accounting policies due to an amendment to a current standard's view of borrowing costs that makes it compulsory to capitalise finance costs on the construction of a property. The cumulative impact at the beginning of 2019 is a €30,000 increase in retained earnings. The effect on profit before tax for 2019 is assumed to be a €10,000 increase, with a resultant impact of increase in tax of €2,000.

Statement of Income and Retained Earnings (Extract)

	2020	**2019 (Restated)**
	€	**€**
Profit before tax (2019: previously stated €60,000)	90,000	70,000
Income tax expense (2019: previously stated €15,000)	(30,000)	(17,000)
Profit for the year (2019: previously stated €45,000)	60,000	53,000
Retained earnings at start of the year		
- As previously stated	165,000	120,000
- Effect of change in accounting policy	38,000	30,000
	203,000	150,000
Retained earnings at the end of the year	263,000	203,000

In addition, in the accounting policy notes to the financial statements, the change in accounting policy would need to be disclosed as follows:

Note 6. Change in Accounting Policy

In 2020, in accordance with an amendment to Section 25 *Borrowing Costs* of FRS 102, the company has changed its accounting policy for borrowing costs. Previously, the company had expensed these costs. The company now capitalises these costs. This change in accounting policy has been accounted for retrospectively and the comparative information for 2019 has been restated. The effect of the change is an increase of €8,000 in profit for the year ended 31 December 2019. Opening retained earnings for 2019 have also been increased by €30,000, which is the amount of adjustment relating to periods before 2019.

When a voluntary change in policy is undertaken, an entity should disclose:
(a) the nature of the change in accounting policy;
(b) the reasons why the new policy provides reliable and more relevant information;
(c) for the current period and for each prior period presented, the adjustment for each line item affected, showing separately the current period, each prior period presented and in aggregate for periods before those presented, to the extent practicable; and
(d) an explanation if it is impracticable to determine the amounts disclosed in (b) and (c).

Example 7.23: Voluntary Change in Accounting Policy (Change in Presentation)

Note 6. Change in Accounting Policy

In 2020 the company voluntarily changed its accounting policy for R&D tax credits. Previously the company had presented these credits as reductions in the tax expense. The company treats the tax credits as a form of government grant. Management judges that this policy provides reliable and more relevant information because the substance of the relief is to encourage more expenditure on R&D activity rather than a general tax relief. There is no retrospective accounting treatment as it is a change in presentation, but the comparative information for 2019 has been restated.

A good real-life example of disclosure of a voluntary change in accounting policy is provided by the IFG Group Plc.

IFG Group Plc

Annual Report and Accounts 2008

NOTES TO THE CONSOLIDATED FINANCIAL STATEMENTS (EXTRACT)

36. Comparative changes

In the current year income statement, some expenses which were historically classified as administrative expenses and other expenses have been reclassified to cost of sales. The prior year comparatives have also been reclassified in order to ensure consistency with the current year disclosure. The Directors believe that the current year disclosure is more appropriate and provides more useful information to the users of the financial statements.

The comparative information for 2007 has been restated as follows:

	Cost of Sales €'000	**Administrative Expenses €'000**	**Other Expenses €'000**	**Gross Profit €'000**
As previously reported	(4,775)	(104,736)	(1,976)	17,342
Professional staff salaries and other costs directly attributable to sales reclassified	(97,535)	95,559	1,976	-
As restated	(102,310)	(9,177)	-	17,342

Changes in Accounting Estimates

Changes in accounting estimates represent adjustments to the carrying amount of assets and liabilities resulting from new information and are not corrections of errors. They should be recognised prospectively by including them in profit or loss in:

(a) the period of change, if the change affects that period only; or
(b) the period of change and future periods, if the change affects both.

Typical examples of changes in estimates include:

- obtaining more accurate information about the amount to be provided for provisions. These are normal revisions of best estimates;

- the reassessment of both the useful life of property, plant and equipment, their residual values and even their method of depreciation; and
- over- or under-estimates of current tax payable to revenue authorities.

If the changes affect assets and liabilities or equity, then entities must adjust the carrying amount of those assets and liabilities in the period of change.

Example 7.24: Change in Accounting Estimate

Douglas Ltd acquired a machine for €100,000 on 1 January 2019 and assessed its life at 10 years at the date of acquisition with a residual value of €Nil. The company adopted the straight-line method of depreciation. Unfortunately, it appears that the machine's useful life will be curtailed due to technological developments such that at 31 December 2023 it is likely that only two more years of benefits will be earned.

The book value at 31 December 2022 would be €100,000 – €40,000* = €60,000. The revised useful life will now be two years and thus in 2019 and 2020, €30,000 depreciation will be charged prospectively in the income statement.

* Accumulated depreciation = (€100,000 ÷ 10 years) × 4 years = €40,000.

Disclosure of a Change in Estimate

An entity should disclose the nature of a change in accounting estimate, and its effect in the current period; and, if practicable, the effect on future periods. If it is impracticable, that fact should be disclosed. Using the facts of the previous example, a possible disclosure note for Douglas Ltd is given below.

Example 7.25: Disclosure of Change in Accounting Estimate

Note 2. Operating Profit

Change in accounting estimate
At 31 December 2022, as a result of a review of the likely future income to be generated from the Linex machine, the company has reassessed its useful life at six years (previously 10 years) from the date of acquisition. This has had the effect of increasing the depreciation charge for the year ended 31 December 2022 by €20,000 (previously €10,000, now €30,000 per annum).

Corrections of Prior Period Errors

The corrections of prior period errors are the corrections of omissions and misstatements for one or more prior periods. These include mathematical mistakes, oversights and fraud. These should be corrected, in the first period discovered, retrospectively by:

(a) restating the comparatives for prior periods; and
(b) if the error occurred before the earliest period presented, restating the opening balances for the earliest period presented.

When that is impracticable for one or more prior years, an entity must restate the opening balances for the earliest period for which retrospective restatement is practicable.

Some examples of items that could be classified as errors include:

- mathematical error in the computation of overheads to be included in the inventory valuation;
- oversight in not including certain overheads, included in previous years, in the construction costs of a property; and
- the deliberate concealment of costs in the income statement (see Greencore Group plc example below).

The correction of the prior period error should be treated similarly to that for changes in accounting policies covered earlier in the chapter.

Disclosure of Prior Period Errors

An entity should disclose the following:

(a) the nature of the prior period error;
(b) for each prior period presented, to the extent practicable, the amount of the correction for each line item affected;
(c) the amount of the correction at the start of the earliest prior period presented; and
(d) an explanation if it is not practicable to determine the amounts to be disclosed in (b) and (c) above.

In essence, the disclosure is the same as that for changes in accounting policies. An example is provided below:

Example 7.26: Correction of Prior Period Error

Notes to the Financial Statements

Note 6. Correction of prior period error

In 2020 the company corrected an oversight that had resulted in the understatement of inventory in the previous year. The correction of the error is accounted for retrospectively and the comparative information for 2019 has been restated. The effect of the change is a €40,000 increase in profit for the year ended 31 December 2019. In addition retained earnings for 2019 have also been increased by €40,000.

Greencore Group plc provides an example of a prior period adjustment caused by a material error arising due to fraudulent activity in previous years in one of its subsidiaries.

Greencore Group plc

Annual Report 2008

NOTES TO THE GROUP FINANCIAL STATEMENTS (EXTRACT)

In June 2008, the Group uncovered a deliberate concealment of costs at its Mineral Water business (part of the Convenience Foods segment) which resulted in a material misstatement of the Group financial position and performance presented in the Annual Reports for the financial years 2006, 2007 and the 2008 Half Yearly Financial Report. The investigation undertaken indicated that this concealment of costs was undertaken by the former Financial Controller of the Mineral Water business who left the business prior to this issue being uncovered. The effect of this restatement on the Group Financial Statements for the year ended 28 September 2007 is summarised below. Opening retained earnings for 2007 have been reduced by €5.2m, which is the amount of the adjustment relating to the year ended 29 September 2006.

	As previously stated 2007 €'000	**As restated 2007 €'000**	Restatement 2007 €'000
Effect on Balance Sheet			
Property, plant and equipment	393,424	**392,164**	(1,260)
Inventory	142,789	**136,905**	(5,884)
Trade and other receivables	114,417	**112,497**	(1,920)
Trade and other payables	(359,278)	**(367,104)**	(7,826)
Deferred tax liabilities	(37,845)	**(33,273)**	4,572
			(12,318)

Retained earnings	38,663	**26,012**	(12,651)
Other reserves	1,659	**1,992**	333
Net decrease in equity			(12,318)

	As previously stated 2007	**As restated 2007**	Restatement 2007
	€'000	**€'000**	€'000
Effect on Income Statement	(903,293)	**(906,021)**	(2,725)
Increase in cost of sales			
Increase in other expenses (pre exceptional)	(272.819)	**(280,161)**	(7,342)
Group operating profit (pre exceptional)	91,041	**80,974**	(10,067)
Taxation	(13,131)	**(10,505)**	2,626
Decrease in result for the period from continuing operations			(7,441)

	As previously stated cent	**As restated cent**	Restatement cent
	2007	**2007**	2007
Effect on Earnings per share	55.5	**51.8**	3.7
Earnings per share			
Adjusted earnings per share	30.6	**26.9**	3.7
Diluted earnings per share	55.3	**51.6**	3.7
Adjusted diluted earnings per share	30.5	**26.8**	3.7

There was no cashflow impact as a result of the restatement other than the consequential adjustments arising as a result of the restatement of the comparative Balance Sheet at 28 September 2007.

A couple of simple examples of how to deal with both a change in accounting policy and a material error are provided below.

Example 7.27: Change in Accounting Policy

Myriad Ltd has recently adopted FRS 102 and has decided to review its existing policy of capitalising interest costs as part of the costs of the construction of a power plant and no longer wishes to apply that policy. The new policy, to be first applied for the financial statements to 31 December 2019, is to recognise interest costs as an expense. Construction work began in 2017 and is being financed by a bank loan. Interest charges directly attributable to the power plant in 2017 of €150,000 and in 2018 of €250,000 were capitalised. Interest charges incurred in 2019 amounted to €300,000 and these have all been written off to income.

The company's draft income statement for the year ended 31 December 2019 (before accounting retrospectively for the change in accounting policy) reveals the following:

	2019	**2018**
	€000	**€000**
Profit before interest and tax	2,500	2,400
Interest charges	(300)	-
Profit before taxation	2,200	2,400
Taxation	(660)	(720)
Profit after taxation	1,540	1,505

No depreciation has been charged in relation to the power plant since it is still not yet in use. Assume taxation is 30% of profit before tax. Retained earnings were reported to be €840,000 on 31 December 2017 and no dividends were paid out during 2018 or 2019.

Solution

Changes in accounting policies should be accounted for as follows under FRS 102:

PROFIT AND LOSS ACCOUNT (EXTRACT)
for the year ended 31 December 2019

	2019	**2018 (restated)**
	€000	**€000**
Profit before interest and taxation	2,500	2,400
Interest charges	(300)	(250)
Profit before taxation	2,200	2,150
Taxation	(660)	(645)
Profits after taxation	1,540	1,505

Retained earnings	€000
Balance as at 31 December 2017, as previously reported	840
Change in accounting policy relating to borrowing costs	(105)
Restated balance as at 31 December 2017	735
Restated profit for the year ended 31 December 2018	1,505
Restated balance as at 31 December 2018	2,240
Profit for the year ended 31 December 2019	1,540
Balance as at 31 December 2019	3,780

Note: interest charges were €150,000 for the year ended 31 December 2017. Treating these as expenses reduces pre-tax profit by €150,000, but also reduces the tax liability by €45,000 (i.e. 30% × €150,000). Thus, the reduction in post-tax profits is €105,000, as shown above.

Example 7.28: Prior Period Error

Molton Ltd has discovered a material error when preparing its financial statements for the year ended 31 December 2019, in that the inventory for 2018 was overstated by €50,000.

The company's draft income statement for the year ended 31 December 2019 (before correcting the error) was as follows:

	2019	2018
	€000	€000
Sales	940	790
Cost of sales	(750)	(540)
Gross profit	190	250
Other expenses	(120)	(110)
Profit before taxation	70	140
Taxation	(14)	(28)
Profits after taxation	56	112

Retained earnings were reported to be €270,000 on 31 December 2017 and no dividends were paid in either 2018 or 2019. Assume taxation to be 30% of profits before tax.

Solution

PROFIT AND LOSS ACCOUNT
for the year ended 31 December 2019

	2019	2018 (restated)
	€000	€000
Sales	940	790
Cost of sales	(700)	(590)
Gross profit	240	200
Other expenses	(120)	(110)
Profit before taxation	120	90
Taxation	(36)	(27)
Profits after taxation	84	63

Retained earnings	**€000**
Balance as at 31 December 2017	270
Restated profit for the year ended 31 December 2018	63
Restated balance as at 31 December 2018	333
Profit for the year ended 31 December 2019	84
Balance as at 31 December 2019	417

7.4 SMALL ENTITIES

There are no explicit minimum disclosure requirements for small entities under FRS 102, Section 1A for either the UK or the Republic of Ireland. However, small entities may need to provide disclosures as required by FRS 102, Sections 23 and 10, if required to give a true and fair view.

7.5 MICRO-ENTITIES

The accounting treatment for both revenue and accounting policies, estimates and errors are identical to that under FRS 102.

Disclosure Checklist: Performance Measurement – FRS 102

(References are to the relevant Section of FRS 102)

	PARA.
Revenue – Section 23	
General disclosures about revenue	
An entity shall disclose: (a) the accounting policies adopted for the recognition of revenue, including the methods adopted to determine the stage of completion of transactions involving the rendering of services; (b) the amount of each category of revenue recognised during the period, showing separately, at a minimum, revenue arising from: (i) the sale of goods, (ii) the rendering of services, (iii) interest, (iv) royalties, (v) dividends, (vi) commissions, (vii) grants, and (viii) any other significant types of revenue.	23.30
Disclosures relating to revenue from construction contracts	
An entity shall disclose the following: (a) the amount of contract revenue recognised as revenue in the period; (b) the methods used to determine the contract revenue recognised in the period; and (c) the methods used to determine the stage of completion of contracts in progress.	23.31
An entity shall present: (a) the gross amount due from customers for contract work as an asset; and (b) the gross amount due to customers for contract work as a liability.	23.32
Accounting Policies, Estimates and Errors – Section 10	
Disclosure of a change in accounting policy	
When an amendment to a FRS or FRC abstract has an effect on the current period or any prior period, or might have an effect on future periods, an entity shall disclose the following: (a) the nature of the change in accounting policy; (b) for the current period and each prior period presented, to the extent practicable, the amount of the adjustment for each financial statement line item affected; (c) the amount of the adjustment relating to periods before those presented, to the extent practicable; and (d) an explanation if it is impracticable to determine the amounts to be disclosed in (b) or (c) above. Financial statements of subsequent periods need not repeat these disclosures.	10.13

	PARA.
When a voluntary change in accounting policy has an effect on the current period or any prior period, an entity shall disclose the following: (a) the nature of the change in accounting policy; (b) the reasons why applying the new accounting policy provides reliable and more relevant information; (c) to the extent practicable, the amount of the adjustment for each financial statement line item affected, shown separately: (i) for the current period, (ii) for each prior period presented, and (iii) in the aggregate for periods before those presented; and (d) an explanation if it is impracticable to determine the amounts to be disclosed in (c) above. Financial statements of subsequent periods need not repeat these disclosures.	10.14
Disclosure of a change in estimate	
An entity shall disclose the nature of any change in an accounting estimate and the effect of the change on assets, liabilities, income and expense for the current period. If it is practicable for the entity to estimate the effect of the change in one or more future periods, the entity shall disclose those estimates.	10.18
Disclosure of prior period errors	
An entity shall disclose the following about prior period errors: (a) the nature of the prior period error; (b) for each prior period presented, to the extent practicable, the amount of the correction for each financial statement line item affected; (c) to the extent practicable, the amount of the correction at the beginning of the earliest prior period presented; and (d) an explanation if it is not practicable to determine the amounts to be disclosed in (b) or (c) above. Financial statements of subsequent periods need not repeat these disclosures.	10.23

Disclosure Checklist: Performance Measurement – Small Entities

(References are to the relevant Appendix of Section 1A FRS 102)

The mandatory disclosure requirements for small entities required under the Companies Act 2014 (ROI) (CA 2014), the Companies Act 2006 (UK) (CA 2006) and the Small Companies and Groups (Accounts and Directors' Report) Regulations 2008 (UK) (S.I. No. 409 of 2008) are as follows:

	Para.
Notes supporting the income statement	
The income statement or the notes to the financial statements shall disclose information on the nature, amount and effect of individual items of income and expenditure that are exceptional by virtue of size or incidence. (Schedule 3A, paragraph 53 CA 2014) (Schedule 1, paragraph 61(2) S.I. 409/2008)	1AD.36 (ROI) 1AC.32 (UK) (similar)
Accounting policies	
A small entity shall disclose in the notes to its financial statements the accounting policies adopted by the small entity in determining: (a) the items and amounts to be included in its statement of financial position; and (b) the items and amounts to be included in its income statement. (Section 321(1) CA 2014) (Schedule 1, paragraph 44 S.I. 409/2008)	1AD.4 (ROI) 1AC.3 (UK) (similar)
If an amount is included in a small entity's statement of financial position in respect of development costs, the following information shall be given in a note to the financial statements: (a) the period over which the amount of those costs originally capitalised is being or is to be written off; and (b) the reasons for capitalising the costs in question. (Schedule 3A, paragraph 24(2) CA 2014) (Schedule 1, paragraph 21(2) S.I. 409/2008)	1AD.5 (ROI) 1AC.4(UK) (similar)
Where development costs are shown as an asset in the small entity's financial statements and the amount is not treated as a realised loss because there are special circumstances justifying this, a note to the financial statements shall state the circumstances and that it is not a realised loss. (Section 120(3) CA 2014) (Section 844 CA 2006)	1AD.6 (ROI) 1AC.5 (UK) (similar)
Where in exceptional cases the useful life of intangible assets cannot be reliably estimated, there must be disclosed in a note to the financial statements the period over which those intangible assets are being written off and the reasons for choosing that period. (Schedule 1, paragraph 22(4) S.I. 409/2008)	1AC.6 (UK only)

	PARA.
In any case where any goodwill acquired by a small entity is shown or included as an asset in the entity's statement of financial position, the period chosen for writing off the consideration for that goodwill and the reasons for choosing that period shall be disclosed in a note to the financial statements. (Schedule 3A, paragraph 25(4) CA 2014)	1AD.7 (ROI only)
Changes in presentation and accounting policies and corrections of prior period errors	
Where any change is made in the format adopted in preparing a statement of financial position or income statement of a small entity, the reasons for the change, together with full particulars of the change, shall be given in a note to the financial statements in which the new format is first adopted. (Schedule 3A, paragraph 3(2) CA 2014) (Schedule 1, paragraph 2(2) S.I. 409/2008)	1AD.8(ROI) 1AC.7(UK) (similar)
Where a small entity changes an accounting policy and has disclosed such change in the notes to the financial statements, the notes to those financial statements shall also disclose: (a) the reason for the change in accounting policy; and (b) to the extent practicable, the impact of the change in accounting policy on the financial statements for the current reporting period and on the financial statements of preceding periods. (Section 321(3) CA 2014) (Schedule 1, paragraph 7(2) S.I. 409/2008)	1AD.9 (ROI) 1AC.8 (UK) (similar)
Where the corresponding amount for the immediately preceding reporting period is not comparable with the amount to be shown for the item in question in respect of the reporting period to which the statement of financial position or income statement relates, the former amount may be adjusted, and particulars of the adjustment and the reasons therefor shall be given in a note to the financial statements. (Schedule 3A, paragraph 5(1) CA 2014)	1AD.10 (ROI only)
Where any amount relating to a preceding reporting period is included in any item in the income statement, the effect must be stated. (Schedule 1, paragraph 61(1) S.I. 409/2008)	1AC.9 (UK only)

Disclosure Checklist: Performance Measurement – Micro-entities

(References are to the relevant Section of FRS 105)

The mandatory disclosure requirements for micro-entities required under FRS 105 and the Companies Act 2014 (ROI) (CA 2014), the Companies Act 2006 (UK) (CA 2006) and the Small Companies and Groups (Accounts and Directors' Report) Regulations 2008 (UK) (S.I. No. 409 of 2008) are as follows:

	Para.
An Irish micro-entity shall disclose information in relation to changes to accounting policies and corrections of material prior period errors in accordance with Appendix B to Section 6 *Notes to the Financial Statements*.	8.10A (ROI only)
Accounting policies	
A micro-entity shall disclose in the notes to its financial statements the accounting policies adopted by the micro-entity in determining: (a) the items and amounts to be included in its statement of financial position; and (b) the items and amounts to be included in its income statement. (Section 321(1) CA 2014)	6B.3 (ROI only)
In any case where any goodwill acquired by a micro-entity is shown or included as an asset in the micro-entity's statement of financial position, the period chosen for writing off the consideration for that goodwill and the reasons for choosing that period shall be disclosed in a note to the financial statements. (Schedule 3B, paragraph 25(4) CA 2014)	6B.4 (ROI only)
Changes in presentation and accounting policies and correcting prior period errors	
Where any change is made in the format adopted in preparing a statement of financial position of a micro-entity, the reasons for the change, together with full particulars of the change, shall be given in a note to the financial statements in which the new format is first adopted. (Schedule 3B, paragraph 3(2) CA 2014)	6B.5 (ROI only)
Where a micro-entity changes an accounting policy and has disclosed such change in the notes to the financial statements, the notes to those financial statements shall also disclose: (a) the reason for the change in accounting policy; and (b) to the extent practicable, the impact of the change in accounting policy on the financial statements for the current reporting period and on the financial statements of preceding periods. (Section 321(3) CA 2014)	6B.6 (ROI only)
Where the corresponding amount for the immediately preceding reporting period is not comparable with the amount to be shown for the item in question in respect of the reporting period to which the statement of financial position or income statement relates, the former amount may be adjusted, and particulars of the adjustment and the reasons therefor shall be given in a note to the financial statements. (Schedule 3B, paragraph 5 CA 2014)	6B.7 (ROI only)

Chapter 8
EMPLOYEE COSTS

8.1 EMPLOYEE BENEFITS (SECTION 28)

Section 28 of FRS 102 covers all forms of consideration given by an entity in exchange for services rendered by employees. There are four distinct types of consideration covered:

(a) short-term employee benefits due within 12 months;
(b) post-employment benefits;
(c) other long-term employee benefits not due within 12 months; and
(d) termination benefits due to early retirement or to voluntary redundancy.

General Recognition Principle for all Employee Benefits

The cost of all employee benefits should be recognised:

(a) as a **liability** after deducting any amounts paid directly to the employees or as a contribution to an employee benefit fund. If the contribution paid exceeds the obligation, then that excess should be treated as an asset, but only to the extent that the prepayment will lead to a reduction in future payments or a cash refund; and
(b) as an **expense**, unless the cost is included within inventories or in the cost of property.

Short-term Employee Benefits

Examples of short-term employee benefits:

(a) wages, salaries and social security contributions;
(b) paid annual leave and paid sick leave;
(c) profit-sharing and bonuses; and
(d) non-monetary benefits, e.g. medical care, housing benefit, cars, free or subsidised goods.

Measurement of Short-term Benefits Generally

Short-term benefits should be measured at the undiscounted amount of short-term employee benefits expected to be paid in exchange for an employee's service.

Recognition and Measurement – Short-term Compensated Absences

Some short-term absences accumulate, e.g. annual vacation leave and sick leave, which can be carried forward into a subsequent accounting period. The expected cost of accumulating compensated absences should be recognised when the employees render service, and be measured at the additional amount the entity expects to pay as a result of the unused entitlement accumulated at the end of the reporting period. These are then presented as current liabilities.

The cost of other non-accumulating absences should be charged when the absences occur and at an undiscounted amount.

Example 8.1: Accrual for Annual Leave

Melrose Ltd has four employees, each entitled to 20 days of paid annual leave. A loading of 17.5% is paid when annual leave is taken. At 1 July 2019 the balance of the provision was €5,264. After annual leave taken during the year had been recorded, the provision had a debit balance of €2,100. All annual leave accumulated at 30 June 2020 is expected to be paid by 30 June 2021. The following information is obtained from the payroll records for the year ended 30 June 2020.

Employee	Wage per day	Annual leave 1.7.2015	Increase in entitlement	Annual leave taken
	€	Days	Days	Days
A	120	10	20	16
B	160	7	20	16
C	180	8	20	14
D	90	8	20	24

Solution

Employee	Annual leave 1.7.2019	Increase entitlement	Annual leave taken	Accumulated 30.6.2020	Liability 30.6.2020
	Days	Days	Days	Days	€
A	10	20	16	14	1,974[1]
B	7	20	16	11	2,068[2]
C	8	20	14	14	2,961[3]
D	8	20	24	4	423[4]
					7,426

Dr Wages and salaries (€7,426 + €2,100 debit balance)	€9,526	
Cr Provision for annual leave		€9,526

1. 14 × €120 × 117.5% = €1,974.
2. 11 × €160 × 117.5% = €2,068.
3. 14 × €180 × 117.5% = €2,961.
4. 4 × €90 × 117.5% = €423.

Recognition – Profit-sharing and Bonus Plans

An expected cost and liability for profit-sharing and bonus plans is only recognised when:

(a) there is a legal or constructive obligation; and
(b) a reliable estimate of the obligation can be made.

Example 8.2: Profit Bonus Scheme

Bigger Ltd has a profit-sharing bonus scheme whereby it agrees to pay its employees 10% of its profit for the year ended 31 December 2019. For that year the company has recorded a profit of €4 million. The bonuses are due to be paid at the end of February 2020.

Solution

Bigger Ltd should account for its profit-sharing scheme as follows:

Dr	Income statement (10% × €4m)	€400,000	
Cr	Accruals		€400,000

Post-employment Benefits

Post-employment benefits include retirement benefits, such as pensions, and other benefits, e.g. medical care. They are all classified as either defined contribution or defined benefit plans, depending on their principal terms and conditions.

(a) **Defined contribution (DC) plans** In these schemes fixed contributions are paid into a separate fund, but the entity has no further obligation to pay any additional contributions. The benefits depend on the contributions paid and the investment returns thereon. All the risk is being borne by the employees and there are no particular accounting problems for the employer.
(b) **Defined benefit (DB) plans** These are schemes other than DC plans. They represent obligations of the entity to provide the agreed benefits based on both actuarial and investment risks. If these are worse than expected, there is a need to increase the obligation of the entity, leading ultimately to increased contributions to be paid by the entity to the fund. Thus the risk and all the accounting problems are borne by the employer.

Multi-employer Plans and State Plans

Multi-employer plans and state plans are classified as DC or DB on the basis of their terms. If there is insufficient information to treat a

DB multi-employer scheme as DB, the entity must account for the scheme as DC and disclose that fact and the reason why it has been accounted for as DC, as well as providing **details of the overall plan's surplus or deficit**. Multi-employer plans and state plans are relatively uncommon in the private sector, but very common in the public sector. State plans should be accounted for in the same way as multi-employer plans.

When a DB multi-employer plan is accounted for as if the plan were a DC scheme, and the entity has entered into an agreement with the plan that determines how the entity will fund a deficit, the entity must recognise a liability for the contributions payable that arise from the agreement (to the extent that they relate to the deficit) and the resulting expense in profit or loss.

Insured Benefits

Insured benefits are DC plans unless the entity has a legal or constructive obligation to pay the employee benefits directly when due or to pay further amounts if the insurer does not pay all future benefits.

Post-employment Benefits: Defined Contribution Plans

Recognition and Measurement The contribution payable for a period should be recognised:

(a) as a **liability** after deducting the amount already paid. If the contributions paid exceed the contributions due, the excess is treated as an asset; and
(b) as an **expense**, unless it is capitalised in inventories or property.

When contributions to a DC plan are not expected to be wholly settled within 12 months after the end of the reporting period in which the employees render the related service, the liability should be discounted to present value. The unwinding of the discount must be recognised as a finance cost in profit or loss in the period in which it arises.

Example 8.3: Defined Contribution Plan

Gala Ltd made a number of payments to a defined contribution plan during the year ended 31 December 2019 amounting to a total of €110,000, but had not paid the last instalment of €10,000 for the month of December.

Solution

Gala Ltd must recognise the full amount incurred during the year of €120,000 as an expense, €110,000 credited to bank and an accrual of €10,000 representing the final instalment still due for the year ended 31 December 2019.

Post-employment Benefits: Defined Benefit Plans

Recognition The following must be recognised for DB plans:

(a) a liability for an entity's obligations net of plan assets should be recognised; and
(b) the net change in the liability treated as the cost for the period of its DB plans.

Measurement of the Defined Benefit Liability The defined benefit liability should be calculated as the net total of the following amounts:

(a) the present value of its obligations at the reporting date; minus
(b) the fair value of the plan assets at the reporting date.

Where a defined benefit obligation is measured using the projected unit credit method, it must not recognise any additional liabilities to reflect differences between the actuarial assumptions and those used for funding purposes. No additional liability to fund a deficit such as a schedule of contributions should be provided.

An exception is made if the asset is an insurance policy that exactly matches the amount and timing of some or all of the benefits payable under the plan, in which case the fair value of the asset is deemed to be the present value of the related obligation.

Example 8.4: Measurement of Defined Benefit Liability

Muck Ltd has a defined benefit plan providing a monthly pension of 0.3% of final salary for each year of service, payable from the age of 65. At 31 December 2019 the present value of the company's obligations under the plan was estimated at €300,000. The fair value of the plan assets out of which the obligations are to be settled was agreed at €220,000.

Solution

At 31 December 2019, Muck Ltd must recognise a liability of €80,000 (€300,000 – €220,000). If the scheme were unfunded, then a liability of €300,000 would be recorded.

Inclusion of both Vested and Unvested Benefits The present value should reflect the estimated benefit that employees have earned in return for both current and prior service, including benefits not yet vested and including the effects of benefit formulas that might provide greater benefits in later years of service. Estimates of demographic variables (e.g. employee turnover, mortality rates) and financial variables (e.g. salary increases, medical costs) must be determined and the actuarial assumptions should be unbiased, mutually compatible and lead to the best estimate of future cash flows that will arise under the plan.

Discounting Entities should refer, at the reporting date, to the market yields on high-quality corporate bonds; if data on the market yields of high-quality corporate bonds is not available in the country, an entity should adopt the rate on government bonds. The currency and term of either the corporate bonds or government bonds should be consistent with the currency and term and estimated period of the future payments.

Actuarial Valuation Method The projected unit credit method should be adopted to determine its DB obligations and related current and past service costs.

Example 8.5: Calculation of Defined Benefit Obligation

Assume a lump sum benefit is payable on termination of service and equal to 1% of final salary for each year of service. The salary is €40,000 in the first year and is expected to increase at 4% each year. The discount rate is 10%. Assume the employee is expected to leave after four years.

	Year 1 €	Year 2 €	Year 3 €	Year 4 €
Benefit				
Current year	450	450	450	450
Cumulative benefit	Nil	450	900	1,350
Total	450	900	1,350	1,800
Obligation				
Opening		338	744	1,227
Interest at 10%		34	74	123
Current service cost	338	372	409	450
Closing obligation	338	744	1,227	1,800

Final salary = €40,000 year 1 × (1 + 0.04 annual increase)^3
= €44,995

Benefit = 1% × €44,995
= €450

FRS 102 does not require an entity to engage an independent actuary to perform the comprehensive actuarial valuation needed to calculate its DB obligation, nor does it require that a comprehensive actuarial valuation be done annually. In the periods between comprehensive actuarial valuations, if the principal actuarial assumptions have not changed significantly, the defined benefit obligation can simply be measured by adjusting the prior period measurement for changes in employee demographics, such as number of employees and salary levels.

Plan Introductions, Changes, Curtailments and Settlements If a DB plan has been introduced or changed during the period, the reporting entity must increase/decrease the DB liability and recognise the change in measuring the profit or loss for the period. Conversely, if a plan has been curtailed or settled, the obligation must be adjusted, with any resulting gain or loss being reported in profit or loss.

EXAMPLE 8.6: CURTAILMENT OF SCHEME

Bearnagh Ltd discontinues one of its businesses and the employees' employment contracts are terminated. The employee will earn no further benefits, thus it is a curtailment. Before the curtailment a present value obligation of €20,000 existed, with plan assets having a fair value of €16,000. The curtailment reduces the obligation by 10% to €18,000.

Solution

The net liability prior to the curtailment is €4,000 (€20,000 – €16,000) and after is €2,000 (€18,000 – €16,000), thus a gain of €2,000 should be recorded in income and a reduction in the net liability recorded on the balance sheet.

If a DB plan has been curtailed (i.e. either the benefits or the group of covered employees are reduced) or settled (the relevant part of the employer's obligation is completely discharged) in the current period, the DB obligation is decreased or eliminated, and the entity must recognise the resulting gain or loss in profit or loss in the current period.

Defined Benefit Plan Asset If a DB plan has a surplus, then an asset is only recognised to the extent that it is able to recover the surplus through reduced contributions or by refunds.

Cost of a Defined Benefit Plan The cost of a defined benefit plan, except if capitalised under Section 17 *Property, Plant and Equipment,* Section 16 *Investment Property,* Section 18 *Intangible Assets other than Goodwill,* etc., should be recognised as follows:

(a) additional service for the year – in profit or loss;
(b) net interest[1] in defined benefit liability – in profit or loss;
(c) curtailments, settlements – in profit or loss; and
(d) remeasurement[2] of defined benefit liability – in other comprehensive income (OCI).

1 Net interest – calculated by multiplying the defined benefit liability by the discount rate at the start of the accounting period, but also must consider any changes to contributions paid in and benefits paid out during the reporting period.
Interest cost equals defined benefit obligation less interest income on plan assets excluding irrecoverable surpluses.

2 Remeasurement – actuarial gains and losses; and return on plan assets less amounts included in interest income.

Some DB plans require employees or third parties to contribute to the cost of the plan. Contributions by employees reduce the cost of the benefits to the entity.

Subsequently, no reclassification is permitted from OCI to profit or loss.

Employee service gives rise to an obligation during the period for a DB plan, even if the benefits are conditional on future employment. This is a constructive obligation. In measuring the obligation, an entity must consider the probability that employees may not satisfy those vesting requirements. Similarly, medical benefits are only payable if a specified event occurs, so the probability of whether or not it will occur affects the measurement of the obligation but not whether or not an obligation actually exists.

If the defined benefits are reduced for the amounts paid to employees under government-sponsored plans, the DB obligation should be measured on a basis that reflects the benefits payable under the government plans, but only if:

(a) those plans were enacted before the reporting date; or
(b) past history or other reliable evidence indicates that those state benefits will change in the future predictably, e.g. by changes in the consumer price index or general salary levels.

Reimbursements If an entity is virtually certain that another party will reimburse the DB obligation, the entity should report the right to reimbursement as a separate asset, at fair value. The cost of a defined benefit plan recognised may be presented net of the amounts relating to changes in the carrying amount of the right to reimbursement.

EXAMPLE 8.7: DEFINED BENEFIT SCHEME

Roseberry Ltd prepares annual accounts to 31 December annually and has operated a defined benefit pension scheme for many years. The scheme is non-contributory. At 31 December 2019 the company's balance sheet revealed a defined benefit liability of €575,000, made up as follows:

	€000
Present value of defined benefit obligation	2,430
Fair value of plan assets	1,855
Defined benefit liability	575

The following figures relate to the year ended 31 December 2020:

	€000
Interest income on pension fund assets	170
Actual returns on pension scheme assets	155
Employer contributions	450
Benefits paid	375
Interest cost	220
Present value of the current service cost for the year	415
Present value of the defined benefit obligation at the end of the year	2,810
Fair value of plan assets at the end of the year	2,190

Assume a corporate bond rate of 9% is adopted, with interest income and cost both based on that rate (and rounded).

Solution

The calculation of the defined benefit expense to be shown in the company's profit and loss account for the year ended 31 December 2020 and the defined benefit liability as at that date are as follows:

	€000
Movement in defined benefit obligation	
Present value of the defined benefit obligation	2,430
Interest cost	220
Present value of the current service cost for the year	415
Benefits paid during the year	(375)
	2,690
Actuarial losses (balancing figure)	120
Present value of defined benefit obligation at the end of the year	2,810

Movement in plan assets	
Fair value of the plan assets at the start of the year	1,855
Interest income on plan assets	170
Employer contributions	450
Benefits paid during the year	(375)
	2,100
Actuarial gains (balancing figure)	90
Fair value of plan assets at end of the year	2,190
Defined benefit expense – profit or loss	
Present value of the current service cost for the year	415
Net interest cost (€220,000 – €170,000)	50
	465
Defined benefit expense – OCI	
Actuarial losses (€120,000 – €90,000)	30
	495
Defined benefit liability	
Present value of defined benefit obligation at the end of the year	2,810
Fair value of plan assets at the end of the year	2,190
Defined benefit liability in the balance sheet	620

The defined benefit expense for the year is €495,000, but the employer's contributions were only €450,000. This explains why the defined liability has increased by €45,000 during the year, from €575,000 to €620,000.

Other Long-term Employee Benefits

Other long-term employee benefits include:

(a) long-term compensated absences, e.g. sabbatical or long-service leave;
(b) long-service benefits;
(c) long-term disability benefits;
(d) profit-sharing and bonuses payable 12 months or more after the period end; and
(e) deferred compensation paid 12 months or more after the period end.

A liability should be measured at the net total of the following amounts:

(a) the present value of the benefit obligation at the reporting date; minus
(b) the fair value of plan assets at the reporting date.

Any change in the liability should be reported in profit or loss or capitalised as inventories, plant, etc.

Termination Benefits due to Early Retirement or Voluntary Redundancy

An entity may be committed to make payments when an employee's service is terminated by taking early retirement or voluntary redundancy.

Recognition

As there are no future economic benefits to the entity, termination benefits should be expensed immediately in profit or loss.

An entity may also have a curtailment of retirement benefits on the termination of employment of employees.

The termination benefits should be recorded as a liability and as an expense only when the entity is demonstrably committed to either:

(a) terminate the employment of an employee or group before normal retirement age; or
(b) provide termination benefits to encourage voluntary redundancy.

There needs to be a detailed formal plan with little realistic possibility of withdrawal from the plan.

Measurement

The termination benefits liability should be measured as the best estimate of expenditure required to settle the obligation at the reporting date and it should be based on the number of employees expected to accept the offer.

If the obligation is not due for more than 12 months after the end of the reporting period, it should be discounted to present value using the methodology mentioned earlier in this section.

Example 8.8: Termination Benefits

Doolong Ltd has decided to close one of its manufacturing sites in Ballyduff on 1 June 2019. It has announced its decision to the employees at the site and has a detailed plan that has been communicated to the employees. The costs of redundancy are likely to be €4 million.

Solution

In this scenario there is either a legal obligation under government regulations to pay out compulsory redundancy or else a constructive obligation to do so as the company has clearly gone public and the employees will now look for alternative employment. The bookkeeping is as follows:

Dr Income statement	€4,000,000	
Cr Provision for termination		€4,000,000

Group Plans

If a company participates in a group scheme and there is a contractual obligation, it must measure the assets and liabilities for the plan as a whole. If there is a contractual agreement or policy to charge each individual entity, that entity must recognise its share of the cost in its own financial statements. If there is no agreement or policy, the whole charge should go to the entity legally responsible for the plan. In that case the other entities should charge their contributions payable to their own financial statements. Recognising a net DB cost requires the recognition of a corresponding net DB asset or liability in the individual financial statements of any group entity recognising a net DB cost.

Disclosures

Short-term Employee Benefits

No specific disclosures are required for short-term employee benefits.

Defined Contribution Schemes

The total amount recognised in profit or loss as an expense should be disclosed.

If a DB multi-employer plan is accounted for as a DC plan because sufficient information is not available to use DB accounting, it must:

(a) disclose the fact that it is a DB plan and the reason why it is being accounted for as a DC plan, along with any available information about the plan's surplus or deficit and the implications, if any, for the entity;

(b) include a description of the extent to which the entity can be liable to the plan for other entities' obligations under the terms and conditions of the multi-employer plan; and

(c) disclose how any liability recognised has been determined.

Defined Benefit Plans

The following should be disclosed, individually or in the most appropriate groupings:

(a) a general description of the type of plan, including funding policy;

(b) the date of the most recent comprehensive actuarial valuation, and, if not carried out at the year end, what adjustments were made to measure the DB obligation at the reporting date;
(c) a reconciliation of the opening and closing balances of the DB obligation, fair value of assets and reimbursement rights;
(d) the above should include:
  (i) change in DB obligation,
  (ii) interest income or expense,
  (iii) remeasurement of DB liability split between actuarial gains and losses and return on assets in excess of interest included in profit, and
  (iv) plan introductions, settlements and curtailments;
(e) the total cost relating to defined benefit plans for the period, disclosing separately the amounts:
  (i) recognised in profit or loss as an expense, and
  (ii) included in the cost of an asset;
(f) for each major class of plan assets, which must include, but is not limited to, equity instruments, debt instruments, property and all other assets, the percentage or amount that each major class constitutes of the fair value of the total plan assets at the reporting date;
(g) the amounts included in the fair value of plan assets for:
  (i) each category of entity's own financial instruments, and
  (ii) any property occupied by entity;
(h) the return on plan assets; and
(i) the principal actuarial assumptions, including:
  (i) the discount rates,
  (ii) the expected rates of salary increases,
  (iii) medical cost trend rates, and
  (iv) any other material actuarial assumptions used.

The reconciliations in (d) and (e) above need not be presented for prior periods.

If the entity participates in a group DB scheme that shares risks between entities under common control, it must disclose the following:
(a) its policy for charging cost or the fact that it has no policy;
(b) its policy for determining the contributions paid to the scheme;
(c) if it allocates part of the cost of the DB scheme in its own accounts, it must disclose the same information, as above, for single company schemes; and
(d) if it accounts for its contributions payable as an expense, it must disclose (a), (b), (c), (f) and (g) above.

The information can be cross-referenced to disclosures in another group entity's financial statements if:
(a) that entity separately identifies and discloses all the required information about the plan; and
(b) that entity's financial statements are available to users on the same terms and the same timings as the financial statements of the entity itself.

Other Long-term Benefits

For each category of long-term benefit, the nature of the benefit, the amount of the obligation and the extent of funding at the reporting date must be disclosed.

Termination Benefits

For each category of termination benefit, the nature of the benefit, its accounting policy, the amount of the obligation and the extent of funding at the reporting date must be disclosed.

Where there is uncertainty regarding the number of employees who are likely to accept the offer of the termination benefits, a contingent liability should be disclosed under Section 21, unless the possibility of settlement is remote – see **Chapter 6**).

The following extract is based on the IASB's *IFRS for SMEs 2009 Illustrative Financial Statements Presentation and Disclosure Checklist* and provides an example of the disclosure required for employee benefits, but only for a long-service agreement.

Example 8.9: Illustrative Financial Statements – Long-service Agreements

Accounting Policies and Explanatory Notes (Extracts)

2. Basis of preparation and accounting policies

Employee benefits – long-service payments
The liability for employee benefit obligations relates to government-mandated long-service payments. All full-time staff, excluding directors, are covered by the programme. A payment is made of 5% of salary (as determined for the 12 months before the payment) at the end of each of five years of employment. The payment is made as part of the December payroll in the fifth year. The Group does not fund this obligation in advance.

The Group's cost and obligation to make long-service payments to employees are recognised during the employees' periods of service. The cost and obligation are measured using the projected unit credit method, assuming a 4% average annual salary increase, with employee turnover based on the Group's recent experience, discounted using the current market yield for high quality corporate bonds.

[...]

19. Employee benefit obligation – long-service payments

The Group's employee benefit obligation for long-service payments under a government-mandated plan is based on a comprehensive actuarial valuation as of 31 December 20X2 and is as follows:

	20X2
	€
Obligation at 1 January 20X2	9,830
Additional accrual during the year	7,033
Benefit payments made in year	(6,240)
Obligation at 31 December 20X2	10,623

The obligation is classified as:

	20X2	20X1
	€	€
Current liability	4,944	4,754
Non-current liability	5,679	5,076
Total	10,623	9,830

A good example of the type of disclosure required is provided by Musgrave Group Plc.

Musgrave Group Plc

ANNUAL REPORT 2018 – NOTES TO THE FINANCIAL STATEMENTS (EXTRACTS)

for the year ending 31 December 2018

Accounting policies

Employment benefits
The Group provides a range of benefits to employees, including annual bonus arrangements, paid holiday arrangements and defined benefit and defined contribution pension schemes.

(i) Short term benefits
Short term benefits, including holiday pay and other similar non-monetary benefits, are recognised as an expense in the period in which the service is received.

(ii) Defined contribution pension schemes
The Group operates certain defined contribution schemes for its employees. A defined contribution scheme is a pension scheme under which the Group pays fixed contributions into a separate entity. Once the contributions have been paid the Group has no

further payment obligations. The contributions are recognised as an expense when they are due. Amounts not paid are shown in other creditors in the balance sheet. The assets of the scheme are held separately from the Group in independently administered funds.

(iii) Defined benefit pension scheme
The Group has certain defined benefit schemes. All these schemes are closed to new entrants and future accrual. A defined benefit scheme defines the pension benefit that the employee will receive on retirement, usually dependent upon several factors including age, length of service and remuneration. A defined benefit scheme is a pension scheme that is not a defined contribution scheme. The liability recognised in the balance sheet in respect of the defined benefit scheme is the present value of the defined benefit obligation at the end of the reporting date less the fair value of the scheme assets at the reporting date.

The defined benefit obligation is calculated using the projected unit credit method. Annually, the Group engages independent actuaries to calculate the obligation. The present value is determined by discounting the estimated future payments using market yields on high quality corporate bonds that are denominated in euro and sterling and that have terms approximating the estimated period of the future payments (discount rate).

The fair value of scheme assets is measured in accordance with the FRS 102 fair value hierarchy and in accordance with the Group's policy for similarly held assets. For most plan assets this is the quoted price in the active market. Where quoted prices are not available appropriate valuation techniques are used to estimate fair value.

The cost or credit relating to defined benefit schemes is recognised in the profit or loss account as employee costs and comprises the cost of benefit changes, curtailments and settlements.

The net interest cost on the defined benefit liability is determined by multiplying the net defined liability by the discount rate (both as determined at the start of the financial year, taking account of any changes in the net defined liability during the financial year as a result of contribution and benefit payments). This cost is recognised in profit or loss as a net interest expense.

Actuarial gains and losses arising from the experience adjustments and changes in actuarial assumptions are charged or credited to other comprehensive income. These amounts together with the return on scheme assets, less amounts included in net interest, are presented as 're-measurement of net defined benefit liability' in other comprehensive income.

The aggregate amounts of net defined benefit assets (for schemes with surpluses) and net defined benefit liabilities (for schemes with deficits) are shown separately in the balance sheets within debtors and pension liability respectively.

(iv) Annual bonus plan
The Group operates an annual bonus plan for employees. An expense is recognised in the profit and loss account when the Group has a present legal or constructive obligation to make payments under the plan as a result of past events and a reliable estimate of the obligation can be made.

(v) Share-based payments
Employees may acquire shares in the Company under profit sharing schemes and long-term incentive plans. Equity-settled arrangements are measured at fair value (excluding the effect of non-market based vesting conditions) at the date of the grant. The fair value of employee services received in exchange for the benefit provided is recognised as an expense with a corresponding credit to other reserves over the period that the employees become unconditionally entitled to shares, share options or cash payments ('the vesting period'). The Company recharges the subsidiaries involved for the share-based payment expense relating to its employees. The fair value of a share option is calculated based on the fair value of the underlying share as adjusted for dividends foregone and the option price.

Share entitlements granted by the Company are subject to certain non-market vesting conditions that are taken into account by adjusting the number of shares or share options included in the measurement of the cost of employee service so that ultimately the amount recognised reflects the number of vested share options.

[...]

6 Employee costs

	2018 Number	2017 Number
Group		
The average number of persons (including directors) employed by the Group during the financial year was:		
Administration and support	1,507	1,395
Wholesale and retail distribution	5,699	5,207
	7,206	6,602

	2018 €m	2017 €m
Staff costs (including directors' remuneration)		
Wages and salaries	280.9	255.7
Social insurance costs	31.2	28.1
Pension costs (note 30)	6.5	15.6
Other compensation costs:		
Share-based payments charge (note 31)	4.7	4.0
	323.3	303.4

[...]

30 Pensions

The pension entitlements of employees arise under defined benefit and defined contribution schemes and are secured by contributions by the Group to separately administered funds in the Republic of Ireland and Northern Ireland.

All defined benefit schemes operated by the Group are closed to new entrants and to the future accrual of pension benefits. The defined benefit schemes provide retirement benefits on the basis of members' salary at the date of scheme closure. Annual contributions are based on the advice of qualified actuaries using the projected unit credit method and the Group had agreed a funding plan for the schemes whereby special contributions are made to reduce the funding deficit where necessary. The funding requirements in relation to the defined benefit schemes are assessed in accordance with the advice of qualified actuaries and valuations are prepared at triennial intervals. The actuarial valuation reports are available for inspection by members of the schemes at the registered office of the Company but are not available for public inspection, An updated actuarial valuation for the purposes of FRS 102 was carried out as at 29 December 2018 by qualified actuaries in respect of the defined benefit schemes.

The defined contribution schemes operated by the Group now provide benefits to all qualifying employees. Contributions in respect of the defined contribution schemes payable at year end amounted to €0.3 million (2017: €Nil million).

	2018 €m	2017 €m
The pension charge for the year is:		
Defined contribution schemes	16.1	15.6
Defined benefit schemes:		
Settlement gains	(10.0)	-
Curtailment losses	0.4	-
	(9.6)	-
Total pension costs (note 6)	**6.5**	**15.6**
Net interest expense – defined benefit pension schemes (note 7)	**2.5**	**3.4**

Pension costs are included with administration and distribution costs as follows:

	2018 €m	2017 €m
Administration costs:		
Defined contribution schemes	3.2	3.1
Settlement gains	(7.6)	-
Curtailment losses	0.3	-
Distribution costs:		
Defined contribution schemes	12.9	12.5
Settlement gains	(2.4)	-
Curtailment losses	0.1	-

During the year Musgrave Limited defined benefit pension scheme members were offered the option to transfer their accumulated benefits, plus an enhancement, to a personal defined contribution scheme. As a result, employer contributions of €14.0 million were paid to the scheme for member fund value enhancements and a €10.0 million settlement gain arose. The costs associated with this programme were €0.7 million. In addition, an adjustment was made to the valuation of defined benefit scheme liabilities in Northern Ireland to reflect a change in legislation in relation to guaranteed minimum pensions and a curtailment loss arose of €0.4 million. The net impact of these two matters was a gain of €8.9 million (2017: €Nil million).

Principal actuarial assumptions at the balance sheet date for defined benefit schemes	2018	2017
Discount rate at year end	2.4%	2.3%
Future pension increases	0.7%	0.7%
Inflation rate	1.6%	1.8%

The percentages set out above are based on the weighted average of the ROI and UK pension schemes.

Mortality assumptions used are as follows:	2018 Years	2017 Years
Longevity at age 65 for current pensioners		
Male	22.4	23.0
Female	24.3	25.0
Longevity at age 65 for future pensioners		
Male	24.2	25.2
Female	26.1	27.3

The following amounts at the balance sheet dates were measured in accordance with the requirements of FRS 102:

	Schemes in surplus 2018 €m	Schemes in deficit 2018 €m	Total 2018 €m
Present value of plan liabilities	(68.3)	(399.4)	(467.7)
Fair value of scheme assets	74.2	333.0	407.2
Pension asset/(liability)	5.9	(66.4)	(60.5)

	Schemes in surplus 2017 €m	Schemes in deficit 2017 €m	Total 2017 €m
Present value of plan liabilities	(51.4)	(513.7)	(565.1)
Fair value of scheme assets	52.0	392.7	444.7
Pension asset/(liability)	0.6	(121.0)	(120.4)

The fair value of scheme assets was:

	2018 €m	2017 €m
Debt instruments	273.7	280.9
Equities	85.9	111.1
Other	47.1	48.4
Cash and cash equivalents	0.5	4.3
	407.2	444.7

The actual return on scheme assets is a loss of €8.4 million (2017: €18.0 million gain).

The amounts recognised in other comprehensive income are as follows:

Other comprehensive income	2018 €m	2017 €m
Return on scheme assets excluding interest income	(18.4)	8.6
Experience gains arising on scheme liabilities	14.0	6.1
Changes in assumptions underlying the present value of scheme liabilities	36.5	22.7
Re-measurement of net defined benefit liability	32.1	37.4

The return on scheme assets excluding interest income of €18.4 million loss (2017: €8.6 million gain) has resulted rom the decline in asset values during the year due to the global fall in investment markets. The experience gains arising on scheme liabilities of €14.0 million (2017: €6.1 million) relates to a revision of scheme membership data following updated valuations.

The impact of the changes in assumptions underlying the present value of scheme liabilities of a €36.5 million gain (2017: €22.7 million gain) primarily relates to reductions in the inflation rates and changes in the mortality assumptions of the ROI schemes.

Movement in scheme assets and liabilities	Scheme assets €m	Scheme liabilities €m	Pension deficit €m
At 31 December 2017	444.7	(565.1)	(120.4)
Employer special contributions – ETV	14.0	-	14.0
Employer special contributions – recurring	6.8	-	6.8

Curtailment losses	-	(0.4)	(0.4)
Settlement gains	-	10.0	10.0
Interest income/(expense)	10.0	(12.5)	(2.5)
Return on scheme assets excluding interest income	(18.4)	-	(18.4)
Actuarial gain	-	50.5	50.5
Benefits paid	(10.4)	10.4	-
Settlement payments from plan assets	(24.2)	24.2	-
Settlement payments from employer	(14.0)	14.0	-
Translation adjustment	(1.3)	1.2	(0.1)
At 29 December 2018	(407.2)	(467.7)	(60.5)

This has been disclosed in the balance sheets as:

	2018 €m	2017 €m
Pension liability (for schemes with pension deficits)	(66.4)	(121.0)
Pension asset (for schemes with pension surpluses – included in note 16)	5.9	0.6
Net defined benefit schemes liabilities	(60.5)	(120.4)

Employer contributions for the financial year ended 28 December 2019 are expected to be €6.0 million.

8.2 SHARE-BASED PAYMENT (SECTION 26)

Reporting entities should apply Section 26 of FRS 102 to all share-based payment transactions, including:

(a) equity-settled transactions;
(b) cash-settled transactions; and
(c) transactions where the entity receives or acquires goods or services and the terms provide either the entity or the supplier with a choice of cash or equity settlement. These are known as hybrids.

An important change was made to Section 26 in the March 2018 version of FRS 102: in a group scenario where one entity in the group receives goods/services but another settles the share-based payment, this should be recognised as an equity-settled transaction ONLY if settled in the settler's own equity – otherwise it must be treated as a cash-settled transaction.

Recognition

Entities should recognise goods or services received in a share-based payment when they obtain the goods or as the services are received. There should be a corresponding increase in equity if they are equity-based, or a liability if cash-settled.

When the goods/services do not qualify as assets, the entity should expense them.

Recognition when there are Vesting Conditions

If the share-based payments granted to employees **vest** immediately, the employee is not required to complete a specified period of service before he/she is entitled to those share-based payments. The entity should presume that the services rendered by the employee as consideration for the share-based payments have been received. In this case, on grant date, the entity must recognise the services received in full, with a corresponding increase in equity or liabilities.

Normally the share-based payments do not vest until the employee completes a specified period of service. The entity must presume that the services to be rendered as consideration will be received in the future, during the vesting period. Entities must account for those services as they are rendered by the employee during the vesting period, with a corresponding increase in equity or liabilities.

Measurement of Equity-settled, Share-based Payment Transactions

Measurement Principle

Equity-settled schemes must be measured when the goods or services are received, and the corresponding increase in equity, at the fair value of the goods or services received, unless that fair value cannot be estimated reliably.

If the entity cannot estimate reliably the fair value of the goods or services received, it must measure their value, and the corresponding increase in equity, by reference to the fair value of the equity granted. To apply this requirement to transactions with employees and others providing similar services, the entity must measure the fair value of the services received by reference to the fair value of the equity granted, because it is not possible to estimate reliably the fair value of the services received.

For transactions with employees, the fair value of the equity must be measured at date of grant.

For transactions with parties other than employees, the measurement date is the date when the entity obtains the goods or renders the service.

A grant of equity might be conditional on employees satisfying specified vesting conditions related to service or performance. For example, a grant of shares or share options to an employee is typically conditional on the employee remaining in the entity's employ for a specified period of time. There might be performance conditions that must be satisfied, such as the entity achieving a specified growth in profit (a non-market vesting condition) or a specified increase in the entity's share price (a market vesting condition). All vesting conditions related solely to employee service or to a non-market performance condition must be taken into account when estimating the number of equity shares that are expected to vest. Subsequently, the entity should revise that estimate, if necessary, if new information indicates that the number of equity shares expected to vest differs from previous estimates. On vesting date, it must revise its estimate to equal the number of equity instruments that ultimately vested.

All market vesting conditions and non-vesting conditions must be taken into account when estimating the fair value of the shares or share options at the measurement date, with no subsequent adjustment, irrespective of the outcome of the market or non-vesting condition, provided that all other vesting conditions are satisfied.

Shares

The fair value of shares must be measured using the following three-tier measurement hierarchy:

(a) if an observable market price is available for the equity granted, use that price;
(b) if an observable market price is not available, measure the fair value of equity granted using entity-specific observable market data, such as:
  (i) a recent transaction in the entity's shares, or
  (ii) a recent independent fair valuation of the entity or its principal assets;
(c) if an observable market price is not available and obtaining a reliable measurement of fair value under (b) is **impracticable**, indirectly measure the fair value of the shares or the share appreciation rights using a valuation method that uses market data to the greatest extent practicable to estimate what the price of those equity shares would be on the grant date in an arm's length transaction between knowledgeable, willing parties.

The entity's directors should use their judgement to apply a generally accepted valuation methodology to determine fair value.

EXAMPLE 8.10: EQUITY-SETTLED, SHARE-BASED SCHEME

On 1 April 2019 the board of directors of Mosside Ltd granted key employees share options that are subject to vesting conditions. Details of the award are as follows: 50 employees can potentially receive 5,000 options each on 31 March 2021. The options that vest (see below) will permit the employees to purchase shares in Mosside Ltd at any time in the year to 31 March 2022 for €15 each. The par value of the shares is €1 per share.

The options only vest if the employees remain as employees of Mosside Ltd until 31 March 2021 and if the share price of Mosside Ltd is at least €20 by that date.

On 1 April 2019 the board of Mosside Ltd estimated that five of the 50 employees would leave in the following two years. Three of the employees left in the year ended 31 March 2020 and at that date the board considered that a further three would leave in 2021.

On 1 April 2019 the share price of Mosside Ltd was €15. The price had risen to €18 by 31 March 2020 and the directors are reasonably confident that the price will exceed €20 by 31 March 2021.

On 1 April 2019 the directors estimated that the fair value of one of the granted options was €4.50. This estimate had risen to €5 by 31 March 2020.

Solution

The total number of share options that can be awarded is 250,000 (50 employees × 5,000 options). At 31 March 2020 it was estimated that only 44 employees (50 – 3 left – 3 expected to leave) would be entitled to their options. Thus a total of 220,000 options (44 employees × 5,000) will be awarded.

The transaction must be measured at fair value at the date of the grant, i.e. €4.50.

The total cost of awarding the options is €990,000 (220,000 options × €4.50).

The vesting period is two years, thus the cost to be recognised for the year ended 31 March 2020 is €495,000 (€990,000 × ½).

The journal entry is as follows:

Dr	Income statement (expense)	€495,000	
Cr	Share option reserve (equity)		€495,000

The income statement for the year ended 31 March 2020 includes an expense of €495,000. This is an employment cost and is included in the cost of sales, distribution costs or administrative expenses, as appropriate.

The balance sheet as at 31 March 2020 includes a corresponding amount of €495,000 relating to the options. This is presented as a separate component within equity (i.e. a share option reserve).

In the year ended 31 March 2021, the employment cost will be €495,000 (i.e. 44 employees × 5,000 options × €4.50 × ½) and is recognised as per the previous year. The amount now recognised in the share option reserve will rise from €495,000 to €990,000.

In the year ended 31 March 2022, assume the number of options exercised will be 220,000 options × 90% = 198,000. The amount of cash invested will be €2,970,000 (198,000 options × €15). There is no impact on the income statement as the date of vesting occurred on 31 March 2021 and the remaining 10% expire and therefore lapse.

The impact on the balance sheet is as follows:

		€000	€000
Dr	Cash	2,970	
Dr	Share option reserve	990	
Cr	Share capital (198,000 shares × €1)		198
Cr	Share premium (198,000 shares × (€14 + €4.50))		3,663
Cr	Retained earnings (990,000 options × 10%)		99

This can be explained as follows:
Only the nominal or par value of the shares can be recorded as share capital, i.e. 198,000 shares × €1 = €198,000.

The share premium increases by €3,663,000, made up of premium paid on exercise of 198,000 shares × €14 plus the cost of the options to the company of €4.50.

The balance on the share options reserve is cleared: €891,000 (€990,000 × 90%) is transferred to share premium and the remaining amount of €99,000 is transferred to retained earnings when the options lapse.

Share Options and Equity-settled Share Appreciation Rights (SARs)

Share options and equity-settled share appreciation rights (SARs) must be measured at fair value using the three-tier measurement hierarchy:

(a) if an observable market price is available for the equity granted, use that price;

(b) if an observable market price is not available, measure the fair value of the share options and SARs granted using entity-specific observable market data, such as a recent transaction in share options;

(c) if an observable market price is not available and obtaining a reliable measurement of fair value under (b) is impracticable, indirectly measure the fair value of share options or SARs using an option pricing model. The inputs for the model (such as the weighted average share price, exercise price, expected volatility, option life, expected dividends, and the risk-free interest rate) should use market data to the greatest extent possible.

Modifications to the Terms and Conditions on which Equity Instruments were Granted

If the vesting conditions are modified in a manner beneficial to the employee, e.g. by reducing the exercise price or reducing the vesting period or modifying or eliminating a performance condition, the entity must take the modified vesting conditions into account in accounting for the share-based payment transaction, as follows.

(a) If the modification increases the fair value of the equity granted measured immediately before and after the modification, the entity must include the incremental fair value granted in the measurement of the amount recognised for services received as consideration for the equity granted. The incremental fair value granted is the difference between the fair value of the modified equity instrument and that of the original equity instrument. Both should be estimated as at the date of the modification. If the modification occurs during the vesting period, the incremental fair value granted is included in the measurement of the amount recognised for services received over the period from the modification date until the date when the modified equity instruments vest, in addition to the amount based on the grant-date fair value of the original equity instruments, which is recognised over the remainder of the original vesting period.

(b) If the modification reduces the total fair value of the share-based payment arrangement, or apparently is not otherwise beneficial to the employee, it must continue to account for the services received as consideration for the equity instruments granted as if that modification had not occurred.

Cancellations and Settlements

A cancellation or settlement of an equity-settled, share-based payment award must be accounted for as an acceleration of vesting, and therefore entities must immediately recognise the amount that otherwise would have been recognised for services received over the remainder of the vesting period.

Measurement of Cash-settled, Share-based Payment Transactions

In cash-settled transactions the goods and services acquired and the liability should be measured at the fair value of the liability. Until that is settled, the fair value must be remeasured at each reporting date and the date of settlement, with any changes in fair value being reported in profit or loss.

Measurement of Share-based Payment Transactions with Cash Alternatives

Entities should account for the transaction as cash-settled if, and to the extent, it has incurred a liability to settle in cash; or as equity-settled if, and to the extent, that no such liability has been incurred. It is treated as cash-settled unless either:

(a) the entity has a past practice of settling by issuing equity, or
(b) the option has no commercial substance because the cash settlement amount bears no relationship to, and is likely to be lower in value than, the fair value of the equity, in which case it is treated as equity-settled.

Group Plans

If a share-based payment award is granted by a **parent** to the employees of one or more **subsidiaries** in the group, the subsidiaries are permitted to recognise and measure a share-based payment expense on the basis of a reasonable allocation of the expense recognised for the group.

Government-mandated Plans

Some jurisdictions have programmes established under law by which equity investors (such as employees) are able to acquire equity without providing goods or services that can be specifically identified.

This indicates that some other consideration has been or will be received (such as past or future employee services). These are equity-settled, share-based payment transactions within the scope of this section. The entity must measure the unidentifiable goods or services received (or to be received) as the difference between the fair value of the share-based payment and the fair value of any identifiable goods or services received (or to be received) measured at the grant date.

Disclosures

The following information about the nature and extent of share-based payment arrangements must be disclosed:

(a) a description of each type of share-based payment that existed at any time during the period, including their general terms and conditions, e.g. vesting requirements, maximum term of options granted, method of settlement. It is possible to aggregate similar types of arrangements;

(b) the number and weighted average exercise prices of share options for each of the following groups of options:

   (i) outstanding at the beginning of the period,
   (ii) granted during the period,
   (iii) forfeited during the period,
   (iv) exercised during the period,
   (v) expired during the period,
   (vi) outstanding at the end of the period, and
   (vii) exercisable at the end of the period.

For equity-settled arrangements, information must be disclosed about how entities measure the fair value of goods or services received or the value of the equity instruments granted. If a valuation methodology has been adopted, entities must disclose the method and their reason for choosing it.

For cash-settled arrangements, entities must disclose information about how the liability was measured.

For share-based payment arrangements that were modified during the period, an entity must disclose an explanation of those modifications.

If the entity is part of a group share-based payment plan, and it recognises and measures its share-based payment expense on the basis of a reasonable allocation of the expense recognised for the group, it must disclose that fact and the basis for the allocation.

Entities must also disclose the following information about the effect of share-based transactions on the entity's profit or loss for the period and on its balance sheet:

(a) the total expense recognised in profit or loss for the period; and

(b) the total carrying amount at the end of the period for liabilities arising from share-based transactions.

A good example of the required reconciliation of the number of options outstanding at both the start and the end of the year as well as the weighted average exercise price is provided by the Musgrave Group Plc.

Musgrave Group Plc

ANNUAL REPORT 2017 – NOTES TO THE FINANCIAL STATEMENTS (EXTRACTS)

Accounting Policies

[...]

(v) Share-based payments
Employees may acquire shares in the Company under profit sharing schemes and long term incentive plans. Equity-settled arrangements are measured at fair value (excluding the effect of non-market based vesting conditions) at the date of the grant The fair value of employee services received in exchange for the benefit provided is recognised as an expense with a corresponding credit to other reserves over the period that the employees become unconditionally entitled to shares, share options or cash payments ('the vesting period'). The Company recharges the subsidiaries involved for the share-based payment expense relating to its employees. The fair value of a share option is calculated based on the fair value of the underlying share as adjusted for dividends foregone and the option price.

Share entitlements granted by the Company are subject to certain non-market vesting conditions that are taken into account by adjusting the number of shares or share options included in the measurement of the cost of employee service so that ultimately the amount recognised reflects the number of vested share options.

Own shares
Shares in the Company have been purchased by employee share trusts to satisfy share-based payment awards. The shares held by the employee share trusts are treated as own shares and the value of these shares is deducted from retained earnings. Any cash consideration received on the subsequent exercise of share awards is credited to retained earnings together with a transfer from other reserves representing the accumulated cost recognised in other reserves.

STATEMENT OF CHANGES IN EQUITY

	Share capital and related reserves €m	Revaluation reserve €m	Other reserves €m	Profit and loss €m	Total €m
At 31 December 2016	34.0	21.1	5.6	188.1	248.8
Movement during 2017:					
Profit for the financial year	-	-	-	71.7	71.7

Other comprehensive income for the financial year	-	-	-	30.0	30.0
Total comprehensive income for the financial year	-	-	-	101.7	101.7
Dividends paid (note 10)	-	-	-	(17.0)	(17.0)
Transfer from retained earnings	-	(0.1)	-	0.1	-
Share award consideration (note 26)	-	-	(5.6)	5.6	-
Share revaluation (note 26)	-	-	0.7	(0.7)	-
Payments to acquire own shares (note 26)	-	-	-	(7.1)	(7.1)
Profit sharing schemes charge (note 31)	-	-	1.7	-	1.7
Long term incentive plans charge (note 31)	-	-	2.3	-	2.3
Total transactions recognised in equity	-	(0.1)	(0.9)	82.6	81.6
At 31 December 2017	34.0	21.0	4.7	270.7	330.4

[...]

31 Share-based payments

The Group operates a number of share-based incentive plans which feature ordinary shares of the Company. The purpose of these plans is to motivate employees to contribute towards the creation of long term shareholder value. These plans are equity-settled share-based payments as defined in Section 26 of FRS 102. A charge has been reported in the profit and loss account of €4.0 million (2016: €4.6 million), comprised of a charge of €1.7 million (2016: €1.6 million) in relation to approved profit sharing schemes and a €2.3 million charge (2016: €3.0 million) for long term incentive plans.

Approved Profit Sharing Schemes ('APSS')

The Group operates share acquisition schemes on terms approved by the Republic of Ireland and United Kingdom revenue authorities. The schemes are open to certain employees based in the Republic of Ireland with more than three years of service and employees in the United Kingdom with more than eighteen months of service. The Company may allocate shares to qualifying employees and the employee is, subject to certain conditions, exempt from income taxes. The directors set aside a certain number of shares to be awarded to employees annually at their discretion. Trusts are established for acquiring shares which must be held by the trustees for a total period of three to five years for the employees to obtain the maximum tax benefit. There were 288,397 shares issued under these schemes during the year (2016: 290,248).

Long term incentive plans
The Group operates long term incentive plans for executive directors and certain senior executives under which conditional share options have been granted that may fully or partly vest depending on the achievement of demanding Group performance measures of growth in profitability and return on capital over a three year performance cycle.

The value of each executive's award is calculated at the conclusion of each performance cycle and may include a cash alternative at the Company's discretion. The plans are accounted for as equity-settled share-based payments consistent with the Company's intention to settle in equity rather than cash.

The cost of these awards is recognised over the three years of each performance cycle based on an estimation of the extent to which the performance measures are likely to be achieved and the fair value at the grant dates.

A summary of activity under the Group's long term incentive plans together with the range of exercise prices of the share options is as follows:

	2017	2016
Number of conditional options:		
Outstanding at beginning of year	2,907,113	3,900,681
Granted	735,073	883,413
Exercised	(621,589)	(1,631,642)
Forfeited	(198,138)	(245,339)
Outstanding at and of year	2,822,459	2,907,113

The options outstanding at 30 December 2017 have a weighted average vesting period of 1.2 years, a weighted average contractual life of 5.2 years and an exercise price of €0.50. Options were exercised during the year at an exercise price of €0.50 (2016: €0.57) and an average share price of €6.30 (2016: €5.17). The fair value of the options granted in 2017 was €4.50 (2016: €4.00). The fair value was measured based on the market value of the underlying share as adjusted for dividends foregone. The shares exercised were provided by the Employee Benefit Trust through purchases of shares from existing shareholders.

There were 474,302 (2016: 272,470) options exercisable at the end of the year.

8.3 SMALL ENTITIES

There are no explicit minimum disclosure requirements for small entities under Section 1A of FRS 102 for either the UK or the Republic of Ireland. However, small entities may need to provide disclosures as required by FRS 102, Sections 28 and 26 if required to give a true and fair view.

If a small entity has a material defined benefit pension share-based payment scheme it would probably be necessary to provide the full FRS 102 disclosures for those transactions to provide a true and fair view.

8.4 MICRO-ENTITIES

The accounting treatment for employee costs is identical to that under FRS 102. While it is unlikely a micro-entity would have either a defined benefit or share-based payment scheme, the general principles in FRS 102 have been retained in FRS 105.

Disclosure Checklist: Employee Costs – FRS 102

(References are to the relevant Section of FRS 102)

	Para.
Employee Benefits – Section 28	
Disclosures about short-term employee benefits	
This section does not require specific disclosures about short-term employee benefits.	28.39
Disclosures about defined contribution plans	
An entity shall disclose the amount recognised in profit or loss as an expense for defined contribution plans.	28.40
If an entity treats a defined benefit multi-employer plan as a defined contribution plan because sufficient information is not available to use defined benefit accounting (see paragraph 28.11), it shall: (a) disclose the fact that it is a defined benefit plan and the reason why it is being accounted for as a defined contribution plan, along with any available information about the plan's surplus or deficit and the implications, if any, for the entity; (b) include a description of the extent to which the entity can be liable to the plan for other entities' obligations under the terms and conditions of the multi-employer plan; and (c) disclose how any liability recognised in accordance with paragraph 28.11A has been determined.	28.40A
Disclosures about defined benefit plans	
An entity shall disclose the following information about defined benefit plans (except for any defined multi-employer benefit plans that are accounted for as a defined contribution plan in accordance with paragraph 28.11, for which the disclosures in paragraph 28.40 apply instead). If an entity has more than one defined benefit plan, these disclosures may be made in total, separately for each plan, or in such groupings as are considered to be the most useful: (a) a general description of the type of plan, including funding policy, including the amount and timing of the future payments to be made by the entity under any agreement with the defined benefit plan to fund a deficit (such as a schedule of contributions); (b) [Deleted]; (c) [Deleted]; (d) the date of the most recent comprehensive actuarial valuation and, if it was not as of the reporting date, a description of the adjustments that were made to measure the defined benefit obligation at the reporting date; (e) a reconciliation of opening and closing balances for each of the following: (i) the defined benefit obligation, (ii) the fair value of plan assets, and (iii) any reimbursement right recognised as an asset;	28.41

	PARA.
(f) each of the reconciliations in paragraph 28.41(e) shall show each of the following, if applicable: (i) the change in the defined benefit liability arising from employee service rendered during the reporting period in profit or loss, (ii) interest income or expense, (iii) remeasurement of the defined benefit liability, showing separately actuarial gains and losses and the return on plan assets less amounts included in (ii) above, and (iv) plan introductions, changes, curtailments and settlements; (g) the total cost relating to defined benefit plans for the period, disclosing separately the amounts: (i) recognised in profit or loss as an expense, and (ii) included in the cost of an asset; (h) for each major class of plan assets, which shall include, but is not limited to, equity instruments, debt instruments, property and all other assets, the percentage or amount that each major class constitutes of the fair value of the total plan assets at the reporting date; (i) the amounts included in the fair value of plan assets for: (i) each class of the entity's own financial instruments, and (ii) any property occupied by, or other assets used by, the entity; (j) the return on plan assets; (k) the principal actuarial assumptions used, including, when applicable: (i) the discount rates, (ii) the expected rates of salary increases, (iii) medical cost trend rates, and (iv) any other material actuarial assumptions used. The reconciliations in (e) and (f) above need not be presented for prior periods.	28.41
If an entity participates in a defined benefit plan that shares risks between entities under common control (see paragraph 28.38), it shall disclose the following information: (a) the contractual agreement or stated policy for charging the cost of a defined benefit plan or the fact that there is no policy; (b) the policy for determining the contribution to be paid by the entity; (c) if the entity accounts for an allocation of the net defined benefit cost, all the information required in paragraph 28.41; (d) if the entity accounts for the contributions payable for the period, the information about the plan as a whole required by paragraph 28.41(a), (d), (h) and (i). This information can be disclosed by cross-reference to disclosures in another group entity's financial statements if: (i) that group entity's financial statements separately identify and disclose the information required about the plan; and (ii) that group entity's financial statements are available to users of the financial statements on the same terms as the financial statements of the entity and at the same time as, or earlier than, the financial statements of the entity.	28.41A

	PARA.
Disclosures about other long-term benefits	
For each category of other long-term benefits that an entity provides to its employees, the entity shall disclose the nature of the benefit, the amount of its obligation and the extent of funding at the reporting date.	28.42
Disclosures about termination benefits	
For each category of termination benefits that an entity provides to its employees, the entity shall disclose the nature of the benefit, its accounting policy, and the amount of its obligation and the extent of funding at the reporting date.	28.43
When there is uncertainty about the number of employees who will accept an offer of termination benefits, a contingent liability exists. Section 21 *Provisions and Contingencies* requires an entity to disclose information about its contingent liabilities unless the possibility of an outflow in settlement is remote.	28.44
Share-based Payment – Section 26	
An entity shall disclose the following information about the nature and extent of share-based payment arrangements that existed during the period: (a) a description of each type of share-based payment arrangement that existed at any time during the period, including the general terms and conditions of each arrangement, such as vesting requirements, the maximum term of options granted, and the method of settlement (e.g. whether in cash or equity). An entity with substantially similar types of share-based payment arrangements may aggregate this information; (b) the number and weighted average exercise prices of share options for each of the following groups of options: (i) outstanding at the beginning of the period, (ii) granted during the period, (iii) forfeited during the period, (iv) exercised during the period, (v) expired during the period, (vi) outstanding at the end of the period, and (vii) exercisable at the end of the period.	26.18
For equity-settled, share-based payment arrangements, an entity shall disclose information about how it measured the fair value of goods or services received or the value of the equity instruments granted. If a valuation methodology was used, the entity shall disclose the method and its reason for choosing it.	26.19
For cash-settled, share-based payment arrangements, an entity shall disclose information about how the liability was measured.	26.20
For share-based payment arrangements that were modified during the period, an entity shall disclose an explanation of those modifications.	26.21
If the entity is part of a group share-based payment plan, and it recognises and measures its share-based payment expense on the basis of a reasonable allocation of the expense recognised for the group, it shall disclose that fact and the basis for the allocation (see paragraph 26.16).	26.22
An entity shall disclose the following information about the effect of share-based payment transactions on the entity's profit or loss for the period and on its financial position: (a) the total expense recognised in profit or loss for the period; and (b) the total carrying amount at the end of the period for liabilities arising from share-based payment transactions.	26.23

Disclosure Checklist: Employee Costs – Small Entities

(References are to the relevant Appendix of Section 1A FRS 102)

The mandatory disclosure requirements for small entities required under the Companies Act 2014 (ROI) (CA 2014), the Companies Act 2006 (UK) (CA 2006) and the Small Companies and Groups (Accounts and Directors' Report) Regulations 2008 (UK) (S.I. No. 409 of 2008) are as follows:

	Para.
Information about employee numbers	
The notes to a small entity's financial statements shall disclose the average number of persons employed by the small entity in the reporting period. (Sections 317(1)(a) and 317(7A) CA 2014) (Section 411 CA 2006)	1AD.37 (ROI) 1AC.33 (UK) (same)

Disclosure Checklist: Employee Costs – Micro-entities

(References are to the relevant Section of FRS 105)

The mandatory disclosure requirements for micro-entities required under FRS 105 and the Companies Act 2014 (ROI) (CA 2014), the Companies Act 2006 (UK) (CA 2006) and the Small Companies and Groups (Accounts and Directors' Report) Regulations 2008 (UK) (S.I. No. 409 of 2008) are as follows:

	Para.
A micro-entity shall disclose any commitment not recognised in the statement of financial position concerning pensions separately from other financial commitments, guarantees and contingencies in accordance with the relevant appendix to Section 6 *Notes to the Financial Statements*.	23.22
An Irish micro-entity shall disclose particulars of retirement benefit commitments included in the statement of financial position in accordance with Appendix B to Section 6 *Notes to the Financial Statements*.	23.23 (ROI only)

Chapter 9

FOREIGN CURRENCY TRANSLATION

9.1 FOREIGN CURRENCY TRANSLATION (SECTION 30)

Entities involved with foreign activities can conduct their affairs in two ways: by buying or selling goods and services abroad (i.e. transaction accounting); and/or by translating foreign operations back into the functional currency of the parent company for consolidation purposes (i.e. translation accounting). However, similar to IAS 21 *The Effects of Changes in Foreign Exchange Rates*, Section 30 of FRS 102 does not cover hedge accounting as it is covered in the financial instruments section (see **Chapter 12**).

Unlike most parts of the FRS, definitions play a key role in this section, in particular, the definition of functional currency.

Functional Currency

This is defined as the currency of the primary economic environment in which an entity operates. Normally, it is the currency of the country where the entity primarily generates and expends cash. Therefore, the most important factors to consider when determining functional currency are:

(a) the currency that mainly influences sales prices and the country whose competitive forces and regulations mainly determine the entity's sales prices; and
(b) the currency that mainly influences labour, material and other costs of providing goods and services.

However, the following factors should also help to provide evidence of the functional currency of an entity:

(a) the currency in which funds from financing are generated; and
(b) the currency in which receipts from operating activities are normally retained.

When investigating a foreign operation, such as a branch, associate or subsidiary, the following additional factors must also be considered:

(a) whether the activities of the foreign operation are an extension of the reporting entity rather than being carried out with a degree of autonomy, e.g. the former only sells goods of the 'parent' entity and remits proceeds directly to, and solely to, that entity;

(b) whether the transactions with the entity are a high or low proportion of the foreign entity's activities;
(c) whether the cash flows of a foreign operation directly affect the cash flows of the reporting entity; and
(d) whether the cash flows of a foreign operation are sufficient to service existing and expected debt without the funds being made available by the entity.

Example 9.1: Functional Currency

Slieve Bloom Ltd set up a wholly-owned subsidiary in Northern Ireland, Slieve Donard Ltd, on 1 June 2018 with a share capital of 400,000 ordinary shares of £1 each. Slieve Bloom Ltd transacts business on a limited basis with Slieve Donard Ltd. It maintains a current account with the company, but very few transactions are processed through this account. Slieve Bloom has assets of €1.5 million and 'normal' profits are approximately €160,000. The management of Slieve Donard are all based locally in Newcastle, County Down, although Slieve Bloom does have a representative on the management board. The prices of the products of Slieve Donard are determined locally and 90% of the sales are made within Northern Ireland. Most of the finance required by Slieve Donard is raised locally, although occasionally short-term finance is raised through borrowing monies from Slieve Bloom. Slieve Donard has made profits of £80,000 and £120,000, after dividend payments, for the two years to 31 May 2020, respectively.

During the year the following transactions have taken place:

1. On 30 September 2019 a dividend from Slieve Donard of £0.15 per share was declared. The dividend was received by Slieve Bloom on 1 January 2020.
2. Slieve Donard sold goods for £24,000 to Slieve Bloom during the year. Slieve Donard made a 25% mark-up on the cost of the goods. The goods were ordered by Slieve Bloom on 30 September 2019, were shipped free on board on 1 January 2020 and were received by Slieve Bloom on 31 January 2020. Slieve Bloom paid the Sterling amount on 31 May 2020 and had not hedged the transaction. All the goods remained unsold at 31 May 2020 (the group's financial year end).
3. Slieve Donard borrowed £15,000 on 31 January 2020 from Slieve Bloom in order to alleviate its working capital problems. At 31 May 2020 Slieve Donard's financial statements showed the amount as owing to Slieve Bloom. The loan is to be treated as permanent and is designated in euro.

On 1 June 2020 the subsidiary was sold for £825,000 and the proceeds were received on that day.

Assume the following exchange rates:

	£ to €1
1 June 2018	1.0
31 May 2019	1.3
30 September 2019	1.1
1 January 2020	1.2
31 January 2020	1.5
31 May 2020	1.6
1 June 2020	1.65
Average rate for year to 31 May 2020	1.44

Solution

There is not any one factor to determine the functional currency of a reporting entity. In this example there are limited transactions between the two companies. There have been sales of goods of £24,000, the payment of a dividend by Slieve Donard Ltd and a loan of €15,000 to Slieve Donard from Slieve Bloom. The management of Slieve Donard Ltd are all based locally, except for a common director, and pricing decisions are made locally. Thus there is limited dependence on the parent. Most of the finance has been raised locally and the goods are invoiced in Sterling. It would therefore appear that the functional currency of Slieve Donard Ltd is Sterling. The translation process is investigated later in the chapter.

Reporting Foreign Currency Transactions in the Functional Currency

Initial Recognition

If a reporting entity based in Ireland has decided, after consideration, that the euro is its functional currency, how should transactions for goods and services outside the euro area be recorded in the entity's own financial statements? This is known as foreign currency transaction accounting.

A foreign currency transaction therefore occurs:

(a) where a company buys or sells goods or services whose prices are denominated in a foreign currency (i.e. in this case, not euro);
(b) an entity borrows or lends funds when the amounts payable/receivable are denominated in a foreign currency; or
(c) otherwise the entity acquires or disposes of assets or incurs liabilities denominated in a foreign currency.

Initially the reporting entity should apply the spot exchange rate on the date of the transaction, but FRS 102 does permit an approximate rate for a large number of similar transactions, e.g. the average rate for a week/month is often used as long as the exchange rates do not fluctuate significantly over the week/month.

Reporting at the End of the Subsequent Reporting Period

At the end of each reporting period an entity should:

(a) translate all foreign currency monetary items at the closing rate of exchange;
(b) translate all non-monetary items at the exchange rate at the date of transaction; and
(c) translate all non-monetary items measured at fair value using exchange rates when the fair value is determined.

Exchange differences on monetary items (i.e. amounts that are receivable/payable in fixed or determinable units of currency) should always be recognised in profit or loss in the period they arise – at both settlement and at period-end dates.

Where a gain/loss on a non-monetary item is recognised directly in equity under another section of FRS 102, any exchange component should also go to equity. Conversely, when a gain/loss on a non-monetary item goes to profit or loss, so should the exchange component.

Example 9.2: Transaction Accounting

A company purchased goods from the US on 30 September for $40,000, half to be paid for on 30 November and the rest on 31 January.

The following exchange rates ruled:

	$ = €1
30 September	1.60
30 November	1.80
31 December	1.90
31 January	1.85

1. On 30 September, to record the transaction:

Dr	Purchases	€25,000	
Cr	Trade payables		€25,000

i.e. $40,000 @ $1.60/€1

2. On 30 November, to record the payment of half of the amount @ $1.80/€1:

Dr	Trade payables	€12,500	
Cr	Cash		€11,111
Cr	Exchange gain		€1,389

i.e. $20,000 @ $1.80/€1 = €11,111

3. At 31 December, translation of the year-end liability @ $1.90/€1

Dr	Trade payables	€1,974	
Cr	Exchange gain		€1,974

i.e. $20,000 @ $1.90/€1 = €10,526
€12,500 – €10,526 = €1,974

4. 31 January, to record the payment of $20,000 @ $1.85/€1:

Dr	Trade payables	€10,526	
Dr	Exchange loss	€285	
Cr	Cash		€10,811

i.e. $20,000 @ $1.85 = €10,811

EXAMPLE 9.3: FOREIGN LOAN

On 30 June, a US company is loaned $10,000 (€5,000 at that day's exchange rate). By

31 December	Year 1	it translates at €4,500
31 December	Year 2	it translates at €5,500
31 June	Year 3	it translates at €5,700 (date of repayment).

1. On 30 June, Year 1

Dr	Loan	€5,000	
Cr	Bank		€5,000

Foreign loan at **actual** euro cost.

2. On 31 December, Year 1

Dr	Exchange loss	€500	
	Cr Loan		€500

Loss charged to profit or loss at the year end.

3. On 31 December, Year 2

Dr	Loan	€1,000	
	Cr Exchange gain		€1,000

Gain credited to profit or loss at the year end.

4. On 30 June, Year 3

Dr	Bank	€5,700	
	Cr Exchange gain		€200
	Cr Loan		€5,500

Gain credited to profit or loss at the date of realisation.

If there are doubts as to the loan's convertibility or marketability, the gain in Year 2 should have been limited to the amount of past exchange losses, i.e. the gain of €1,000 is limited to €500 resulting in a €700 gain on realisation.

Example 9.4: Individual Transactions

Using the facts from **Example 9.1** and assuming that the subsidiary's functional currency is Sterling, the following should be the accounting required for the individual transactions between the parent and the foreign subsidiary.

Dividend
The dividend should be recorded in the parent's financial statements at the exchange rate when the dividend was declared, i.e. at 30 September 2019.

£400,000 × 0.15 × 1/1.1 = €54,545

An exchange difference will arise when the dividend is received in Slieve Bloom Ltd's financial statements. At 1 January 2020, Slieve Bloom will receive £400,000 × 0.15 × 1/1.2 = €50,000.

Thus an exchange loss of €4,545 will be taken to its profit and loss account and will be included in the consolidated profit and loss account.

The dividend paid in the translated financial statements of Slieve Donard Ltd will be £400,000 × 0.15 × 1/1.44 = €41,667, i.e. translated at the average rate.

There is, therefore, a difference between the dividend received in Slieve Bloom's income statement of €50,000 and the dividend paid by Slieve Donard of €41,667. The consolidated profit and loss account should reflect the subsidiary's profits translated at the average rate. Therefore the exchange loss of €8,333 should be treated as a movement in reserves. Although it is possible to take the dividend to the profit and loss account at the euro amount received, doing so would not retain the elements of the profit and loss account of Slieve Donard at the average rate.

Inter-company sales

The goods received from Slieve Donard would be recorded at the date that the risks and rewards of ownership pass to Slieve Bloom, which would be the shipping date if they are free on board. That is £24,000 × 1/1.2 = €20,000.

The profit made on the transaction will be €20,000 × 25/125 = €4,000. This would be eliminated from both inventory and group profit. This method of treating intragroup profit is consistent with the use of the weighted average rate. There would be a gain on the settlement of the liability by Slieve Bloom. The amount paid would be £24,000 × 1/1.60 = €15,000. Thus a gain on the settlement of the liability of €5,000 would be made, and reported, in the profit and loss account of the parent and thus the group accounts.

Loan

Where the loan is deemed to be permanent, it is really part of the net investment in the foreign subsidiary and exchange differences arising on such loans should be dealt with through reserves. The loan would be stated at £15,000 × 1/1.5 = €10,000 in Slieve Bloom's balance sheet. At 31 May 2018 it would be stated at £15,000 × 1/1.6 = €9,375 in the subsidiary's balance sheet. The exchange difference of €625 would be taken to reserves.

Sale of subsidiary

The net assets in Slieve Donard as at 31 May 2020 will be:

	£000
Share capital	400
Profit (£80,000 + £120,000)	200
	600

The net assets will be included in the consolidated financial statements at £600,000 × 1/1.6 = €375,000 less the inter-company profit in inventory of €4,000 = €371,000.

The sale proceeds at 1 June 2020 were £825,000 × 1/1.65 = €500,000. Thus a profit of €129,000 would be shown in the consolidated financial statements for the year ended 31 May 2021. On disposal of the foreign entity, the cumulative amount of exchange differences should be recognised as a transfer from unrealised to realised reserves but **not** recorded in profit, i.e. no reclassification is permitted.

Net Investment in a Foreign Operation

An entity may have a monetary item receivable or payable from a foreign operation. If the settlement is neither planned nor likely to occur soon, it is, in substance, part of the entity's net investment in the foreign operation. This could include long-term receivables or loans.

Exchange differences on a monetary item that forms part of an entity's net investment in a foreign operation should be recognised in profit or loss in the entity's statements or foreign operations as appropriate, except that any unrealised gain should be recognised in other comprehensive income. In the consolidated accounts, exchange differences may be recognised directly as a separate component of equity, but subsequently they are not recycled to profit on disposal. However, it does mean that a separate translation reserve needs to be created to keep a running record of all accumulated exchange differences, which are effectively temporarily 'parked' in that reserve until the investment is sold and are then transferred to retained earnings.

An example of this approach is provided by Oxford Instruments Plc with its creation of a foreign exchange translation reserve.

Oxford Instruments Plc

Report and Financial Statements 2018

CONSOLIDATED STATEMENT OF CHANGES IN EQUITY (EXTRACT)

Year ended 31 March 2018	Share capital £m	Share premium account £m	Other reserves £m	Foreign exchange translation reserve £m	Retained earnings £m	Total £m
Balance at 1 April 2017	2.9	61.5	0.2	22.8	45.1	132.5
Total comprehensive income/(expense):						
Profit for the year	—	—	—	—	65.5	65.5
Other comprehensive income:						
– Foreign exchange translation differences	—	—	—	(8.8)	—	(8.8)
– Net foreign exchange gain on disposal of subsidiaries recycled to the Income Statement	—	—	—	(4.8)	—	(4.8)
– Remeasurement gain in respect of post-retirement benefits	—	—	—	—	2.2	2.2
– Tax on items recognised directly in other comprehensive income	—	—	—	—	(0.9)	(0.9)
Total comprehensive income/(expense) attributable to equity Shareholders of the parent	—	—	—	(13.6)	66.8	53.2
Transactions with owners recorded directly in equity:						
– Proceeds from issue of shares	—	0.2	—	—	—	0.2
– Charge in respect of employee service costs settled by award of share options	—	—	—	—	1.1	1.1
– Dividends paid	—	—	—	—	(7.4)	(7.4)
Total transactions with owners recorded directly in equity	—	0.2	—	—	(6.3)	(6.1)
Balance at 31 March 2018	2.9	61.7	0.2	9.2	105.6	179.6

[...]

The foreign exchange translation reserve comprises all foreign exchange differences arising since 1 April 2004 from the translation of the Group's net investments in foreign subsidiaries into Sterling.

Change in Functional Currency

If there is a change in the functional currency of a reporting entity, the entity should apply translation procedures prospectively to the new currency from the date of change.

However, a change is only permitted if there is a change to the underlying transactions. The effect of a change in functional currency is accounted for prospectively, i.e. use the exchange rate at the date of change. The resulting translated amounts are then treated as the new historical cost. A good example of this was the decision taken by Greencore Group plc in 2011 to change its functional currency from euro to Sterling as a result of a major acquisition in the United Kingdom.

Greencore Group plc

Annual Report and Accounts 2011

GROUP STATEMENT OF ACCOUNTING POLICIES (EXTRACT)

Basis of Preparation

The Group Financial Statements, which are presented in sterling and rounded to the nearest thousand (unless otherwise stated), have been prepared under the historical cost convention, as modified by the measurement at fair value of certain financial assets and financial liabilities, including share options at grant date and derivative financial instruments. The carrying values of recognised assets and liabilities that are hedged are adjusted to record the changes in the fair values attributable to the risks being hedged. Share options and share awards granted to employees are recognised at fair value at the date of grant.

The accounting policies set out below have been applied consistently by all the Group's subsidiaries and associates and have been consistently applied to all years presented, unless otherwise stated.

Following the acquisition of Uniq plc, the Group changed its reporting currency from euro to sterling. This change aligns the Group's external financial reporting with the currency profile of the Group. At the same time, Greencore Group plc has changed its functional currency from euro to sterling. This change reflects the increased concentration of the Group's activities in sterling. The change in functional currency has been accounted for prospectively from completion of the acquisition while the change in presentation currency has been applied retrospectively.

Use of a Presentation Currency other than the Functional Currency

Translation to the Presentation Currency

Entities can present their financial statements in any currency they wish, but the group must present in a common currency for consolidation purposes.

If the functional currency is not that of a hyperinflationary economy, the entity must adopt the following procedures:

(a) assets and liabilities are translated at the closing rate;
(b) income and expenses are translated at the rates of exchange at the dates of the transactions; and
(c) all exchange differences are recognised within other comprehensive income.

For practical reasons, entities may adopt a rate that approximates actual rates, e.g. average rates, but not if the rates fluctuate significantly.

The exchange differences result from:

(a) translating income and expenses at transaction dates, not closing rate; and/or
(b) translating opening net assets at closing rate that differs from the previous closing rate.

When exchange differences relate to an operation with non-controlling interests, then part of those differences must be allocated to them.

Any entity whose functional currency is the currency of a hyperinflationary economy must adjust its results and financial position using the procedures specified in Section 31 *Hyperinflation* (see **Section 9.2** below) before translating them into a different presentation currency as follows:

(a) all amounts (i.e. assets, liabilities, equity, income and expenses) should be translated at the closing rate at the date of the most recent statement of financial position;
(b) comparative amounts should be those presented as current period amounts in the prior period financial statements.

Translation of a Foreign Operation into the Investor's Presentation Currency

Reporting entities should follow normal consolidation procedures, e.g. the elimination of intragroup balances and transactions (Section 9 – see **Chapter 11**). However, an intragroup monetary asset (or liability) cannot be eliminated against the corresponding intragroup liability (or asset) without showing the results of currency fluctuations in the consolidated financial statements. This is because the monetary item represents a commitment to convert one currency into another and thus exposes the reporting entity to a gain or loss through currency fluctuations.

Accordingly, in the consolidated financial statements, a reporting entity must continue to recognise exchange differences in profit or loss or, if it arises, in equity.

Any goodwill arising on the acquisition of a foreign operation and any fair value adjustments to the **carrying amounts** of assets and liabilities arising on the acquisition of that foreign operation must be treated as assets and liabilities of the foreign operation. Thus, they must be expressed in the functional currency of the foreign operation and be translated at the closing rate.

EXAMPLE 9.5: TRANSLATION OF A FOREIGN OPERATION INTO THE INVESTOR'S PRESENTATION CURRENCY

Boghill Ltd owns 75% of the ordinary share capital of Downward Ltd situated in Ruritania. Boghill Ltd acquired Downward Ltd on 1 May 2018 for R$120,000 when the retained profits of Downward Ltd were R$80,000. Downward Ltd has not revalued its assets nor issued any share capital since its acquisition by Boghill Ltd. The following financial statements relate to both companies.

BALANCE SHEETS
as at 30 April 2019

	Boghill Ltd	Downward Ltd
	€000	**R$000**
Tangible Assets		
Property, plant and equipment	297	146
Investment in Downward Ltd	48	–
Loan to Downward Ltd	5	–
	350	146
Current Assets	355	102
Less: *Creditors amounts falling due within one year:*		
Current liabilities	205	60
Net current assets	150	42
Creditors amounts falling due after more than one year:		
Non-current liabilities	30	41
Net assets	470	147
Capital and Reserves		
Ordinary shares of €1/ R$1	60	32
Share premium account	50	20
Retained earnings	360	95
Equity	470	147

PROFIT AND LOSS ACCOUNTS
for the year ended 30 April 2019

	Boghill Ltd	Downward Ltd
	€000	**R$000**
Revenue	200	142
Cost of sales	(120)	(96)
Gross profit	80	46

Distribution and administration expenses	(30)	(20)
Operating profit	50	26
Interest receivable	4	–
Interest payable	–	(2)
Profit before taxation	54	24
Income tax expense	(20)	(9)
Profit after taxation	34	15

The following information is relevant to the preparation of the consolidated financial statements of Boghill Ltd and its subsidiary:

(a) Goodwill is to be amortised over 10 years but, as at 30 April 2019, R$4,200 has been written off as an impairment.

(b) During the year Downward Ltd purchased raw materials from Boghill and denominated the purchase in R$ in its financial records. The details of the transaction are:

Date of transaction:	Purchase price:	Mark-up on selling price: 20%.
01/02/2019	€6,000	

At the year end, 50% of the raw materials were still in the inventory of Downward Ltd. The intragroup transactions have not been eliminated from the financial statements and the goods were recorded by Downward Ltd at the exchange rate ruling on 1 February 2019. A payment of R$6,000 was made to Boghill Ltd when the exchange rate was R$2.2 to €1. Any exchange gain or loss arising on the transaction is still held in the current liabilities of Downward Ltd.

(c) Boghill Ltd had made an interest-free loan to Downward Ltd of €5,000 on 1 May 2018. The loan was repaid on 30 May 2019. Boghill Ltd had included the loan in non-current liabilities and had recorded it at the exchange rate at 1 May 2018.

(d) The fair value of the net assets of Downward Ltd at the date of acquisition is assumed to be the same as their carrying value.

(e) The functional currency of Downward Ltd is the R$.

(f) The following exchange rates are relevant to the financial statements:

	R$ to €1
1 May 2018	2.5
1 November 2018	2.6
1 February 2019	2
30 April 2019	2.1
Average rate for year to 30 April 2019	2

(g) Boghill Ltd has paid a dividend of €800,000 for the year ended 30 April 2019 which is not included in the income statement.

Solution

Boghill Ltd and its Subsidiary
CONSOLIDATED PROFIT AND LOSS ACCOUNT
for the year ended 30 April 2019

	€000
Revenue (€200,000 + €71,000 – €6,000)	265
Cost of sales (€120,000 + €48,000 – €6,000 + €600) *(W7)*	(163)
Gross profit	102
Distribution costs and administrative expenses	(40)
Goodwill amortisation	(2)
Finance costs	(1)
Interest receivable	4
Exchange gains *(W7)*	1
Profit before tax	64
Income tax expense	(24)
Profit after tax	40

Boghill Ltd and its Subsidiary
CONSOLIDATED BALANCE SHEET
as at 30 April 2019

	€000
Tangible Assets	
Property, plant and equipment	367
Intangible Assets	
Goodwill (*W4*)	8
	375
Current Assets (€355,000 + €48,600 – €600) (*W7*)	403
Less: Creditors amounts falling due within one year	
Current liabilities	234
Net current assets	169
Less: Creditors amounts falling due after more than one year	
Non-current liabilities (€30,000 + €18,600 – €5,000)	44
Net assets	500

	€000
Capital and Reserves	
Share capital	60
Share premium	50
Retained earnings (*W5*)	363
Translation reserve (*W9*)	9
	482
Non-controlling interests (*W6*)	18
Equity	500

WORKINGS

W1 Group Structure

Boghill Ltd	75% Downward Ltd 01/05/2018
	25% non-controlling interests

W2 Translation of Balance Sheet

	R$000	Rate	€000
Property, plant and equipment	146.0	2.1	69.5
Current assets	102.0	2.1	48.6
	248.0		118.1
Share capital	32.0	2.5	12.8
Share premium	20.0	2.5	8.0
Retained earnings			
Pre-acquisition	80.0	2.5	32.0
Post-acquisition (R$15,000 + R$2,000 – R$1,200) (*W7*)	15.8	2.0	7.9
Translation reserve	–		9.7
	147.8		70.4
Non-current liabilities (R$41,000 – R$2,000) (*W7*)	39.0	2.1	18.6
Current liabilities (R$60,000 + R$1,200) (*W7*)	61.2	2.1	29.1
	248.0		118.1

W3 Translation of Profit and Loss Account

	R$000	Rate	€000
Revenue	142	2	71
Cost of sales	(96)	2	48
Gross profit	46		23

Distribution and administrative expenses	(20)	2	(10)
Interest payable	(2)	2	(1)
Exchange gain (R$2,000 – R$1,200) *(W7)*	0.8	2	0.4
Profit before tax	24.8		12.4
Income tax expense	(9)	2	(4.5)
Profit after tax for the year	15.8		7.9

W4 Goodwill

	R$000	R$000	Rate	€000
Cost of investment		120.0		
Less: fair value of net assets acquired				
Share capital	32			
Share premium	20			
Retained earnings	80			
	132			
Group share (75%)		99.0		
Goodwill		21.0	2.5	8.4
Impairment		(4.2)	2.1	(2.0)
Foreign exchange gain				1.6
Balance as at 30 April 2019		16.8		8.0

W5 Retained Earnings

	€000
Boghill Ltd	360
Downward Ltd (75% × €7,900) *(W3)*	5.9
Provision for unrealised profit *(W8)*	(0.6)
Impairment of goodwill *(W4)*	(2.0)
	363.3

W6 Non-controlling Interests

	€000
Non-controlling interests – share of net assets (25% × €70,400) *(W2)*	17.6

W7 Exchange Gains and Losses in Downward Ltd

	R$
Loan to Downward Ltd (non-current liabilities)	
At 1 May 2017 (€5,000 × 2.5)	12,000
At 30 April 2018 (€5,000 × 2.1)	10,500
Exchange gain	2,000

	R$
Intragroup balances	
Purchase of goods from Boghill Ltd (€600,000 × 2)	12,000
Payment made (€600,000 × 2.2)	13,200
Exchange loss	1,200

	€
Exchange differences in profit and loss account	
Gain on loan (R$2,000 ÷ 2)	1,000
Loss on current liability/purchases (R$1,200 ÷ 2)	600
	400

W8 Provision for Unrealised Profit

	€000
Intragroup sale (€6,000 × 20% × 50%)	0.60

W9 Translation Reserve

	€000
Closing net assets at closing rate *(W2)*	70.4
Less: opening net assets at opening rate *(W2)*	(52.8)
	17.6
Less: reported profit *(W3)*	(7.9)
	9.7
Group (75%)	7.3
Exchange gain on re-translation of goodwill *(W4)*	1.6
	8.9

Disclosures

An entity shall disclose:

(a) the amount of exchange differences recognised in profit or loss except for financial instruments measured at fair value through profit or loss; and

(b) the exchange differences recognised in other comprehensive income during the period.

The presentation currency must be disclosed and, if different from the functional currency, that fact and the reason for the adoption of a different presentation currency.

Where there is a change in functional currency, that fact and the reason for that change must also be disclosed.

9.2 HYPERINFLATION (SECTION 31)

Scope

Section 31 of FRS 102 applies to an entity whose **functional currency** is the currency of a hyperinflationary economy. It requires such an entity to prepare financial statements that have been adjusted for the effects of hyperinflation.

Hyperinflationary Economy

This section does not establish an absolute rate at which an economy is deemed hyperinflationary. That is a judgement made by considering all the available information, including, but not limited to, the following possible indicators of hyperinflation:

(a) The general population prefers to keep its wealth in non-monetary assets or in a relatively stable foreign currency. Amounts of local currency held are immediately invested to maintain purchasing power.
(b) The general population regards monetary amounts not in terms of the local currency but in terms of a relatively stable foreign currency. Prices may be quoted in that currency.
(c) Sales and purchases on credit take place at prices that compensate for the expected loss of purchasing power during the credit period, even if the period is short.
(d) Interest rates, wages and prices are linked to a price index.
(e) The cumulative inflation rate over three years is approaching, or exceeds, 100 per cent.

Measuring Unit in the Financial Statements

All amounts in the financial statements of an entity whose functional currency is the currency of a hyperinflationary economy must be restated in terms of the measuring unit current at the end of the **reporting period**. The comparative information for the previous period must also be stated in terms of the measuring unit current at the **reporting date**.

The restatement requires the use of a general price index that reflects changes in general purchasing power. In most economies there is a recognised general price index, published by government.

Procedures for Restating Historical Cost Financial Statements

Statement of Financial Position

Statement of financial position amounts are restated by applying a general price index.

Monetary items are not restated because they are expressed in terms of the measuring unit current at the end of the reporting period.

Assets and liabilities linked by agreement to changes in prices, such as index-linked bonds and loans, are adjusted in accordance with the agreement and presented at this adjusted amount in the restated statement of financial position.

All other assets and liabilities are non-monetary:

(a) Some non-monetary items are carried at amounts current at the end of the reporting period, such as net realisable value and fair value, so they are not restated. All other non-monetary assets and liabilities are restated.

(b) Most non-monetary items are carried at cost or cost less depreciation; thus they are expressed at the amounts current at their date of acquisition. The restated cost, or cost less depreciation, of each item is determined by applying to its historical cost and accumulated depreciation the change in a general price index from the date of acquisition to the end of the reporting period.

(c) Some non-monetary items are carried at amounts that are neither current at the end of the reporting period nor at cost less depreciation, for example, property, plant and equipment that has been revalued at an earlier date. In these cases, the carrying amounts are restated by applying the change in a general price index to the revalued amount, from the date of revaluation.

(d) The restated amount of a non-monetary item is reduced, in accordance with Section 27, when it exceeds its **recoverable amount** (see **Chapter 3, Section 3.4**).

At the beginning of the first period of application of this section, the components of **equity**, except retained earnings and any revaluation surplus, are restated by applying a general price index from the dates the components were contributed or otherwise arose. Any revaluation surplus that arose in previous periods is not restated. Restated retained earnings are derived from all the other amounts in the restated statement of financial position.

At the end of the first period and in subsequent periods, all components of owners' equity are restated by applying a general price index from the beginning of the period or the date of contribution, if later. The changes for the period in owners' equity are disclosed in accordance with Section 6 (see **Chapter 1, Section 1.4**).

Statement of Comprehensive Income and Profit and Loss Account

All items in the statement of comprehensive income (and in the profit and loss account, if presented) must be expressed in terms of the measuring unit current at the end of the reporting period. Therefore, all amounts need to be restated by applying the change in the general price index from the dates when the items of income and expenses were initially recognised in the financial statements. If general inflation is approximately even throughout the period, and the items of income and expense arose approximately evenly throughout the period, an average rate of inflation may be appropriate.

Statement of Cash Flows

All items in the statement of cash flows must be expressed in terms of the measuring unit current at the end of the reporting period.

Gain or Loss on Net Monetary Position

In a period of inflation, an entity holding an excess of monetary assets over monetary liabilities loses purchasing power, and an entity with an excess of monetary liabilities over monetary assets gains purchasing power, to the extent the assets and liabilities are not linked to a price level. Reporting entities must therefore include in profit or loss the gain or loss on the net monetary position, except any unrealised gain which should be recognised in other comprehensive income. An entity should offset the adjustment to those assets and liabilities linked by agreement to changes in prices against the gain or loss on the net monetary position.

Economies Ceasing to be Hyperinflationary

When an economy ceases to be hyperinflationary and an entity discontinues the preparation and presentation of financial statements prepared in accordance with this section, it must treat the amounts expressed in the presentation currency at the end of the previous reporting period as the basis for the **carrying amounts** in its subsequent financial statements.

Disclosures

An entity to which this section applies shall disclose the following:

(a) the fact that the financial statements and other prior period data have been restated for changes in the general purchasing power of the functional currency;

(b) the identity and level of the price index at the reporting date and changes during the current reporting period and the previous reporting period; and

(c) the amount of any gain or loss on monetary items.

Example 9.6: Hyperinflation

On 30 November 2018 Annoy Ltd set up a subsidiary in a foreign country where the local currency is forcurs (F). The principal asset of this subsidiary was a hotel, the cost of which was F2 million. The rate of inflation for the period 30 November 2018 to 30 November 2019 has been significantly high. The following information is relevant to the economy of the foreign country.

	Forcurs in exchange for €	**Consumer price index for foreign country**
30 November 2018	1.34	100
30 November 2019	17.87	3,254

There is no depreciation charged in the financial statements as the hotel has been maintained to a high standard and the useful life is assumed to be infinite. There has also been no impairment arising from a review of the property at 30 November 2019.

Solution

	Value		**Exchange rate**	**Value**
	Fm			**€m**
30 November 2018	2		1.34	1.493
30 November 2019	2		17.87	0.120

If the above approach were adopted, the reduction in cost would be solely caused by severe exchange rate movements and have nothing to do with trading performance. Instead, the following is required under FRS 102:

30 November 2019	2	3,254/100	17.87	36.420

9.3 SMALL ENTITIES

There are no explicit minimum disclosure requirements for small entities under Section 1A of FRS 102 for either the UK or the Republic of Ireland. However, small entities may need to provide disclosures as required by FRS 102, Sections 30 and 31 if required to give a true and fair view.

9.4 MICRO-ENTITIES

Though FRS 105 does not distinguish between functional and presentational currencies, it does state that if a micro-entity has a foreign branch it should refer to Section 30 of FRS 102 to determine if the foreign branch has a different functional currency. If the foreign branch does have a different functional currency, the requirements of FRS 102, Section 30 should be applied.

Under FRS 105, micro-entities follow the same general principles in the full version of FRS 102 regarding foreign exchange transactions, with one key exception: when a trading transaction is to be settled at a contracted rate, or is covered by a related or matching forward contract, the rate specified in the contract should be used.

Disclosure Checklist: Foreign Currency Translation – FRS 102

(References are to relevant Sections of FRS 102)

	Para.
Foreign Currency Translation – Section 30	
In paragraphs 30.26 and 30.27, references to 'functional currency' apply, in the case of a group, to the functional currency of the parent.	30.24
An entity shall disclose the following: (a) the amount of exchange differences recognised in profit or loss during the period, except for those arising on financial instruments measured at fair value through profit or loss in accordance with Sections 11 and 12; and (b) the amount of exchange differences recognised in other comprehensive income arising during the period.	30.25
An entity shall disclose the currency in which the financial statements are presented. When the presentation currency is different from the functional currency, an entity shall state that fact and shall disclose the functional currency and the reason for using a different presentation currency.	30.26
When there is a change in the functional currency of either the reporting entity or a significant foreign operation, the entity shall disclose that fact and the reason for the change in functional currency.	30.27
Hyperinflation – Section 31	
An entity to which this section applies shall disclose the following: (a) the fact that financial statements and other prior period data have been restated for changes in the general purchasing power of the functional currency; (b) the identity and level of the price index at the reporting date and changes during the current reporting period and the previous reporting period; and (c) the amount of the gain or loss on monetary items.	31.15

Disclosure Checklist: Foreign Currency Translation – Small Entities

There are no mandatory disclosures.

Disclosure Checklist: Foreign Currency Translation – Micro-entities

There are no mandatory disclosures.

Chapter 10

DISCLOSURE SECTIONS

10.1 EVENTS AFTER THE END OF THE REPORTING PERIOD (SECTION 32)

Events after the end of the reporting period are defined as those events, both favourable and unfavourable, between the end of the reporting period and the date that the financial statements are authorised for issue.

There are two types:

(a) adjusting events – those that provide evidence of conditions existing at the end of the reporting period; and

(b) non-adjusting events – those that are indicative of conditions arising after the end of the reporting period.

Events after the end of the reporting period include all those incurred by the date when the financial statements are authorised for issue, even if those events occur after the public announcement of profit or loss or other comprehensive income.

Recognition and Measurement

Adjusting Events after the End of the Reporting Period

Entities should adjust the amounts recognised in the financial statements to reflect adjusting events. The following are examples:

(a) the settlement of a court case confirming a present obligation – the entity must adjust the provision or create a new one, not merely disclose a contingent liability;

(b) the receipt of information that an asset was impaired, e.g. the bankruptcy of a customer, the sale of obsolete inventories at NRV in cases where this is below cost;

(c) the determination of the cost of assets purchased or the proceeds of assets sold;

(d) the determination of profit-sharing or bonus payments if a legal or constructive obligation exists; and

(e) the discovery of fraud or errors showing the financial statements to be incorrect.

EXAMPLE 10.1: ADJUSTING EVENT

On 1 March 2020 an entity's financial statements for the year ended 31 December 2019 were authorised for issue. On 1 February 2020 a competitor settled a claim with the entity for breach of one of its patents by paying the entity €600,000. The entity had opened the case in question against the competitor in 2019. However, until 1 February 2020 the competitor disputed the entity's case.

Solution

The settlement of the case provides evidence of conditions that existed at the end of the reporting period. The entity must report a €600,000 receivable at 31 December 2019 with a corresponding increase in profit for the year ended 31 December 2019.

EXAMPLE 10.2: ADJUSTING EVENT

An entity gives warranties at the time of sale to purchasers of its products. On 31 December 2019 an entity assessed its warranty obligation as €100,000. Immediately before the 31 December 2019 annual financial statements were authorised for issue, the entity discovered a latent defect in one of its product lines (i.e. a defect that was not discoverable by reasonable or customary inspection). As a result of the discovery, the entity reassessed its estimate of its warranty obligation at 31 December 2019 at €150,000.

Solution

The discovery of the latent defect is an adjusting event after the end of the reporting period. The condition – the latent defect – existed in products sold before 31 December 2019.

The obligation for the warranty provision must be measured at €150,000 at 31 December 2019, with a corresponding decrease in profit for the year ended 31 December 2019.

EXAMPLE 10.3: ADJUSTING EVENT

On 28 February 2020 an entity's financial statements for the year ended 31 December 2019 were authorised for issue. The entity sells some products on credit to a customer before 31 December 2019.

At 31 December 2019 the entity's management had no doubt about the customer's ability to pay the outstanding trade receivable of €200,000. However, in February 2020, during the process of finalising the financial statements, the entity is informed that the customer is going into liquidation because it has significant debt, has virtually no cash inflows and its accounting records are poorly maintained. Because of this, the trade receivables are deemed worthless.

Solution

A full allowance for bad debts of €200,000 should be made against the trade receivable, giving a corresponding loss of €200,000 in profit or loss. A customer's bankruptcy after the year-end will be, in nearly all cases, the culmination of a sequence of events that started before year-end, indicating that the trade receivable is impaired as at 31 December 2019.

However, if the financial instability of the debtor had arisen after 31 December 2019 (i.e. the debtor's financial position was strong at 31 December 2019), then the event would be non-adjusting, e.g. when the debtor's bankruptcy was caused by a unique, catastrophic event that occurred after 31 December 2019.

Example 10.4: Distinction between Correction of Error and Adjusting Event

In March 2023 the entity discovers that an error was made in the inventory reported in its balance sheet at 31 December 2020, resulting in an overstatement of income for that year. No error was made in the inventory that was reported for 31 December 2021. Therefore, the effect of the error on profit for 2020 was 'reversed' in measuring profit for 2021.

Solution

If historical data are presented that include 2020 and 2021, these years should be restated even though there is no effect in 2022 or 2023, not even on retained earnings at 1 January 2022. This is a correction of an error (dealt with in Section 10 (see **Chapter 7**), not an event after the end of the reporting period covered by Section 32.

Non-adjusting Events after the End of the Reporting Period

A reporting entity should not adjust the financial statements for non-adjusting events after the end of the reporting period. An example would be a decline in the market value of investments after the balance sheet date as this does not reflect their value at the end of the reporting period but circumstances that have arisen subsequently.

The following are examples of non-adjusting events after the end of the reporting period:

(a) a major business combination or disposal of a major subsidiary;
(b) an announcement of a plan to undertake a major restructuring of the entity;
(c) a plan to discontinue an operation;
(d) major purchases of assets;
(e) the destruction of a major production plant by fire;
(f) major ordinary share transactions;
(g) abnormally large changes in asset prices or foreign exchange rates;
(h) changes in tax rates announced;
(i) the entering into significant commitments or contingent liabilities; and
(j) the commencement of major litigation.

Example 10.5: Non-adjusting Event

On 1 March 2020 an entity's financial statements for the year ended 31 December 2019 were authorised for issue. At 31 December 2019 the entity had significant unhedged foreign currency exposures. By 1 March 2020 a significant loss had been incurred on these exposures because of a material weakening of the entity's functional currency against the foreign currencies to which it is exposed.

Solution

The deterioration of the exchange rate is a non-adjusting event after the end of the reporting period. It is indicative of conditions that arose after the end of the reporting period. The decline in exchange rate does not usually relate to conditions that existed at the end of the reporting period, but reflects circumstances that have arisen subsequently (i.e. the exchange rate at the end of the reporting period took account of conditions that existed at that date). Therefore, the entity does not adjust the amounts recognised during the year for the change in the exchange rate. Similarly, the entity does not update the amounts disclosed for the foreign-currency denominated liabilities (and assets) as at the end of the reporting period, although it may need to provide additional disclosure.

EXAMPLE 10.6: NON-ADJUSTING EVENT

On 28 February 2020 an entity's financial statements for the year ended 31 December 2019 were authorised for issue. On 20 February 2020 a fire destroyed one of the entity's manufacturing plants, which had a carrying amount of €2 million at 31 December 2019. The entity does not have insurance against fire damage. The entity remains a going concern.

Solution

The destruction of the plant by fire is a non-adjusting event after the end of the reporting period. The fire is a condition that arose after the end of the reporting period. The entity does not adjust the amounts recognised in its financial statements. However, it must give additional disclosure.

EXAMPLE 10.7: NON-ADJUSTING EVENT

On 28 February 2020 an entity's financial statements for the year ended 31 December 2019 were authorised for issue. At 31 December 2019 the fair value of the entity's investment in the ordinary shares of a publicly traded entity accounted for at fair value through profit or loss in accordance with Section 11 (see **Chapter 12**) was €20,000.

On 28 February 2020 the fair value of the shares was €25,000.

Solution

The change in the fair value of the publicly traded shares is a non-adjusting event after the end of the reporting period. The change in the fair value is a result of conditions that arose after the end of the reporting period. The entity does not adjust the amounts recognised in its financial statements. However, it must give additional disclosure.

Dividends

If an entity declares dividends after the period end, no liability should be recognised at the end of that reporting period. They may be shown, however, as a segregated component of retained earnings at the end of the reporting period.

Example 10.8: Proposed Dividends

On 1 March 2020 an entity's financial statements for the year ended 31 December 2019 were authorised for issue. On 28 February 2020 the entity declared a final dividend of €100,000 in respect of profits earned in the year ended 31 December 2019.

Solution

The declaration of the dividend is a non-adjusting event after the end of the reporting period. At 31 December 2019 the entity did not have an obligation to pay a dividend and therefore it cannot record a liability for those dividends at 31 December 2019. Proposed dividends do not meet the criteria for recognition as a liability under Section 21 (see **Chapter 6**) until they are appropriately authorised, e.g. usually passed at the annual general meeting, and are therefore no longer at the discretion of the reporting entity.

Example 10.9: Proposed Dividends before Year End but Paid after the Year End

On 1 March 2020 an entity's financial statements for the year ended 31 December 2019 were authorised for issue. On 28 February 2020 the entity paid a final dividend of €100,000 to its shareholders in respect of profits earned in the year ended 31 December 2019. The entity declared the dividend on 31 December 2019.

Solution

The payment of the dividend is not relevant to the existence of the obligation at 31 December 2019. At 31 December 2019, the entity had an obligation to pay the dividend and therefore must record €100,000 liability for those dividends at 31 December 2019.

Going Concern

Financial statements are **not** prepared on a going concern basis if management determines after the reporting date either that it intends to liquidate the entity or to cease trading, or that it has no realistic alternative but to do so.

Deterioration in operating results and financial position after the reporting date may indicate a need to consider whether the going concern assumption is still appropriate. If it is no longer appropriate, it requires a fundamental change in the basis of accounting, i.e. preparation on a break-up basis.

Disclosure

Date of Authorisation for Issue

An entity should disclose the date when the financial statements are authorised and provide details of those persons who gave the authorisation.

Non-adjusting Events after the End of the Reporting Period

An entity must disclose the following for each category of non-adjusting event:

(a) the nature of the event; and
(b) an estimate of its financial effect or a statement that such an estimate cannot be made.

Example 10.10: Disclosure of Non-adjusting Events

On 1 March 2020 an entity's financial statements for the year ended 31 December 2019 were authorised for issue. At 31 December 2019 the spot exchange rate was €2:FC1. The entity therefore measured its FC2 million unhedged non-current liability at €4 million in its balance sheet at 31 December 2019.

On 1 March 2020 the exchange rate was €2.5:FC1.

Solution

Note 20 Events after the end of the reporting period

The financial statements were authorised for issue on 1 March 2020 when the exchange rate was €2.5:FC1. The deterioration of the exchange rate from €2:FC1 at 31 December 2019 has increased the expected settlement amount of the FC-denominated liability by €1 million.

Example 10.11: Disclosure of Non-adjusting Events

An entity's financial statements for the year ended 31 December 2019 were authorised for issue on 28 February 2020.

On 20 February 2020 a fire destroyed one of the entity's manufacturing plants, which had a carrying amount of €2 million in the entity's balance sheet at 31 December 2019. The entity does not have insurance against fire damage. The destroyed plant has no value. It will be replaced at an estimated cost of €3 million. The entity remains a going concern.

Solution

Note 20 Events after the end of the reporting period

On 20 February 2020, one of the entity's uninsured manufacturing plants was destroyed by fire, resulting in plant with a carrying amount of €2 million at 31 December 2019 being impaired to €nil during 2020. The plant will be replaced at an estimated cost of €3 million.

Example 10.12: Disclosure of Non-adjusting Events

On 15 May 2020 an entity's financial statements for the year ended 31 March 2020 were authorised for issue. The entity has three major product lines: A, B and C. On 1 May 2020 the entity announced that it intends closing its Product A operations. The Product A operations did not meet the criteria to be classified as discontinued at 31 March 2020. The announcement to discontinue the Product A operations is a non-adjusting event.

The condition did not exist at 31 March 2020. This non-adjusting event must be disclosed in its 31 March 2020 financial statements.

Solution

Note 20 Events after the end of the reporting period

On 1 May 2020 the entity announced the closure of its Product A operations in Area A. During the year ended 31 March 2020, Product A accounted for operating profits of €20,000. At 31 March 2020 the carrying amount of the net assets related to Product A operations was €0.5 million.

The following extract, based on the IASB's *IFRS for SMEs 2009 Illustrative Financial Statements Presentation and Disclosure Checklist*, shows a disclosure note on non-adjusting events after the end of the reporting period.

Example 10.13: Illustrative Financial Statements – Items after the End of the Reporting Period

Accounting Policies and Explanatory Notes (Extract)

25. Events after the end of the reporting period

On 25 January 20X3 there was a flood in one of the candle storage rooms. The cost of refurbishment is expected to be €36,000. The reimbursements from insurance are estimated to be €16,000.

On 14 February 20X3 the directors voted to declare a dividend of €1.00 per share (€30,000 total), payable on 15 April 20X3, to shareholders registered on 31 March 20X3.

Because the obligation arose in 20X3, a liability is not shown in the balance sheet at 31 December 20X2.

Examples from Published Financial Statements

The following are real-life examples of the disclosure of non-adjusting events prepared under FRS 102 and full IFRS.

Ornua Co-operative Ltd

ANNUAL REPORT 2016 – NOTES TO THE FINANCIAL STATEMENTS (EXTRACT)

30. Post balance sheet events

Except for the following, there have been no significant event since the period end which require disclosure in the financial statements:

- In January 2017, the Group announced that it has signed an agreement to acquire F.J. Need (Foods) Limited, the Cheshire-based cheese ingredients' company. F.J. Need supplies a comprehensive range of British and Irish cheese ingredients to the foodservice and food manufacturing sectors. Ornua has been a supplier of high quality Irish cheese to F.J. Need for many years and the acquisition will strengthen this important supply channel. Completion of the acquisition is subject to UK competition approval.

Bibby Line Group Ltd

NOTES TO THE FINANCIAL STATEMENTS (EXTRACT)
for the year ending 5 March 2016

28. Post balance sheet events

Subsequent to the year end, on 5 March 2016, the group sold its entire shareholding in Bibby Ship Management Group Limited, realising a profit on sale of £6.0 million.

Interim dividends of £56.45 and £112.90 per share to the holders of the £1,000 Ordinary Shares were paid on 4 January 2016 and 24 March 2016. This constitutes a total dividend for the year ended 31 December 2015 of £169.35 per Ordinary share (2014 – £168.00 per share).

Interim dividends of £191.68 and £383.36 per share to the holders of the £1 Ordinary A Shares were paid on 4 January 2016 and 24 March 2016.

This constitutes a total dividend for the year ended 31 December 2015 of £575.04 per Ordinary A share (2014 – £nil).

No adjustments to the 2015 year end financial statements arose as a result of these transactions.

Musgrave Group Plc

NOTES TO THE FINANCIAL STATEMENTS (EXTRACT)
for the year ended 31 December 2017

34. Events after the balance sheet date

In January 2018, the Group purchased 100 per cent of the share capital of La Rousse Foods Limited, a food services company, for a consideration €49.0 million.

Aer Lingus Group Plc

Annual Report 2011

NOTES TO THE CONSOLIDATED FINANCIAL STATEMENTS (EXTRACT)

(Prepared under full IFRS)

36. Events after the reporting period

On 14 March 2012, Aer Lingus and its Aer Lingus Regional franchise partner, Aer Arann, announced an expansion of the existing franchise relationship. Aer Arann will operate all of its services between Ireland and the UK, France and the Isle of Man under the Aer Lingus Regional brand from 25 March 2012. Aer Arann will continue to assume full operational and commercial responsibility for the services covered by the franchise agreement, with Aer Lingus receiving a franchise fee in recognition for providing its brand and product suite to Aer Arann.

The EU emissions trading system ("EU ETS") became effective for Airlines from 1 January 2012. Under the EU ETS, all flights departing from and arriving at EU airports must pay for a portion of their carbon emissions. Aer Lingus has received free allowances amounting to 80% of its 2012 requirement under the EU ETS. The Group has purchased the balance of its 2012 requirements for €1.66 million.

On 23 March 2012, Aer Lingus Group plc subscribed for an additional 64,000,000 ordinary shares of €1.25 each in its wholly owned subsidiary, Aer Lingus Limited. The shares were issued at par and the total consideration was €80.0m. The amount payable was offset against the intercompany loan due to Aer Lingus Group plc from Aer Lingus Limited.

10.2 RELATED PARTY DISCLOSURES (SECTION 33)

This section of FRS 102 requires an entity to include disclosures to draw attention to the possibility that its financial position and performance could be affected by the existence of related parties and by transactions and outstanding balances with such parties.

In addition, FRS 102 has permitted exemption from disclosure for intra-group transactions provided any subsidiary involved is 100% owned, i.e. both members of the group must be 100% owned by the parent.

Related Party Defined

A related party is a person or entity who is related to the entity that is preparing its financial statements. It includes the following:

"(a) a person or a close member of that person's family is related to a reporting entity if that person:
  - (i) has control or joint control over the reporting entity,
  - (ii) has significant influence over the reporting entity, or
  - (iii) is a member of the key management personnel of the reporting entity or of a parent of the reporting entity;

(b) an entity is related to a reporting entity if any of the following conditions applies:
  - (i) the entity and the reporting entity are members of the same group (which means that each parent, subsidiary and fellow subsidiary is related to the others),
  - (ii) either entity is an associate or joint venture of the other entity (or of a member of a group of which the other entity is a member),
  - (iii) both entities are joint ventures of a third entity,
  - (iv) either entity is a joint venture of a third entity and the other entity is an associate of the third entity,
  - (v) the entity is a post-employment benefit plan for the benefit of employees of either the reporting entity or an entity related to the reporting entity. If the reporting entity is itself such a plan, the sponsoring employers are also related to the plan,
  - (vi) the entity is controlled or jointly controlled by a person identified in (a), or
  - (vii) a person identified in (a)(i) has significant influence over the entity or is a member of the key management personnel of the entity,
  - (viii) a person defined in (a) (i) who is a member of the key management personnel of the entity."

In all cases it is essential to assess the substance of the relationship, and not merely its legal form.

The following are not related parties:

(a) two entities having common directors or key management;

(b) two venturers simply because they share joint control over a joint venture;

(c) any of the following simply by normal dealings with an entity:
  (i) providers of finance,
  (ii) trade unions,
  (iii) public utilities, and
  (iv) government departments and agencies; and
(d) economically dependent customers, suppliers, franchisors, etc. with whom the entity does a significant volume of business.

However, FRS 102 clarifies that an associate includes subsidiaries of that associate and a joint venture includes its subsidiaries as well, i.e. an associate's subsidiary and the investor **do have** related party implications.

Disclosure

Disclosure of Parent–Subsidiary Relationships

Relationships between parents and subsidiaries should be disclosed irrespective of whether or not there are transactions between the parties. Entities should disclose the name of the entity's parent and, if different, its ultimate controlling party. If neither entity publishes accounts for public use, then the next most senior parent that does so should be disclosed.

Disclosure of Key Management Personnel Compensation

Key management personnel are those persons having authority and responsibility to plan, direct and control the activities of the entity. Compensation includes all forms of employee benefits provided in exchange for services rendered to the entity. It also includes consideration paid on behalf of a parent of the entity in respect of the entity.

Key management personnel (KMP) compensation should be disclosed in total, but not by individual categories. FRS 102 was amended in March 2018 so that an entity that has to disclose directors' remuneration in its Directors' Report (and the KMP are the same persons as the directors) need not make the above disclosure.

Disclosure of Related Party Transactions

A related party transaction is a transfer of resources, services or obligations between related parties regardless of whether a price is charged. Examples include:
(a) transactions between an entity and its principal owners;
(b) transactions between an entity and another entity where both are under the common control of a single entity; and
(c) transactions where an entity or individual that controls the reporting entity incurs expenses directly that otherwise would be borne by the reporting entity.

The nature of the relationship as well as transactions and outstanding balances should be provided. These are in addition to the key management personnel compensation disclosure above. At a minimum, the disclosures shall include:

(a) the amount of transactions;
(b) the amount of outstanding balances and their terms and conditions and details of any guarantees given or received;
(c) provisions for uncollectible receivables; and
(d) the expense recognised in the period for bad and doubtful debts due from related parties.

The disclosures should be provided separately for each of the following categories:

(a) entities over which there is joint control or significant influence, i.e. associates and jointly controlled arrangements;
(b) key management personnel; and
(c) other related parties.

An entity is exempt from the disclosure requirements in relation to:

(a) a **state** (a national, regional or local government) that has control, joint control or significant influence over the reporting entity; and
(b) another entity that is a related party because the same state has control, joint control or significant influence over both the reporting entity and the other entity.

However, the entity must still disclose a parent–subsidiary relationship as required above.

The following are examples of transactions that are disclosed if they are with a related party:

(a) purchases or sales of goods;
(b) purchases or sales of property;
(c) rendering or receiving of services;
(d) leases;
(e) transfers of research and development;
(f) transfers under licence agreements;
(g) transfers under financing arrangements;
(h) provision of guarantees;
(i) settlement of liabilities on behalf of the entity; and
(j) participation by a parent or subsidiary in a defined benefit plan.

Entities cannot state that they are using arm's length prices for their transactions unless this can be substantiated. An entity may disclose similar items in aggregate except when separate disclosure is necessary in order to understand their effect on the financial statements.

A good example of the 'two of three' sets of disclosures required by FRS 102 is provided by Eason & Son Ltd.

Eason & Son Ltd

ANNUAL REPORT – NOTES TO THE FINANCIAL STATEMENTS (EXTRACT)

for the year ended 28 January 2018

23 Related party transactions

During the year the Company traded with EM News Distribution (Ireland) Limited, joint venture company between the Company and Menzies Distribution Limited. This joint venture ceased on 27 May 2017. The material charges and balances up to this date are as follows:

	2018 €'000	2017 €'000
E M News Distribution (Ireland) Limited		
Amounts charged as interest from Eason & Son Limited	9	24
Amounts due as loan from Eason & Son Limited	-	1,461
Foreign exchange contracts entered into by Eason & Son Limited during the year* on behalf of EMND.	6,456	33,094

* E M News Distribution (Ireland) Limited bear full exposure for all foreign exchange contracts entered into on their behalf. For the year ended 28 January 2018 the foreign exchange contracts entered into were €6,456k (2017 €33,094k).

Eason and Son Limited is wholly owned within the Eason Holdings PLC group. Transactions with the holding company and fellow subsidiaries are not disclosed as the Company has taken advantage of the exemption available under FRS 102 from disclosing such transactions.

A good example of the three sets of disclosures required by FRS 102 is that provided by First Derivatives plc (albeit the financial statements are prepared under full IFRS).

First Derivatives plc
Annual Report and Accounts 2018
NOTES TO THE ACCOUNTS (EXTRACT)

31. Related parties transactions

Parent and ultimate controlling party
There is no one party who is the ultimate controlling party of the Group and Company.

Group
Key management personnel compensation
Key management personnel have been deemed to be the Directors of the Company. The remuneration of the Directors is set out in note 12.

The Group is charged rent monthly for the use of apartments located in London owned by Brian Conlon. The charge incurred during the financial year amounted to £55k (2017: £55k). Rent deposits of £26k (2017: £26k) have been paid to Brian Conlon in respect of these apartments. The balance owed to Brian Conlon at 28 February 2018 is £nil (2017: £nil).

A 15 year lease was entered into for the rental of office space for the head office in Newry. The lessor is Oncon Properties, a partnership in which Brian Conlon is a partner. £140k (2017: £140k) rental charge was incurred in the year. The balance owed to Oncon Properties at 28 February 2018 is £nil (2017: £nil) and an amount of £168k (2017: £207k had been repaid.

The Group holds an interest in an associate, together with other instruments as disclosed in note 18.

Company
Other related party transactions

	Revenue		**Administrative expenses incurred from**	
	2018	2017	**2018**	2017
	£'000	£'000	**£'000**	£'000
Subsidiaries	**8,488**	12,408	**22,976**	17,862

	Receivables outstanding		**Payables outstanding**	
	2018	2017	**2018**	2017
	£'000	£'000	**£'000**	£'000
Subsidiaries	**20,165**	25,805	**17,786**	18,270

Development costs of £281k (2017: £218k) were recharged from a subsidiary to the Company.

Interest is charged on inter-company loans at market rates.

Dividends paid by the Company to the Directors during the period were as follows:

	2018	2017
	£'000	£'000
B G Conlon	1,649	1,414
R G Ferguson	24	28
K MacDonald	10	9
S Keating	5	5
V Gambale	2	1
	1,690	1,457

An example of possible disclosure, based on the IASB's *IFRS for SMEs 2009 Illustrative Financial Statements Presentation and Disclosure Checklist*, is shown below.

Example 10.14: Illustrative Financial Statements – Related Party Transactions

26. Related party transactions

Transactions between the Company and its subsidiary, which is a related party, have been eliminated in consolidation.

The Group sells goods to its associate (see note 12), which is a related party, as follows:

	Sales of goods		Amounts owed to the Group by the related party and included in trade receivables at year-end	
	20X2	20X1	20X2	20X1
	€	€	€	€
Associate	10,000	8,000	800	400

The payments under the finance lease (see note 20) are personally guaranteed by a principal shareholder of the Company. No charge has been requested for this guarantee.

The total remuneration of directors and other members of key management in 20X2 (including salaries and benefits) was €249,918 (20X1: €208,260).

Example 10.15: Possible Related Party Relationships

Which of the following would be included as a related party of Portnoo Ltd:

1. An employee of Portnoo Ltd?
2. A shareholder holding 30% of the equity shares in Portnoo Ltd?
3. A director of Portnoo Ltd?
4. The sister of a director of Portnoo Ltd?
5. Otway Ltd, which supplies 90% of its output to Portnoo Ltd and which is economically dependent on its transactions with Portnoo Ltd?

Solution

1. In general an employee is not regarded as a related party simply because he or she is employed by the company.
2. A 30% shareholding would normally give significant influence over a company. If this is the case, the shareholder is a related party of Portnoo Ltd.
3. A director is a member of the company's key management personnel and is a related party.
4. The sister of a director is a close family member of a related party and is therefore also considered to be a related party of the entity.
5. The fact that Otway Ltd is economically dependent on Portnoo Ltd does not by itself mean that Otway Ltd is a related party of Portnoo Ltd.

Example 10.16: Disclosure of Related Party Transactions

Enniskerry Ltd has the following transactions with parties connected with the company.

Every month, Enniskerry Ltd sells €5,000 of goods per month to Mr O'Neill, the financial director. He has set up a small retail business for his son and the goods are purchased at cost price for him. The annual sales revenue of Enniskerry Ltd is €3 million. Additionally, Mr O'Neill has purchased his company car from the company for €30,000 (market value €45,000). Mr O'Neill earns a salary of €150,000 per annum.

Solution

Disclosure is only required if the transactions are material. Materiality must be assessed at both the entity and at the individual director level. Mr O'Neill has purchased €60,000 (12 months at €5,000 per month) of goods from the company and a car for €30,000, the market value of which is 50% higher. Based on Mr O'Neill's annual salary the goods purchased and €15,000 car benefit are material to him and thus must be disclosed in the notes to the financial statements.

EXAMPLE 10.17: DISCLOSURE OF RELATED PARTY TRANSACTIONS

A hotel property has been sold to Mr Strange, a brother of the managing director of Clare Ltd, for €1.85 million (net of selling costs of €50,000). The market value of the property was €2 million, but property prices are falling rapidly. The carrying value of the hotel was €3.5 million and its value in use €3 million. There was an over-supply of hotel accommodation due to government subsidies in an attempt to encourage the tourist industry.

Solution

This is clearly a related party transaction as Mr Strange's brother is a member of his close family and the transaction was not at arm's length. The property itself should be reduced to its recoverable amount of €3 million (higher of €3 million or €2m – €0.05m = €1.95 million). The property has been sold at €100,000 below its impaired value and this is the nature of the disclosure required.

EXAMPLE 10.18: DISCLOSURE OF RELATED PARTY TRANSACTIONS IN GROUP CONTEXT

Mr Oddball owns several companies and the structure of the group is as follows:

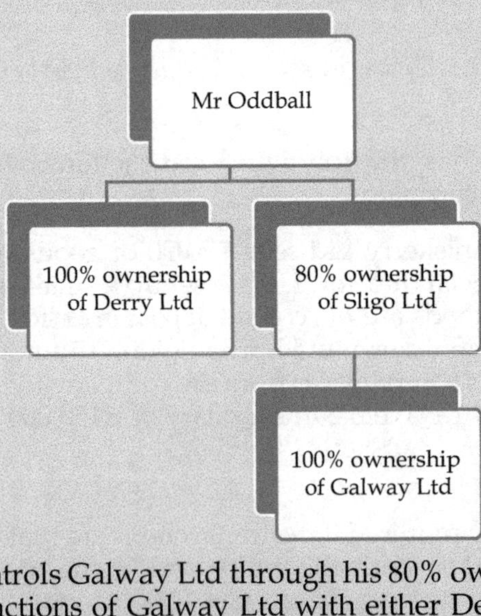

Mr Oddball controls Galway Ltd through his 80% ownership of Sligo Ltd. Any transactions of Galway Ltd with either Derry Ltd or Sligo Ltd will have to be disclosed as they are under the common control of Mr Oddball.

10.3 SMALL ENTITIES

There are no explicit minimum disclosure requirements for small entities under Section 1A of FRS 102 for either the UK or the Republic of Ireland. However, small entities may need to provide disclosures as required by FRS 102, Sections 32 and 33 if required to give a true and fair view.

10.4 MICRO-ENTITIES

The accounting treatment in FRS 105 for post-balance sheet events is identical to that under FRS 102 and there are no disclosures required of non-adjusting events in either jurisdiction.

There are also no disclosures required for related party transactions in the UK, but the Republic of Ireland has included a number of legal requirements (see Disclosure Checklist for micro-entities at the end of this chapter).

DISCLOSURE CHECKLIST: DISCLOSURE SECTIONS – FRS 102

(References are to the relevant Section of FRS 102)

	PARA.
Events after the End of the Reporting Period – Section 32	
An entity shall disclose the date when the financial statements were authorised for issue and who gave that authorisation.	32.9
An entity shall disclose the following for each category of non-adjusting event after the end of the reporting period: (a) the nature of the event; and (b) an estimate of its financial effect, or a statement that such an estimate cannot be made.	32.10
The following are examples of non-adjusting events after the end of the reporting period that would generally result in disclosure; the disclosures will reflect information that becomes known after the end of the reporting period but before the financial statements are authorised for issue: (a) a major business combination or disposal of a major subsidiary; (b) announcement of a plan to discontinue an operation; (c) major purchases of assets, disposals or plans to dispose of assets, or expropriation of major assets by government; (d) the destruction of a major production plant by a fire; (e) announcement, or commencement of the implementation, of a major restructuring; (f) issues or repurchases of an entity's debt or equity instruments; (g) abnormally large changes in asset prices or foreign exchange rates; (h) changes in tax rates or tax laws enacted or announced that have a significant effect on current and deferred tax assets and liabilities; (i) entering into significant commitments or contingent liabilities, e.g. by issuing significant guarantees; and (j) commencement of major litigation arising solely out of events that occurred after the end of the reporting period.	32.11
Related Party Disclosures – Section 33	
Disclosures required by this section need not be given of transactions entered into between two or more members of a group, provided that any subsidiary which is a party to the transaction is wholly owned by such a member.	33.1A
Disclosure of parent–subsidiary relationships	
Relationships between a parent and its subsidiaries shall be disclosed irrespective of whether there have been related party transactions. An entity shall disclose the name of its parent and, if different, the ultimate controlling party. If neither the entity's parent nor the ultimate controlling party produces financial statements available for public use, the name of the next most senior parent that does so (if any) shall also be disclosed.	33.5
Disclosure of key management personnel compensation	
Key management personnel are those persons having authority and responsibility for planning, directing and controlling the activities of the entity, directly or indirectly, including any director (whether executive or otherwise) of that entity. Compensation includes all employee benefits (as defined in Section 28 *Employee Benefits*), including those in the form of share-based payment (see Section 26 *Share-based Payment*). Employee benefits include all forms of consideration paid, payable or provided by the entity, or on behalf of the entity (e.g. by its parent or by a shareholder), in exchange for services rendered to the entity. It also includes such consideration paid on behalf of a parent of the entity in respect of goods or services provided to the entity.	33.6

	PARA.
An entity shall disclose key management personnel compensation in total.	33.7
When an entity is subject to a legal or regulatory requirement to disclose directors' remuneration (or equivalent), it is exempt from the requirements of paragraph 33.7 if the key management personnel and directors are the same.	33.7A
Disclosure of related party transactions	
A related party transaction is a transfer of resources, services or obligations between a reporting entity and a related party, regardless of whether a price is charged. Examples of related party transactions that are common to SMEs include, but are not limited to: (a) transactions between an entity and its principal owner(s); (b) transactions between an entity and another entity when both entities are under the common control of a single entity or person; (c) transactions in which an entity or person that controls the reporting entity directly incurs expenses that otherwise would have been borne by the reporting entity.	33.8
If an entity has related party transactions, it shall disclose the nature of the related party relationship as well as information about the transactions, outstanding balances and commitments necessary for an understanding of the potential effect of the relationship on the financial statements. Those disclosure requirements are in addition to the requirements in paragraph 33.7 to disclose key management personnel compensation. At a minimum, disclosures shall include: (a) the amount of the transactions; (b) the amount of outstanding balances and: (i) their terms and conditions, including whether they are secured, and the nature of the consideration to be provided in settlement, and (ii) details of any guarantees given or received; (c) provisions for uncollectible receivables related to the amount of outstanding balances; (d) entities that provide key management personnel services to the entity; and (e) the expense recognised during the period in respect of bad or doubtful debts due from related parties. Such transactions could include: purchases, sales, or transfers of goods or services; leases; guarantees; and settlements by the entity on behalf of the related party or vice versa.	33.9
An entity shall make the disclosures required by paragraph 33.9 separately for each of the following categories: (a) entities with control, joint control or significant influence over the entity; (b) entities over which the entity has control, joint control or significant influence; (c) key management personnel of the entity or its parent (in the aggregate); and (d) other related parties.	33.10

An entity is exempt from the disclosure requirements of paragraph 33.9 in relation to: (a) a state (a national, regional or local government) that has control, joint control or significant influence over the reporting entity; and (b) another entity that is a related party because the same state has control, joint control or significant influence over both the reporting entity and the other entity. However, the entity must still disclose a parent–subsidiary relationship as required by paragraph 33.5.	33.11
The following are examples of transactions that shall be disclosed if they are with a related party: (a) purchases or sales of goods (finished or unfinished); (b) purchases or sales of property and other assets; (c) rendering or receiving of services; (d) leases; (e) transfers of research and development; (f) transfers under licence agreements; (g) transfers under finance arrangements (including loans and equity contributions in cash or in kind); (h) provision of guarantees or collateral; (i) settlement of liabilities on behalf of the entity or by the entity on behalf of another party; (j) participation by a parent or subsidiary in a defined benefit plan that shares risks between group entities.	33.12
An entity shall not state that related party transactions were made on terms equivalent to those that prevail in arm's length transactions unless such terms can be substantiated.	33.13
An entity may disclose items of a similar nature in the aggregate except when separate disclosure is necessary for an understanding of the effects of related party transactions on the financial statements of the entity.	33.14

DISCLOSURE CHECKLIST: DISCLOSURE SECTIONS – SMALL ENTITIES

(References are to the relevant Appendix of Section 1A FRS 102)

The mandatory disclosure requirements for small entities required under the Companies Act 2014 (ROI) (CA 2014), the Companies Act 2006 (UK) (CA 2006) and the Small Companies and Groups (Accounts and Directors' Report) Regulations 2008 (UK) (S.I. No. 409 of 2008) are as follows:

	PARA.
Other	
The particulars and financial impact of material events that have occurred after the end of the reporting period shall be given in the notes to the financial statements. (Schedule 3A, paragraph 56 CA 2014) (Schedule 1, paragraph 64 S.I. 409/2008)	1AD.54 (ROI) 1AC.39 (UK) (similar)
Related party disclosures	
Directors' remuneration (sections 305 and 306 CA 2014)	
The notes to the financial statements of a small entity shall disclose both for the current and the preceding reporting period the following amounts in relation to persons who at any time during the financial year were directors of the small entity: (a) the aggregate amount of emoluments paid to or receivable by directors in respect of qualifying services; (b) the aggregate amount of the gains by the directors on the exercise of share options during the reporting period; (c) the aggregate amount of the money or value of other assets, including shares but excluding share options, paid to or receivable by the directors under long term incentive schemes in respect of qualifying services; (d) the aggregate amount of any contributions paid, treated as paid, or payable during the reporting period to a retirement benefit scheme in respect of qualifying services of directors, identifying separately the amounts relating to: (i) defined contribution schemes; and (ii) defined benefit schemes; and in each case showing the number of directors, if any, to whom retirement benefits are accruing under such schemes in respect of qualifying services, (e) the aggregate amount of any compensation paid or payable to directors in respect of loss of office or other termination payments in the reporting period, distinguished between: (i) amounts in respect of the office of director of the small entity; and (ii) amounts in respect of other offices. (Sections 305(1) and 305(12)(b) CA 2014) The aggregate amounts in sub-paragraph (e) above should also be distinguished between amounts paid by or receivable from: (i) the small entity; (ii) the small entity's subsidiaries; (iii) any parent of the small entity; and (iv) any other person. (Section 305(13)(b) CA 2014)	1AD.38 (ROI only)

	PARA.
The notes to the financial statements of a small entity shall disclose both for the current and the preceding reporting period the following amounts in relation to the one or more persons who are past directors of it or past directors of its parent: (a) the aggregate amount paid or payable for such directors' retirement benefits analysed between: (i) retirement benefits for services as director of the small entity; and (ii) other retirement benefits; (Sections 305(2) and 305(10) CA 2014) (b) the aggregate amount of any compensation paid or payable to such directors in respect of loss of office or other termination benefits distinguished between: (i) amounts in respect of the office of director of the small entity; and (ii) amounts in respect of other offices. (Sections 305(2) and 305(12)(b) CA 2014) The aggregate amounts in sub-paragraph (b) above should also be distinguished between amounts paid by or receivable from: (i) the small entity; (ii) the small entity's subsidiaries; (iii) any parent of the small entity; (iv) and any other persons. (Section 305(13)(b) CA 2014) The disclosures in paragraphs 1AD.38 and 1AD.39 shall include all amounts paid or payable to a person connected with a director (Section 306(1)) and shall include all relevant sums paid by or receivable from the small entity, its subsidiaries, any parent of the small entity, and any other person. (Section 305(13)(a) CA 2014)	1AD.39 (ROI only)
Payments to third parties for services of directors (sections 305A and 306 CA 2014)	
The notes to the financial statements of a small entity shall disclose, both for the current and the preceding reporting period, the aggregate amount of any consideration paid to, or receivable by, third parties for making available the services of any person: (a) as a director of the small entity; (b) as director of any of its subsidiaries; or (c) otherwise in connection with the management of the small entity's affairs or any of its subsidiaries. This disclosure shall include all relevant sums paid by or receivable from, and shall distinguish between the sums respectively paid by, or receivable from, the small entity, its subsidiaries, any parent of the small entity and any other persons. (Section 305A(1) and 305A(2) CA 2014) The nature of any consideration paid to, or receivable by, the third parties identified above, shall also be disclosed. (Section 305A(4)(a)(ii) CA 2014)	1AD.40 (ROI only)
Transactions with directors (sections 307 to 309 CA 2014)	
The financial statements of a small entity shall disclose, both for the current and the preceding reporting period, in the notes to the financial statements the particulars of the following arrangements (see paragraphs 1AD.42 to 1AD.45).	1AD.41 (ROI only)

	PARA.
Loans, quasi-loans and credit transactions	
The particulars required in respect of loans, quasi-loans and credit transactions entered into by the small entity with or for persons who at any time during the reporting period, were directors of the company or of its parent or persons connected with such directors, separately for each director or other person, are: (a) the name of the person for whom the arrangements were made and where that person is or was connected with a director of the small entity or its parent, the name of the director; (b) the value of the arrangements at the beginning and end of the reporting period; (c) advances made under the arrangements during the reporting period; (d) amounts repaid under the arrangements during the reporting period; (e) the amounts of any allowance made during the reporting period in respect of any failure or anticipated failure by the borrower to repay the whole or part of the outstanding amount; (f) amounts outstanding under the arrangements waived during the reporting period; (g) an indication of the interest rate; and (h) the arrangements' other main conditions. (Section 307(3) CA 2014) Additionally, a separate total of the amounts stated for the purposes of each of paragraphs (b) to (f) above, and the amounts stated for the purposes of paragraph (b) expressed as a percentage of the net assets of the small entity at the beginning and end of the reporting period shall be disclosed. (Section 307(8)(a) and (c) CA 2014) These additional requirements are extended to persons who are officers (but not directors) of the small entity or its parent, and separate disclosure in respect of these officers is required on an aggregate basis, as well as the number of officers for whom such arrangements were made. (Section 307(9) CA 2014)	1AD.42 (ROI only)
The particulars required in respect of an agreement to enter into loans, quasi-loans or credit transactions by the small entity with or for persons who at any time during the reporting period, were directors of the small entity or directors of its parent or persons connected with such directors, are those of subparagraphs (a), (g) and (h) of paragraph 1AD.42, and additionally the value of the arrangements agreed to. (Section 307(4) CA 2014) The disclosures shall be made separately for each director or other person.	1AD.43 (ROI only)
Guarantees and security provided by the small entity	
The particulars required for guarantees entered into and security provided by the small entity on behalf of persons who at any time during the reporting period were directors of the small entity or of its parent or persons connected with such directors in connection with a loan, quasi-loan or credit transaction entered into with or for those directors or other persons, separately for each director or other person, are: (a) the name of the person for whom the arrangements were made and where that person is or was connected with a director of the small entity or its parent, the name of the director;	1AD.44 (ROI only)

	PARA.
(b) the amount of the maximum liability that may be incurred by the small entity; (c) any amount paid and any liability incurred by the small entity for the purpose of fulfilling the guarantee or on foot of the provision of security (including any loss incurred by reason of enforcement of the guarantee or loss of the security); and (d) the arrangements' main terms. (Section 307(5) CA 2014) Additionally, a separate total of the amounts stated for the purposes of each of paragraphs (b) and (c) above is required. (Section 307(8)(b) CA 2014) This requirement is extended to persons who are officers (but not directors) of the small entity or its parent and separate disclosure in respect of these officers is required on an aggregate basis, as well as the number of officers for whom such arrangements were made. (Section 307(9) CA 2014)	1AD.44 (ROI only)
The particulars required in respect of agreements by the small entity to enter into guarantees or provide security on behalf of persons who at any time during the reporting period were directors of the small entity or of its parent or persons connected with such directors in connection with a loan, quasi-loan or credit transaction entered into with or for those directors or other persons, are those of subparagraphs (a), (b) and (d) of paragraph 1AD.44. (Section 307(6) CA 2014) The disclosures shall be made separately for each director or other person.	1AD.45 (ROI only)
Additional requirements	
Where at any time during the reporting period the aggregate of the amounts of: (a) the amount outstanding under arrangements waived comprising loans, quasi-loans and credit transactions; and (b) the amount of the maximum liability that may be incurred by the small entity in respect of arrangements comprising guarantees entered into or security provided in connection with a loan, quasi-loan or credit transaction amount to more than 10% of the net assets of the small entity, the aggregate amount shall be stated and the percentage of net assets that the total represents. (Section 307(10) CA 2014)	1AD.46 (ROI only)
In the event that the small entity is a parent and is taking an exemption from the requirement to prepare group financial statements, it shall provide the information required by paragraphs 1AD.41 to 1AD.46 in its financial statements in relation to both the small entity and its subsidiaries. (Section 308(4) CA 2014)	1AD.47 (ROI only)
The financial statements of a small entity shall disclose, both for the current and the preceding reporting period, in the notes to the financial statements the following particulars of any other arrangement or transaction not dealt with in paragraphs 1AD.38 to 1AD.47, entered into by the small entity in which a person, who at any time during the reporting period was a director, a director of its parent or a person connected with such a director, had, directly or indirectly, a material interest: (a) particulars of the principal terms of the arrangement or transaction; (b) the name of the director or other person with the material interest; and (c) the nature of the interest. (Section 309 CA 2014)	1AD.48 (ROI only)

	PARA.
Disclosure is not required in relation to transactions or arrangements with a small entity in which a director of the small entity or of its parent, or a person connected with such a director, had directly or indirectly, a material interest if: (a) they are excluded by virtue of section 309(5) CA 2014; or (b) (i) the value of each transaction or arrangement in which that director, or other person, had directly or indirectly a material interest and which was made after the commencement of the financial year with the small entity; and (ii) the value of each such transaction or arrangement which was made before the commencement of the reporting period, less the amount, if any, by which the liabilities of the person for whom the transaction or arrangement was made have been reduced (that is, the value outstanding), did not at any time in the reporting period exceed in aggregate €5,000 or, if more, did not exceed the lesser of €15,000 and 1% of the value of the small entity's net assets. (Section 309(6) CA 2014) In the event that the small entity is a parent and is taking an exemption from the requirement to prepare group financial statements, it shall provide the information required by this paragraph in its financial statements in relation to both the small entity and its subsidiaries. (Section 309(7) CA 2014) A small entity that is not a company shall provide the disclosures required by paragraphs 1AD.38 to 1AD.48 in relation to members of its governing body.	1AD.48 (ROI only)
Other related party disclosures	
Where a small entity, or a nominee of the small entity or a person acting in that person's own name but on behalf of the small entity, holds shares in the small entity or an interest in such shares, the notes to the financial statements shall give separately: (a) the number and aggregate nominal value of those shares and, where shares of more than one class have been acquired, the number and aggregate nominal value of each class of such shares, at the beginning and end of the reporting period together with the consideration paid for such shares; (b) a reconciliation of the number and nominal value of each class of such shares from the beginning of the reporting period to the end of the reporting period showing all changes during the reporting period, including further acquisitions, disposals and cancellations, in each case showing the value of the consideration paid or received, if any; (c) the reasons for any acquisitions made during the reporting period; (d) the proportion of called-up share capital held at the beginning and end of The reporting period; and (e) particulars of any restriction on profits available for distribution by virtue of the application of Section 320. (Section 320 CA 2014)	1AD.49 (ROI only)
Where a small entity is a parent and a subsidiary, the following information shall be stated with respect to the parent of the smallest group for which consolidated financial statements are drawn up and of which the small entity is a member: (a) the name of the parent; and (b) if the parent is incorporated, the address of the parent's registered office whether in or outside of the Republic of Ireland; or (c) if the parent is unincorporated, the address of its principal place of business.	1AD.50 (ROI) 1AC.34 (UK) (similar)

	PARA.
(Schedule 3A, paragraphs 57 and 58 CA 2014) (Schedule 1, Paragraph 65 S.I. 409/2008) Paragraph 33.5 addresses a similar requirement to paragraph (a).	1AD.50 (ROI) 1AC.34 (UK) (similar)
Particulars shall be given in the notes to the financial statements of transactions which have been entered into with related parties by the small entity if such transactions are material and have not been concluded under normal market conditions. The particulars shall include the amount of such transactions, the nature of the related party relationship and other information about the transactions which is necessary for an understanding of the financial position of the small entity. The provision of particulars and other information about individual transactions may be aggregated according to their nature, except where separate information is necessary for an understanding of the effects of related party transactions on the financial position of the small entity. Particulars need not be given of transactions which are entered into between two or more members of a group if any subsidiary which is party to the transaction is wholly owned by such a member. These requirements apply only to related parties that are: (a) the holders of participating interests in the small entity; (b) entities in which the small entity holds a participating interest; and (c) directors of the small entity or of a parent of the small entity. (Schedule 3A, paragraph 55 CA 2014) A small entity that is not a company shall provide the disclosures required by this paragraph in relation to members of its governing body. Although disclosure is only required of material transactions with the specified related parties that have not been concluded under normal market conditions, small entities disclosing all transactions with such related parties would still be compliant with company law. Transactions with directors, or members of a small entity's governing body, include dividends paid to directors. Paragraphs 33.9 and 33.14 address similar requirements for all related parties.	1AD.51 (ROI) 1AC.35 (UK) (similar)
Details of advances and credits granted by the small entity to its directors and guarantees of any kind entered into by the small entity on behalf of its directors must be shown in the notes to the financial statements. The details required of an advance or credit are: (a) its amount; (b) an indication of the interest rate; (c) its main conditions; (d) any amounts repaid; (e) any amounts written off; and (f) any amounts waived. There must also be stated in the notes to the financial statements the totals of amounts stated under (a), (d), (e) and (f). The details required of a guarantee are: (a) its main terms; (b) the amount of the maximum liability that may be incurred by the small entity; and (c) any amount paid and any liability incurred by the small entity for the purpose of fulfilling the guarantee (including any loss incurred by reason of enforcement of the guarantee). There must also be stated in the notes to the financial statements the totals of amounts stated under (b) and (c). (Section 413 CA 2006) Paragraph 33.9 addresses similar requirements for all related parties. A small entity that is not a company shall provide this disclosure in relation to members of its governing body.	1AC.36 (UK only)

Disclosure Checklist: Disclosure Sections – Micro-entities

(References are to the relevant Section of FRS 105)

The mandatory disclosure requirements for micro entities required under FRS 105, the Companies Act 2014 (ROI) (CA 2014), the Companies Act 2006 (UK) and the Small Companies and Groups (Accounts and Directors' Report) Regulations 2008 (UK) (S.I. No. 409 of 2008) are as follows:

	PARA.
Related party disclosures	
Transactions with directors (sections 307 and 308 CA 2014)	
The financial statements of a micro-entity shall disclose, both for the current and the preceding reporting period, in the notes to the financial statements the particulars of the following arrangements (see paragraphs 6B.20 to 6B.23).	6B.19 (ROI only)
Loans, quasi-loans and credit transactions	
The particulars required in respect of loans, quasi-loans and credit transactions entered into by the micro-entity with or for persons who at any time during the reporting period, were directors of the company or of its parent or persons connected with such directors, separately for each director or other person, are: (a) the name of the person for whom the arrangements were made and where that person is or was connected with a director of the micro-entity or its parent, the name of the director; (b) the value of the arrangements at the beginning and end of the reporting period; (c) advances made under the arrangements during the reporting period; (d) amounts repaid under the arrangements during the reporting period; (e) the amounts of any allowance made during the reporting period in respect of any failure or anticipated failure by the borrower to repay the whole or part of the outstanding amount; (e) amounts outstanding under the arrangements waived during the reporting period; (g) an indication of the interest rate; and (h) the arrangements' other main conditions. (Section 307(3) CA 2014) Additionally, a separate total of the amounts stated for the purposes of each of paragraphs (b) to (f) above, and the amounts stated for the purposes of paragraph (b) expressed as a percentage of the net assets of the micro-entity at the beginning and end of the reporting period shall be disclosed. (Section 307(8)(a) and (c) CA 2014) These additional requirements are extended to persons who are officers (but not directors) of the micro-entity or its parent, and separate disclosure in respect of these officers is required on an aggregate basis, as well as the number of officers for whom such arrangements were made. (Section 307(9) CA 2014)	6B.20 (ROI only)
The particulars required in respect of an agreement to enter into loans, quasi-loans or credit transactions by the micro-entity with or for persons who at any time during the reporting period, were directors of the company or directors of its parent or persons connected with such directors, are those of subparagraphs (a), (g) and (h) of paragraph 6B.20, and additionally the value of the arrangements agreed to. (Section 307(4) CA 2014) All the above disclosures shall be made separately for each director or other person.	6B.21 (ROI only)

	PARA.
Guarantees and security provided by the micro-entity	
The particulars required for guarantees entered into and security provided by the micro-entity on behalf of persons who at any time during the reporting period were directors of the micro-entity or of its parent or persons connected with such directors in connection with a loan, quasi-loan or credit transaction entered into with or for those directors or other persons, separately for each director or other person, are: (a) the name of the person for whom the arrangements were made and where that person is or was connected with a director of the micro-entity or its parent, the name of the director; (b) the amount of the maximum liability that may be incurred by the micro-entity; (c) any amount paid and any liability incurred by the micro-entity for the purpose of fulfilling the guarantee or on foot of the provision of security (including any loss incurred by reason of enforcement of the guarantee or loss of the security); and (d) the arrangements' main terms. (Section 307(5) CA 2014) Additionally, a separate total of the amounts stated for the purposes of each of paragraphs (b) and (c) above is required. (Section 307(8)(b) of the Companies Act 2014) This requirement is extended to persons who are officers (but not directors) of the micro-entity or its parent and separate disclosure in respect of these officers is required on an aggregate basis, as well as the number of officers for whom such arrangements were made. (Section 307(9) CA 2014)	6B.22 (ROI only)
The particulars required in respect of agreements by the micro-entity to enter into guarantees or provide security on behalf of persons who at any time during the reporting period were directors of the micro-entity or of its parent or persons connected with such directors in connection with a loan, quasi-loan or credit transaction entered into with or for those directors or other persons, are those of subparagraphs (a), (b) and (d) of paragraph 6B.22. (Section 307(6) CA 2014) The disclosures shall be made separately for each director or other person.	6B.23 (ROI only)
Additional requirements	
Where at any time during the reporting period the aggregate of the amounts of: (a) the amount outstanding under arrangements waived comprising loans, quasi loans and credit transactions; and (b) the amount of the maximum liability that may be incurred by the micro-entity in respect of arrangements comprising guarantees entered into or security provided in connection with a loan, quasi-loan or credit transaction amount to more than 10% of the net assets of the micro-entity, the aggregate amount shall be stated and the percentage of net assets that the total represents. (Section 307(10) CA 2014)	6B.24 (ROI only)
A micro-entity that is a parent shall provide the information required by paragraphs 6B.19 to 6B.24 in its financial statements in relation to both the micro-entity and its subsidiaries. (Section 308(4) CA 2014) The micro-entities regime is not available if consolidated financial statements are prepared.	6B.25 (ROI only)

	PARA.
Other related party disclosures	
Where a micro-entity, or a nominee of the micro-entity or a person acting in that person's own name but on behalf of the micro-entity, holds shares in the micro-entity or an interest in such shares, the notes to the financial statements shall give separately: (a) the number and aggregate nominal value of those shares and, where shares of more than one class have been acquired, the number and aggregate nominal value of each class of such shares, at the beginning and end of the reporting period together with the consideration paid for such shares; (b) a reconciliation of the number and nominal value of each class of such shares from the beginning of the reporting period to the end of the reporting period showing all changes during the reporting period, including further acquisitions, disposals and cancellations, in each case showing the value of the consideration paid or received, if any; (c) the reasons for any acquisitions made during the reporting period; (d) the proportion of called-up share capital held at the beginning and end of the reporting period; and (e) particulars of any restriction on profits available for distribution by virtue of the application of section 320. (Section 320 CA 2014)	6B.26 (ROI only)

Chapter 11

GROUP ACCOUNTING

11.1 BUSINESS COMBINATIONS AND GOODWILL (SECTION 19)

Business Combinations Defined

A business combination is defined as "a bringing together of separate entities into one reporting entity". In a combination, an acquirer obtains control over the financial and operating policies of an acquiree. The date of acquisition is the date that the acquirer effectively obtains control over the acquiree.

A business combination may be structured in a variety of ways, e.g. the purchase of an entity or all the net assets, the assumption of liabilities, or the purchase of another entity that together forms one or more businesses.

It may be achieved by the issue of shares, the transfer of cash or a combination thereof. It may even involve setting up a new entity or the restructuring of one or more of the combining entities. In essence, the definition is very broad so that all types of business combinations are captured by the FRS.

Accounting

All business combinations should be accounted for using the acquisition (purchase) method. The merger method that was permitted in certain defined circumstances in local accounting standards has been banned, with the exception of group reorganisations and public benefit entity (PBE) combinations that are in substance a gift or are mergers. Under the acquisition method, the following steps should be followed in accounting for a combination:

1. identify one of the two parties as the acquirer;
2. determine the acquisition date;
3. measure the cost of the business combination, i.e. the purchase consideration;
4. allocate, at acquisition date, the purchase consideration to the net assets acquired, including any contingent liabilities assumed and recognising and measuring any non-controlling interest (NCI) in the acquiree; and
5. recognise and measure goodwill.

1. Identifying the Acquirer

An acquirer should be identified for all business combinations and is the party which obtains control over the other party. Control is defined as the power to govern the operating and financial policies of an entity so as to gain benefits from its activities.

Normally it would be fairly obvious which party is the acquirer, but the FRS provides preparers with some indicators on how to identify an acquirer where it may not be so clear.

The following are the indicators provided to determine an acquirer:

(a) an acquirer is identified if the fair value of one of the combining entities is significantly greater than the other; or
(b) if the combination is via an exchange of voting ordinary shares for cash, the entity giving up cash is usually the acquirer; or
(c) if the combination results in the management of one of the parties being able to dominate the selection of the management team of the combined entity, then that party is usually the acquirer.

These must be regarded as helpful guidelines. Ultimately, it will be the decision of the two parties and will reflect the substance of the new arrangement.

2. Determining the Acquisition Date

The application of the acquisition method starts from the date of acquisition, i.e. the date that control is obtained, though it is not necessary for a transaction to be closed or finalised in law before obtaining control. It is essential, however, that all pertinent facts and circumstances be considered.

3. Measuring Cost of a Business Combination

The cost of a business combination (i.e. the purchase consideration) is the aggregate of:

(a) the fair value at the date of exchange of assets given, liabilities incurred and equity issued by the acquirer in exchange for control of the acquiree; plus
(b) any directly attributable costs.

Where control is achieved following a series of transactions, i.e. piecemeal, the cost of the business combination is the aggregate of the fair values of the assets given, liabilities assumed and equity instruments issued by the acquirer at the date of each transaction in the series.

Adjustments to the Cost of a Business Combination involving Earn-out Clauses The amount of the adjustment (i.e. earn-out clauses) should be included in the cost of the combination if it will probably happen and can be reliably measured.

If, however, it is not recognised at the acquisition date but can subsequently be measured reliably and is probable, then the additional consideration should be adjusted to the cost of the combination.

4. Allocating the Cost of a Business Combination to the Assets Acquired and Liabilities and Contingent Liabilities Assumed, and Recognising and Measuring any Non-controlling Interest in the Acquiree

The cost of the combination should be allocated to the identifiable assets and liabilities at their fair value at the date of the business combination.

Any difference between the cost and the acquirer's interest in the net fair value of identifiable net assets is accounted for as goodwill/negative goodwill.

At acquisition date, the NCI in the acquiree is stated at the NCI's share of the net amount of the identifiable assets, liabilities and provisions for contingent liabilities (i.e. no goodwill is allocated to NCIs).

Identifiable net assets can only be recognised separately if they satisfy the following criteria at that date:

(a) it is **probable**, for an **asset**, that future economic **benefits will flow** to the acquirer and the fair value can be **reliably measured**; and
(b) it is **probable**, in a **liability**, that an **outflow of resources** will be required to settle the obligation and the fair value can be **reliably measured**; and
(c) for **contingent liabilities**, their fair value can be **reliably measured**.

However, there are two exceptions to the above:

(a) deferred tax assets and liabilities are recognised and measured as per Section 29 *Income Tax*; and
(b) share-based payment is recognised as per Section 26 *Share-based Payment*.

The profit and loss account should incorporate the acquiree's profits and losses after the acquisition date based on costs identified at the acquisition date, e.g. depreciation should be based on the fair values at that date and not on the original historical costs.

Only assets and liabilities that are separately identified at acquisition may be recognised in the financial statements. Therefore:

(a) only existing restructuring provisions in the books of an acquiree may be included. No future restructuring that may occur as a result of an acquisition may be included; and
(b) no provision for future losses is permitted.

If the initial accounting is incomplete by the end of the reporting period in which the combination took place, provisional amounts may be used, but within the next 12 months the acquirer must retrospectively adjust the provisional amounts to reflect any new information obtained. Any adjustments after that period are accounted for as errors under Section 10 (see **Chapter 7**).

Contingent Liabilities These should be recognised separately as liabilities at the date of acquisition, but only if their fair value can be measured reliably. If they cannot be measured reliably:

(a) this will affect the amount recognised as goodwill; and
(b) the acquirer should disclose the information about the contingent liability as required by Section 21 (see **Chapter 6**).

After initial recognition an acquirer should measure the recognised contingent liabilities at the higher of:

(a) the amount that would be recognised under Section 21 (see **Chapter 6**); or
(b) the amount initially recognised less amounts previously recognised as revenue under Section 23 (see **Chapter 7**).

5. Recognising and Measuring Goodwill

The acquirer at acquisition date should:

(a) recognise goodwill as an asset; and
(b) measure goodwill as the excess of the cost of combination over the acquirer's interest in the net fair value of the identifiable net assets recognised.

After initial recognition, goodwill should be measured at cost less accumulated amortisation and impairment losses and should follow the principles of Section 18 (see **Chapter 4**). If there is no reliable estimate of the useful life, then it should be presumed to be 10 years. Entities should also follow Section 27 for the impairment rules (see **Chapter 3**).

Negative Goodwill If an acquirer's interest in the fair value of the net assets exceeds their cost, this will create negative goodwill or a gain from a bargain purchase. In these circumstances, the acquirer must:

(a) reassess the identification and measurement of the net identifiable assets acquired and the measurement of cost to ensure they have been correctly assessed; and, if still negative, then recognise and separately disclose the resulting excess on the face of the balance sheet on the acquisition date, immediately below goodwill, and followed by a subtotal of the net amount of goodwill and the excess; and
(b) recognise any excess after reassessment in profit or loss in the periods in which the non-monetary assets acquired are recovered.

Example 11.1: Goodwill

Lambeg Ltd purchased 75% of the issued share capital of Hilden Ltd and 40% of the issued share capital of Drumbeg Ltd on 1 April 2019.

Details of the purchase consideration at the date of purchase are:

- Hilden Ltd – A share exchange of two shares in Lambeg Ltd for every three shares in Hilden Ltd plus an issue to the shareholders of Hilden Ltd of 8% loan notes redeemable at par on 30 June 2021 on the basis of €100 loan note for every 250 shares held in Hilden Ltd.

- Drumbeg Ltd – A share exchange of three shares in Lambeg Ltd for every four shares in Drumbeg Ltd plus €1 per share acquired in cash. The market price of Lambeg Ltd's shares at 1 April 2019 was €6 per share.

SUMMARISED PROFIT AND LOSS ACCOUNTS
for the year ended 30 September 2019

	Lambeg Ltd	Hilden Ltd	Drumbeg Ltd
	€000	€000	€000
Revenue	75,000	40,700	31,000
Cost of sales	(47,400)	(19,700)	(15,300)
Gross profit	27,600	21,000	15,700
Operating expenses	(10,480)	(9,000)	(9,700)
Operating profit	17,120	12,000	6,000
Finance costs	(170)	Nil	Nil
Profit before tax	16,950	12,000	6,000
Income tax expense	(4,800)	(3,000)	(2,000)
Profit after tax for the period	12,150	9,000	4,000

The following information is also relevant:

1. A fair value exercise carried out for Hilden Ltd at the date of its acquisition is as follows:

	Book value	Fair value
	€000	€000
Land	20,000	23,000
Plant	25,000	30,000

The fair values have not been reflected in Hilden Ltd's financial statements. The increase in the fair value of the plant would create additional depreciation of €500,000 in the post-acquisition period in the consolidated financial statements to 30 September 2019.

Depreciation of plant is charged to cost of sales.

2. The details of each company's share capital and reserves at 1 October 2018 are:

	Lambeg Ltd	Hilden Ltd	Drumbeg Ltd
	€000	€000	€000
Equity shares of €1 each	20,000	10,000	5,000
Share premium	5,000	4,000	2,000
Retained earnings	18,000	7,500	6,000

3. In the post-acquisition period Lambeg Ltd sold goods to Hilden Ltd for €10 million. Hilden Ltd made a profit of €4 million on these sales. Some 25% of these goods were still in the inventory of Hilden Ltd at 30 September 2019.
4. Goodwill is amortised on a straight-line basis over a period of 10 years.
5. Lambeg Ltd paid a dividend of €5 million on 20 September 2019, but Hilden Ltd and Drumbeg Ltd did not make any dividend payments.
6. Lambeg Ltd measures non-controlling interests at their proportionate share of net assets.

Solution

The example illustrates a number of different aspects of group accounting, including elements of IAS 27 *Consolidated and Separate Financial Statements,* IFRS 3 *Business Combinations* and IAS 28 *Accounting for Associates* that are contained in FRS 102.

The consolidation procedures required to calculate the elimination of intragroup balances and the calculations for both the allocation of profits attributable to and the amount recorded within equity for non-controlling interests are described in **Chapter 1, Section 1.7**.

CONSOLIDATED PROFIT AND LOSS ACCOUNT
for the year ended 30 September 2019

	€000
Sales (*W2*)	85,350
Cost of sales (*W2*)	(48,750)
Gross profit	36,600
Operating expenses *(W2)*	(15,605)
Finance costs	(170)
Share of profit of associate *(W3)*	800
Profit before tax	21,625
Income tax expense (€4,800,000 + (6/12ths × €3,000,000))	(6,300)
Profit for the year	15,325
Profits attributable to:	
Owners of the parent	14,325
Non-controlling interests (*W4*)	1,000
	15,325

WORKINGS

W1 Group structure as at 30 September 2019

Hilden Ltd:	Lambeg Ltd owns 75%	Non-controlling interest 25%
Drumbeg Ltd:	Lambeg Ltd owns 40%	Associate presumed as over 20% holding

W2 Revenue and expenses

	Revenue	Cost of sales	Operating expenses
	€000	€000	€000
Parent	75,000	47,400	10,480
Subsidiary (6 months)	20,350	9,850	4,500
Elimination of inter-company balances	(10,000)	(10,000)	–
Additional depreciation on fair values	–	500	–
Unrealised profit (€4m × 25%)	–	1,000	–
Goodwill amortised (W5)	–	–	625
	85,350	48,750	15,605

W3 Share of profit of associate

40% × 6/12ths × profit after tax of €4 million = €800,000

W4 Non-controlling interest

	€000
Subsidiary – profit after tax (6/12ths × €9m)	4,500
Less additional depreciation on fair valuation	(500)
	4,000
25% non-controlling interest	1,000

W5 Computation of fair values and goodwill

	€000
Goodwill in Hilden Ltd	
Cost of combination	
Share exchange (2/3rds × 75% × 10m shares × €6)	30,000
Loan note (100/250 × 75% × 10m shares × €1)	3,000
	33,000

Fair value of net assets acquired	
Share capital	10,000
Share premium	4,000
Retained earnings at 1 October 2018	7,500
Profit after tax for year (6/12ths × €9m)	4,500
Fair value of land (€23,000 – €20,000)	3,000
Fair value of plant (€30,000 – €25,000)	5,000
	34,000
Group share (75%)	25,500
Goodwill	7,500
Amortisation (6/12ths × 10% × €7,500,000)	375
Carrying amount at 30 September 2019	7,125
Goodwill in Drumbeg Ltd	
Cost of combination	
Share exchange (3/4ths × 40% × 5m shares × €6)	9,000
Cash (€1 × 40% × 5m shares)	2,000
	11,000
Share capital	5,000
Share premium	2,000
Retained earnings at 1 October 2018	6,000
Profit after tax for year 6/12ths × €4m	2,000
	15,000
Group share 40%	(6,000)
Goodwill	5,000
Amortisation (€5,000,000 × 10% × 6/12ths)	(250)
Carrying amount as at 30 September 2019	4,750

Disclosures

Disclosure for Business Combinations Effected During the Reporting Period

For each combination effected during the reporting period, an acquirer should disclose:

(a) the names and descriptions of combining entities;
(b) the acquisition date;
(c) the percentage of voting equity acquired;
(d) the cost of the combination and description of its components (i.e. cash, equity, debt);
(e) the amounts recognised for each class of acquiree's assets, liabilities and contingent liabilities, including goodwill;

(f) a qualitative description of the nature of intangible assets included in goodwill;
(g) the useful life of goodwill and, if this exceeds 10 years, supporting reasons for why; and
(h) the periods in which negative goodwill will be recognised in profit or loss.

In addition, FRS 102 requires that for each material business combination disclosure, either in aggregate or separately, the amount of revenue and profit or loss since the date of acquisition be included in the consolidated profit and loss account.

Good examples of the above disclosure can be found from Irish listed companies. In particular, the fair value table covering the acquisition of a subsidiary by Cpl Resources plc shows the adjustments made to the book values of the subsidiary to arrive at fair values. Note the introduction of new intangible assets, such as purchased brands and customer databases. The description of the components of the cost of the combination has been split between cash paid and deferred consideration. Note also that the figures are provisional in the year of combination and these needed to be finalised in the 2011 financial statements. In the full IFRS 3 *Business Combinations*, but not in FRS 102, there is a requirement to explain the reasons for goodwill arising.

Cpl Resources plc

Annual Report and Accounts 2011

NOTES, FORMING PART OF THE FINANCIAL STATEMENTS (EXTRACT)

20 Business combinations

On 11 November 2010, the Group acquired PHC Care Management Limited and Emoberry Limited. On 13 April 2011, the Group acquired Runway Personnel Limited.

The provisional fair values of the assets and liabilities which were acquired, determined in accordance with IFRS, were as follows:

	Book Value 2011 €'000	Fair Value adjustment 2011 €'000	Fair Value 2011 €'000
Property, plant and equipment	20	–	20
Brands	–	600	600
Customer databases	–	200	200
Trade and other receivables	928	–	928
Trade and other payables	(637)	–	(637)
Deferred tax liability	–	(25)	(25)

Net identifiable assets and liabilities acquired	311	775	1,086
Goodwill arising on acquisition			459
			1,545
Satisfied by:			
Cash consideration			1,510
Cash acquired			(444)
Bank overdraft assumed on acquisition			149
Deferred consideration accrued			330
Total consideration			**1,545**

The acquisitions contributed profit before tax of €109,000 on revenues of €1.9 million for the period from their acquisition dates to 30 June 2011. The combined profit before tax for the period assuming the business had been purchased on 1 July 2010 would have been approximately €366,000 on revenues of approximately €6.8 million.

The initial assignment of fair values to identifiable net assets acquired has been performed on a provisional basis in respect of the above business combinations. Any amendments to these fair values within the twelve month timeframe from the date of acquisition will be reflected in the 2012 Annual Reports as stipulated by IFRS 3, *Business Combinations*.

Prior year acquisitions

[...]

(i) Included, in property, plant & equipment was land valued at €150,000 which was included in assets classified as held for sale in the balance sheet at 30 June 2010. The land was sold for €150,000 during the current year.

The acquisitions contributed profit before tax of €222,000 on revenues of €9.5 million for the period from their acquisition dates to 30 June 2010. The combined profit before tax for the year ended 30 June 2010 assuming the businesses had been purchased on 1 July 2009 would have been approximately €530,000 on revenues of approximately €17.6 million.

Disclosure for all Business Combinations

For all business combinations, the acquirer should disclose a reconciliation of the carrying amount of goodwill at the start and end of the period, showing separately:

(a) changes arising from new combinations;
(b) impairment losses;

(c) disposals of previously acquired businesses;
(d) amortisation; and
(e) any other changes.

This reconciliation need not be presented for prior periods.

A reconciliation is required of the carrying amount of the negative goodwill at the beginning and end of the reporting period, showing separately:

(a) changes arising from new business combinations;
(b) amounts recognised in profit or loss;
(c) disposals of previously acquired businesses; and
(d) other changes.

This reconciliation need not be presented for prior periods.

Group Reconstructions

Group reconstructions can adopt merger accounting as there is no acquirer. A group reconstruction happens when a restructuring takes place within a group, e.g. a new holding company set up to take over the existing group entities. An example was the setting up of Viridian Plc to take over the group entities formerly under the Northern Ireland Electricity parent company, with no outside parties involved.

Merger accounting is only permitted if:

1. it is not prohibited by company law;
2. the ultimate equity holders are the same, the rights of equity holders are the same relative to each other; and
3. no non-controlling interest is altered by the transfer.

Merger Accounting

When applying merger accounting, the carrying amount of assets and liabilities are **not** adjusted to fair value, but they still need to be adjusted to ensure uniformity of accounting policies.

The results and cash flows of all combining parties are included from the start of the accounting period and **not** from the date of acquisition in the year of acquisition.

The combined entity needs to restate the corresponding figures of the previous year to ensure comparability.

Any differences between the nominal value of equity issued and the NBV is recognised as a movement in reserves and is also shown in the statement of changes in equity.

Merger expenses are **not** part of the adjustment to reserves, **but** instead are charged to profit or loss.

Disclosure

For each combination under common control the following must be disclosed:

1. the names of the combining entities;
2. whether acquisition or merger accounting has been adopted; and
3. the date of the combination.

11.2 INVESTMENTS IN ASSOCIATES (SECTION 14)

Definition of Associates

Associates are defined as entities over which an investor exercises significant influence and is neither a subsidiary nor a joint venture.

The key phrase is *significant influence,* which is the power to participate in the financial and operating policy decisions of the associate, but this power does not constitute control or joint control over the entity.

FRS 102 provides some guidance in interpreting the definition, as follows:

(a) it is assumed that a holding of 20% plus voting power gives significant influence;
(b) it is assumed also that a holding of 20% or less voting power does not give significant influence; and
(c) a majority ownership by another investor does not preclude an investor from having significant influence. In other words, A could own 60% but B, which owns 25%, could still have significant influence.

The decision as to whether an associate relationship exists will depend on the judgement of the investing entity's directors and all facts and circumstances should be investigated. In group situations, the holdings of the parent and subsidiaries are added together in deciding total holding, **but not** an associate's holding in another potential associate.

Example 11.2: Definition of Associates

Example A has a 100% holding in B and B has a 30% holding in C. Is C an associate of A?

There is a rebuttable presumption that, via its control over B, A can exercise significant influence over C.

Example A has 20% of shares in C and B has 10%, with A still holding 100% of the shares in B. Is this an associate relationship with C?

Again there is a rebuttable presumption that because A controls B, then we can add both A and B's share together and 30% normally gives rise to significant influence, giving rise to an associate relationship.

Example A has 15% of the shares in B and B has 20% of the shares in C. Can both be included in deciding an associate relationship?

The holding of B in C must be excluded as B is an associate of A and not part of the group, thus there appears to be no significant influence and therefore no associate relationship.

Measurement after Initial Recognition: Accounting Policy Election

An investor that is **not a parent** should account for associates using either:

(a) the cost model;
(b) the fair value through other comprehensive income model; or
(c) the fair value through profit or loss model.

However, an investor that **is a parent** must adopt the equity method unless the associates are held as part of an investment portfolio, in which case the entity must adopt the fair value model with any changes being reported in profit or loss (i.e. it does not use the associate to carry out business but instead it is treated as part of a 'basket' of investments).

Cost Model

Under this model associates are measured at cost less accumulated impairment losses. Income is only recognised to the extent that it receives distributions, regardless of whether these have been paid out of accumulated profits pre- or post-acquisition.

EXAMPLE 11.3: COST MODEL

X acquired 25% of the shares in Y for €400,000 and meets the criteria for an associate. For the year ended 31 December 2019 a profit of €360,000 was recognised by Y and it paid out a dividend of €100,000 for the year. The fair value of X's investment in Y is €500,000, but there is no published price quotation for shares in Y.

Solution

X should recognise dividend income of €25,000 for the year ended 31 December 2019.

X must report its investment at €400,000 cost, but also consider whether there are any indicators that its investment is impaired. As the fair value is €100,000 above cost, there is no impairment.

Note: if Y had proposed a dividend for 2018 of €80,000 for the previous year, then the income statement would also have to include an additional dividend received of €20,000 (25% × €80,000) as this would only be included in the 2019 financial statements.

If the fair value had been €380,000, then an impairment would need to be recognised and €20,000 written off to profit and loss.

Equity Method

Under the equity method of accounting, an equity investment is initially recognised at the transaction price (including transaction costs) of acquiring the associate, which is then subsequently adjusted to reflect the investor's share of the **profit or loss** and **other comprehensive income** of the associate.

(a) **Distributions and Other Adjustments to Carrying Amount** Distributions received from the associate have the effect of reducing the carrying amount of the investment. Adjustments to the carrying amount may also be required as a consequence of changes in the associate's equity arising from items of other comprehensive income.

(b) **Potential Voting Rights** Although potential voting rights are considered in deciding whether or not significant influence exists, an investor must measure its share of the profit or loss of the associate and its share of changes in the associate's equity on the basis of its present ownership interests.

(c) **Implicit Goodwill and Fair Value Adjustments** On the acquisition of the investment in an associate, an investor must account for any difference (whether positive or negative) between the cost of acquisition and the investor's share of the fair values of the net identifiable assets of the associate as goodwill. The investor must adjust its share of the associate's profits or losses after acquisition to account for additional depreciation on the basis of the excess of their fair values over their carrying amounts at the time the investment was acquired.

(d) **Impairment** If there is an indication that an investment in an associate may be impaired, an investor must test the entire carrying amount of the investment for impairment as a single asset. Any goodwill in the associate is not tested separately for impairment, but rather as part of the test for impairment of the investment as a whole.

(e) **Investor's Transactions with Associates** If an associate is accounted for using the equity method, the investor must eliminate unrealised profits and losses resulting from transactions upstream (associate to investor) and downstream (investor to associate), **but only to the extent of the investor's interest in the associate**. Unrealised losses on such transactions, however, may provide evidence of an impairment of the asset transferred.

(f) **Date of Associate's Financial Statements** In applying the equity method, the investor must use the financial statements of the associate as of the same date as the financial statements of the investor unless it is **impracticable** to do so. If it is impracticable, the investor should use the most recent available financial statements of the associate, with adjustments made for the effects of any significant transactions or events occurring between the accounting period dates.

(g) **Associate's Accounting Policies** If the associate uses accounting policies that differ from those of the investor, the investor must adjust the associate's financial statements to reflect the investor's accounting policies for the purpose of applying the equity method unless it is impracticable to do so.

(h) **Losses in Excess of Investment** If an investor's share of losses of an associate equals or exceeds the carrying amount of its investment in the associate, the investor must discontinue recognising its share of further losses. After the investor's interest is reduced to zero, the investor should recognise additional losses by a provision (Section 21 – see **Chapter 6**), but only to the extent that the investor has incurred legal or constructive obligations or has made payments on behalf of the associate. If the associate subsequently reports profits, the investor can only resume recognising its share of those profits after its share of the profits equals the share of losses not recognised in previous accounting periods.

(i) **Discontinuing the Equity Method** An investor must stop using the equity method from the date that significant influence ceases. This includes the following:

1. If the associate becomes a subsidiary or a joint venture, the investor should apply the rules in Section 19 *Business Combinations and Goodwill* or Section 15 *Investments in Joint Ventures*.
2. If an investor loses significant influence over an associate as a result of a full or partial disposal, it must derecognise that associate and recognise in profit or loss the difference between, on the one hand, the sum of the proceeds received plus the fair value of any retained interest and, on the other hand, the carrying amount of the investment in the associate at the date when significant influence was lost. Thereafter, the investor must

account for any retained interest using Section 11 *Basic Financial Instruments* or Section 12 *Other Financial Instruments Issues*, as appropriate (see **Chapter 12**).

3. If an investor loses significant influence for reasons other than a partial disposal of its investment, the investor must regard the carrying amount of the investment at that date as a new cost basis and must account for the investment using Sections 11 or 12, as appropriate (see **Chapter 12**).

Example 11.4: Equity Method

Scenario 1 X acquired 25% of the shares in Y for €400,000 and meets the criteria for an associate. For the year ended 31 December 2019, a profit of €360,000 was recognised by Y and it paid out a dividend of €100,000 for the year. The fair value of X's investment in Y is €500,000, but there is no published price quotation for shares in Y.

Solution

X must recognise its share of the profit in Y in its profit and loss account of €90,000 (25% × €360,000).

X must recognise its investment in Y at €465,000 (€400,000 + €90,000 – dividend €25,000).

Scenario 2 Assume the same facts as above except that X buys goods from Y for €80,000, of which 40% were still in X's inventory at the year end. Y's mark-up on its sales to X is 25% on cost.

Solution

X must recognise its share of profit from the associate in its profit and loss account, calculated as:

25% × €360,000 = €90,000
€90,000 – (40% × €80,000 × 25/125)
€90,000 – €6,400
= €83,600

X must recognise its investment in Y at €458,600 (€400,000 + €90,000 – €6,400 – €25,000).

An example of accounting for associates (including a subsidiary) using the equity method, together with the calculation of goodwill, the introduction of new intangibles and the calculation of deferred tax, is provided below.

EXAMPLE 11.5: EQUITY METHOD

Arklow Ltd holds investments in two other companies, Barrow Ltd and Conor Ltd. All three entities prepare financial statements to 31 March 2019 and the balance sheets of the three companies were as follows:

	Arklow Ltd	Barrow Ltd	Conor Ltd
	€000	€000	€000
Fixed assets			
Property, plant and equipment	125,000	85,000	75,000
Investments (Note 2)	32,000	–	–
	157,000	85,000	75,000
Current assets			
Inventories (Note 3)	33,000	30,000	28,000
Trade receivables (Note 4)	43,000	30,000	31,000
Cash and cash equivalents	11,000	10,000	9,000
	87,000	70,000	68,000
Less Creditors: amounts falling due within one year			
Trade and other payables (Note 4)	25,000	17,000	20,000
Current tax payable	9,000	7,000	6,000
Total current liabilities	34,000	24,000	26,000
Net current assets	53,000	46,000	42,000
Creditors: amounts falling due after more than one year			
Long-term borrowings	50,000	25,000	22,000
Deferred tax	35,000	12,000	17,000
Total non-current liabilities	85,000	37,000	39,000
Net assets	125,000	94,000	78,000
Capital and reserves			
Share capital (€1 shares)	70,000	50,000	50,000
Retained earnings	55,000	44,000	28,000
Total equity	125,000	94,000	78,000

NOTES

1. Purchase of shares in Barrow Ltd

On 1 April 2018 Arklow Ltd purchased 40 million shares in Barrow Ltd by issuing one share in Arklow Ltd for every two shares purchased in Barrow Ltd. The share issue has not yet been recorded.

The fair value of an Arklow Ltd share at 1 April 2018 was €6 and the fair value of a Barrow Ltd share at the same date was €2.40. Arklow Ltd incurred costs of €800,000 in relation to the cost of issuing the shares. These costs have been charged as an expense in the profit and loss account of Arklow Ltd for the year ended 31 March 2019.

The retained earnings of Barrow Ltd, as shown in its balance sheet at 31 March 2018, was €35 million. The directors of Arklow Ltd carried out a fair value exercise on the net assets of Barrow Ltd at that date. The following matters arose out of the exercise:

(a) Property, plant and equipment comprised non-depreciable land with a carrying amount of €50 million and a market value of €60 million, plus plant with a carrying amount of €30 million and a market value of €38 million. The estimated future economic life of plant at 1 April 2018 was four years (straight-line). None of the property, plant and equipment had been sold by 31 March 2019.

(b) At 1 April 2018 Barrow Ltd was in legal action against a supplier in respect of damages caused by the supply of faulty products. Barrow Ltd was claiming damages of €5 million. In the middle of March 2018 the supplier had offered an out-of-court settlement of €3 million and Barrow Ltd's lawyers advised that this was a fair offer given the likelihood of success in court. However, Barrow Ltd refused the offer, took the case to court, and subsequently won the case. The directors of Barrow Ltd had not recognised any receivable in respect of the case in the balance sheet because the claim was a contingent asset. The directors of Arklow Ltd considered that the fair value of the contingent asset at 1 April 2018 was €3 million.

(c) At 1 April 2018 Barrow Ltd had a long-standing portfolio of loyal customers who regularly ordered goods and services from Barrow Ltd. In addition, the assembled workforce of Barrow Ltd was highly trained and their expertise was seen by the directors as conferring significant competitive advantage to Barrow Ltd. The customer relationships and the expertise of the workforce were not included in the balance sheet of

Barrow Ltd at 31 March 2018 because the directors did not consider that they met the recognition criteria of Section 19 of FRS 102. The directors of Arklow Ltd considered that the customer relationships had a market value of €20 million at 1 April 2018 and that based on the life cycle of the existing products, the existing customers would continue to order goods and services from Barrow Ltd for at least five years from that date. They estimated that the fair value of the competitive advantage conferred by the workforce was €15 million at 1 April 2018 and the average period to retirement for a typical employee was 20 years.

(d) The financial director of Arklow Ltd has stated that the fair value adjustments will create temporary differences for deferred taxation purposes.

2. Purchase of shares in Conor Ltd

On 1 April 2017 Arklow Ltd purchased 20 million shares in Conor Ltd for cash of €1.60 per share. The retained earnings of Conor Ltd were €15 million at 1 April 2017. This shareholding has resulted in the directors of Arklow Ltd being able to exercise a significant influence over the operating and financial policies of Conor Ltd. The fair value of the net assets of Conor Ltd at 1 April 2017 was equal to their carrying amounts in Conor Ltd's balance sheet.

3. Inventories

The inventories of Barrow Ltd and Conor Ltd at 31 March 2019 included components purchased from Arklow Ltd during the year at a cost of €20 million to Barrow Ltd and €16 million to Conor Ltd. Arklow Ltd supplied these components at cost plus a mark-up of 25%.

4. Trade receivables and payables

The trade receivables of Arklow Ltd included €5 million receivable from Barrow Ltd and €4 million receivable from Conor Ltd in respect of the purchase of components (see Note 3). The trade receivables of Barrow Ltd and Conor Ltd include an equivalent amount payable to Arklow Ltd.

5. Other information

(a) Neither the goodwill arising on acquisition of Barrow Ltd nor the investment in Conor Ltd has suffered any impairment since the dates of investment by Arklow Ltd in these entities. Goodwill is being amortised over a 10-year period.

(b) The rate of tax to apply to temporary differences is 25%.

Solution

The consolidation procedures required to calculate the elimination of intragroup balances and the calculations of both the allocation of profits attributable to and the amount recorded within equity for non-controlling interests are described in **Chapter 1, Section 1.7**.

WORKINGS

1. Group structure

   Arklow Ltd owns 80% of the ordinary shares in Barrow Ltd; it is assumed this gives control, therefore Barrow Ltd is a subsidiary of Arklow Ltd.

   Arklow Ltd owns 40% of the ordinary shares in Conor Ltd; it is assumed there is an associate relationship.

2. Calculation of goodwill

Fair value adjustments

	Date of acquisition	Change	Year end
	€000	**€000**	**€000**
Land	10,000	Nil	10,000
Plant	8,000	(2,000)	6,000
Contingencies	3,000	(3,000)	Nil
Customer relationships	20,000	(4,000)	16,000
	41,000	(9,000)	32,000
Deferred tax on temporary differences (25%)	(10,250)	2,250	(8,000)
	30,750	6,750	24,000

Recognition of the competitive advantage of the workforce would not be permitted as it is not reliably measurable.

Goodwill

	€000	€000
Cost of combination (using gross method)		
Fair value of shares issued (€40,000 × ½ × €6)		120,000
Fair value of non-controlling interest (20% × €115,750)		23,150
		143,150
Fair value of net assets acquired		
Share capital	50,000	
Retained earnings	35,000	
Fair value adjustments (see note 2 above)	30,750	
		(115,750)
Goodwill		27,400

Amortisation (10% straight-line)	(2,740)
Net book value at 31 March 2019	24,660

3. Investment in associate

	€000	€000
Cost of purchase in associate, Conor Ltd (20m shares × €1.60)		32,000
Share of post-acquisition retained reserves ((€78m – €65m) × 40%)		5,200
Goodwill amortisation adjustment		(1,200)
Less provision for unrealised profit (25/125 × €16m × 40%)		(1,280)
		34,720
Goodwill		
Purchase price (20m × €1.60)	32,000	
Net assets at acquisition (40% × €65m)	26,000	
	6,000	
Amortisation (2 years at 10%)	(1,200)	
	4,800	

4. Non-controlling interest

	€000	€000
Net assets of Barrow Ltd at reporting date		94,000
Fair value adjustments (see Note 2)		24,000
		118,000
		23,600

5. Retained earnings

	Arklow Ltd	Barrow Ltd	Conor Ltd
	€000	€000	€000
As per balance sheet	55,000	44,000	28,000
Acquisition costs (already written off)			
Provision for unrealised profit			
Barrow Ltd (25/125 × €20m)	(4,000)		
Conor Ltd (25/125 × €16m × 40%)	(1,280)		
Deferred tax (€5.28m × 25%)	1,320		
Fair value adjustments		(6,750)	
Pre-acquisition retained earnings	Nil	(35,000)	(15,000)
	51,040	2,250	13,000

	€000
Barrow Ltd	
Share of post-acquisition retained earnings (€2.25m × 80%)	1,800
Conor Ltd	
Share of post-acquisition retained earnings (€13m × 40%)	5,200
Deferred tax (€5.2m × 25%)	(1,300)
Amortisation of goodwill (€2.740m + €1.2m)	(3,940)
	52,800

Arklow Ltd and its Subsidiary
Consolidated Balance Sheet
as at 31 March 2019

	€000
Fixed assets	
Property, plant and equipment (€125m + €85m + €10m (land) + €6m (plant))	226,000
Goodwill *(W2)*	24,660
Intangible assets *(W2)*	16,000
Investment in associate *(W3)*	34,720
	301,380
Current assets	
Inventories (€33m + €30m – €4m unrealised profit)	59,000
Trade receivables (€43m + €30m – €5m intercompany)	68,000
Cash and cash equivalents (€11m + €10m)	21,000
	148,000
Creditors: amounts falling due within one year	
Trade and other payables (€25m + €17m – €5m intercompany)	37,000
Current tax payable (€9m + €7m)	16,000
Current liabilities	53,000
Net current assets	95,000
Creditors: amounts falling due after more than one year	
Long-term borrowings (€50m + €25m)	75,000
Deferred tax (€35m + €12m + €8m(*W2*) + €1.3m (*W5*) – €1.32m (*W5*))	54,980

Non-current liabilities	129,980
Net assets	266,400
Capital and reserves	
Share capital (€70m + €20m)	90,000
Share premium (20m shares × €5)	100,000
Retained earnings (*W5*)	52,800
	242,800
Non-controlling interest (*W4*)	23,600
Total equity	266,400

Fair Value Model

Initially, where investors are **not parents**, associates are measured at cost exclusive of any transaction costs. Parents must adopt the fair value model, with changes in fair values in equity being reported in the revaluation reserve (equity) and also reported in other comprehensive income.

Dividends are reported in profit and loss regardless of whether paid out of pre- or post-acquisition accumulated profits.

Financial Statement Presentation

The following is an example of the presentation required in a parent's books for its investment in associates.

Example 11.6: Presentation of Associates in Parent's Books

		2019	2018
	Note	**€**	**€**
Assets			
Non-current assets			
Investment in associates	12	500,000	400,000

Disclosures

An entity must disclose:

(a) its accounting policy;
(b) the carrying amount of its investments in associates; and
(c) the fair value of investments in associates using the equity method for which there are published prices.

For the cost model, the amount of dividends recognised as income must be disclosed.

For the equity method, an entity's share of the profit/loss on discontinued operations must be disclosed separately.

For the fair value model, the disclosures required are those required by Section 11 *Basic Financial Instruments* of FRS 102 (see **Chapter 12**).

The individual financial statements of an investor that is not a parent must disclose summarised financial information about the investments in the associates, along with the effect of including those investments as if they had been accounted for using the equity method. Investing entities that are exempt from preparing consolidated financial statements, or would be exempt if they had subsidiaries, are exempt from this requirement.

An illustrative example, based on the IASB's *IFRS for SMEs 2009 Illustrative Financial Statements Presentation and Disclosure Checklist*, of a company adopting the cost model when accounting for investment in an associate is shown below.

Example 11.7: Illustrative Financial Statements – Investment in Associate

Accounting Policies and Explanatory Notes (Extracts)

2. Basis of preparation and accounting policies

Investments in associates
Investments in associates are accounted for at cost less any accumulated impairment losses.

Dividend income from investments in associates is recognised when the Group's right to receive payment has been established. It is included in other income.

12. Investment in associate

The Group owns 35 per cent of an associate whose shares are not publicly traded.

	2019	**2018**
	€	**€**
Cost of investment in associate	107,500	107,500
Dividend received from associate (included in other income)	25,000	25,000

11.3 INVESTMENTS IN JOINT VENTURES (SECTION 15)

Joint Ventures Defined

A joint venture is a contractual arrangement whereby two or more parties undertake an economic activity subject to *joint control*. Joint ventures can be jointly controlled operations, jointly controlled assets or jointly controlled entities.

Joint control is a contractually agreed sharing of control over an economic activity – it can only exist when strategic financial and operating decisions require the unanimous consent of all parties sharing control.

EXAMPLE 11.8: DEFINITION OF JOINT VENTURE

X, Y and Z (all unrelated) each own 33.33% of the ordinary shares in M that carry voting rights, but all strategic decisions in M require only a simple majority interest of investors. Therefore no joint control exists.

X, Y and Z each own 33.3% of the ordinary shares in M, but all three investors have contractually agreed to exercise joint control of Z. Joint control therefore exists.

1. Jointly Controlled Operations

Jointly controlled operations can involve the use of assets and other resources rather than the establishment of a separate entity. Usually joint control provides the means by which revenue from the sale of a joint product and any relevant expenses are shared amongst the venturers.

Each venturer should recognise in its own financial statements:

(a) the assets that it controls and liabilities it incurs itself; and
(b) the expenses it incurs itself and its share of the income that it earns from the sale of goods and services by the joint venture.

An example given by the IASB suggests that two separate pharmaceutical companies might get involved in a jointly controlled operation, with one company concentrating on the manufacture of a drug and the other concentrating on its distribution, but ultimately both parties share in the rewards.

Example 11.9: Jointly Controlled Operation

Kill Ltd and Rush Ltd have jointly tendered for and been awarded a government contract to build a new hospital. The contract is a fixed-price contract for €30 million. Kill Ltd has agreed to construct the main building and Rush Ltd to incorporate the interior. Both use their own equipment and staff. The core building will cost €8 million and the interior €10 million. Both companies share equally in the revenue. The contract is started and completed in 2019.

Solution

Kill Ltd

			€m	€m
Dr	Profit or loss (construction costs)		8	
	Cr	Bank		8

Being recognition of construction costs incurred in 2019 (assumed paid).

Dr	Bank		15	
	Cr	Profit or loss		15

Being recognition of the construction revenue earned in 2019.

Rush Ltd

			€m	€m
Dr	Profit or loss (construction costs)		10	
	Cr	Bank		10

Being recognition of construction costs incurred in 2019 (assumed paid).

Dr	Bank		15	
	Cr	Profit or loss		15

Being recognition of the construction revenue earned in 2019.

2. Jointly Controlled Assets

Some joint ventures involve joint control over one or more assets. Each venturer should recognise in its own financial statements:

(a) its share of any jointly controlled assets, classified as to their nature;
(b) any liabilities it has incurred itself;

(c) its share of any liabilities incurred jointly with other venturers;
(d) any income from the sale or use of its share of the output of the joint venture together with its share of any expenses incurred by the joint venture; and
(e) any expenses it has incurred in respect of its interest in the joint venture.

An example would be where a number of companies purchase an aircraft and each has the right to use the aircraft for 40–50 days per annum. The costs of running the aircraft, including depreciation, pilot salaries and maintenance costs, are all shared by the joint venturers.

EXAMPLE 11.10: JOINTLY CONTROLLED ASSETS

On 1 January 2019 Able Ltd, Better Ltd, Corry Ltd and Derry Ltd jointly purchase an IT network for €2 million cash. Each has a right to use the system for 90 days per annum. Each paid €12,000 to meet the running costs of the system. Assume Able Ltd has incurred €8,000 maintenance costs and that the asset has a life of 10 years.

Solution

Able Ltd

		€	€
Dr	Property, plant and equipment	500,000	
	Cr Bank		500,000
Being the initial recognition of share of the IT network.			
Dr	Profit or loss	12,000	
	Cr Bank		12,000
Being the running costs for the year.			
Dr	Profit or loss	50,000	
	Cr Accumulated depreciation on PP&E		50,000
Being the first year's depreciation on the share of the IT network.			
Dr	Profit or loss	8,000	
	Cr Bank		8,000
Being maintenance costs incurred.			

3. Jointly Controlled Entities

Most people, when they think of a joint venture, regard a jointly controlled entity relationship as the norm. It involves the establishment of a corporation, partnership or other entity in which each venturer has an interest. It operates like any other entity except that there is a contractual arrangement involving joint control by the venturers. However, the entity must publish its own separate set of financial statements and the IFRS has decided to permit three options in how a joint venture might subsequently account for its investment in such an entity, but initially it will be recorded at cost. Under FRS 102, however, only two models are permitted in most situations.

Measurement after Initial Recognition – Accounting Policy Election

A venturer that is not a parent but has one or more interests in jointly controlled entities, must adopt either:

(a) the cost model; or
(b) the fair value through other comprehensive income model; or
(c) the fair value through profit or loss model.

In its consolidated accounts, however, a venturer must adopt the equity method of accounting. However, if it is a venturer that is a parent with investments in jointly controlled entities held as part of an investment portfolio, the investments must be measured at fair value with changes in fair value being recognised in profit or loss in the consolidated financial statements.

The proportionate consolidation method, which was permitted until fairly recently as an option under the full IAS 31 *Joint Ventures* (now superceded by IAS 28 *Investments in Associates and Joint Ventures*) is **not** permitted by the standard.

Cost Model Venturers measure their investments at cost less accumulated impairment losses. Income is only recognised to the extent that the venturer receives distributions regardless of whether these have been paid out of accumulated profits pre- or post-acquisition.

Example 11.11: Cost Model

Scenario 1 X and Y each acquired 50% of the ordinary shares in Z for €800,000 on 1 January 2019. Both agreed to share control over Z. For the year ended 31 December 2019 a profit of €900,000 was recognised.

A dividend of €300,000 was declared and paid on 30 November 2019. Assume that the fair value in Z was €1,200,000.

Solution

	€
Income statement – dividend income (50% × €300,000)	150,000
Balance sheet – investment in joint venture	800,000 (cost)

There is no impairment as the fair value of €1,200,000 exceeds the cost of €800,000.

Scenario 2 Assume the facts are the same except on 31 March 2019 a final dividend of €200,000 was also paid for the year ended 31 December 2018 and the fair value was €1,100,000.

Solution

	€
Income statement – dividend income (50% × (€300,000 + €200,000))	250,000
Balance sheet – investment in joint venture	800,000 (cost)

As the dividend was paid out of pre-acquisition profits, a review for impairment is needed. In this case, fair value of €1,100,000 exceeds the cost of €800,000 so there is no impairment.

Fair Value Model If an entity adopts the fair value model, fair value is initially the transaction price.

If the venture is not a parent, it must measure its jointly controlled entities at fair value, with any changes in fair value included within equity (revaluation reserve) and also reported as other comprehensive income.

Dividends from both pre- and post-acquisition accumulated profits are reported in the profit and loss account.

Example 11.12: Fair Value Model

Assume the facts are same as in Scenario 1 in **Example 11.11** but that there is a reliable price quotation for Z.

Solution

	€
Income statement – dividend income (50% × €300,000)	150,000
– increase in fair value (50% × (€1,200,000 – €800,000))	200,000
Balance sheet – investment in joint venture (€800,000 + €200,000)	1,000,000

Equity Method Entities should adopt the procedures in Section 14 of FRS 102, outlined in **Section 11.2** above.

EXAMPLE 11.13: EQUITY METHOD

Scenario 1 X and Y each acquired 50% of the ordinary shares in Z for €800,000 on 1 January 2019. Both agreed to share control over Z. For the year ended 31 December 2019 a profit of €900,000 was recognised.

A dividend of €300,000 was declared and paid on 30 November 2019. Assume that the fair value in Z was valued at €1,200,000 but there is no published price quotation for Z.

Solution

	€	€
Income statement – share of joint venture profit (50% × €900,000)		450,000
Statement of financial position – investment in joint venture:		
Cost	800,000	
Add share of profit (50% × €900,000)	450,000	
Less share of dividend (50% × €300,000)	(150,000)	
	1,100,000	

Scenario 2 Assume the facts are the same except on 31 March 2019 a final dividend of €200,000 was paid for the year ended 31 December 2018 and the fair value was €1,100,000.

Solution

	€	€
Income statement – share of joint venture profit (50% × €900,000)		450,000
Statement of financial position – investment in joint venture:		
Cost	800,000	
Add share of profit (50% × €900,000)	450,000	
Less share of dividend (50% × (€300,000 + €200,000))	(250,000)	
	1,000,000	

As the dividend was paid out of pre-acquisition profits it is necessary to check for impairment, but the fair value is €1,100,000 so there is no impairment.

Scenario 3 Assume the facts with regard to the cost of investment are the same but that the joint venture incurs a loss of €200,000 for the year and no dividend was paid out. The recoverable amount of the investment is €650,000.

Solution

	€	€
Income statement – share of joint venture loss (50% × €200,000)		(100,000)
Statement of financial position – investment in joint venture:		
Cost	800,000	
Less share of loss	(100,000)	
	700,000	
Impairment – profit and loss	(50,000)	
	650,000	

Transactions between a Venturer and a Joint Venture

Gains and losses must reflect the substance of transactions. If assets are retained by the joint venture, provided the venturer has transferred the significant risks and rewards of ownership, the venturer should only recognise in its consolidated financial statements that portion of the gain or loss attributable to the interests of the other venturers. However, if there is evidence of impairment, the full loss should be recognised.

When a venturer purchases an asset from a joint venture, the venturer should **not** recognise its share of the profits until it resells the asset to an independent party or otherwise realises its carrying amount. Losses should be recognised similarly, except that they should be recognised immediately if they represent impairments.

Example 11.14: Inter Venturer–Joint Venture Transactions

Scenario 1 A has a 50% interest in a joint venture and on 11 December 2019 it sells goods to the joint venture for €90,000. They are still in the joint venture's inventory at the year end. A sells goods at a mark-up of 50% on cost.

Solution

The elimination of unrealised profit should be 50% × €30,000 = €15,000. A must reduce its investment in the joint venture by €15,000 and, in addition, reduce its sales by €45,000 and cost of sales by €30,000.

Scenario 2 A purchases goods for €120,000 from its joint venture. At 31 December 2019, €90,000 of the goods were still in A's inventory. The joint venture has a 50% mark-up on goods sold.

Solution

A must reduce its investment by €15,000 (50% × €30,000) and profit for the year by the same amount.

If an Investor does not have Joint Control

If an investor does not have joint control, the investment should be recorded in accordance with Section 11 *Basic Financial Instruments* (see **Chapter 12**) and be treated as a trade investment or, if the entity exercises significant influence, the investment should be recorded in accordance with Section 14 (see **Section 11.2** above) and treated as an associate.

Disclosures

An investor in a joint venture must disclose:

(a) the **accounting policy** it uses for recognising its interests in jointly controlled entities;
(b) the **carrying amount** of investments in jointly controlled entities;
(c) the fair value of investments in jointly controlled entities accounted for using the equity method for which there are published price quotations; and
(d) the aggregate amount of its commitments relating to joint ventures.

For jointly controlled entities accounted for under the equity method, the venturer should disclose separately its share of the profit or loss of such investments and its share of any discontinued operations of such jointly controlled entities.

If a venturer has to adopt the fair value model, the disclosures required are those required under the fair value model in Section 11 of FRS 102 (see **Chapter 12**).

The individual financial statements of a venturer that is not a parent should disclose summarised financial information about the investments in the jointly controlled entities, along with the effect of including those investments as if they had been accounted for using the equity method. Investing entities that are exempt from preparing consolidated financial statements, or would be exempt if they had subsidiaries, are exempt from this requirement.

An example of an equity-accounted accounting policy note is provided by Fyffes Ltd. Fyffes Ltd adopts the equity method for both associates and joint ventures.

Fyffes Ltd
Annual Report 2017
SIGNIFICANT ACCOUNTING POLICIES (EXTRACT)

Joint ventures and associates
The Group's interests in equity-accounted investees comprise interests in joint ventures and associates, A joint venture is an arrangement in which the Group has joint control, whereby the Group has rights to the net assets of the arrangement, rather than rights to its assets and obligations for its liabilities. Associates are those entities in which the Group has significant influence, but not control or joint control, over the financial and operating policies. Interests in joint ventures and associates are accounted for using the equity method. They are recognised initially at cost, which includes transaction costs. Subsequent to initial recognition, the consolidated financial statements include the Group's share of the profit or loss and other comprehensive income of equity-accounted investees, until the date on which significant influence or joint control ceases.

EXAMPLE 11.15: ADOPTION OF EQUITY METHOD

Moneygall Ltd is a parent company with several wholly-owned subsidiaries. Cong Ltd is jointly controlled by Moneygall Ltd and three other co-venturers. The draft consolidated balance sheet of Moneygall Ltd as at 31 March 2019 and the balance sheet of Cong Ltd at that date are as follows:

	Moneygall Ltd and subsidiaries	Cong Ltd
	€	€
Fixed assets		
Property, plant and equipment	644,000	244,000
Investment in joint venture at cost	70,000	–
	714,000	244,000
Current assets	238,000	88,000
Creditors: amounts falling due within one year	135,000	48,000
Net current assets	103,000	40,000
Net assets	817,000	284,000

Capital and reserves		
Ordinary share capital	500,000	120,000
Retained earnings	317,000	164,000
Equity	817,000	284,000

The following information is also available:

(a) On 1 April 2016, Moneygall Ltd paid €70,000 to acquire 25% of the shares in Cong Ltd. On that date the retained earnings of Cong Ltd were €72,000 and the fair value of the company's non-current assets was €40,000 more than their book value. This revaluation has not been reflected in the books of Cong Ltd.

(b) Cong Ltd has issued no shares since Moneygall Ltd acquired its holding and there have been no impairment losses for goodwill, which is being amortised over a 10-year period.

Solution

1. Investment in joint venture

	€		€
Purchase price			70,000
Less: Fair value of net assets acquired:			
Share capital	120,000		
Retained earnings	72,000		
Fair value adjustment	40,000		
	232,000	× 25%	58,000
Goodwill			12,000
Amortisation (10% × €12,000 × 3 years)			(3,600)
Net book value			8,400
Investment at cost			70,000
Share of post-acquisition retained earnings (see below)			19,400
			89,400
OR			
Share of net assets at 31 March 2019 (25% × €284,000)			71,000
Share of fair value adjustments (25% × €40,000)			10,000
Share of goodwill (see above)			8,400
			89,400

2. Retained earnings

	€
Moneygall Ltd balance as at 31 March 2019	317,000
Share of joint venture post-acquisition retained earnings	
€164,000 – €72,000 = €92,000	
€92,000 × 25% = €23,000	
€23,000 – €3,600 amortisation	19,400
	336,400

CONSOLIDATED BALANCE SHEET OF MONEYGALL LTD AND ITS SUBSIDIARIES
as at 31 March 2019

	€	€
Fixed assets		
Property, plant and equipment	644,000	
Investment in joint venture *(W1)*	89,400	
		733,400
Current assets	238,000	
Creditors: amounts falling due within one year	(135,000)	
Net current assets		103,000
		836,000
Capital and reserves		
Ordinary share capital		500,000
Retained earnings *(W2)*		336,400
Equity		836,400

11.4 SMALL ENTITIES

There are no explicit minimum disclosure requirements for small entities under Section 1A of FRS 102 for either the UK or the Republic of Ireland. However, small entities may need to provide disclosures as required by FRS 102, Sections 19, 14 and 15 if required to give a true and fair view.

11.5 MICRO-ENTITIES

Under FRS 105, the same general principles are applied as the full version of FRS 102 regarding business combinations and goodwill. They are required to apply FRS 102, Section 19, with the exceptions that a micro-entity:

(a) shall not separately identify and recognise intangible assets;
(b) shall not recognise a deferred tax asset or liability;
(c) is not required to provide any of the disclosures.

An entity that is required, or chooses to, present consolidated financial statements is excluded from the micro-entities regime and must not apply FRS 105.

Disclosure Checklist: Group Accounting – FRS 102

(References are to the relevant Section of FRS 102)

	Para.
Business Combinations and Goodwill – Section 19	
Disclosures for business combinations effected during the reporting period	
For each business combination that was effected during the period, the acquirer shall disclose the following: (a) the names and descriptions of the combining entities or businesses; (b) the acquisition date; (c) the percentage of voting equity instruments acquired; (d) the cost of the combination and a description of the components of that cost (e.g. cash, equity instruments and debt instruments); (e) the amounts recognised at the acquisition date for each class of the acquiree's assets, liabilities and contingent liabilities, including goodwill; (f) [not used]; (fA) a qualitative description of the nature of intangible assets included in goodwill; (g) the useful life of goodwill and, if this exceeds five years, supporting reasons for this; (h) the periods in which the excess recognised in accordance with paragraph 19.24 will be recognised in profit or loss.	19.25
Disclosures for all business combinations	
The acquirer shall disclose, either in aggregate or separately for each material business combination that occurs during the reporting period, the amounts of revenue and profit or loss of the acquiree since the acquisition date included in the consolidated statement of comprehensive income for the reporting period.	19.25A
An acquirer shall disclose a reconciliation of the carrying amount of goodwill at the beginning and end of the reporting period, showing separately: (a) changes arising from new business combinations; (b) amortisation; (c) impairment losses; (d) disposals of previously acquired businesses; and (e) other changes. This reconciliation need not be presented for prior periods.	19.26
An acquirer shall disclose a reconciliation of the carrying amount of the excess recognised in accordance with paragraph 19.24 at the beginning and end of the reporting period, showing separately: (a) changes arising from new business combinations; (b) amounts recognised in profit or loss in accordance with paragraph 19.24(c); (c) disposals of previously acquired businesses; and (d) other changes. This reconciliation need not be presented for prior periods.	19.26A
Disclosure for group reconstructions	
For each group reconstruction that was effected during the period, the combined entity shall disclose the following: (a) the names of the combining entities (other than the reporting entity); (b) whether the combination has been accounted for as an acquisition or a merger; and (c) the date of the combination.	19.33

	PARA.
Investments in Associates – Section 14	
An investor in an associate shall disclose the following: (a) its accounting policy for investments in associates; (b) the carrying amount of investments in associates; and (c) the fair value of investments in associates accounted for using the equity method for which there are published price quotations.	14.12
For investments in associates accounted for by the cost model, an investor shall disclose the amount of dividends and other distributions recognised as income.	14.13
For investments in associates accounted for in accordance with paragraph 14.4(c), an investor shall disclose separately its share of the profit or loss of such associates and its share of any discontinued operations of such associates.	14.14
For investments in associates accounted for by the fair value model, an investor shall make the disclosures required by paragraphs 11.43 and 11.44.	14.15
The individual financial statements of an investor that is not a parent shall disclose summarised financial information about the investments in the associates, along with the effect of including those investments as if they had been accounted for using the equity method. Investing entities that are exempt from preparing consolidated financial statements, or would be exempt if they had subsidiaries, are exempt from this requirement.	14.15A
Investments in Joint Ventures – Section 15	
An investor in a joint venture shall disclose: (a) the accounting policy it uses for recognising its interests in jointly controlled entities; (b) the carrying amount of investments in jointly controlled entities; (c) the fair value of investments in jointly controlled entities accounted for using the equity method for which there are published price quotations; and (d) the aggregate amount of its commitments relating to joint ventures, including its share in the capital commitments that have been incurred jointly with other venturers, as well as its share of the capital commitments of the joint ventures themselves.	15.19
For jointly controlled entities accounted for in accordance with the equity method, the venturer shall disclose separately its share of the profit or loss of such investments and its share of any discontinued operations of such jointly controlled entities.	15.20
For jointly controlled entities accounted for in accordance with paragraph 15.9(c), the venturer shall make the disclosures required by paragraphs 11.43 and 11.44.	15.21
The individual financial statements of a venturer that is not a parent shall disclose summarised financial information about the investments in the jointly controlled entities, along with the effect of including those investments as if they had been accounted for using the equity method. Investing entities that are exempt from preparing consolidated financial statements, or would be exempt if they had subsidiaries, are exempt from this requirement.	15.21A

Disclosure Checklist: Group Accounting – Small Entities

(References are to the relevant Appendix of Section 1A FRS 102)

The mandatory disclosure requirements for small entities required under the Companies Act 2014 (ROI) (CA 2014), the Companies Act 2006 (UK) (CA 2006) and the Small Companies and Groups (Accounts and Directors' Report) Regulations 2008 (UK) (S.I. No. 409 of 2008) are as follows:

	Para.
Accounting policies	
Where in exceptional cases the useful life of intangible assets cannot be reliably estimated, there must be disclosed in a note to the financial statements the period over which those intangible assets are being written off and the reasons for choosing that period. (Schedule 1, paragraph 22(4) S.I. 409/2008) Intangible assets include goodwill. Paragraphs 18.27(a) and 19.25(g) address similar requirements.	1AC.6 (UK only)
In any case where any goodwill acquired by a small entity is shown or included as an asset in the entity's statement of financial position, the period chosen for writing off the consideration for that goodwill and the reasons for choosing that period shall be disclosed in a note to the financial statements. (Schedule 3A, paragraph 25(4) CA 2014)	1AD.7 (ROI only)

Disclosure Checklist: Group Accounting – Micro-entities

(References are to the relevant Section of FRS 105)

The mandatory disclosure requirements for micro-entities required under FRS 105, the Companies Act 2014 (ROI) (CA 2014), the Companies Act 2006 (UK) (CA 2006) and the Small Companies and Groups (Accounts and Directors' Report) Regulations 2008 (UK) (S.I. No. 409 of 2008) are as follows:

	Para.
A micro-entity shall disclose information in relation to financial commitments, guarantees and contingencies not recognised in the statement of financial position for trade and asset acquisitions in accordance with the relevant appendix to Section 6 *Notes to the Financial Statements*.	14.3
An Irish micro-entity shall disclose information in relation to goodwill acquired in accordance with Appendix B to Section 6 *Notes to the Financial Statements*.	14.4 (ROI only)
Accounting policies	
In any case where any goodwill acquired by a micro-entity is shown or included as an asset in the micro-entity's statement of financial position, the period chosen for writing off the consideration for that goodwill and the reasons for choosing that period shall be disclosed in a note to the financial statements. (Schedule 3B, paragraph 25(4) CA 2014)	6B.4 (ROI only)

Chapter 12

FINANCIAL INSTRUMENTS

12.1 BASIC FINANCIAL INSTRUMENTS (SECTION 11)

Scope

Section 11 of FRS 102 applies to basic financial instruments and is relevant to all entities reporting under the Standard. Section 12 applies to more complex instruments, which may not be relevant to all entities.

FRS 102 also covers the accounting treatment for concessionary loans (for public benefit entities), which are covered in **Chapter 14**.

Accounting Policy Choice

Every entity must choose whether or not to apply either:

(a) the provisions of both Sections 11 and 12 in full; or
(b) the IAS 39 *Financial Instruments: Recognition and Measurement* (and eventually IFRS 9 *Financial Instruments*) recognition and measurement provisions (as adopted in the EU) but, in addition, also apply the disclosure requirements in Sections 11 and 12.

The choice between (a) and (b) above is an accounting policy choice. Most entities will obviously opt for (a), but there could be reasons why subsidiaries might want to apply full IAS 39, possibly to facilitate the easy application of their consolidation procedures.

Introduction to Section 11

A financial instrument is a contract giving rise to a financial asset in one entity and a financial liability or equity instrument in another entity.

Examples of financial instruments included in Section 11 are:

(a) cash;
(b) demand deposits (e.g. bank accounts), loan receivables or payables;
(c) commercial paper;
(d) accounts receivable and payable;
(e) bonds;
(f) investments in non-convertible preference shares and non-puttable ordinary and preference shares; and
(g) commitments to receive a loan if it cannot be settled in cash.

However, Section 11 also provides examples of financial instruments that are **not** normally included within Section 11 and these include:

(a) asset-backed securities;
(b) options, warrants, futures contracts, forward contracts and interest rate swaps;
(c) financial instruments qualifying as hedging instruments;
(d) commitments to make a loan and to receive a loan if settled net in cash.

These are of a more complex nature and fit into Section 12.

Scope of Section 11

Section 11 applies to all financial instruments **except** the following:

(a) interests in subsidiaries, associates and joint ventures (Sections 9, 14 and 15 – see **Chapter 11**);
(b) an entity's own equity (Section 22 – see **Chapter 6**);
(c) leases (Section 20 – see **Chapter 4**);
(d) employee benefit plans (Section 28 – see **Chapter 8**);
(e) share-based payments (Section 26 – see **Chapter 8**);
(f) insurance contracts (apply FRS 103 *Insurance Contracts* instead);
(g) financial instruments with discretionary participation features (apply FRS 103 *Insurance Contracts* instead);
(h) reimbursement assets (Section 21 – see **Chapter 6**); and
(i) financial guarantee contracts (Section 21 – see **Chapter 6**).

Basic Financial Instruments

Every company will have some basic financial instruments since all have cash balances, trade receivables and payables, bank overdrafts and loans. The definition of financial instruments is very broad and encompasses a whole range of instruments. Many companies that are not involved in complex derivatives will probably only have to be concerned with Section 11 and can ignore Section 12.

Entities must account for the following as basic financial instruments in accordance with Section 11:

(a) cash;
(b) a debt instrument, e.g. accounts payable, accounts receivable, loans, etc.;
(c) a commitment to receive a loan that cannot be settled in cash; and
(d) an investment in non-convertible preference shares and non-puttable ordinary or preference shares.

A debt instrument satisfying **all** the conditions (a)–(d) below must be accounted for under Section 11, paragraph 11.9:

(a) returns to the holder are:
    (i) a fixed amount;
    (ii) a fixed rate of return over the life of the instrument; or
    (iii) [Deleted]

(iv) some combination of such fixed rate and variable rates (such as LIBOR plus 200 basis points), provided that both the fixed and variable rates are positive (e.g. an interest rate swap with a positive fixed rate and negative variable rate would not meet this criterion);[1]

(b) there is no contractual provision that could result in the holder losing the principal amount or any interest attributable to the current period or prior periods;
(c) contractual provisions that permit the issuer (the borrower) to prepay a debt instrument or permit the holder (the lender) to put it back to the issuer before maturity are not contingent on future events;
(d) extensions to debt instruments may be permitted provided their returns satisfy (a) to (c) above.

Examples that would normally satisfy the conditions are:
(a) bank loans and overdraft facilities to extent of the facility used;
(b) trade receivables; and
(c) a debt instrument that would become immediately receivable if the issuer defaults on an interest or principal payment.

Examples of financial instruments that do not satisfy the conditions (and are therefore within the scope of Section 12) include:
(a) an investment in another entity's equity instruments other than non-convertible preference shares and non-puttable ordinary and preference shares;
(b) an interest rate swap that returns a cash flow that is positive or negative, or a forward commitment to purchase a commodity or financial instrument that is capable of being cash-settled and that, on settlement, could have positive or negative cash flow;
(c) options and forward contracts, because the returns to the holder are not fixed and the conditions above are not met; and
(d) investments in convertible debt, because the return to the holder can vary with the price of the issuer's equity shares rather than just with market interest rates.

Initial Recognition of Financial Assets and Liabilities

Financial assets and liabilities should only be recognised when an entity becomes a party to the contractual provisions of the instrument. Firm commitments are not recognised until one of the parties has performed under the agreement.

Initial Measurement

At each reporting date an entity should typically measure the following instruments at transaction price (i.e. cost) unless it is a financing

[1] As a result of feedback from stakeholders, in the March 2018 version of FRS 102, the FRC expanded the definition of a basic financial instrument by incorporating a more principles-based definition to support the detailed conditions in paragraph 11.9. Readers should refer to the Standard for detailed examples of such instruments.

transaction, e.g. a payment deferred beyond normal business terms or financed at non-market rates. The interest cost should be measured at the present value of future payments discounted at a market rate of interest for a similar debt instrument.

There is an option to designate debt instruments to be measured subsequently at fair value through profit and loss to avoid an accounting mismatch.

Example 12.1: Financial Assets

Goods sold to a customer on short-term credit A receivable is recognised at the undiscounted amount of cash receivable from that entity, which is normally the invoice price.

Long-term loan A receivable is recognised at the present value of cash receivable (including interest payments and repayment of principal) from that entity.

Sale on two-year interest-free credit A receivable is recognised at the current cash sale price for that item. If the current cash sale price is not known, it may be estimated as the present value of the cash receivable discounted using the prevailing market rate(s) of interest for a similar receivable.

Purchase of another entity's ordinary shares The investment is recognised at the amount of cash paid to acquire the shares.

Example 12.2: Financial Liabilities

Goods purchased from a supplier on short-term credit A payable is recognised at the undiscounted amount owed to the supplier, which is normally the invoice price.

Loan received from a bank A payable is recognised initially at the present value of cash payable to the bank (e.g. including interest payments and repayment of principal).

Example 12.3: Financing Arrangements

Examples of present value calculations:

Interest-free deferred payment sale or purchase agreement The entity must initially measure the financial asset/liability at the present value of the future payments discounted at a market rate of interest for a similar debt instrument.

Loan not made at a market rate for a similar loan Should initially recognise the loan at the present value of the future payments discounted at a market rate of interest for a similar debt instrument.

Transaction costs, as long as they are clearly incremental to the creation of the instrument, are included in the initial amount recognised – added to financial assets and deducted from financial liabilities. However, for fair value instruments they must be charged to income.

Subsequent Measurement

At the end of each **reporting period**, an entity must measure financial instruments as follows, without any deduction for transaction costs on disposal:

Debt instruments that meet the basic instrument conditions These should be subsequently measured at **amortised cost** using the **effective interest method**.

Debt instruments that are classified as current assets or current liabilities These must be measured at the undiscounted amount of the cash or other consideration expected to be paid or received unless the arrangement constitutes, in effect, a financing transaction.

Debt instruments that constitute a financing transaction These must be measured at the present value of the future payments discounted at a market rate of interest for a similar debt instrument.

Debt instruments meeting the basic instrument conditions but initially designated at fair value through profit or loss This is permitted provided that doing so results in more relevant information, because either:

1. it eliminates or significantly reduces a measurement or recognition inconsistency (i.e. 'an accounting mismatch') that would otherwise arise from measuring assets or debt instruments or recognising the gains and losses on them on different bases; or
2. a group of debt instruments or financial assets and debt instruments is managed and its performance is evaluated on a fair value basis, in accordance with a documented risk management or investment strategy, and information about the group is provided internally on that basis to the entity's key management personnel.

Commitments to receive a loan that meet the basic instrument conditions These must be measured at cost (sometimes nil) less impairment.

Investments in non-convertible preference shares and non-puttable ordinary or preference shares that meet the basic instrument conditions

1. If the shares are publicly traded or their fair value can otherwise be measured reliably, the investment should be measured at fair value with any changes in fair value recognised in profit.

2. All other such investments should be measured at cost less impairment.

Impairment or uncollectibility must be assessed for all financial instruments measured at cost or amortised cost. That is not required for fair value measurements as these would already incorporate any impairment in value.

Amortised Cost and Effective Interest Method

The amortised cost of a financial asset or financial liability at each reporting date is the net of the following amounts:

(a) the amount at which the financial asset or financial liability is measured at initial recognition;
(b) minus any repayments of the principal;
(c) plus or minus the cumulative amortisation using the effective interest method of any difference between the amount at initial recognition and the maturity amount; and
(d) minus, in the case of a financial asset, any reduction (directly or through the use of an allowance account) for impairment or uncollectibility.

Financial assets and financial liabilities that have no stated interest rate and are classified as current assets or current liabilities are initially measured at an undiscounted amount.

The effective interest method is a method of calculating the amortised cost of a financial asset or liability and of allocating the interest income or interest expense over the relevant period.

The effective interest rate is the rate that exactly discounts the estimated future cash payments or receipts through the expected life of the financial instrument or, when appropriate, a shorter period, to the carrying amount of the financial asset or financial liability. The effective interest rate is determined on the basis of the carrying amount of the financial asset or liability at initial recognition. It really represents the true interest cost or income of a financial instrument.

Under the effective interest method:

(a) the amortised cost of a financial asset (liability) is the present value of future cash receipts (payments) discounted at the effective interest rate; and
(b) the interest expense (income) in a period equals the carrying amount of the financial liability (asset) at the beginning of a period multiplied by the effective interest rate for the period.

When calculating the effective interest rate, entities must estimate cash flows after taking into consideration all the contractual terms of the financial instrument and taking into account any known credit losses that have been incurred, but it must not consider possible future credit losses not yet incurred.

When calculating the effective interest rate, an entity must amortise any related fees, finance charges paid or received, transaction costs and other premiums or discounts over the expected life of the instrument, except as follows:

- entities must use a shorter period if that is the period to which the fees, etc. relate. This will be the case when the variable to which the fees, etc. relate is re-priced to market rates before the expected maturity of the instrument. In such a case, the appropriate amortisation period is the period to the next such re-pricing date.

For variable rate financial assets and liabilities, periodic re-estimation of cash flows to reflect changes in market rates of interest alters the effective interest rate. If a variable rate financial asset or liability is recognised initially at an amount equal to the principal receivable or payable at maturity, re-estimating the future interest payments normally has no significant effect on the carrying amount of the asset or liability.

If an entity revises its estimates of payments or receipts, it must adjust the carrying amount of the financial asset or financial liability (or group of financial instruments) to reflect the actual and revised estimated cash flows. The carrying amount must be recalculated by computing the present value of estimated future cash flows at the financial instrument's original effective interest rate. The adjustment must be recognised as an income or an expense in profit or loss at the date of the revision.

Section 11 provides a worked example of the determination of amortised cost, which is reproduced below. Note that the interest income is calculated using the internal rate of return.

Example 12.4: Determining Amortised Cost for a Five-year Loan using the Effective Interest Method

On 1 January 2019, an entity acquires a bond for €900, incurring transaction costs of €50. Interest of €40 is receivable annually, in arrears, over the next five years (31 December 2019–31 December 2023). The bond has a mandatory redemption of €1,100 on 31 December 2023.

Year	Carrying amount at beginning of period	Interest income at 6.9583%*	Cash inflow	Carrying amount at end of period
	€	€	€	€
2019	950.00	66.10	(40.00)	976.11
2020	976.11	67.92	(40.00)	1,004.03
2021	1,004.03	69.86	(40.00)	1,033.89

Year	Carrying amount at beginning of period	Interest income at 6.9583%*	Cash inflow	Carrying amount at end of period
	€	€	€	€
2022	1,033.89	71.94	(40.00)	1,065.83
2023	1,065.83	74.16	(40.00)	1,100.00
			(1,100.00)	0

* The effective interest rate of 6.9583 per cent is the rate that discounts the expected cash flows on the bond to the initial carrying amount:

$40/(1.069583)^1 + 40/(1.069583)^2 + 40/(1.069583)^3 + 40/(1.069583)^4 + 1{,}140/(1.069583)^5 = 950$

Impairment of Financial Instruments Measured at Cost or Amortised Cost

Recognition

At the end of each reporting period an entity should assess all financial assets measured at cost or amortised cost for impairment. If there is objective evidence of any impairment loss, it should be recognised immediately in profit or loss.

The objective evidence to be considered includes observable data about the following loss events:

(a) a significant financial difficulty of the issuer;
(b) a breach of contract, e.g. default in interest or principal payments;
(c) a creditor has granted a debtor a concession not normally considered;
(d) it is probable that a debtor will enter bankruptcy; and
(e) there is a measurable decrease in the estimated future cash flows from a group of financial assets even though individual assets cannot be identified, e.g. due to adverse national economic conditions.

Other factors to be considered could include technological, market, economic or legal environmental factors in which the issuer operates.

Financial assets that are significant should be assessed separately for impairment as well as all equity instruments, but others may be grouped in similar credit risk categories.

Example 12.5: Impairment of Trade Receivables

Townly Ltd has sold goods on credit to its customers. At 31 December 2019 (year end) it still has €30,000 outstanding. Last year 3% of the trade receivables were never paid. Townly would like to recognise an allowance for bad debts this year of 3% of €30,000. One of its customers has already gone into liquidation owing €5,000.

Solution

No allowance is permitted for bad debts for a general allowance of 3% against all balances. Section 11 requires a separate assessment to be undertaken of impairment of any trade receivable balance that is individually significant and then to group other assets on the basis of similar credit risk characteristics. €5,000 is significant and clearly an allowance should be created for that amount if unrecoverable, but this would be reduced by any amounts likely to be recovered from the liquidation of the customer.

Townly then needs to break up the remaining €25,000 into credit risk groupings and, provided there is objective evidence of impairment on an individual group, further allowances may be provided.

Measurement

Entities should measure an impairment loss as follows:

(a) for amortised cost less impairment assets – it is the difference between the carrying amount and the present value of estimated future cash flows discounted at the original effective discount rate; and

(b) for cost less impairment assets – it is the difference between the carrying amount and the best estimate of the amount that would be received for the asset if sold at the reporting date.

Example 12.6: Measurement of Impairment of Trade Receivables

Joburg Ltd granted a loan of €10,000 to one of its customers for four years at a rate of interest of 8%, interest being paid in arrears. The market rate of interest for similar loans is also 8%.

At the year-end 31 December 2019, the customer informed the company that it could not keep up the present level of payments due to severe financial difficulties. As a result, Joburg agreed to restructure the agreement and, under the revised terms, the customer is not required to pay any interest for two years, i.e. 2019 and 2020. However, interest due in 2021 and 2022 is expected to be paid and the principal repaid on 31 December 2022.

Solution

Initially, as the interest was at market rate, the loan receivable should be recorded at its transaction price of €10,000. The amortised cost is as follows:

Period	Book value at 01.01	Interest at 8%	Cash inflow	Book value at 31.12
	€	€	€	€
2019	10,000	800	(800)	10,000
2020	10,000	800	(800)	10,000
2021	10,000	800	(800)	10,000
2022	10,000	800	(10,800)	Nil

At the end of 2019 the book value is €10,800, i.e. principal plus first year's interest. Estimated cash flows are now reassessed at 8%, i.e. (€800 × 0.857) + (€10,800 × 0.794) = €685 + €8,575 = €9,260. An impairment loss of €9,260 – €10,800 = €1,540 is created and this is charged to the income statement and the loan receivable reduced by the same amount.

Reversal

If, subsequently, an impairment loss decreases, e.g. there is an improvement in a debtor's credit rating, the loss should be reversed directly or, alternatively, by adjusting an allowance account. It should not result, however, in the carrying amount exceeding what would have been stated had the impairment not previously been recognised. The reversal should be reported in profit or loss.

Example 12.7: Reversal of Impairment Loss

Arko Ltd purchases a debt instrument with a five-year term for a fair value of €1,000 (including transaction costs). The instrument has a principal amount of €1,250 payable on redemption and carries fixed interest of 4.7% annually. The annual cash income is therefore €59 (€1,250 × 0.047). The effective interest rate is 10%.

During 2019 the issuer of the instrument is in financial difficulties and likely to be put into administration. The fair value of the instrument at the end of 2020 is estimated to be €636 by discounting the expected future cash flows at 10%. No cash flows were received in 2021. However, at the end of 2021 the issuer is released from administration and Arko Ltd received a letter from the administrator/

receiver that the issuer will be able to meet all of its remaining commitments, including interest and principal.

The following table sets out the cash flows and interest income for each period using the effective interest rate of 10%:

Year	Amortised cost At start of year	Interest income 10%	Cash flows	Amortised cost At end of year
	€	€	€	€
2018	1,000	100	59	1,041
2019	1,041	104	59	1,086
2020	1,086	109	59	1,136
2021	1,136	113	59	1,190
2022	1,190	119	59 + 1,250	–

Solution

The journal entries are as follows:

			€	€
2018	Dr	Investment	1,000	
		Cr Bank		1,000
	Dr	Investment	41	
	Dr	Bank	59	
		Cr Interest income		100
2019	Dr	Investment	41	
	Dr	Bank	59	
		Cr Interest income		104
2020	Dr	Investment	50	
	Dr	Bank	59	
		Cr Interest income		109
2020	Dr	Profit or loss (impairment) (€1,136 – €636 fair value)	500	
		Cr Investment		500

There are no cash flows during 2021, but the effective interest of 10% × €636 should be reported as interest income for the year as follows:

			€	€
2021	Dr	Investment (10% × €636)	64	
		Cr Interest income		64

At the end of 2022 there is objective evidence that the impairment loss has been reversed. The limit on the amount of the reversal is what the amortised cost of the asset would have been at the date of reversal had the impairment loss not been recorded, i.e. €1,190 at the end of 2021. The asset's carrying value at the end of 2021 was €700 (€636 + €64), so the reversal of the impairment loss is €490 (€1,190 – €700) and the journal entry recorded as follows:

				€	€
2021	Dr	Investment		490	
		Cr	Profit or loss (reversal of impairment)		490

The final journal entries for 2022 would be as follows:

				€	€
2022	Dr	Investment		60	
	Dr	Bank		59	
		Cr	Interest income		119
	Dr	Bank		1,250	
		Cr	Investment		1,250

Fair Value

Entities must measure an investment in non-puttable ordinary or non-convertible preference shares at fair value, if the fair value can be reliably measured. The following hierarchy should be used:

(a) the best evidence of fair value is a quoted price in an active market; or
(b) the price for a recent transaction for an identical asset; or
(c) if there is no active market nor a recent transaction, entities can adopt a valuation technique to estimate what the transaction price would have been on the measurement date in an arm's length exchange.

Valuation Technique Valuation techniques include using recent arm's length market transactions for an identical asset between knowledgeable, willing parties. If available, reference should be made to the current fair value of another asset that is substantially the same as the asset being measured or adopt discounted cash flow analysis and option pricing models. If there is a valuation technique commonly used by market participants to price the asset and that technique has been demonstrated to provide reliable estimates of prices obtained in actual market transactions, the entity should adopt that technique.

The objective of using a valuation technique is to establish what the transaction price would have been on the measurement date in an arm's length exchange motivated by normal business considerations. Fair value is estimated on the basis of the results of a valuation technique that makes maximum use of market inputs, and relies as little as possible on entity-determined inputs. A valuation technique would be expected to arrive at a reliable estimate of the fair value if:

(a) it reasonably reflects how the market could be expected to price the asset; and
(b) the inputs to the valuation technique reasonably represent market expectations and measures of the risk–return factors inherent in the asset.

No Active Market The fair value of ordinary shares or preference shares that do not have a quoted market price in an active market is reliably measurable if:

(a) the variability in the range of reasonable fair value estimates is not significant for that asset; or
(b) the probabilities of the various estimates within the range can be reasonably assessed; and used in estimating fair value.

There are many situations in which the variability in the range of reasonable fair value estimates of assets that do not have a quoted market price is unlikely to be significant. Normally it is possible to estimate the fair value of an asset that an entity has acquired from an outside party. However, if the range of reasonable fair value estimates is significant and the probabilities of the various estimates cannot be reasonably assessed, an entity is precluded from measuring the asset at fair value.

If a reliable measure of fair value is no longer available for an asset measured at fair value (e.g. an equity instrument measured at fair value through profit or loss), its carrying amount at the last date the asset was reliably measurable becomes its new cost. Entities must measure the asset at this cost amount less impairment until a reliable measure of fair value becomes available.

Derecognition of a Financial Asset

The derecognition of a financial asset from the balance sheet is only permitted when:

(a) the contractual rights to the cash flows from a financial asset have expired or been settled;
(b) the entity transfers to another party all significant risks and rewards relating to the asset; or
(c) the entity, despite retaining some significant risks and rewards, has transferred control of an asset to another party and the other party has the practical ability to sell the asset in its entirety to an unrelated third party. In this case the assets should be derecognised and any rights and obligations that are retained should be recorded separately.

The carrying amount of a transferred asset should be allocated between the rights and obligations retained and those transferred based on their relative fair values at the transfer date. New rights and obligations should be valued at fair values at that date with any differences reported in profit or loss.

If a transfer does not result in the derecognition of a financial asset, the entity should continue to recognise the transferred asset in its entirety, together with a financial liability for the consideration received. The asset and liability should not be offset. Subsequently, the entity should recognise any income on the asset transferred and expense incurred on the liability in profit or loss.

If a transferor provides non-cash collateral, the accounting treatment will depend on whether or not the transferee has the right to sell or re-pledge the collateral and on whether or not the transferor has defaulted. Both parties should account for the collateral as follows:

(a) if the transferee has the right, by contract, to sell or re-pledge the collateral, the transferor should reclassify the asset in its balance sheet, e.g. as a loaned asset, separately from other assets;
(b) if the transferee sells the collateral pledged to it, it should recognise the proceeds from sale and a liability measured at fair value;
(c) if the transferor defaults and is no longer entitled to redeem the collateral, it should derecognise the collateral and the transferee recognise the collateral as its asset initially at fair value or, if already sold, derecognise its obligation;
(d) apart from (c), the transferor should continue to carry the collateral as its asset and the transferee should not recognise the collateral as an asset.

Section 11 offers two examples of the derecognition of a financial asset, both of which are reproduced below (**Examples 12.8** and **12.9**).

Example 12.8: A Transfer that Qualifies for Derecognition

An entity sells a group of its accounts receivable to a bank at less than their face value. The entity continues to handle collections from the debtors on behalf of the bank, including sending monthly statements, and the bank pays the entity a market-rate fee for servicing the receivables. The entity is obliged to remit promptly to the bank any and all amounts collected, but it has no obligation to the bank for slow payment or non-payment by the debtors.

In this case, the entity has transferred to the bank substantially all of the risks and rewards of ownership of the receivables. Accordingly, it removes the receivables from its statement of financial position (i.e. derecognises them), and it shows no liability in respect of the proceeds received from the bank.

The entity recognises a loss calculated as the difference between the carrying amount of the receivables at the time of sale and the proceeds received from the bank. The entity recognises a liability to the extent that it has collected funds from the debtors but has not yet remitted them to the bank.

Example 12.9: A Transfer that does not Qualify for Derecognition

The facts are the same as the preceding example except that the entity has agreed to buy back from the bank any receivables for which the debtor is in arrears as to principal or interest for more than 120 days.

In this case, the entity has retained the risk of slow payment or nonpayment by the debtors – a significant risk with respect to receivables. Accordingly, the entity does not treat the receivables as having been sold to the bank, and it does not derecognise them. Instead, it treats the proceeds from the bank as a loan secured by the receivables. A continues to recognise the receivables as an asset until they are collected or written off as uncollectible.

In effect, the principle of applying the doctrine of enforcing the economic substance of a transaction over its legal form has been implemented in the derecognition rules.

Example 12.10: Derecognition on Factoring of Debts

Wolfgang Ltd sells its trade debts with a book value of €50,000 less bad debt allowance of €4,000 to a finance company. The finance company agrees to pay Wolfgang €43,000 for the debts. Based on past experience, both parties estimate that 92% of the trade debts will be settled. No guarantee, however, has been given to the finance company that this will happen. Wolfgang will continue to collect the debts and pass on the proceeds to the finance company.

Assume that one particular customer, owing €5,000, went into liquidation and thus only €41,000 was passed on to the finance company.

Solution

The agreement can only result in derecognition of the financial asset if substantially all of the risks are transferred to the finance company. Clearly this has happened as Wolfgang is not responsible for any excess debts over €4,000. In addition, Wolfgang will not benefit if more than €41,000 of the debts were collected.

The journal entries should therefore be as follows:

	€	€
Dr Cash	43,000	
Dr Income statement fee on disposal of trade receivables	3,000	
Cr Trade receivables		46,000

Cash will be collected gradually from Wolfgang's customers and the total remittance back to the finance company should add up to the following:

	€	€
Dr Cash	41,000	
Cr Financial liability		41,000
Proceeds from customers		
Dr Financial liability	41,000	
Cr Cash		41,000
Payment to finance company		

Derecognition of a Financial Liability

A financial liability should only be derecognised when it is either extinguished, cancelled or expired.

If an existing borrower and lender exchange debt instruments with substantially different terms, the borrower should account for the transaction as an extinguishment of the original financial liability and the creation of a new financial liability. Similarly, a substantial modification should result in the same accounting treatment.

Any difference between the carrying amount of a financial liability extinguished and the new revised liability is reported in profit or loss.

Presentation

A financial asset and a financial liability can only be offset and the net amount presented in the balance sheet when, and only when, an entity:

(a) currently has a legally enforceable right to set off the recognised amounts; and

(b) intends either to settle on a net basis, or to realise the asset and settle the liability simultaneously.

Disclosures

This part of Section 11 only applies to financial liabilities measured at fair value through profit or loss. If an entity has only basic financial instruments, it will not have any and thus no fair value disclosures will be required.

Accounting Policies for Financial Instruments

Entities should disclose the measurement basis for financial instruments and other accounting policies that are relevant to understanding the financial statements.

Balance Sheet: Categories of Financial Assets and Financial Liabilities

An entity must disclose the carrying amounts of:
- financial assets measured at fair value through profit or loss;
- financial liabilities measured at fair value through profit or loss – in addition, in FRS 102, financial liabilities that are not held as part of a trading portfolio and are not derivatives must be disclosed separately.

A typical example of the disclosure required for financial assets and liabilities is shown in the financial statements for the Northern Ireland company Brett Martin Limited.

Brett Martin Limited

ACCOUNTING POLICIES AND NOTES TO THE FINANCIAL STATEMENTS (EXTRACTS)
for the year ended 31 December 2017

3.14 Financial Instruments
The company has chosen to adopt Sections 11 and 12 of FRS 102 in respect of financial instruments.

(i) Financial assets
Basic financial assets, including trade and other receivables and cash and bank balances and are initially recognised at transaction price, unless the arrangement constitutes a financing transaction, where the transaction is measured at the present value of the future receipts discounted at a market rate of interest. Such assets are subsequently carried at amortised cost using the effective interest method.

At the end of each reporting period financial assets measured at amortised cost are assessed for objective evidence of impairment. If an asset is impaired the impairment loss is the difference between the carrying amount and the present value of the estimated cash flows discounted at the asset's original effective interest rate. The impairment loss is recognised in the statement of income and retained earnings.

If there is a decrease in the impairment loss arising from an event occurring after the impairment was recognised, the impairment is reversed. The reversal is such that the carrying amount does not exceed what the carrying amount would have been had the impairment not previously been recognised. The impairment reversal is recognised in the statement of income and retained earnings.

Financial assets are derecognised when (a) the contractual rights to the cash flows from the asset expire or are settled, or (b) substantially all the risks and rewards of the ownership of the asset are transferred to another party or (c) despite having retained some significant risks and rewards of ownership, control of the asset has been transferred to another party who has the practical ability to unilaterally sell the asset to an unrelated third party without imposing additional restrictions.

(ii) Financial liabilities

Basic financial liabilities, including trade and other payables, bank loans and amounts payable in respect of invoice discounting facilities, are initially recognised at transaction price, unless the arrangement constitutes a financing transaction, where the debt instrument is measured at the present value of the future receipts discounted at a market rate of interest. Debt instruments are subsequently carried at amortised cost, suing the effective interest rate method.

Fees paid on the establishment of loan facilities are recognised as transaction costs of the loan to the extent that it is probable that some or all of the facility will be drawn down. In this case, the fee is deferred until the draw-down occurs. To the extent there is no evidence that it is probable that some or all of the facility will be drawn down, the fee is capitalised as a prepayment for liquidity services and amortised over the period of the facility to which it relates.

Trade payables are obligations to pay for goods or services that have been acquired in the ordinary course of business from suppliers. Accounts payable are classified as current liabilities if payment is due within one year or less. If not, they are presented as non-current liabilities. Trade payables are recognised initially at transaction price and subsequently measured at amortised cost using the effective interest rate method.

Derivatives, including forward exchange contracts are not basic financial instruments.

Derivatives are initially recognised at fair value on the date a derivative contract is entered into and are subsequently remeasured at their fair value. Changes in the fair value of derivatives are recognised in profit or loss in finance costs or finance income as appropriate, unless they are included in a hedging arrangement.

Financial liabilities are derecognised when the liability is extinguished, that is when the contractual obligation is discharged, cancelled or expires.

(iii) Offsetting
Financial assets and liabilities are offset and the net amounts presented in the financial statements when there is a legally enforceable right to set off the recognised amounts and there is an intention to settle on a net basis or to realise the asset and settle the liability simultaneously.

[...]

26. Derivative financial instruments

The principal amount of the company's US$ forward exchange contracts as at 31 December 2017 was £5,804,449 (2016: £4,149,528). The principal amount of the company's AUS$ forward contracts as at 31 December 2017 was £647,678 (2016: £1,552,459). The fair value gain or loss is not considered material.

[...]

18. Creditors: amounts falling due after more than one year

	2017 £	2016 £
Bank loans	**734,496**	1,151,052
Government grants received	**196,193**	196,193
	930,689	1,347,245

19. Loans
Analysis of the maturity of loans is given below:

	2017 £	2016 £
Amounts falling due within one year		
Bank loans	**545,712**	866,656
Amounts due in respect of invoice discounting	**17,592,200**	12,156,582
	18,137,912	13,023,238
Amounts falling due 1–2 years		
Bank loans	**416,556**	416,556

Amounts falling due 2–5 years		
Bank loans	**317,940**	734,496
	18,872,408	14,174,290

The information must be disclosed in such a manner as to enable users to evaluate the significance of financial instruments in understanding the financial position and performance of the entity. For example, the terms and conditions of long-term debt, restrictions, repayment schedules, etc. should be provided.

An example of this type of disclosure might be as follows.

EXAMPLE 12.11: DISCLOSURE OF FINANCIAL LIABILITIES

Note 19 Bank overdrafts and loans

	2019	**2018**
	€	**€**
Bank overdraft	16,600	12,000
Fixed rate bank loan	155,000	130,000
Variable rate bank loan	80,000	-
Total	251,600	142,000

The bank overdraft is repayable on demand. Interest is payable on the bank overdraft at 5%.

Interest is payable on the seven-year bank loan at a fixed rate of 6% of the principal amount. The bank loan is fully repayable in 2023. Early payment is permitted without penalty.

The bank overdraft and fixed rate bank loan are secured by a floating lien over the entity's land and buildings, with a book amount of €220,000 at 31 December 2019 (€265,000 at 31 December 2018).

Interest is payable on the variable rate loan at LIBOR plus 1%. The variable rate bank loan is fully repayable on 30 June 2020. Early payment is prohibited. The variable rate loan is secured by €90,000 of trade receivables (see note 18).

For all financial assets and liabilities measured at fair value, the basis for determining that value should be disclosed, together with details of active markets or assumptions used in the valuation techniques.

Example 12.12: Disclosure of Fair Values in Financial Assets

Note 14 Investments in equity securities

	2019 €	2018 €
Listed non-puttable ordinary shares	9,300	10,000
Unlisted non-puttable ordinary shares	2,600	1,400
Total	11,900	11,400

The fair value of the entity's investments in listed equity securities is based on quoted market prices at the reporting date on the Irish Stock Exchange. The quoted market price used is the current bid price.

The fair value of the entity's investments in unlisted equity securities is determined using a discounted cash flow analysis based on assumptions that are supported by observable market data, where available. For the discounted cash flow analysis, an earnings growth factor of 5%, equal to the industry average, is used. A risk-free interest rate of 7% is used to discount the cash flows as the estimated cash flows themselves are adjusted for risk.

If a reliable measure of fair value is no longer available, that fact should be disclosed.

Derecognition

If an entity has transferred financial assets to another party in a transaction that does not qualify for derecognition, the entity should disclose for each class of such financial assets:

(a) the nature of the assets;
(b) the nature of the risks and rewards of ownership to which the entity remains exposed; and
(c) the carrying amounts of the assets and associated liabilities it continues to recognise.

Example 12.13: Disclosure of Derecognition of Financial Assets

Note 15 Trade and other receivables

	2019 €	2018 €
Trade receivables	385,000	440,000
Prepayments	1,500	1,300
Total	386,500	441,300

During 2019 the company sold €200,000 of its trade receivables to a bank for €250,000. The company continues to handle collections from the debtors on behalf of the bank. The company will buy back any receivables for which the debtor is in arrears as to principal or interest for more than 160 days. The company continues to recognise the full carrying amount of the receivables sold (€200,000) and has recognised the cash received on the transfer as a secured loan for €250,000. At 31 December 2019 the book value of the loan is €256,000, including accrued interest of €6,000 under the effective interest method. The bank is not entitled to sell the trade receivables or use them as security for its own borrowings.

Collateral

When an entity has pledged financial assets as collateral for liabilities, it must disclose:

(a) the carrying amount of the financial assets pledged; and
(b) the terms and conditions relating to the pledge.

Defaults and Breaches on Loans Payable

For loans payable an entity should disclose:

(a) details of any defaults during the period of principal, interest or redemption terms;
(b) the carrying amount of loans payable in default; and
(c) whether the default has been remedied or the terms renegotiated before the financial statements were authorised for issue.

Items of Income, Expense, Gains and Losses

The following items should be disclosed on the face of the financial statements or in the notes:

(a) the net gains or net losses recognised on:
  (i) financial assets measured at fair value through profit or loss,
  (ii) financial liabilities measured at fair value through profit or loss. In the FRS, separate disclosure of movements on those which are not held as part of a trading portfolio and are not derivatives is required,
  (iii) financial assets measured at amortised cost less impairment, and
  (iv) financial liabilities measured at amortised cost;
(b) the total interest income and expense for financial assets or liabilities that are not measured at fair value through profit or loss; and
(c) the amount of any impairment loss for each class of financial asset.

FRS 102 has inserted, for legal reasons, additional disclosure requirements for financial instruments at fair value which are outlined below.

The following disclosures are required only for financial instruments at fair value that are not equity investments, are not held as part of a trading portfolio and are not derivatives:

(a) the amount of change, during the period and cumulatively, in the fair value of the financial liability that is attributable to changes in the credit risk of that liability, determined either:
    (i) as the amount of change in its fair value that is not attributable to changes in market conditions that give rise to market risk, or
    (ii) using an alternative method the entity believes more faithfully represents the amount of change in its fair value that is attributable to changes in the credit risk of the liability;
(b) the method used to establish the amount of change attributable to changes in own credit risk or, if the change cannot be measured reliably or is not material, that fact;
(c) the difference between the financial liability's carrying amount and the amount the entity would be contractually required to pay at maturity to the holder of the obligation;
(d) if an instrument contains both a liability and an equity feature, and the instrument has multiple features that substantially modify the cash flows and the values of those features are interdependent (such as a callable convertible debt instrument), the existence of those features;
(e) any difference between the fair value at initial recognition and the amount that would be determined at that date using a valuation technique, and the amount recognised in profit or loss; and
(f) information that enables users of the entity's financial statements to evaluate the nature and extent of relevant risks arising from financial instruments to which the entity is exposed at the end of the reporting period. These risks typically include, but are not limited to, credit risk, liquidity risk and market risk. The disclosure should include both the entity's exposure to each type of risk and how it manages those risks.

An illustrative example, based on the IASB's *IFRS for SMEs 2009 Illustrative Financial Statements Presentation and Disclosure Checklist*, is shown below.

Example 12.14: Illustrative Financial Statements – Basic Instruments

Accounting Policies and Explanatory Notes (Extracts)

2. Basis of preparation and accounting policies

Trade and other receivables
Most sales are made on the basis of normal credit terms, and the receivables do not bear interest. Where credit is extended beyond normal credit terms, receivables are measured at amortised cost

using the effective interest method. At the end of each reporting period, the carrying amounts of trade and other receivables are reviewed to determine whether there is any objective evidence that the amounts are not recoverable. If so, an impairment loss is recognised immediately in profit or loss.

Trade payables
Trade payables are obligations on the basis of normal credit terms and do not bear interest. Trade payables denominated in a foreign currency are translated into € using the exchange rate at the reporting date. Foreign exchange gains or losses are included in other income or other expenses.

10. Trade and other receivables

	20X2 €	20X1 €
Trade debtors	528,788	528,384
Prepayments	56,760	45,478
	585,548	573,862

17. Trade payables

Trade payables at 31 December 20X2 include €42,600 denominated in foreign currencies (nil at 31 December 20X1).

Financial Institutions and Retirement Benefit Plans

A financial institution must, in addition, apply the relevant requirements of Section 34 *Specialised Activities* (see **Chapter 13**).

A retirement benefit plan must also apply additional relevant requirements of Section 34.

12.2 OTHER FINANCIAL INSTRUMENTS ISSUES (SECTION 12)

Scope

Section 12 applies to more complex financial instruments and transactions. If an entity has only basic financial instruments, it is exempt from Section 12.

Accounting Policy Choice

Similarly to Section 11, an entity should choose to apply either:

(a) the provisions of both Sections 11 and 12 in full; or
(b) IAS 39/IFRS 9 recognition and measurement provisions, but also apply the disclosures in Sections 11 and 12.

The choice between (a) and (b) is an accounting policy choice.

Scope of Section 12

Section 12 applies to all financial instruments except the following:

(a) those covered by Section 11;
(b) interests in subsidiaries (Section 9 – see **Chapter 11**), associates (Section 14 – see **Chapter 11**) and joint ventures (Section 15 – see **Chapter 11**);
(c) employers' rights and obligations under employee benefit plans (Section 28 – see **Chapter 8**);
(d) insurance and reinsurance contracts (see FRS 103 *Insurance Contracts*);
(e) financial instruments that meet the definition of an entity's own equity (Section 22 – see **Chapter 6;** Section 26 – see **Chapter 8**);
(f) leases (Section 20 – see **Chapter 4**) unless the lease could result in a loss to the lessor;
(g) contracts for contingent consideration in a business combination (Section 19 – see **Chapter 11**). This exemption applies only to the acquirer;
(h) any forward contract to buy/sell in the future an acquiree in a business combination provided the deal does not exceed a reasonable period to complete;
(i) share-based payments under Section 26 – see **Chapter 8**;
(j) financial instruments issued by an entity with a discretionary participation feature (see FRS 103 *Insurance Contracts*);
(k) reimbursement assets accounted for in accordance with Section 21 – see **Chapter 6**; and
(l) financial guarantee contracts under Section 21 – see **Chapter 6**.

Most contracts to buy or sell a non-financial item, such as a commodity, inventory or property, are excluded because they are not financial instruments. However, it applies to all contracts that impose risks on the buyer or seller that are not typical of contracts to buy or sell tangible assets. For example, Section 12 applies to contracts that could result in a loss to the buyer or seller as a result of contractual terms that are unrelated to changes in the price of the non-financial item, changes in foreign exchange rates, or a default by one of the counterparties.

In addition to the contracts above, Section 12 applies to contracts to buy or sell non-financial items if the contract can be settled net in cash or another financial instrument, or by exchanging financial instruments as if the contracts were financial instruments, with the following exception:

- contracts that were entered into and continue to be held for the purpose of the receipt or delivery of a non-financial item in accordance with the entity's expected purchase, sale or usage requirements.

Initial Recognition of Financial Assets and Liabilities

Financial assets and liabilities may only be recognised when an entity becomes a party to the contractual provisions of the instrument.

Initial Measurement

Initially an entity should measure the instruments covered in Section 12 at fair value, which is normally the transaction price. It includes transaction costs, unless they are at fair value through profit or loss.

If payment for an asset is deferred beyond normal business terms or is financed at a rate of interest that is not a market rate, the asset must be measured at the present value of the future payments discounted at a market rate of interest for a similar debt instrument.

Subsequent Measurement

At the end of each **reporting period**, an entity must measure all financial instruments within the scope of Section 12 at fair value and recognise changes in fair value in profit or loss, except as follows:

1. equity instruments that are not publicly traded and whose fair value cannot otherwise be measured reliably;
2. hedging instruments in a designated hedging relationship;
3. small entities must adopt amortised cost.

If a reliable measure of fair value is no longer available for an equity instrument that is not publicly traded but it is measured at fair value through profit or loss, its fair value at the last date the instrument was reliably measurable is treated as the cost of the instrument. The entity must then measure the instrument at this cost amount less impairment until a reliable measure of fair value becomes available.

Fair Value

Entities must apply the guidance on fair value in accordance with Section 12 as well as with Section 11.

The fair value of a financial liability that is due on demand is not less than the amount payable on demand, discounted from the first date that the amount could be required to be paid.

Impairment of Financial Instruments Measured at Cost or Amortised Cost

Entities must apply the guidance on impairment of a financial instrument measured at cost as per Section 11.

Derecognition of a Financial Asset or Financial Liability

Entities must apply the derecognition requirements in Section 11 to financial assets and financial liabilities to which Section 12 applies.

Hedge Accounting

It is possible to designate a hedging relationship between a hedging instrument and a hedged item and if certain specified criteria are met, then a gain/loss on that instrument and on the hedged item may be recognised in profit or loss at the same time.

In order to qualify, however, an entity must comply with all of the following conditions:

(a) the relationship must be designated and documented so that the risk, hedging instrument and hedged item are clearly identified;
(b) the designation of the relationship must be consistent with the entity's risk-management objectives and hedge strategy;
(c) the only hedge instruments permitted:
    (i) must be an external contract,
    (ii) it is designated in full or a portion of the nominal value is designated, and
    (iii) it is not a written option;
(d) the only hedged items permitted:
    (i) a recognised asset or liability,
    (ii) an unrecognised firm commitment,
    (iii) a highly probable present transaction, and
    (iv) a net investment in a foreign operation.

    } Must be reliably measured; and must be external party in consolidated accounts

A fair value hedge is a hedge of the exposure to changes in the fair value of a recognised asset or liability or an unrecognised firm commitment. An example would be inventory whose price is likely to vary and therefore, in order to ensure it 'locks in' a selling price that will be realised, a company might enter a forward contract to sell the inventory at a fixed price.

A cash flow hedge is a hedge of the exposure to variability in cash flows that is attributable to a particular risk associated with a recognised asset or liability. Often it involves a future purchase where a buyer is concerned about having to pay a foreign currency and so hedges the risk by entering into a forward contract to buy the foreign currency; the company is therefore 'locked into' cash flows.

Examples of a fair value hedge and a cash flow hedge are given below.

Example 12.15: Fair Value Hedge

On 30 June 2019 Lismore Ltd issues €10 million fixed interest debt at 7.5% (six-month rate). The liability is expected to be volatile and Lismore is worried about changes in the value of the liability, so on the same day it enters into an interest rate **swap** (fixed to floating) arrangement to hedge the liability.

From 1 July–31 December 2019 LIBOR is 6%.

At 31 December 2019:

	€
Fair value of the liability	10,125,000
Fair value of the swap (an asset)	(125,000)

Lismore Ltd is now exposed to variable rates, as the required rate of return on the market changes the value of the fixed rate debt and the swap will change in tandem. If we think of it as a synthetic instrument (i.e. borrowing + swap), the company's cash flows change as does the market's view of them. The overall value remains constant.

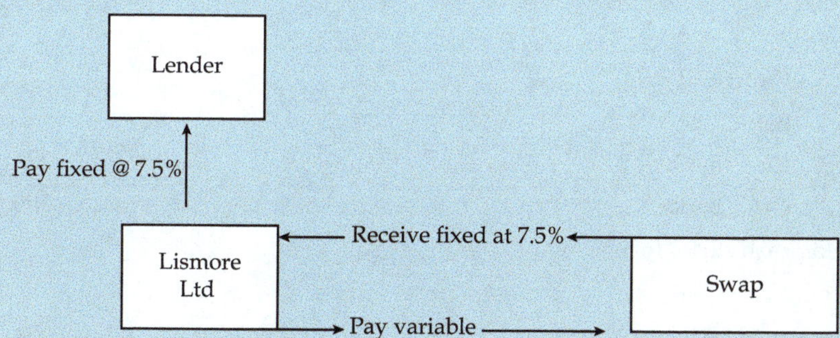

The value of the liability has increased because it is now in demand. The fair value of the swap is an asset because it gives Lismore Ltd the right to pay 6% for 7.5%.

The value of the cash flows are as follows:

Cash flows	Gross €	Net €
Lismore Ltd pays 7.5% to lender	375,000	375,000
Lismore Ltd receives 7.5% from the counterparty to the swap	(375,000)	
Lismore Ltd pays 6% to the counterparty to the swap	300,000	(75,000)
Outflow	300,000	300,000

Solution

The following journal entries are required:

		€000	€000
Dr	Cash	10,000	
	Cr Liability		10,000
Being initial issue of €10m debt.			
Dr	Swap	125	
	Cr Profit and loss		125
Being fair value changes for the year.			
Dr	Profit and loss	125	
	Cr Swap		125
Being fair value changes for the year.			
Dr	Profit and loss	300	
Dr	Bank	375	
	Cr Bank		375
	Cr Bank		300
Being cash flows for the year.			

EXAMPLE 12.16: CASH FLOW HEDGE

Carrick Ltd has contracted to buy a machine for 100,000 CHF (Swiss Francs). The spot rate of exchange at that date was 2.5 CHF = €1. It enters into a forward contract to buy CHF/sell € at a rate of 2.5 CHF = €1.

At year end 31 December 2019:

The spot rate is 2.4 CHF = €1

The fair value of the forward contract is given as:

	€
100,000 CHF @ 2.4 =	41,667
100,000 CHF @ 2.5 =	40,000
	1,667

At 31 March 2020:

The machine is purchased with the exchange rate at 2.3 CHF = €1

The fair value of the forward contract is given as:

	€
100,000 CHF @ 2.3 =	43,478
100,000 CHF @ 2.5 =	40,000
	3,478

Solution

	Note	Forward Dr	Forward Cr	Reserve Dr	Reserve Cr
30 September	(1)				
31 December	(2)	1,667			1,667
31 March	(3)	1,811			1,811
	(5)		3,478		
	(5)			3,478	

	Note	Cash Dr	Cash Cr	Machine Dr	Machine Cr
30 September					
31 December					
31 March	(4)		43,478	43,478	
	(5)	3,478			3,478
	(6)				40,000
				43,478	43,478
Balance b/f	(6)			40,000	

Notes:

1. Spot rate is 2.5, which is same as forward rate, therefore the fair value of the forward contract is zero.
2. Fair value of the forward contract at year end (difference between spot rate and contracted rate).
3. Increase in fair value of the forward contract to the date of the purchase of the machine.
4. Purchase of the asset at the spot rate.
5. Recognising the amount by which the forward contract reduces the cash flow.
6. Recognises that the asset's real cost was only €40,000.

The following journal entries are required:

		€000	€000
31 December:			
	Dr Forward contract asset	1,667	
	Cr Cash flow hedge reserve		1,667
31 March:			
	Dr Forward contract asset	1,811	
	Cr Cash flow hedge reserve		1,811
	Dr Machine	43,478	
	Cr Cash		43,478
	Dr Cash flow hedge reserve	3,478	
	Cr Forward contract asset		3,478
	Dr Cash	3,478	
	Cr Machine		3,478

Accounting for Qualifying Hedge Relationships

There are three types of hedging relationship:

(a) fair value hedge – hedge to exposure to changes in fair values of recognised assets or liabilities;
(b) cash flow hedge – hedge to variability in cash flows; and
(c) hedge in net investments in a foreign operation.

Fair Value Hedges

- Gain/loss on hedging instrument must be recognised in profit or loss; and
- holding gain/loss on hedged item is adjusted to carrying amount of hedged item and recognised in profit or loss.

Cash Flow Hedges

- Cash flow hedge reserve (in equity) is adjusted to the lower of:
  - cumulative gain/loss on hedging instrument from inception of hedge, or
  - cumulative change in fair value of expected future cash flows on hedged item from the inception of the hedge;
- effective portion is recognised in other comprehensive income;
- ineffective gain/loss is recognised in profit and loss;
- if a hedge of a forecast transaction subsequently results in a recognised non-financial asset or liability, the amount must be transferred from the hedge reserve to the carrying amount of the asset/liability;
- for other cash flow hedges, the amount should be recycled to profit and loss in the same period when the hedged future expected cash flows affect profit or loss.

Hedges in Net Investment of a Foreign Operation These are accounted for similarly to cash flow hedges:

- effective hedge gains and losses through other comprehensive income;
- ineffective hedge gains and losses through profit and loss.

However, there is no recycling to profit and loss on the disposal of a foreign operation.

Discontinuing Hedge Accounting

An entity must discontinue hedge accounting if:

(a) the holding instrument is sold or terminated;
(b) the hedge fails the criteria for hedge accounting;
(c) if, for a hedge of a foreign transaction, the forecast is no longer probable; or
(d) the entity revokes the designation.

In cash flow hedges, if previously expected cash flows are no longer expected, then cumulative gains and losses must be immediately recycled to the profit and loss account.

Presentation

A financial asset and a financial liability can only be offset and the net amount presented in the balance sheet when, and only when, an entity:

(a) currently has a legally enforceable right to set off the recognised amounts; and
(b) intends either to settle, or to realise the asset and settle the liability simultaneously.

Disclosures

Entities must make all the disclosures required by Section 11, but in addition must also provide the following.

An entity should disclose the following separately for hedges of each of the three types of hedging relationship:

(a) a description of the hedge;
(b) a description of the financial instruments designated as hedging instruments and their fair values at the reporting date; and
(c) the nature of the risks being hedged, including a description of the hedged item.

For fair value hedges the following must be disclosed:

(a) the amount recognised in profit and loss for changes in fair value – hedged item; and
(b) the amount recognised in profit and loss for changes in fair value – hedged instrument.

For cash flow hedges the following must be disclosed:

(a) the periods when cash flows are expected to occur and when they affect profit and loss;
(b) a description of any foreign translation for fair value hedge accounting no longer expected to occur;
(c) the amount of changes to the fair value of hedging instruments recognised in other comprehensive income;
(d) the amount recycled from other comprehensive income to profit and loss; and
(e) the amount of any excess of fair value of hedging instrument over the change in the fair value of the expected cash flows recognised in profit or loss.

For hedge accounting a net investment in a foreign operation, the following must be separately disclosed:

(a) the amounts recognised in other comprehensive income; and
(b) the amounts recognised in profit and loss.

EXAMPLE 12.17: SIMPLE FAIR VALUE HEDGE

Boyle Ltd has an investment in an equity instrument. The cost of the investment on 1 July 2019 was €250,000. On 1 September 2018, Boyle Ltd enters into a derivatives future contract to hedge the fair value of the investment. Assume all the conditions for hedge accounting are met and also that it qualifies as a fair value hedge as it is a hedge of an exposure to changes in the fair value of a recognised asset.

At the next reporting date, 30 September 2019, the fair value of the investment (hedged item) was €230,000 based on quoted market prices. The fair value of the derivative (hedging instrument) at that date was €18,000. The journal entries required would be as follows:

			€	€
1 July 2019:				
	Dr	Investment	250,000	
		Cr Bank		250,000
	Being the initial recognition of the investment.			

There are no entries required for the futures contract as the net fair value is zero.

30 September 2019:				
	Dr	Profit or loss (expense)	20,000	
		Cr Investment		20,000
	Being remeasurement of the investment.			
	Dr	Futures contract	18,000	
		Cr Profit or loss (income)		18,000
	Being settlement of futures contract.			

EXAMPLE 12.18: CASH FLOW HEDGE OF A FIRM COMMITMENT

Carrick Ltd enters into a forward exchange contract on 30 June 2019 to receive 100,000 FC and deliver local currency of €109,600 on 30 June 2020. It designates the forward exchange contract as a hedging instrument in a cash flow hedge of a firm commitment to purchase a specified quantity of paper on 31 March 2020. Payment for the paper is due on 30 June 2020. All hedge accounting criteria are assumed to be met.

Assume the following exchange rates at different dates:

Date	Spot rate	Forward rate to 30.06.20	Fair value of forward contract
30 June 2019	1.072	1.096	–
31 December 2019	1.080	1.092	(388)
31 March 2020	1.074	1.076	(1,971)
30 June 2020	1.072	–	(2,400)

The journal entries would be as follows:

		€	€
30 June 2019:			
Dr	Forward contract	Nil	
	Cr Bank		Nil
	On initial recognition the forward contract has a fair value of zero.		
31 December 2019:			
Dr	Equity	388	
	Cr Forward contract		388
	Being recording of the change in fair value of the forward contract.		
31 March 2020:			
Dr	Equity	1,583	
	Cr Forward contract		1,583
	Being recording of the change in fair value of the forward contract (€1,971 – €388).		
Dr	Purchases	107,400	
Dr	Purchases (hedging loss)	1,971	
	Cr Equity		1,971
	Cr Trade payables		107,400
	Being recording of hedging loss and paper at spot rate in cost of purchased paper. The paper is effectively recognised at the forward rate.		
30 June 2020:			
Dr	Equity	429	
	Cr Forward contract		429
	Being recording of change in fair value of the forward contract (€2,400 – €1,971)		

Dr	Trade payables	107,400	
Dr	Forward contract	2,400	
Cr	Bank		109,600
Cr	Profit or loss		200

Being repayment of liability at the forward rate of €109,600.

Dr	Profit or loss	2,400	
Cr	Equity		2,400

Being recycling of previous gains/losses on the forward contract to profit or loss.

12.3 SMALL ENTITIES

There are no explicit minimum disclosure requirements for small entities under Section 1A FRS 102 for either the UK or the Republic of Ireland. However, small entities may need to provide disclosures as required by FRS 102, Sections 11 and 12 if required to give a true and fair view.

12.4 MICRO-ENTITIES

The main differences between accounting under FRS 105 and FRS 102 is that fair value reporting is not permitted for micro-entities. All financial instruments must be reported at amortised cost or at cost less impairment.

Disclosure Checklist: Financial Instruments – FRS 102

(References are to the relevant Section of FRS 102)

	Para.
Basic Financial Instruments – Section 11	
Disclosure of accounting policies for financial instruments	
In accordance with paragraph 8.5, an entity shall disclose, in the summary of significant accounting policies, the measurement basis (or bases) used for financial instruments and the other accounting policies used for financial instruments that are relevant to an understanding of the financial statements.	11.40
Statement of financial position – categories of financial assets and financial liabilities	
An entity shall disclose separately the carrying amounts at the reporting date of financial assets and financial liabilities measured at fair value through profit or loss. This disclosure may be made separately by category of financial instrument. Financial liabilities that are not held as part of a trading portfolio and are not derivatives shall be shown separately.	11.41
An entity shall disclose information that enables users of its financial statements to evaluate the significance of financial instruments for its financial position and performance. For example, for long-term debt such information would normally include the terms and conditions of the debt instrument (such as interest rate, maturity, repayment schedule and restrictions that the debt instrument imposes on the entity). When the risks arising from financial instruments are particularly significant to the business (e.g. because they are principal risks for the entity), additional disclosure may be required. Paragraphs 34.19 to 34.30, which set out disclosure requirements for financial institutions, include examples of disclosure requirements for risks arising from financial instruments that may be relevant in such cases.	11.42
For all financial assets and financial liabilities measured at fair value, the entity shall disclose the basis for determining fair value, e.g. quoted market price in an active market or a valuation technique. When a valuation technique is used, the entity shall disclose the assumptions applied in determining fair value for each class of financial assets or financial liabilities. For example, if applicable, an entity discloses information about the assumptions relating to prepayment rates, rates of estimated credit losses, and interest rates or discount rates.	11.43
If a reliable measure of fair value is no longer available for an equity instrument measured at fair value through profit or loss, the entity shall disclose that fact.	11.44
Derecognition	
If an entity has transferred financial assets to another party in a transaction that does not qualify for derecognition (see paragraphs 11.33–11.35), the entity shall disclose the following for each class of such financial assets: (a) the nature of the assets; (b) the nature of the risks and rewards of ownership to which the entity remains exposed; and (c) the carrying amounts of the assets and of any associated liabilities that the entity continues to recognise.	11.45

	PARA.
Collateral	
When an entity has pledged financial assets as collateral for liabilities or contingent liabilities, it shall disclose the following: (a) the carrying amount of the financial assets pledged as collateral; and (b) the terms and conditions relating to its pledge.	11.46
Defaults and breaches on loans payable	
For loans payable recognised at the reporting date for which there is a breach of terms or default of principal, interest, sinking fund, or redemption terms that has not been remedied by the reporting date, an entity shall disclose the following: (a) details of that breach or default; (b) the carrying amount of the related loans payable at the reporting date; and (c) whether the breach or default was remedied, or the terms of the loans payable were renegotiated, before the financial statements were authorised for issue.	11.47
Items of income, expense, gains or losses	
An entity shall disclose the following items of income, expense, gains or losses: (a) income, expense, gains or losses, including changes in fair value, recognised on: (i) financial assets measured at fair value through profit or loss, (ii) financial liabilities measured at fair value through profit or loss, (iii) financial assets measured at amortised cost, and (iv) financial liabilities measured at amortised cost; (v) when an entity has made the accounting policy choice in paragraphs 11.2(c) and 12.2(c) to apply the recognition and measurement provisions of IFRS 9, financial instruments measured at fair value through other comprehensive income. (b) total interest income and total interest expense (calculated using the effective interest method) for financial assets or financial liabilities that are not measured at fair value through profit or loss; and (c) the amount of any impairment loss for each class of financial asset. A class of financial asset is a grouping that is appropriate to the nature of the information disclosed and that takes into account the characteristics of the financial assets. When an entity has made the accounting policy choice in paragraph 11.2(c) and 12.2(c) to apply the recognition and measurement provisions of IFRS 9, the groupings shall be based on whether the amount is equal to 12-month expected credit risk losses, equal to the lifetime expected credit losses or financial assets that are purchased or originated credit-impaired.	11.48
Financial instruments at fair value through profit or loss	
The following disclosures are required only for financial instruments at fair value that are not held as part of a trading portfolio and are not derivatives: (a) the amount of change, during the period and cumulatively, in the fair value of the financial instrument that is attributable to changes in the credit risk of that instrument, determined either: (i) as the amount of change in its fair value that is not attributable to changes in market conditions that give rise to market risk, or (ii) using an alternative method the entity believes more faithfully represents the amount of change in its fair value that is attributable to changes in the credit risk of the instrument;	11.48A

	PARA.
(b) the method used to establish the amount of change attributable to changes in own credit risk, or, if the change cannot be measured reliably or is not material, that fact; (c) the difference between the financial liability's carrying amount and the amount the entity would be contractually required to pay at maturity to the holder of the obligation; (d) if an instrument contains both a liability and an equity feature, and the instrument has multiple features that substantially modify the cash flows and the values of those features are interdependent (such as a callable convertible debt instrument), the existence of those features; (e) any difference between the fair value at initial recognition and the amount that would be determined at that date using a valuation technique, and the amount recognised in profit or loss; and (f) information that enables users of the entity's financial statements to evaluate the nature and extent of relevant risks arising from financial instruments to which the entity is exposed at the end of the reporting period. These risks typically include, but are not limited to, credit risk, liquidity risk and market risk. The disclosure should include both the entity's exposure to each type of risk and how it manages those risks.	11.48A
Other Financial Instruments Issues – Section 12	
An entity applying this section shall make all of the disclosures required in Section 11 incorporating in those disclosures, financial instruments that are within the scope of this section as well as those within the scope of Section 11. For financial instruments in the scope of this section that are not held as part of a trading portfolio and are not derivative instruments, an entity shall provide additional disclosures as set out in paragraph 11.48A. In addition, if the entity uses hedge accounting, it shall make the additional disclosures in paragraphs 12.27 to 12.29A.	12.26
An entity shall disclose the following separately for each type of hedging relationship described in paragraph 12.19: (a) a description of the hedge; (b) a description of the financial instruments designated as hedging instruments and their fair values at the reporting date; and (c) the nature of the risks being hedged, including a description of the hedged item.	12.27
An entity uses hedge accounting for a fair value hedge it shall disclose the following: (a) the amount of the change in fair value of the hedging instrument recognised in profit or loss for the period; and (b) the amount of the change in fair value of the hedged item recognised in profit or loss for the period.	12.28
If an entity uses hedge accounting for a cash flow hedge it shall disclose the following: (a) the periods when the cash flows are expected to occur and when they are expected to affect profit or loss; (b) a description of any forecast transaction for which hedge accounting had previously been used, but which is no longer expected to occur;	12.29

	PARA.
(c) the amount of the change in fair value of the hedging instrument that was recognised in other comprehensive income during the period; (d) the amount, if any, that was reclassified from equity to profit or loss for the period; and (e) the amount, if any, of any hedge ineffectiveness recognised in profit or loss for the period.	12.29
If an entity uses hedge accounting for a net investment in a foreign operation it shall disclose separately the amounts recognised in other comprehensive income in accordance with paragraph 12.24(a) and the amounts recognised in profit or loss in accordance with paragraph 12.24(b).	12.29A

DISCLOSURE CHECKLIST: FINANCIAL INSTRUMENTS – SMALL ENTITIES

(References are to the relevant Appendix of Section 1A FRS 102)

The mandatory disclosure requirements for small entities required under the Companies Act 2014 (ROI) (CA 2014), the Companies Act 2006 (UK) (CA 2006) and the Small Companies and Groups (Accounts and Directors' Report) Regulations 2008 (UK) (S.I. No. 409 of 2008) are as follows:

	PARA.
Fair value measurement	
Where financial instruments or assets other than financial instruments have been measured in accordance with the fair value accounting rules there shall be stated: (a) the significant assumptions underlying the valuation models and techniques where fair values have been determined otherwise than by reference to market price in an active market; (b) for each category of financial instruments or assets other than financial instruments, the fair value of the financial instruments or assets other than financial instruments in that category and the change in value: (i) included in the income statement; or (ii) credited or debited to the fair value reserve, in respect of those financial instruments or assets other than financial instruments. (Schedule 3A, paragraphs 46(2)(a) and (b) CA 2014) (Schedule 1, paragraphs 51(2)(a) and (b) S.I. 409/2008) This does not apply where financial instruments or assets other than financial instruments are measured at fair value only on initial recognition. This applies where financial instruments, investment property and biological assets are subsequently measured at fair value through profit or loss, which is permitted or required by paragraphs 9.26(c), 11.14(b), 11.14(d)(i), 12.8, 14.4(d), 15.9(d), 16.7 and 34.4, 9.26(c), 11.14(b), 11.14(d)(iii), 11.14(d)(iv), 12.8, 13.4A, 14.4(d), 15.9(d), 16.7 and 34.4. Paragraphs 11.41, 11.43, 11.48(a)(i), 11.48(a)(ii), 12.28, 12.29(c), and 12.29(e) address similar disclosure requirements for financial instruments. Paragraphs 16.10(a) and 16.10(e)(ii) address similar disclosure requirements for investment property. Paragraphs 34.7(b) and 34.7(c)(i) address similar disclosure requirements for biological assets.	1AD.22 (ROI) 1AC.22 (UK) (similar)
Where financial instruments or assets other than financial instruments have been measured in accordance with the fair value accounting rules there shall be stated for each class of derivatives, the extent and nature of the instruments, including significant terms and conditions that may affect the amount, timing and certainty of future cash flows. (Schedule 3A, paragraph 46(2)(c) CA 2014) (Schedule 1, paragraph 51(2)(c) S.I. 409/2008)	1AD.23(ROI) 1AC.23(UK) (similar)

	PARA.
Where financial instruments or assets other than financial instruments have been measured in accordance with the fair value accounting rules there shall be stated in tabular form, the movements in the fair value reserve during the reporting period. (Schedule 3A, paragraph 46(2)(d) CA 2014) (Schedule 1, paragraph 51(3) S.I. 409/2008) Paragraphs 6.3A, 12.29(c) and 12.29(d) address similar requirements.	1AD.24 (ROI) 1AC.24 (UK) (similar)
Financial instruments measured at fair value	
Financial instruments that under international financial reporting standards (IFRS) may be accounted for in financial statements at fair value, may be so accounted for in financial statements to which the provisions of Schedule 3A apply, provided that the disclosures required by IFRS are made. (Schedule 3A, paragraph 38(1) CA 2014) (Schedule 1, paragraph 36(4) S.I. 409/2008) This applies to all financial instruments measured in accordance with the fair value accounting rules. The disclosures required by Section 11 that relate to financial assets and financial liabilities measured at fair value, including paragraph 11.48A, shall be given.	1AD.25 (ROI) 1AC.26 (UK) (similar)

DISCLOSURE CHECKLIST: FINANCIAL INSTRUMENTS – MICRO-ENTITIES

There are no mandatory disclosures.

Chapter 13

SPECIALISED ACTIVITIES

13.1 AGRICULTURE (SECTION 34)

An entity engaged in **agricultural activity** applying FRS 102 must determine its accounting policy for each class of its **biological assets** (living animals or plants) and its related agricultural produce (the harvested products from biological assets) as follows.

Recognition

Similar to other assets, biological assets or agricultural produce are only recognised when, and only when:

(a) the entity controls the asset as a result of past events;
(b) it is probable that future economic benefits will flow to the entity; and
(c) the fair value or cost of the asset can be measured reliably without undue cost or effort.

Measurement

Entities must initially recognise and measure a biological asset using either:

(a) its fair value less costs to sell. That measurement should be repeated at each reporting date. Any changes in the fair value less costs to sell must be recognised in profit or loss; or
(b) the cost model.

Entities are not allowed to switch their accounting policy to the cost model if they have initially adopted the fair value model.

If agricultural produce harvested from an entity's biological assets is measured at its fair value less costs to sell, this is measured at its point of harvest. At that point, that measurement becomes the cost at that date when applying Section 13 *Inventories* (see **Chapter 5**) or another applicable section of the FRS.

In determining fair value, an entity must consider the following:

(a) if an active market exists for a biological asset or agricultural produce in its present location and condition, use the quoted price. If there is access to different active markets, the price existing in the market that an entity expects to use should be adopted;

(b) if there is no active market, one or more of the following methods should be adopted:
    (i) the most recent market transaction price, provided there are no significant changes in economic circumstances between the transaction date and the end of the reporting period;
    (ii) market prices for similar assets with an adjustment to reflect differences; and
    (iii) sector benchmarks, e.g. the value of an orchard expressed per export tray, bushel or hectare, and the value of cattle expressed per kilogram of meat;

(c) (a) or (b) may suggest different conclusions, so an entity must consider the reasons for those differences to ensure the most reliable estimate of fair value within a relatively narrow range of reasonable estimates; and

(d) in some circumstances, fair value may be readily determinable without undue cost or effort despite a lack of availability of market prices. In those circumstances, entities must consider whether or not the present value of the expected net cash flows from the asset discounted at a current market-determined rate results in a reliable measure of fair value.

If fair values cannot be reliably measured, then the cost model must be adopted.

Disclosures: Fair Value Model

The following must be disclosed if the fair value model is adopted:

(a) a description of each class of its biological assets;

(b) the methods and significant assumptions applied for each category of biological assets; and

(c) a reconciliation of changes in the carrying amount of biological assets between the beginning and the end of the current period. The reconciliation must include:
    (i) the gain or loss arising from changes in the fair value less costs to sell;
    (ii) increases resulting from purchases;
    (iii) decreases from sales;
    (iv) decreases from harvest;
    (v) increases from business combinations; and
    (vi) other changes.

The reconciliation is not required for prior periods.

Measurement: Cost Model

If the cost model is adopted, biological assets must be measured at cost less any accumulated **depreciation** and any accumulated **impairment** losses.

Harvested agricultural produce must be measured at either:

(a) fair value less estimated costs to sell at the point of harvest; or
(b) the lower of cost and estimated selling price less costs to complete and sell.

Disclosures: Cost Model

Entities must disclose the following with respect to its biological assets measured using the cost model:

(a) a description of each class of its biological assets;
(b) the depreciation method adopted;
(c) the useful lives of the assets or the depreciation rates used; and
(d) a reconciliation of the changes in the carrying value of each class of biological asset measured at cost. This includes purchases, sales, harvest, business combinations, impairments and any other changes.

A reconciliation is not required for prior periods.

Example 13.1: Fair Value in an Active Market

Clonmel Ltd owns dairy cattle. The market value is calculated by reference to the quantity in litres of milk able to be produced and the lactation rate of the cows. The cattle have an active market price as they are sold regularly at auction, with average transportation costs of €500 per cattle truck. The normal capacity of the truck is 200 cattle. Based on the latest auction prices close to the year end, a mature cow's market value is 5,000 litres × lactation rate of 0.5 × price of milk € 0.35 = €875 and a heifer's market value is 2,000 litres × lactation rate of 0.5 × price of milk €0.35 = €350.

At the end of the year Clonmel Ltd had 1,000 mature cows and 400 heifers. The cost per cow of transport costs is €500/200 cows = €2.50. Thus the market value for each cow is €850 – €2.50 = €847.50 and a heifer is €350 – €2.50 = €347.50. The fair value at the end of the reporting period is therefore as follows:

	€
1,000 cows × €847.50 =	847,500
400 heifers × €347.50 =	139,000
	986,500

EXAMPLE 13.2: FAIR VALUE IN AN INACTIVE MARKET

Ardara Ltd owns and manages an orchard that produces apples. In 2017 it spent €450,000 in establishing the orchard as follows:

	€	
Cost of the land	350,000	
Cost of the seedlings	30,000	
Plant and equipment	50,000	(useful life 10 years)
Fertilizers, feed, etc.	10,000	
Salaries and wages	10,000	
	450,000	

During 2018 and 2019 it incurred further costs of €20,000 on salaries and €5,000 on feed. At the end of 2019 the trees were three years old and the company expected its first harvest in 2021. The life of the orchard is expected to be 30 years from the date of the first harvest. There is no active market for immature apple trees.

Ardara Ltd should determine fair value (unless there is undue effort or expense involved) from either:

(a) recent transaction prices;
(b) market prices of similar assets; or
(c) sector benchmarks.

As any of these three are unlikely to exist, Ardara Ltd must consider whether or not discounting future cash flows represents a reliable fair value. The process could be as follows:

Future cash inflows from the orchard:

	€
2021	50,000
2022	90,000
2023	150,000
2024	200,000
2025 onwards	200,000

Operating costs for 2020 will be €25,000, but thereafter €40,000 per annum and an appropriate discount rate to use is 6% up until and including 2023 and 15% thereafter due to increased risk. Selling costs are estimated at 1% of sales (from 2021 onwards).

The present value of the expected net cash flows at the end of 2019 are as follows:

	Cash inflows	Cash outflows	Net cash flows	Present value (6% and 15%)
	€	€	€	€
2020	–	(25,000)	(25,000)	(23,585)
2021	50,000	(40,000 + 500)	9,500	8,482
2022	90,000	(40,000 + 900)	49,100	41,260
2023	150,000	(40,000 + 1,500)	108,500	86,111
2024	200,000	(40,000 + 2,000)	158,000	117,910
2025	200,000	(40,000 + 2,000)	158,000	111,268
2026–2039	200,000	(40,000 + 2,000)	158,000	443,443
				784,889

A biological asset of an orchard would be recorded at €784,889 initially as follows:

Dr	Biological asset – orchard	€784,889	
	Cr Profit or loss		€784,889

The land of €350,000 and plant of €50,000 would be capitalised in the normal way, as per **Chapter 3**, and the other costs to establish the orchard written off as expenses (although a case could possibly be made for capitalising the seedlings as well).

Example 13.3: Illustration of Disclosure Requirements

Rathkeale Ltd owns dairy cattle and has a reporting period ending 30 June each year. At 1 July 2018 it had 900 cows and 200 heifers with a fair value of €800 per cow and €320 per heifer.

During the year ended 30 June 2019 the following events occurred:

1. 200 new cows were bought for €810 each;
2. 50 heifers matured into cows;
3. 5 heifers died; and
4. 100 cows were sold for €830 each.

Salaries and other operating costs were €60,000.

The farmland was acquired for €1.5 million and the land is measured at cost, but by 30 June 2019 its market value had increased to €5.6 million.

Plant was acquired for €1 million and is depreciated over an expected useful life of 10 years. It was two years old at the start of 2018/19.

At the 30 June 2019 the fair value is now reliably determined at €850 per cow and €350 per heifer. Assume that is also the fair value of any transfers to cows and deaths. Milk of €500,000 was produced during the year.

Solution

Reconciliation of movements in livestock:

	Cows	Fair value (per unit)	Fair value (total)	Heifers	Fair value (per unit)	Fair value (total)
	Units	**€**	**€**	**Units**	**€**	**€**
Balance as at 1 July 2018	900	800	720,000	200	320	64,000
Purchases	200	810	162,000	–		
Sales	(100)	830	(83,000)	–		
Transfer to cows	50	850	17,500	(50)	850	(17,500)
Deaths	–		–	(5)	850	(1,750)
Increase in fair value (bal. fig.)	–		76,000	–		6,000
Balance as at 30 June 2019	1,050		892,500	145		50,750

Profit and Loss Account (Extract)
for the year ended 30 June 2019

	€
Fair value of milk produced	500,000
Net gains arising from changes in fair value of dairy livestock (€76,000 + €6,000 – €1,750)	80,250
Depreciation of plant (€1m ÷ 10 years)	(100,000)
Other operating expenses	(60,000)
Operating profit	420,250

Balance Sheet (Extract)
as at 30 June 2019

	2019	2018
	€	€
Non-current assets		
Dairy livestock – immature	50,750	64,000
Dairy livestock – mature	892,500	720,000
Biological assets	943,250	784,000
Property, plant and equipment (€1.5m + €0.7m)	2,200,000	2,300,000

An actual example of an Irish company which reports under IFRS for biological assets is Fyffes Ltd. It provides a reconciliation of its fair values for the year as well as an accounting policy note, as follows.

Fyffes Ltd

Annual Report 2017

SIGNIFICANT ACCOUNTING POLICIES (EXTRACT)

Biological assets

Certain of the Group's subsidiaries involved in the production of fresh produce recognise biological assets, which includes agricultural produce due for harvest on plantations. Biological assets are stated at fair value less estimated point of sale costs, with any resultant gain or loss recognised in the income statement. Point of sale costs include all costs that would be necessary to sell the assets.

[...]

NOTES TO THE GROUP FINANCIAL STATEMENTS (EXTRACT)

[...]

14. Biological assets

	2017	2016
	€'000	€'000
Balance at start of year	**27,746**	21,314
Harvested fruit transferred to inventories	**(131,854)**	(135,273)
Additions to unharvested fruit	**131,584**	138,369
Fair value adjustment	**380**	(1,362)
Arising on acquisition of business	**--**	3,907
Exchange movements	**(3,078)**	791
Balance at end of year -- current	**24,778**	27,746

Biological assets represent the fair value of unharvested fruit in a number of the Group's subsidiaries involved in the production of tropical produce in Costa Rica, Panama, Honduras and Guatemala and mushrooms in Canada. At 31 December 2017, unharvested fruit comprised mainly pineapple plants farmed on approximately 3,300 hectares (owned and leased), winter season melons farmed on approximately 8,600 hectares (owned and leased), banana plants farmed on approximately 800 hectares (owned) and mushrooms grown in 166 growing rooms over approximately 600 acres (owned and leased). All have been categorised as Level 3 fair values based on the inputs to the valuation techniques used. The Group's biological assets are exposed to the risk of damage from climatic events, diseases and other natural forces. The fair value estimate of the biological assets reflects a prudent estimate of the fair value of unharvested crops in the context of the stage of the growing season.

The estimated fair value may increase or decrease depending on changes in the significant unobservable inputs below:

Description	Valuation Technique	Significant unobservable inputs and relationship to fair value measurement
Unharvested produce	Discounted cash flows	Estimated future market prices of produce Estimated harvest and transportation costs

13.2 EXTRACTIVE INDUSTRIES (SECTION 34)

An entity that is engaged in exploration for, evaluation or extraction of mineral resources should apply IFRS 6 *Exploration for and Evaluation of Mineral Resources* (as adopted in the EU).

Despite the above, when applying paragraph 21 of IFRS 6, a cash-generating unit (CGU) or group of CGUs must be no larger than an operating segment and the reference to IFRS 8 *Operating Segments* is therefore ignored.

On first-time adoption of FRS 102, if it is not practical to apply a particular requirement of paragraph 18 of IFRS 6 to previous comparative amounts, that fact should be disclosed.

13.3 SERVICE CONCESSION ARRANGEMENTS (SECTION 34)

A service concession arrangement is where a public sector body (the grantor) contracts with a private operator to develop (or upgrade), operate and maintain the grantor's infrastructure assets, such as roads, bridges, tunnels, airports, energy distribution networks, prisons or hospitals.

A service concession arrangement exists when the following conditions apply:

(a) the grantor controls or regulates what services the operator must provide using the infrastructure assets, to whom, and at what price; and
(b) the grantor controls any significant residual interest in the assets at the end of the arrangement.

Where the infrastructure assets have no significant residual value at the end of the term of the arrangement (i.e. the arrangement is for its entire useful life), then the arrangement must be accounted for as a service concession if the conditions in (a) are met.

For condition (b), the grantor's control over any significant residual interest should both restrict the operator's practical ability to sell or pledge the infrastructure assets and give the grantor a continuing right of use throughout the concession period.

A service concession arrangement may contain a group of contracts and sub-arrangements as elements of the service concession arrangement as a whole. These are treated as a whole when the group of contracts and sub-arrangements are linked in such a way that the commercial effect cannot be understood without reference to them as a whole. Accordingly, the contractual terms of certain contracts or arrangements may meet both the scope requirements of service concessions and Section 20 *Leases*. Where this is the case, the requirements of Section 34 shall prevail.

Where the arrangement fails the definition of a service concession, then it must be accounted for under Section 17 *Property, Plant and Equipment*, Section 18 *Intangible Assets other than Goodwill*, Section 20 *Leases* or Section 23 *Revenue*, based on the nature of the arrangement.

Accounting by Grantors: Finance Lease Liability Model

The infrastructure assets are recognised as assets of the grantor together with a liability for its obligations under the service concession arrangement.

The grantor initially recognises the infrastructure assets and associated liability under Section 20. If, however, the grantor has not recognised a liability to make payments to the operator, it cannot recognise the infrastructure assets.

The liability is recognised as a finance lease liability and subsequently accounted for in accordance with Section 20.

The infrastructure assets should be recognised as property, plant and equipment or as intangible assets, as appropriate, and subsequently accounted for in accordance with Section 17 or Section 18.

Accounting by Operators

Treatment of the Operator's Rights over the Infrastructure

Infrastructure assets must not be recognised as property, plant and equipment by the operator because the contractual service arrangement does not convey the right to control the use of the public service assets to the operator. The operator, instead, has access to operate the infrastructure to provide the public service on behalf of the grantor in accordance with the terms specified in the arrangement.

The operator should never report a physical asset on its balance sheet (e.g. bridge, hospital, road, school, etc.), but instead should record either a financial asset or an intangible asset on its balance sheet.

Thus there are two principal categories of service concession arrangements:

(a) **Financial asset** – an unconditional right to receive a cash or another financial asset from the grantor (usually a government department) in return for constructing or upgrading a public sector asset, and then operating and maintaining the asset for a specified period of time. This includes any guarantees given by the government to pay for any shortfall between the amounts received from users of the public service and specified or determinable amounts.

(b) **Intangible asset** – a right to charge for the use of a public sector asset that it constructs or upgrades and then operates and maintains for a specified period of time. A right to charge users is not an unconditional right to receive cash because the amounts are contingent on the extent to which the public uses the service.

Sometimes a single contract may contain both types: to the extent that the grantor has given an unconditional guarantee of payment for the construction of the public sector asset, the operator has a financial asset; to the extent that the operator has to rely on the public using the service in order to obtain payment, the operator has an intangible asset. The classic example in Ireland of this approach has been the creation of toll roads, where the government has guaranteed to subsidise the creation of the toll road as the income from the toll itself would not be sufficient to fully compensate the operator.

Accounting: Financial Asset Model

The operator must recognise a financial asset to the extent that it has an unconditional contractual right to receive cash or another financial asset from the grantor for the construction services. The operator should measure the financial asset at fair value. Thereafter, it must follow Section 11 and Section 12 (see **Chapter 12**) in accounting for the financial asset. Specifying payments as being dependent on infrastructure meeting specified quality or efficiency requirements does not, in itself, prevent financial assets being classed as basic.

Accounting: Intangible Asset Model

The operator must recognise an intangible asset to the extent that it receives a right (e.g. a licence) to charge users for the use of a public service. The operator must initially measure the intangible asset at fair value. Thereafter, it should follow Section 18 (see **Chapter 4**) in accounting for the intangible asset.

Operating Revenue

The operator of a service concession arrangement should recognise, measure and disclose revenue in accordance with Section 23 for the services it performs (see **Chapter 7**).

Borrowing Costs

Borrowing costs attributable to the arrangement are recognised as an expense, in accordance with Section 25 *Costs*, in the period in which they are incurred unless the operator has an intangible asset. In this case borrowing costs may be capitalised in accordance with Section 25 where a policy of capitalisation has been adopted.

Disclosures

An operator and grantor should disclose information to enable users of the financial statements to evaluate the nature and extent of risks arising from service concession arrangements. This information should include, but is not limited to, a description of the arrangements, including any rights, obligations or options arising and any terms that may affect the amount, timing and certainty of cash flows.

An operator should disclose the amount of revenue, profits or losses and other income recognised in the period on exchanging construction services for a financial asset or an intangible asset. The following is an example of the disclosure required for service concession arrangements.

Example 13.4: Service Concession Arrangements

Concession Terms The terms of a concession require an operator to construct a road, completing the construction within two years, and to maintain and operate the road to a specified standard for 48 years thereafter (i.e. years 3–50). The terms of the concession also require the operator to bear the handover costs at the end of the concession period. At the end of year 50, the concession will come to its end. The operator estimates that the costs it will incur in fulfilling its obligations will be:

Table 1: Costs of Service Concession Arrangement

	Year	€m
Construction (cost)	1	800.0
	2	800.0
Concession right	1	2.5
Operation and maintenance (per year)	3–50	Initially 5; growth in line with inflation
Handover costs	50	80 (5% of the initial investment)

Contract Revenues The operator has the right to operate and collect tolls from drivers/the grantor during the concession period. The operator forecasts that vehicle numbers (average daily traffic – ADT) will increase at a rate of approximately 26% per year in the first five years of the concession and at a rate of 3% per year thereafter.

The 'ramp-up' effect in the early years of the concession is included because industry experts agree that in the majority of toll road concessions, the growth in the ADT is higher in the early years, as users take several years to get used to paying for the use of the infrastructure. In this example, for simplicity, the ramp-up effect is concentrated in the first five years. In practice, it might be less steep and continue for longer than in the example, but the overall impact would be similar.

Tariffs are forecast in each model to increase by the forecast rate of inflation (2.5%).

Finance Structuring 20% of the initial investment will be funded by capital calls from shareholders. The remaining 80% will be funded by a loan granted by credit institutions. The fixed interest rate on the loan is 5%. The loan will be repaid over 40 years (years 3–42).

Solution - Intangible Asset Model

This model would be applicable if the terms of the concession allowed the operator to collect tolls from drivers using the road and where no subsidy is being provided by the grantor.

Intangible Asset The operator provides construction services to the grantor in exchange for an intangible asset, i.e. a right to collect tolls from road users in years 3–50. In accordance with Section 18, the operator recognises the intangible asset at cost, i.e. the fair value of the construction services.

FRS 102 does not specify when the intangible asset should be recognised. It could be recognised:

(a) from the outset (with a corresponding amount recognised in respect of the obligation to provide construction services in exchange);
(b) as construction services are provided, by reference to the stage of completion; or
(c) once construction has been completed.

For the purpose of this illustration, it is assumed that the operator receives the intangible asset as construction services are provided, by reference to the stage of completion. The operator estimates that the fair value of its construction services is equal to the forecast construction costs + 5%. The cost of the intangible asset recognised at that date comprises:

TABLE 2: INITIAL MEASUREMENT OF THE INTANGIBLE ASSET

	€m
Fair value of construction in year 1 (€800m + 5%)	840.00
Fair value of construction in year 2 (€800m + 5%)	840.00
Concession right payment	2.50
	1,682.50

In accordance with Section 18, the intangible asset is amortised over the period in which it is expected to be available for use by the operator, i.e. years 3–50.

Construction Costs and Revenue The exchange of construction services for an intangible asset is regarded as a transaction that generates revenue. The operator recognises the revenue and costs in accordance with Section 23 *Revenue*, i.e. by reference to the stage of completion of the construction. It measures contract revenue at the fair value of the consideration receivable. Thus, in each of years 1 and 2 it recognises in its income statement construction costs of €800m, construction revenue of €840m (cost + 5%) and, hence, a construction profit of €40m.

Toll Revenue The road users pay for the concession services at the same time as they receive them, i.e. when they use the road. The operator therefore recognises toll revenue when it collects the tolls.

Handover Costs The operator's obligation to pay handover costs is excluded from the consideration given for the intangible asset. It is recognised and measured in accordance with Section 21 *Provisions and Contingencies*, i.e. at the best estimate of the expenditure required to settle the present obligation at the balance sheet date. The operator expects to incur the handover costs at a cost of €80m at the end of year 50. The terms of the operator's contractual obligation in this example are such that the cost of fulfilling the obligation at any date is proportional to the number of vehicles that have used the road by that date. The operator discounts the provision to its present value in accordance with Section 21.

TABLE 3: INCOME STATEMENT (IN CURRENCY UNITS)
(from the concession operator's point of view)

INCOME STATEMENT – CUMULATIVE											
	Years 1–5	**Years 6–10**	**Years 11–15**	**Years 16–20**	**Years 21–25**	**Years 26–30**	**Years 31–35**	**Years 36–40**	**Years 41–45**	**Years 46–50**	**TOTAL**
Operating revenues	1,749.97	259.49	352.59	462.46	606.57	795.58	1,043.49	1,368.66	1,795.15	2,354.54	**10,788.48**
Operating expenses	(1,616.61)	(30.57)	(34.58)	(39.13)	(44.27)	(50.09)	(56.67)	(64.12)	(72.54)	(82.07)	**(2,090.64)**
EBITDA	**133.36**	**228.93**	**318.00**	**423.33**	**562.30**	**745.49**	**986.82**	**1,304.54**	**1,722.61**	**2,272.46**	8,697.84
Amortisation	110.16	183.61	183.61	183.61	183.61	183.61	183.61	183.61	183.61	183.61	**1,762.63**
EBIT	**23.20**	**45.32**	**134.40**	**239.72**	**378.69**	**561.89**	**803.22**	**1,120.93**	**1,539.00**	**2,088.86**	6,935.22

Hand-over accrual	(0.14)	(0.66)	(1.17)	(1.95)	(3.16)	(5.03)	(7.90)	(12.26)	(18.87)	(28.86)	**(80.00)**
Financial expenses (accrual)	(189.19)	(300.16)	(278.85)	(246.80)	(203.86)	(155.78)	(107.71)	(57.07)	(3.62)	0.01	**(1,543.01)**
EBT	**(166.14)**	**(255.49)**	**(145.63)**	**(9.03)**	**171.67**	**401.07**	**687.62**	**1,051.61**	**1,516.51**	**2,060.01**	**5,312.21**
TAX	58.15	89.42	50.97	3.16	(60.09)	(140.38)	(240.67)	(368.06)	(530.78)	(721.00)	**(1,859.27)**
NET INCOME	**(107.99)**	**(166.07)**	**(94.66)**	**(5.87)**	**111.59**	**260.70**	**446.95**	**683.55**	**985.73**	**1,339.01**	**3,452.93**

Solution - Financial Asset Model

This model would be applicable if the terms of the concession required the grantor to pay the operator. In this example, the operator is assumed to be entitled to collect from the grantor an amount per year in years 3–50 for making the road available to the public.

Contract Revenue The operator recognises contract revenue and costs in accordance with Section 23 *Revenue*. The costs of each activity, namely construction, operation, maintenance and resurfacing, are recognised as expenses by reference to the stage of completion of the related activity. Contract revenue, i.e. the fair value of the amount due from the grantor for the activity undertaken, is recognised at the same time.

The total amounts receivable from the grantor reflect the fair values of each of the activities, which are as follows:

TABLE 4: FAIR VALUES OF SERVICES PROVIDED BY THE OPERATOR

	Fair Value
Construction (capital expenditure)	Forecast cost + 5%
Operation and maintenance	Forecast cost + 20%
Handover costs	Forecast cost + 20%
Lending rate to grantor	5.34% per year

In year 1, construction costs are €800m while construction revenue is €840m (cost + 5%), giving a profit of €40m that is recognised in the income statement.

Financial Asset The operator determines that the amount due from the grantor meets the definition of a receivable in Section 11 *Basic Financial Instruments* and Section 12 *Other Financial Instrument Issues*. The receivable is measured initially at fair value and it is subsequently measured at amortised cost.

If the cash flows and fair values remain the same as those forecast, the effective interest rate is 5.34% and the receivable recognised at the end of years 1–10 will be as follows:

TABLE 5: MEASUREMENT OF RECEIVABLE

Fin. Asset	1	2	3	4	5	6	7	8	9	10
Initial	0.00	842.50	1,727.48	1,808.20	1,888.83	1,967.07	2,040.30	2,105.61	2,171.76	2,238.63
CAPEX	840.00	840.00	0.00	0.00	0.00	0.00	0.00	0.00	0.00	0.00
O&M	0.00	0.00	6.48	6.64	6.81	6.98	7.15	7.33	7.51	7.70
HAND-OVER	0.00	0.00								
FIN. INCOME (effective interest rate on receivable)	0.00	44.98	92.23	96.54	100.85	105.02	108.93	112.42	115.95	119.52
COLLEC-TIONS FROM THE GRANTOR	2.50	0.00	(18.00)	(22.55)	(29.42)	(38.77)	(50.78)	(53.61)	(56.59)	(59.75)
Final	842.50	1,727.48	1,808.20	1,888.83	1,967.07	2,040.30	2,105.61	2,171.76	2,238.63	2,306.11

TABLE 6: INCOME STATEMENT (IN CURRENCY UNITS)
(from the point of view of the concession operator)

INCOME STATEMENT – CUMULATIVE

	Years 1–5	Years 6–10	Years 11–15	Years 16–20	Years 21–25	Years 26–30	Years 31–35	Years 36–40	Years 41–45	Years 46–50	TOTAL
Operating revenues	1,699.93	36.68	41.50	46.95	53.12	60.10	68.00	76.94	87.05	194.49	**2,364.77**
Operating expenses	(1,616.61)	(30.57)	(34.58)	(39.13)	(44.27)	(50.09)	(56.67)	(64.12)	(72.54)	(82.07)	**(2,090.64)**
EBITDA	**83.32**	**6.11**	**6.92**	**7.83**	**8.85**	**10.02**	**11.33**	**12.82**	**14.51**	**112.41**	**274.13**
Amortisa-tion	0.00	0.00	0.00	0.00	0.00	0.00	0.00	0.00	0.00	0.00	**0.00**
EBIT	**83.32**	**6.11**	**6.92**	**7.83**	**8.85**	**10.02**	**11.33**	**12.82**	**14.51**	**112.41**	**274.13**
Handover costs	0.00	0.00	0.00	0.00	0.00	0.00	0.00	0.00	0.00	(80.00)	**(80.00)**
Financial expenses (accrual)	(269.32)	(300.16)	(278.85)	(246.80)	(203.86)	(155.78)	(107.71)	(57.07)	(3.62)	0.01	**(1,623.14)**
Financial income (on receivable)	334.60	561.86	652.02	742.20	824.59	885.78	904.92	850.35	675.00	309.88	**6,741.21**
EBT	**148.61**	**267.82**	**380.09**	**503.22**	**629.59**	**740.02**	**808.55**	**806.11**	**685.89**	**342.31**	**5,312.21**
TAX	**(52.01)**	**(93.74)**	**(133.03)**	**(176.13)**	**(220.35)**	**(259.01)**	**(282.99)**	**(282.14)**	**(240.06)**	**(119.81)**	**(1,859.27)**
NET INCOME	**96.60**	**174.08**	**247.06**	**327.10**	**409.23**	**481.01**	**525.56**	**523.97**	**445.83**	**222.50**	**3,452.93**

13.4 FINANCIAL INSTITUTIONS: DISCLOSURES (SECTION 34)

In order to provide sufficient information to make their financial statements more relevant to the user, FRS 102 requires, in addition to the disclosure in Section 11 *Basic Financial Instruments* and Section 12 *Other Financial Instrument Issues*, a number of additional disclosures by financial institutions.

The disclosures are required to be provided in:

(a) the individual financial statements of a financial institution; and
(b) the consolidated financial statements of a group containing a financial institution when the financial instruments held by the financial institution are material to the group. These disclosures apply regardless of whether the principal activity of the group is being a financial institution or not. For a group, the disclosures are only required by entities within the group that are financial institutions.

The definition of a financial institution is essentially one of the following:

(a) a bank;
(b) a building society;
(c) a business carrying out insurance contract work, including both life and general;
(d) an investment trust, venture capital trust, mutual fund, open-ended investment company, stockbroker, etc.;
(e) a credit union;
(f) an incorporated friendly society;
(g) an investment trust, unit trust, etc.; or
(h) any other entity whose principal activity is similar to those listed in (a)–(g).

A financial institution should disclose the following under Section 34:

(a) information to help users evaluate the significance of financial instruments with regard to financial position and performance, which therefore requires a disaggregation by class of instrument, taking into account the characteristics of those instruments;
(b) if a separate allowance account is used for impairments, a reconciliation of changes in that account for each class of financial asset (unless it has made the accounting policy choice to apply the recognition and measurement provisions of IFRS 9 *Financial Instruments*);
(c) when it has made the accounting policy choice to apply the recognition and measurement provisions of IFRS 9, it should disclose information enabling users of its financial statements to understand the effect of credit risk on the amount, timing and uncertainty of cash flows, including:
    (i) an explanation of credit risk management practices and how they relate to the recognition and measurement of expected credit losses;

(ii) a reconciliation of the loss allowance from opening to closing balance detailing the changes during the period for:
  I. the loss allowance measured as 12 month expected credit losses;
  II. the loss allowance measured as lifetime expected credit losses;
  III. financial assets purchased or originated credit-impaired;

(iii) the gross carrying amount of financial assets and exposure to credit risk on loan commitments and financial guarantee contracts by credit risk rating grade.

(d) an analysis of financial instruments held at fair value using the three-tier hierarchy; and

(e) information about the nature and extent of the key risks arising from financial instruments to which the entity is exposed at the end of the reporting period, including exposures to risk and how arisen, the policies and strategies to manage the risk and any changes from the previous period.

For individual risks the following must also be provided:

Credit Risk By class:

(a) maximum exposure to risk unless carrying amount represents that exposure;
(b) description of any collateral held as security;
(c) amount of any credit derivatives mitigating that exposure to credit risk; and
(d) information about the credit quality of financial assets neither past due nor impaired.

Maturity Analysis By class of financial assets:

(a) for assets that are past due but not impaired at the end of the reporting period; and
(b) individually impaired at the end of the reporting period, including factors considered in making that judgement.

If take-up collateral is held as security:

(a) the nature and carrying amount of assets obtained; and
(b) when not easily convertible into cash, the entity's policies for their disposal or future use.

Liquidity Risk A maturity analysis for financial liabilities, undiscounted, separated between derivative and non-derivative financial liabilities.

Market Risk A sensitivity analysis for each type of market risk exposed to (e.g. interest rate, currency, etc.), showing impact on profit and equity. Details of assumptions and methods should also be provided. A value-at-risk sensitivity analysis can be used instead if the entity uses that approach to manage financial risks.

Capital Information that enables users to evaluate the entity's objectives, policies and processes for managing capital should be provided. The following, therefore, must be disclosed:

(a) qualitative information about its objectives, policies and processes for managing capital, including:
    (i) a description of what it manages as capital;
    (ii) the nature of any externally imposed capital requirements and how they are incorporated into the management of capital; and
    (iii) how it is meeting its objectives for managing capital.
(b) summary quantitative data about what it manages as capital. Some entities regard some financial liabilities (e.g. some forms of subordinated debt) as part of capital. Other entities regard capital as excluding some components of equity (e.g. components arising from cash flow hedges);
(c) any changes in (a) and (b) from the previous period;
(d) whether during the period it complied with any externally imposed capital requirements to which it is subject;
(e) if externally imposed capital requirements are not complied with, the consequences of such non-compliance.

The disclosures should be based on the information provided internally to key management personnel.

Capital may be managed in a number of ways and be subject to a number of different capital requirements, e.g. a conglomerate may include entities that undertake insurance activities and banking activities and those entities may operate in several jurisdictions.

When an aggregate disclosure of capital requirements and how capital is managed would not provide useful information or would distort a user's understanding of the capital resources, separate information should be disclosed for each capital requirement to which an entity is subject.

Reporting Cash Flows on a Net Basis

Financial institutions may report cash flows arising from each of the following activities on a net basis:

(a) cash receipts and payments for the acceptance and repayment of deposits with a fixed maturity date;
(b) the placement of deposits with and withdrawal of deposits from other financial institutions; and
(c) cash advances and loans made to customers and the repayment of those advances and loans.

13.5 RETIREMENT BENEFIT PLANS: FINANCIAL STATEMENTS (SECTION 34)

Retirement benefit plans must comply with Section 34 in addition to complying with the rest of FRS 102 when preparing their financial statements.

There are two main types of scheme – defined contribution (DC) and defined benefit (DB) – as well as hybrids. DC and DB must be distinguished, where material.

Defined Contribution and Defined Benefit Plans

These plans do not have to prepare the same complete set of financial statements as required for non-listed companies. Instead the financial statements should include:

(a) a statement of changes in net assets available for benefits (a fund account);
(b) a statement of net assets available for benefits; and
(c) notes, comprising its significant accounting policies and other explanatory information.

Net assets should be measured at fair value, with any changes being reported in the statements of changes in net assets available for benefits.

Statement of Changes in Net Assets Available for Benefits (Fund Account)

This should include:

- employer and employee contributions;
- investment income – dividends and interest;
- other income;
- benefits paid or payable – split death, retirement, disability and lump sums;
- administration expenses;
- other expenses;
- taxes on income;
- profits and losses on disposal of investments and changes in their value;
- transfers in; and
- payments to and on account of leavers.

Statement of Net Assets Available for Benefits

This must include:

(a) assets at the end of the period, suitably classified; and
(b) liabilities other than the actuarial present value of promised retirement benefits.

The basis of valuation of assets must also be presented in the notes.

Disclosures

Assets other than Financial Instruments Held at Fair Value

The entity must apply the disclosure requirements in the relevant sections of FRS 102 to assets other than financial instruments held at fair value, e.g. for investment property, the entity must provide the disclosures detailed in Section 16 *Investment Properties* (see **Chapter 3**).

Significance of Financial Instruments for Financial Position and Performance

Entities must provide information to evaluate the significance of financial instruments in assessing its financial position and performance. That includes a disaggregation of financial instruments by class.

Fair Value

For each class of financial instrument held, the level of hierarchy into which it is categorised, i.e. level 1, 2 or 3 – see Section 11 *Basic Financial Instruments* (**Chapter 12**).

Nature and Extent of Risks Arising from Financial Instruments

Users must be able to evaluate a plan's exposure to both credit and market risk arising from financial instruments at the end of the period.

For each type of risk a retirement benefit plan must disclose:

(a) the exposures to risk and how they have arisen;
(b) its objectives, policies and processes for managing risk and methods to measure risk; and
(c) any changes from the previous period.

Credit Risk

A plan must disclose by class of financial instrument:

(a) its maximum exposure to credit risk at the end of the reporting period;
(b) a description of collateral held as security and how it mitigates risk;
(c) the amount by which any related credit derivatives mitigate that maxium exposure to risk; and
(d) information about the credit quality of financial assets that are neither impaired nor overdue.

If a plan takes possession of collateral assets, it must disclose the nature and carrying amount of assets obtained and its policies for disposing of them or retaining them if they are not readily convertible into cash.

Defined Benefit Plans – Actuarial Liabilities

No liability is required to be recognised for future promised benefits.

A DB plan, however, must disclose, in a separate report, but with the financial statements, the following information regarding the actuarial present value of promised retirement benefits:

- a statement of the actuarial present value of promised retirement benefits based on the most recent valuation of the scheme;
- the date of the latest valuation of the scheme; and
- the significant actuarial assumptions made and the method to calculate the present value of its promised retirement benefits.

13.6 HERITAGE ASSETS (SECTION 34)

Heritage assets are those with historic, artistic, scientific, technological, geophysical or environmental qualities that are held and maintained principally for their contribution to knowledge and culture. They include a wide variety of assets, such as the Book of Kells, the Giant's Causeway, National Trust properties, etc.

However, works of art and similar objects are sometimes held by commercial entities but are not heritage assets because they are not maintained principally for their contribution to knowledge and culture. These assets must therefore be accounted for in accordance with Section 17 *Property, Plant and Equipment*. Heritage assets in use by the entity, e.g. historic buildings, such as Trinity College, must also be accounted for under Section 17 as they are still operational assets.

Recognition and Measurement

Heritage assets should be reported in accordance with Section 17 or Section 18 (i.e. using the cost model or revaluation model), subject to the requirements set out below.

Heritage assets must be recognised in the balance sheet separately from other assets.

However, if the cost or value of a heritage asset is not available, and cannot be obtained at a cost which is commensurate with the benefits to users, then the assets should not be capitalised, but instead must be disclosed as below.

Each year an entity must apply Section 27 *Impairment of Assets* to determine whether or not a heritage asset is impaired and, if so, how to recognise and measure the impairment loss.

Disclosure

The following should be disclosed for all heritage assets held:

(a) an indication of the nature and scale of heritage assets held by the entity;
(b) the policy for the acquisition, preservation, management and disposal of heritage assets;
(c) accounting policies adopted for heritage assets;
(d) for heritage assets that have not been recognised in the balance sheet, the notes to the financial statements must:
  (i) explain the reasons why,
  (ii) describe the significance and nature of those assets, and
  (iii) disclose information that is helpful in assessing the value of those heritage assets;

(e) where heritage assets are recognised in the balance sheet, the following disclosure is required:
   (i) the carrying amount at the start of the reporting period and the reporting date – split between cost and valuation, and
   (ii) where assets are recognised at valuation, sufficient information to assist in understanding the valuation (date of valuation, method used, if carried out by external valuer, their qualification);

(f) a summary of transactions relating to heritage assets for the reporting period and each of the previous four reporting periods, disclosing:
   (i) the cost of acquisitions of heritage assets,
   (ii) the value of heritage assets acquired by donations,
   (iii) the carrying amount of heritage assets disposed and proceeds, and
   (iv) any impairment recognised in the period;

(g) in exceptional circumstances, where it is not practicable to obtain a valuation of heritage assets acquired by donation, the reason shall be stated.

Disclosures can be aggregated for groups or classes of heritage assets, provided this does not obscure significant information.

The disclosures required by (f) above need not be given for any accounting period earlier than the period immediately before the period in which FRS 102 is first applied where it is not practicable to do so, and a statement to the effect that it is not practicable is made.

13.7 FUNDING COMMITMENTS (SECTION 34)

A liability and corresponding expense is recognised when an entity has made a final commitment to provide resources to another party, but only if:

(a) the definition and recognition criteria for a liability are met;
(b) there is no realistic chance of withdrawing from the obligation; and
(c) the entitlement of the other party to the resources does not depend on satisfying any performance conditions.

Any recognised liability should be measured at the present value of resources committed.

The following should be disclosed:

(a) the commitment made;
(b) the timeframe of the commitment;
(c) any performance-related conditions; and
(d) details of how the commitment will be funded.

These may be aggregated provided that aggregation does not obscure any significant information.

13.8 SMALL ENTITIES

There are no explicit minimum disclosure requirements for small entities under Section 1A of FRS 102 for either the UK or the Republic of Ireland. However, small entities may need to provide disclosures as required by FRS 102, Section 34 if required to give a true and fair view.

13.9 MICRO-ENTITIES

FRS 105 only provides guidance on agriculture as it is unlikely that a micro-entity would be involved in any of the other specialised activities.

Unlike under FRS 102, Section 34, micro-entities do not have an option to recognise biological assets or agricultural produce at fair value – they must be recognised at cost.

Disclosure Checklist: Specialised Activities – FRS 102

(References are to the relevant Section of FRS 102)

	Para.
Agriculture – Section 34	
Disclosures: fair value model	
An entity shall disclose the following for each class of biological asset measured using the fair value model: (a) a description of each class of biological asset; (b) the methods and significant assumptions applied in determining the fair value of each class of biological asset; (c) a reconciliation of changes in the carrying amount of each class of biological asset between the beginning and the end of the current period. The reconciliation shall include: (i) the gain or loss arising from changes in fair value less costs to sell, (ii) increases resulting from purchases, (iii) decreases attributable to sales, (iv) decreases resulting from harvest, (v) increases resulting from business combinations, and (vi) other changes. This reconciliation need not be presented for prior periods.	34.7
If an entity measures any individual biological assets at cost in accordance with paragraph 34.6A, it shall explain why fair value cannot be reliably measured. If the fair value of such a biological asset becomes reliably measurable during the current period, an entity shall explain why fair value has become reliably measurable and the effect of the change.	34.7A
An entity shall disclose the methods and significant assumptions applied in determining the fair value at the point of harvest of each class of agricultural produce.	34.7B
Disclosures: cost model	
An entity shall disclose the following for each class of biological asset measured using the cost model: (a) a description of each class of biological asset; (b) the depreciation method used; (c) the useful lives or the depreciation rates used; and (d) a reconciliation of changes in the carrying amount of each class of biological asset between the beginning and the end of the current period. The reconciliation shall include: (i) increases resulting from purchases, (ii) decreases attributable to sales, (iii) decreases resulting from harvest, (iv) increases resulting from business combinations, (v) impairment losses recognised or reversed in profit or loss in accordance with Section 27 *Impairment of Assets*, and (vi) other changes. This reconciliation need not be presented for prior periods.	34.10
An entity shall disclose, for any agricultural produce measured at fair value less costs to sell, the methods and significant assumptions applied in determining the fair value at the point of harvest of its agricultural produce.	34.10A

	PARA.
Financial Institutions – Section 34	
Significance of financial instruments for financial position and performance	
A financial institution shall disclose information that enables users of its **financial statements** to evaluate the significance of financial instruments for its **financial position** and **performance.**	34.19
A financial institution shall disclose a disaggregation of **the statement of financial position** line item by class of financial instrument. A class is a grouping of financial instruments that is appropriate to the nature of the information disclosed and that takes into account the characteristics of those financial instruments.	34.20
Impairment	
Unless a financial institution has made the accounting policy choice in paragraphs 11.2(c) and 12.2(c) to apply the recognition and measurement provisions of IFRS 9 *Financial Instruments* (as adopted in the EU), when it uses a separate allowance account to record impairments, it shall disclose a reconciliation of changes in that account during the period for each class of **financial asset.**	34.21
When a financial institution has made the accounting policy choice in paragraphs 11.2(c) and 12.2(c) to apply the recognition and measurement provisions of IFRS 9, it shall disclose information that enables users of its financial statements to understand the effect of credit risk on the amount, timing and uncertainty of future cash flows. This shall include: (a) An explanation of the financial institution's credit risk management practices and how they relate to the recognition and measurement of expected credit losses. (b) A reconciliation from the opening balance to the closing balance of the loss allowance, in a table, showing separately the changes during the period for: (i) the loss allowance measured at an amount equal to 12-month expected credit losses; (ii) the loss allowance measured at an amount equal to lifetime expected credit losses (showing separately the amount relating to financial instruments for which credit risk has increased significantly since initial recognition); and (iii) financial assets that are purchased or originated credit-impaired. (c) By credit risk grade, the gross carrying amount of financial assets and the exposure to credit risk on loan commitments and financial guarantee contracts (showing separately information for financial instruments for which the loss allowance is measured at an amount equal to 12-month expected credit losses, for which the loss allowance is measured at an amount equal to lifetime expected credit losses, and that are purchased or originated credit-impaired financial assets).	34.21A
Fair value	
For financial instruments held at **fair value** in the statement of financial position, a financial institution shall disclose for each class of financial instrument an analysis of the level in the fair value hierarchy (as set out in paragraph 11.27) into which the fair value measurements are categorised.	34.22

	PARA.
Nature and extent of risks arising from financial instruments	
A financial institution shall disclose information that enables users of its financial statements to evaluate the nature and extent of **credit risk, liquidity risk** and **market risk** arising from financial instruments to which the financial institution is exposed at the end of the **reporting period.**	34.23
For each type of risk arising from financial instruments, a financial institution shall disclose: (a) the exposures to risk and how they arise; (b) its objectives, policies and processes for managing the risk and the methods used to measure the risk; and (c) any changes in (a) or (b) from the previous period.	34.24
Credit risk	
For financial instruments within the scope of Sections 11 or 12 to which the impairment requirements of IFRS 9 are not applied, a financial institution shall disclose by class of financial instrument: (a) the amount that best represents its maximum exposure to credit risk at the end of the reporting period. This disclosure is not required for financial instruments whose **carrying amount** best represents the maximum exposure to credit risk; (b) a description of collateral held as security and of other credit enhancements and the extent to which these mitigate credit risk; (c) the amount by which any related credit derivatives or similar instruments mitigate that maximum exposure to credit risk; (d) information about the credit quality of **financial assets** that are neither past due nor impaired.	34.25
Unless a financial institution has made the accounting policy choice in paragraphs 11.2(c) and 12.2(c) to apply the recognition and measurement provisions of IFRS 9, it shall provide, by class of financial asset, an analysis of: (a) the age of financial assets that are past due as at the end of the reporting period but not impaired; and (b) the financial assets that are individually determined to be impaired as at the end of the reporting period, including the factors the financial institution considered in determining that they are impaired.	34.26
When a financial institution obtains financial or non-financial assets during the period by taking possession of collateral, it holds as security or calling on other credit enhancements (e.g. guarantees), and such **assets** meet the **recognition** criteria in other sections, a financial institution shall disclose: (a) the nature and carrying amount of the assets obtained; and (b) when the assets are not readily convertible into **cash**, its policies for disposing of such assets or for using them in its operations.	34.27
Liquidity risk	
A financial institution shall provide a maturity analysis for **financial liabilities** that shows the remaining contractual maturities at undiscounted amounts separated between derivative and non-derivative financial liabilities.	34.28
Market risk	
A financial institution shall provide a sensitivity analysis for each type of market risk (e.g. interest rate risk, currency risk, other price risk) it is exposed to, showing the impact on **profit or loss** and **equity**. Details of the methods and assumptions used should be provided.	34.29

	PARA.
If a financial institution prepares a sensitivity analysis, such as value-at-risk, that reflects interdependencies between risk variables (e.g. interest rates and exchange rates) and uses it to manage financial risks, it may use that sensitivity analysis instead.	34.30
Capital	
A financial institution shall disclose information that enables users of its financial statements to evaluate the entity's objectives, policies and processes for managing capital. A financial institution shall disclose the following: (a) qualitative information about its objectives, policies and processes for managing capital, including: (i) a description of what it manages as capital, (ii) when an entity is subject to externally imposed capital requirements, the nature of those requirements and how those requirements are incorporated into the management of capital, and (iii) how it is meeting its objectives for managing capital; (b) summary quantitative data about what it manages as capital. Some entities regard some financial liabilities (e.g. some forms of subordinated debt) as part of capital. Other entities regard capital as excluding some components of equity (e.g. components arising from cash flow hedges); (c) any changes in (a) and (b) from the previous period; (d) whether during the period it complied with any externally imposed capital requirements to which it is subject; (e) when the entity has not complied with such externally imposed capital requirements, the consequences of such non-compliance. A financial institution bases these disclosures on the information provided internally to key **management personnel.**	34.31
A financial institution may manage capital in a number of ways and be subject to a number of different capital requirements. For example, a conglomerate may include entities that undertake insurance activities and banking activities and those entities may operate in several jurisdictions. When an aggregate disclosure of capital requirements and how capital is managed would not provide useful information or would distort a financial statement user's understanding of the financial institution's capital resources, the financial institution shall disclose separate information for each capital requirement to which the entity is subject.	34.32
Retirement Benefit Plans: Financial Statements – Section 34	
Assets other than financial instruments held at fair value	
Where a retirement benefit plan holds assets other than financial instruments at fair value, in accordance with paragraph 34.36, it shall apply the disclosure requirements of the relevant section of this FRS, e.g. in relation to investment property, it shall provide the disclosures required by paragraph 16.10.	34.39
Significance of financial instruments for financial position and performance	
A retirement benefit plan shall disclose information that enables users of its financial statements to evaluate the significance of financial instruments for its financial position and performance.	34.40
A retirement benefit plan shall disclose a disaggregation of the statement of net assets available for benefits by class of financial instrument. A class is a grouping of financial instruments that is appropriate to the nature of the information disclosed and that takes into account the characteristics of those financial instruments.	34.41

	PARA.
Fair value	
For financial instruments held at fair value in the statement of net assets available for benefits, a retirement benefit plan shall disclose, for each class of financial instrument, an analysis of the level in the fair value hierarchy (as set out in paragraph 11.27) into which the fair value measurements are categorised.	34.42
Nature and extent of risks arising from financial instruments	
A retirement benefit plan shall disclose information that enables users of its financial statements to evaluate the nature and extent of credit risk and market risk arising from financial instruments to which the retirement benefit plan is exposed at the end of the reporting period.	34.43
For each type of credit and market risk arising from financial instruments, a retirement benefit plan shall disclose: (a) the exposures to risk and how they arise; (b) its objectives, policies and processes for managing the risk and the methods used to measure the risk; and (c) any changes in (a) or (b) from the previous period. In relation to credit risk, a retirement benefit plan shall, in addition, provide the disclosures set out in paragraphs 34.45 and 34.46.	34.44
Credit risk	
A retirement benefit plan shall disclose by class of financial instrument: (a) the amount that best represents its maximum exposure to credit risk at the end of the reporting period. This disclosure is not required for financial instruments whose carrying amount best represents the maximum exposure to credit risk; (b) a description of collateral held as security and of other credit enhancements, and the extent to which these mitigate credit risk; (c) the amount by which any related credit derivatives or similar instruments mitigate that maximum exposure to credit risk; (d) information about the credit quality of financial assets that are neither past due nor impaired.	34.45
When a retirement benefit plan obtains financial or non-financial assets during the period by taking possession of collateral it holds as security or calling on other credit enhancements (e.g. guarantees), and such assets meet the recognition criteria in other sections, a retirement benefit plan shall disclose: (a) the nature and carrying amount of the assets obtained; and (b) when the assets are not readily convertible into cash, its policies for disposing of such assets or for retaining them.	34.46
Defined benefit plans: actuarial liabilities	
A defined benefit plan is not required to recognise a liability in relation to the promised retirement benefits.	34.47

	PARA.
A defined benefit plan shall disclose, in a report alongside the financial statements, information regarding the actuarial present value of promised retirement benefits, including: (a) a statement of the actuarial present value of promised retirement benefits, based on the most recent valuation of the scheme; (b) the date of the most recent valuation of the scheme; and (c) the significant actuarial assumptions made and the method used to calculate the actuarial present value of promised retirement benefits.	34.48
Funding Commitments – Section 34	
An entity that has made a commitment shall disclose the following: (a) the commitment made; (b) the time-frame of that commitment; (c) any performance-related conditions attached to that commitment; and (d) details of how that commitment will be funded.	34.62
The above disclosures may be made in aggregate, providing that such aggregation does not obscure significant information. However, separate disclosure shall be made for recognised and unrecognised commitments.	34.63
Heritage Assets – Section 34	
An entity shall disclose the following for all heritage assets it holds: (a) an indication of the nature and scale of heritage assets held by the entity; (b) the policy for the acquisition, preservation, management and disposal of heritage assets (including a description of the records maintained by the entity of its collection of heritage assets and information on the extent to which access to the assets is permitted); (c) the accounting policies adopted for heritage assets, including details of the measurement bases used; (d) for heritage assets that have not been recognised in the statement of financial position, the notes to the financial statements shall: (i) explain the reasons why, (ii) describe the significance and nature of those assets, and (iii) disclose information that is helpful in assessing the value of those heritage assets; (e) where heritage assets are recognised in the statement of financial position the following disclosure is required: (i) the carrying amount of heritage assets at the beginning of the reporting period and the reporting date, including an analysis between classes or groups of heritage assets recognised at cost and those recognised at valuation, and (ii) where assets are recognised at valuation, sufficient information to assist in understanding the valuation being recognised (date of valuation, method used, whether carried out by external valuer and if so their qualification and any significant limitations on the valuation); (f) a summary of transactions relating to heritage assets for the reporting period and each of the previous four reporting periods, disclosing: (i) the cost of acquisitions of heritage assets, (ii) the value of heritage assets acquired by donations, (iii) the carrying amount of heritage assets disposed of in the period and proceeds received, and (iv) any impairment recognised in the period. The summary shall show separately those transactions included in the statement of financial position and those that are not;	34.55

Heritage Assets – Section 34 (continued)	PARA.
(g) in exceptional circumstances, where it is impracticable to obtain a valuation of heritage assets acquired by donation, the reason shall be stated. Disclosures can be aggregated for groups or classes of heritage assets, provided this does not obscure significant information.	
Where it is impracticable to do so, the disclosures required by paragraph 34.55(f) need not be given for any accounting period earlier than the previous comparable period, and a statement to the effect that it is impracticable shall be made.	34.56

Disclosure Checklist: Specialised Activities – Small Entities

There are no mandatory disclosures.

Disclosure Checklist: Specialised Activities – Micro-entities

(References are to the relevant Section of FRS 105)

The mandatory disclosure requirements for micro-entities required under FRS 105, the Companies Acts 2014 (ROI) (CA 2104), Companies Act 2006 (UK) (CA 2006) and the Small Companies and Groups (Accounts and Directors' Report) Regulations 2008 (UK) (S.I. No. 409 of 2008) are as follows:

	Para.
A micro-entity shall disclose information in relation to the following items in accordance with the relevant appendix to Section 6 *Notes to the Financial Statements*: (a) financial commitments, guarantees and contingencies not recognised in the statement of financial position for the acquisition of a biological asset; and (b) a biological asset or item of agricultural produce given as security in respect of its commitments, guarantees and contingencies.	27.5
Indebtedness, guarantees and financial commitments	
Particulars and the total amount or estimated total amount shall be given with respect to any other financial commitment, guarantee or contingency not provided for in the statement of financial position. (Schedule 3B, paragraph 35(2) CA 2014) The aggregate amount of any such commitments, guarantees or contingencies which are undertaken on behalf of or for the benefit of: (a) any parent or fellow subsidiary of the micro-entity; (b) any subsidiary of the micro-entity; or (c) any undertaking in which the micro-entity has a participating interest, shall be separately stated and those within each of clauses (a), (b) and (c) shall also be stated separately from those within any other of those clauses. (Schedule 3B, paragraph 35(6) CA 2014)	6B.14 (ROI only)

Chapter 14

PUBLIC BENEFIT ENTITIES

14.1 PUBLIC BENEFIT ENTITIES – BACKGROUND

Public benefit entities (PBEs) are defined as entities whose primary objective is to provide goods or services for the general public or community rather than with a view to providing a financial return to equity holders, shareholders or members.

The FRC realised that once the micro-entity standard (FRS 105) and the small entity standard (Section 1A, FRS 102) were implemented, there was a gap in financial reporting relating to PBEs. HM Treasury in London had already implemented full IFRS, with suitable adaptations and interpretations, for the public sector in the UK from March 2010. With listed companies already implementing full IFRS from 2005 for their consolidated accounts and now the rest of the private sector following suit, it meant the death of local accounting standards. There would therefore be no standards specifically geared to meet the needs of not-for-profit entities.

Originally, the Accounting Standards Board (ASB) had proposed the development of a specialised standard for PBEs and issued FRED 45 *Financial Reporting Standard for Public Benefit Entities* in March 2011, as well as recommending the internationalisation of the not-for-profit Statements of Recommended Practice (SORPS) on charities, housing associations, etc.

However, after receiving the comment letters, it was clear that it would be unwieldly and expensive for preparers to have to use three separate documents to prepare their financial statements – the SORP, FRED 45 and FRS 102. As a result, the FRC, having taken over from the ASB, abandoned the idea of a separate PBE standard and instead opted for including specialised sections solely for PBEs within FRS 102. However, SORPs have also been revised in line with international standards.

Most of the specific PBE sections of FRS 102 are contained in Section 34 *Specialised Activities*, but there are references in two earlier sections:

(a) Section 11 *Basic Financial Instruments*: PBEs that make or receive concessionary loans are referred to Section 34 on how to account for such loans; and
(b) Section 19 *Business Combinations and Goodwill*: PBEs must refer to Section 34 when looking at PBE combinations and not to Section 19.

Section 34 deals with specific issues that can only apply to PBEs:
(a) incoming resources from non-exchange transactions (NETs);
(b) public benefit entity combinations; and
(c) public benefit entity concessionary loans.

The relevant paragraphs are prefixed by 'PBE' to distinguish them. Each of these issues is discussed in more detail below.

14.2 INCOMING RESOURCES FROM NON-EXCHANGE TRANSACTIONS (NETs)

Grants are specifically excluded from this section and instead preparers are referred to Section 24 *Government Grants* (see **Chapter 3**) for the appropriate accounting treatment.

NETs are defined as transactions whereby a reporting entity receives value from another entity without giving approximately equal value in exchange (e.g. donations, legacies, etc.).

Receipts from NETs are accounted for as follows:
- if no future performance conditions are required – immediately in income;
- if future performance conditions required – in income when the conditions are met; and
- if the resources are received in advance of conditions being met – as a liability.

Restrictions limiting or directing the purpose for which a resource is used, however, by themselves should not prevent income being recognised.

NETs may not be recorded unless they are reliably measured and it is clear that the benefits exceed the costs of recognising those resources. If that is not the case, then they can be recorded in income when the resources are sold or distributed.

A liability to repay any of these resources will only be required when it is probable that the resource has to be repaid.

Donations are normally reported in income and expenses, but they can be capitalised if they result in the creation of an asset.

Resources should all be measured at the fair value of resources receivable.

There are three disclosure requirements for NETs:
(a) the nature and amounts receivable from NETs;
(b) any unfulfilled conditions where resources are not yet recognised in income; and
(c) an indication of other forms of resources from NETs from which the entity has benefited.

In addition to the above principles, Appendix B to Section 34 provides additional guidance on how incoming resources from NETs should be recognised and measured in the financial statements. These are summarised below.

Recognition

Normally a receipt of resources results in both an asset and income being created at their fair value. However, that may not happen if the resources are in the form of services or if there are performance conditions attached to those resources that are still to be fulfilled.

There is a need to consider materiality and cost–benefit when deciding on recognition of resources received and they must be reliably measured.

If it is impracticable to recognise resources from NETs, then the income is recognised in the period in which the resources are sold or distributed, e.g. high volume, low value, second-hand goods donated for sale.

Legacies

Legacies should only be recognised following probate and after ensuring that there are sufficient assets in the estate, after settling liabilities, to pay the legacy. If the executor has agreed, prior to year end, that a legacy can be paid, it can be accrued. A portfolio approach may be taken if there are numerous immaterial legacies.

Donated Services

Donated services are expensed immediately but, if used to create another asset (e.g. plumbing, electrical services, etc.), they can be capitalised. If they can be reasonably quantified (e.g. office accommodation, legal fees, etc.), donated services should be recognised, but for volunteer services recognition is not required as they would be difficult to quantify. However, these services should be disclosed.

No income should be recognised until performance conditions are met. However, if the conditions are so broad that they do not actually impose a performance condition, then the income can be recognised on the receipt of the transfer of resources.

Measurement

Fair value is normally the price that an entity would pay on the open market for an equivalent item, but if there is no direct evidence of this, a price may be derived from sources such as:

(a) the cost of the item to the donor; or
(b) the estimated resale value of goods expected to be sold after deducting the cost to sell the goods.

Donations of services are recognised as income and an equivalent amount recognised as an expense unless it qualifies to be capitalised.

14.3 PUBLIC BENEFIT ENTITY COMBINATIONS

Section 34 covers two different types of PBE combination:

- combinations that are essentially a gift; and
- combinations that meet the definition of a merger.

If a combination fails to pass the definition of a merger, it must be accounted for using the acquisition method under Section 19 *Business Combinations and Goodwill.*

Combinations: In Substance Gifts

If a combination is for nil or nominal consideration, i.e. in substance it is a gift, the combination must be accounted for under Section 19 except that the excess of the fair values of assets received over the fair value of liabilities assumed is treated as a gain or, if liabilities exceed assets, as a loss.

Combinations: Mergers

The definition of a merger is similar to that in the local standard FRS 6 *Acquisitions and Mergers* (which was replaced by FRS 102). A merger results in a new reporting entity being created from the combining parties and they come together for the mutual sharing of risks and rewards and no one party is able to control the other nor be seen to be dominant.

An entity combination that is a merger must apply merger accounting as prescribed below.

Any entity combination that is neither a combination that is in substance a gift nor a merger must be accounted for as an acquisition in accordance with Section 19.

Accounting Treatment

The carrying value of the assets and liabilities of the parties to the combination are not adjusted to fair value, although adjustments have to be made to achieve uniformity of accounting policies.

The results and cash flows of all the combining entities should be brought into the financial statements of the newly formed entity from the beginning of the financial period in which the merger occurs.

Comparative amounts are restated by including the results for all the combining entities for the previous accounting period and their balance sheets, for the previous reporting date. The comparative figures shall be marked as 'combined' figures.

All merger costs are expensed immediately.

Disclosure

For each merger the following must be disclosed in the newly formed entity's financial statements:

(a) the names and descriptions of the combining entities or businesses;
(b) the date of the merger;
(c) an analysis of the principal components of the current year's total comprehensive income to indicate:
  (i) the amounts relating to the newly formed merged entity for the period after the date of the merger, and
  (ii) the amounts relating to each party to the merger up to the date of the merger;
(d) an analysis of the previous year's total comprehensive income between each party to the merger;
(e) the aggregate carrying value of the net assets of each party to the merger at the date of the merger; and
(f) the nature and amount of any significant adjustments required to align accounting policies and an explanation of any further adjustments made to net assets as a result of the merger.

14.4 PUBLIC BENEFIT ENTITY CONCESSIONARY LOANS

Concessionary loans are loans made or received at below market rates between the PBE and a third party that are not repayable on demand.

A PBE can adopt either of the following two options for accounting purposes:

(a) apply Section 11 *Basic Financial Instruments* – initially measure at fair value but subsequently adopt the amortised cost approach using the effective interest method; or
(b) apply the following:
  - **Initial Measurement** At the amount received or paid and recognise them in the balance sheet.
  - **Subsequent Measurement** In subsequent years, the carrying amounts of concessionary loans are adjusted to reflect any accrued interest payable or receivable. To the extent that a loan is irrecoverable, an impairment loss must be recognised in income and expenditure.

Presentation and Disclosure

Concessionary loans made and received can be presented either as separate line items on the face of the balance sheet or in the notes.

Concessionary loans must be presented separately between amounts repayable or receivable within one year and amounts repayable or receivable after more than one year.

A summary of significant accounting policies applied to concessionary loans, the measurement basis adopted and any other accounting policies relevant to understanding the transactions in the financial statements must be presented.

The following should be disclosed:

(a) the terms and conditions of concessionary loan arrangements, e.g. the interest rate, any security provided and the terms of the repayment; and
(b) the value of concessionary loans which have been committed but not taken up at the year end.

Concessionary loans made or received must be disclosed separately. However, multiple loans made or received may be disclosed in aggregate, providing that such aggregation does not obscure significant information.

Example 14.1: Two Options of Reporting Concessionary Loans

A public benefit entity makes an interest-free unsecured loan to another entity repayable in five years' time. The market rate of interest would normally be 10%.

Option 1 Section 11 Approach

		€	€
Dr	Receivable	62,092	
Dr	Interest in suspense	37,908	
	Cr Bank		100,000

Being loan provided by PBE to another entity at below market rate.

		€	€
Dr	Interest receivable	6,209	
	Cr Interest in suspense		6,209

Being calculation of interest on suspense for interest receivable for year.

Option 2 Alternative PBE Approach

		€	€
Dr	Receivable	100,000	
	Cr Bank		100,000

Being loan provided by PBE to another entity at below market rate.

Note: No interest is receivable in year one.

Small Entities

There are no explicit minimum disclosure requirements for small entities under Section 1A of FRS 102 for either the UK or the Republic of Ireland. However, small entities may need to provide disclosures as required by FRS 102, Section 34 if required to give a true and fair view.

Micro-entities

The accounting treatment for public benefit entities is identical to that of both small entities under Section 1A and those preparing their financial statements under the full version of FRS 102.

Disclosure Checklist: Public Benefit Entities – FRS 102

(References are to the relevant Section of FRS 102)

	Para.
Specialised Activities – Section 34	
Incoming resources from non-exchange transactions	
An entity shall disclose the following: (a) the nature and amounts of resources receivable from non-exchange transactions recognised in the financial statements; (b) any unfulfilled conditions or other contingencies attaching to resources from non-exchange transactions that have not been recognised in income; and (c) an indication of other forms of resources from non-exchange transactions from which the entity has benefited.	PBE34.74
Public benefit entity combinations	
For each business combination accounted for as a merger in the reporting period the following shall be disclosed in the newly formed entity's financial statements: (a) the names and descriptions of the combining entities or business; (b) the date of the merger; (c) an analysis of the principal components of the current year's total comprehensive income to indicate: (i) the amounts relating to the newly formed merged entity for the period after the date of the merger, and (ii) the amounts relating to each party to the merger up to the date of the merger; (d) an analysis of the previous year's primary financial statements between each party to the merger; (e) the aggregate carrying value of the net assets of each party to the merger at the date of the merger; and (f) the nature and amount of any significant adjustments required to align accounting policies and an explanation of any further adjustments made to net assets as a result of the merger.	PBE34.86
Concessionary loans	
The entity shall disclose, in the summary of significant accounting policies, the measurement basis used for concessionary loans and any other accounting policies that are relevant to understanding these transactions within the financial statements.	PBE34.95
The entity shall also disclose the following information relating to concessionary loans: (a) the terms and conditions of concessionary loan arrangements, e.g. the interest rate, any security provided and the terms of the repayment; and (b) the value of concessionary loans which have been committed but not taken up at the year end.	PBE34.96
Concessionary loans made or received shall be disclosed separately. However, multiple loans made or received may be disclosed in aggregate, providing that such aggregation does not obscure significant information.	PBE34.97

Disclosure Checklist: Public Benefit Entities – Small Entities

There are no mandatory disclosures.

Disclosure Checklist: Public Benefit Entities – Micro-entities

There are no mandatory disclosures.

Chapter 15

TRANSITIONAL ARRANGEMENTS TO IMPLEMENTING FRS 102

15.1 BACKGROUND

Section 35 applies to a first-time adopter of FRS 102 regardless of whether it has been previously using national GAAP or full IFRSs. The section is only applied to the first set of financial statements conforming to FRS 102. If an entity subsequently stops using the FRS, it cannot avail of the special exemptions, simplifications, etc. on re-adoption.

However, the Section does apply to entities whose most recent accounts have previously adopted FRS 102 but failed to make an explicit and unreserved statement of compliance with the FRS. An entity could, as an alternative, apply FRS 102 retrospectively in accordance with Section 10 *Accounting Policies, Changes in Estimates and Errors* (see **Chapter 7**).

An entity's first financial statements that conform with the FRS are the first annual statements in which the entity makes an explicit and unreserved statement of compliance with the FRS. These are the first statements if:

(a) the entity did not present financial statements in previous periods;
(b) the entity presented its most recent previous financial statements under national standards (FRS 102, Section 1A, FRS 102 and FRS 105) and rules; or
(c) the entity presented its most recent previous financial statements in conformity with full IFRSs.

Example 15.1: Statement of Compliance

The financial statements have been prepared under the historical cost convention as modified by the revaluation of certain assets. The financial statements of the company for the year ended 31 December 2018 have been prepared in accordance with the Financial Reporting Standard applicable in the United Kingdom and Republic of Ireland (FRS 102) and issued by the Institute of Chartered Accountants in Ireland [in UK, by the Financial Reporting Council]. These are the company's first set of financial statements prepared in accordance with FRS 102.

FRS 102 requires a complete set of financial statements to disclose comparatives for the previous comparable period for all monetary amounts reported in the statements, as well as specified narrative and descriptive information. Comparatives for more than one prior period may be presented. The date of transition, therefore, is the start of the earliest period for which the entity presents full comparative information in accordance with the FRS. For most companies it will probably only be one year.

Example 15.2: Date of Transition

If an entity adopts FRS 102 for the first time from 1 January 2019, then for the year ended 31 December 2018 it must present full comparative information. That makes the date of transition to be the first day of that comparative year, i.e. 1 January 2018.

15.2 PROCEDURES FOR PREPARING FINANCIAL STATEMENTS AT THE DATE OF TRANSITION

Opening Balance Sheet

At the date of transition an entity must prepare an opening balance sheet. This is a four-step process, as outlined below.

1. **Recognise all assets and liabilities required by FRS 102.**

Example 15.3: Holiday Pay Accrual

Colin Ltd has never accrued for holiday pay, under local GAAP, that its employees have earned between the holiday year end of 31 December 2018 and the accounting year end of 31 March 2019. From personnel records, it is estimated that staff have earned €12,000 holiday pay during those three months.

Colin Ltd must accrue the €12,000 as at 31 March 2019 as follows:

Dr	Profit and loss account	€12,000	
	Cr Accruals		€12,000

2. **Do not recognise assets or liabilities if FRS 102 does not permit their recognition**. (This is likely to be rare in UK/Irish accounting due to the close alignment with the IFRS view of assets and liabilities.)

Example 15.4: Previous Capitalisation of Inherent Intangibles

Glen Ltd has capitalised €100,000 of costs that it had incurred in developing a very successful brand name, 'Glanbread', on the grounds that it generates probable future benefits.

Internally developed brand names should not appear on the balance sheet under UK/Irish GAAP, but it has been attempted by some companies in the past, e.g. Hovis bread and Mr Kipling cakes in the accounts of RHM Plc. Under FRS 102 they are definitely not permitted and therefore must be removed from the balance sheet as follows:

Dr	Profit and loss reserve	€100,000	
	Cr Intangible assets		€100,000

3. **Reclassify items recognised previously as one type of asset, liability, equity, etc., but which are a different type under FRS 102.**

Example 15.5: Reclassification of Equity

Under previous GAAP, the opening balances as at 1 January 2018 for Farset Ltd are as follows:

	€	€
Fixed assets at cost	180,000	
Less accumulated depreciation	52,500	
		127,500
Investment property		300,000
Tangible assets		427,500
Current assets		
Trade debtors	150,000	
Bank and cash	112,500	
	262,500	
Creditors: amounts falling due within one year		
Trade creditors	63,000	
Accruals	15,000	
VAT	3,150	
Other taxation	10,800	
	91,950	
Net current assets		170,550
		598,050

Creditors: amounts falling due after more than one year	
Deferred tax	1,650
	596,400
Capital and reserves	
Ordinary shares €1, fully paid up	150
Revaluation reserve	60,000
Profit and loss account	536,250
	596,400

Assuming the revaluation reserve relates to the investment property, it will have to be reclassified to the profit and loss account as Section 16 of FRS 102 requires investment properties to record all gains and losses through profit or loss.

The double entry required will be:

Dr	Revaluation reserve	€60,000	
	Cr Profit and loss reserve		€60,000

4. Apply FRS 102 in measuring all recognised assets and liabilities.

Example 15.6: Remeasurement of Liability

Ards Ltd has provided €40,000 on its timing differences for deferred taxation. The company has revalued its investment property on a regular basis and estimates that it would have to pay €50,000 capital gains tax if it were to be sold. In addition, the company acquired Newtown Ltd a few years ago and carried out a fair value exercise at that time. It is estimated that this could result in €30,000 tax having to be paid to the government if the assets were to be sold.

Ards Ltd will have to remeasure its deferred tax liability under FRS 102 as it has adopted a timing differences plus approach to deferred tax and does require deferred tax to be reported on the balance sheet for both revaluations and fair value exercises as a result of a business combination.

The additional journal entry would therefore be:

Dr	Profit and loss reserve	€80,000	
	Cr Deferred tax (€50,000 + €30,000)		€80,000

The accounting policies adopted in the opening balance sheet may differ from those adopted under previous frameworks and thus any adjustments must be recognised directly in retained earnings at the date of transition to the FRS.

15.3 NO RETROSPECTION PERMITTED

On first-time adoption of the FRS, an entity is not permitted to change the accounting treatment that it has followed previously for any of the following transactions:

(a) derecognition of financial assets and liabilities;
(b) accounting estimates; and
(c) measurement of non-controlling interests.

15.4 PERMITTED EXEMPTIONS

An entity may adopt one or more of the following exemptions in preparing its first statements under FRS 102:

(a) Business Combinations, including Group Reconstructions

The entity may elect not to adopt Section 19 *Business Combinations and Goodwill* (see **Chapter 11**) for past combinations, but if it does restate any previous combination, the entity must restate all later combinations.

Example 15.7: Business Combinations before the Date of Transition

In 2014, Perth Ltd acquired a wholly-owned subsidiary and applied the requirements of previous GAAP on group reporting. In accordance with those rules, Perth Ltd recognised the following opening fair values:

	€	€
Property, plant and equipment	45,000	
Goodwill	15,000	
		60,000
Stock	5,000	
Debtors	5,500	
Net current assets	3,000	
Creditors	(4,000)	
Net current liabilities		(9,500)
Net assets acquired at fair value		50,500

Adjustment on transition 1 January 2018:

(i) Goodwill
FRS 102 presumes the life of goodwill to be 10 years or less unless the goodwill has a longer economic life.

On acquisition in 2010, Perth Ltd decided that, in accordance with previous group reporting standards, goodwill had a probable economic life of 20 years. At 31 December 2017, the carrying amount for the goodwill is €12,000 and, in accordance with its previous amortisation rate, it has a remaining life of six years.

Perth Ltd considers there is evidence to support the remaining economic life of six years and provides adequate evidence to support this. It is therefore not required to adjust the carrying amount of goodwill or the expected amortisation profile.

(ii) Fair Values at Acquisition
As the acquisition occurred prior to the date of transition, the entity is not required to review the acquired identifiable assets and liabilities, either to determine whether additional items would have been recognised if FRS 102 had been applicable at the date of acquisition, or to restate their fair values at that date if application of FRS 102 would have required recognition at a different value.

(b) Share-based Payment Transactions

Entities are not required to apply Section 26 *Share-based Payment* (see **Chapter 8**) to equity instruments granted before the date of transition or to liabilities settled before the date of transition.

Any first-time adopter who has previously applied FRS 20 *Share-based Payment* is not permitted to make any amendments on transition to FRS 102.

(c) Fair Value as Deemed Cost

Entities may measure property, plant and equipment at the date of transition at fair value and adopt that as its deemed cost under the FRS. That can apply to property, plant and equipment, investment properties and intangible assets (the latter only if it meets the criteria for revaluation).

(d) Revaluation as Deemed Cost

An entity may use the revaluation under previous GAAP as its deemed cost at the date of revaluation. That applies also to property, plant and equipment, investment properties and intangible assets.

Example 15.8: Revaluation as Deemed Cost

Inverness Ltd has two properties, A and B, and is preparing its transition-date balance sheet as at 1 January 2018. Neither property A nor property B is an investment property.

Inverness Ltd had previously made an accounting policy choice to revalue its properties.

Property A was acquired in 1989 at a cost of €70,000 and has been revalued on a regular basis, the last time in 2015, where its value was recorded in the financial statements at €250,000. The directors do not consider there to have been any subsequent change in the value of property A.

Property B was acquired in 2015 at a cost of €200,000. Property B has never been revalued (because it was purchased in the year of the most recent valuation and its cost was the best available evidence of its valuation). It is not considered that there has been any impairment in its value.

If Inverness Ltd decides not to continue its policy of revaluation, it has a choice in relation to property A: it could elect, in accordance with FRS 102, to use the 2015 revaluation as its deemed cost and no further adjustment is required; or it could restate the property to cost.

If the revalued amount were used as deemed cost, in order to comply with company law, the revaluation reserve would be retained and the excess depreciation would continue to be offset against it.

If the property is restated to cost, the following adjustment would be required, assuming annual transfer from revaluation reserve to retained profits and ignoring the effects of deferred tax and assuming a useful economic life of 50 years:

			€	€
Dr	Revaluation reserve		189,400*	
	Cr	Accumulated depreciation		9,400
	Cr	Property, plant and equipment		180,000

No adjustment is required on transition for property B as cost is its fair value.

* Surplus = €250,000 – €33,600 = €216,400
Surplus – Excess depreciation = €216,400 – €27,000 = €189,400

(e) Individual and Separate Financial Statements

Entities must measure their investments in subsidiaries, associates and jointly controlled entities either at cost or at fair value.

If entities adopt the cost model, cost must be determined in accordance with either:

1. Section 9 *Consolidated and Separate Financial Statements*, Section 14 *Investments in Associates*, or Section 15 *Investments in Joint Ventures*; or
2. at deemed cost (i.e. previous GAAP carrying value at the date of transition).

(f) Compound Financial Instruments

There is no need to separate out the two components of compound financial instruments into debt and equity if the debt component is no longer outstanding at the date of transition.

(g) Service Concession Arrangements: Accounting by Operators

Entities are not required to apply Section 34 *Specialised Activities* (see **Chapter 13**) to service concession arrangements entered into before the date of transition to the FRS. The same accounting policies being applied at the date of transition should continue.

(h) Extractive Activities

If an entity has adopted full cost accounting under previous GAAP (i.e. it accounted for exploration and development costs in cost centres in a large geographical area), it may elect to measure oil and gas assets on the date of transition as follows:

1. at the amount determined under the entity's previous GAAP;
2. assets in the development or production phases at the amount recognised under previous GAAP and the amount allocated on a pro rata basis using reserve volumes or reserve values as of the date of transition.

These assets must be tested for impairment at the date of transition to the FRS in accordance with Section 34 *Specialised Activities* or Section 27 *Impairment of Assets*, respectively.

(i) Arrangements Containing a Lease

An entity may elect to determine whether an arrangement existing at the date of transition contains a lease on the basis of the facts and circumstances existing at that date, rather than when the arrangement was entered into.

(j) Decommissioning Liabilities included in the Cost of Property, Plant and Equipment

An entity may elect to measure this component of the cost of an item of property at the date of transition, rather than on the date(s) when the obligation initially arose.

(k) Dormant Companies[1]

Dormant companies may elect to retain their existing accounting policies for the measurement of assets, liabilities and equity at the date of transition to the FRS until there is a change to those balances or new transactions are undertaken.

(l) Deferred Development Costs as a Deemed Cost

An entity can elect to measure the carrying amount for deferred development costs at the date of transition in accordance with previous GAAP as its deemed cost at that date.

Example 15.9: Development Costs

Green Hedges Ltd had previously made an accounting policy choice to capitalise development costs meeting the criteria set out in previous GAAP.

In 2015, Green Hedges Ltd undertook a programme to develop the products it acquired as part of an acquisition in order to be compatible with its own products. In accordance with previous GAAP, it capitalised €10,000 of expenditure which it is amortising over four years. At 31 December 2019 the carrying amount was €5,000.

FRS 102 permits an entity to recognise an intangible asset arising from the development phase of an internal project providing it meets certain criteria. Green Hedges Ltd makes the accounting policy choice to capitalise development costs meeting the criteria set out in the FRS. FRS 102 permits an entity to measure deferred development costs on transition at the amount determined in accordance with previous GAAP. Therefore, although in this example it is unlikely that there is a material difference between the carrying value of the development costs measured using previous GAAP or FRS 102, for ease Green Hedges Ltd elects to retain the value determined in accordance with previous GAAP as the deemed cost of deferred development costs and makes no adjustment to its transition date balance sheet.

---

[1] Only UK, as Irish law has no equivalent.

A number of additional sections, (m) to (q), are included in FRS 102 as follows:

(m) Borrowing Costs

An entity can elect to capitalise borrowing costs from the date of transition as the date on which capitalisation commences.

Example 15.10: Borrowing Costs

Wear Ltd decided to construct a new building. Work on the construction commenced during 2018. Wear Ltd capitalises tangible fixed assets on the basis of cost, in accordance with previous GAAP, but had not previously constructed any significant assets and its accounting policy did not include capitalising finance costs (although previous GAAP permitted this as an accounting policy choice).

As at 31 December 2018, Wear Ltd had capitalised costs of €80,000 and estimated that it still had approximately nine months of construction work ahead. Finance costs that could have been capitalised, had Wear Ltd had a policy of capitalisation, amounted to €1,000.

During 2019 Wear Ltd completes construction of the building. The total cost to be capitalised in accordance with FRS 102 (excluding borrowing costs) is €120,000. Qualifying borrowing costs, calculated in accordance with FRS 102, relating to the project as a whole are €3,500.

On adoption of FRS 102, Wear Ltd reviews its accounting policies and decides that it will now elect to capitalise borrowing costs in accordance with FRS 102, and so elects to capitalise costs prospectively from 1 January 2019. As a result, no adjustment is made to the transition balance sheet, and the €1,000 previously written off is not capitalised, but €2,500 (€3,500 – €1,000) of borrowing costs are capitalised.

Wear Ltd has no evidence that the overall value of the building is less than €122,500.

(n) Lease Incentives

Section 20 *Leases* does not need to be applied to lease incentives provided the lease commenced before the date of transition.

(o) Public Benefit Entity Combinations

An entity need not apply Section 34 to public benefit entity combinations effected before the date of transition. However, if it does restate any combination, then all later combinations must also be restated.

(p) Assets and Liabilities of Subsidiaries, Associates and Joint Ventures

If a subsidiary, associate or joint venture adopts FRS 102 later than its parent, it must measure its assets and liabilities at either:

1. the carrying amounts in the parent's consolidated accounts based on the parent's date of transition; or
2. the carrying amounts required by the rest of the FRS based on the subsidiary's date of transition. They could differ from 1. due to exemptions being applied at different dates or differences in accounting policies (e.g. the subsidiary uses the cost model, but the group adopts the revaluation model).

However, if a parent adopts FRS 102 later than its subsidiary, associate or joint venture, for consolidation purposes, it must measure the assets and liabilities of those entities at the same carrying amounts as in those entities.

(q) Designation of Previously Recognised Financial Instruments

Entities can designate a financial instrument at fair value through profit or loss at the date of transition provided it meets the criteria in Section 11 *Basic Financial Instruments*.

(r) Hedge Accounting

In March 2018 an additional section was added to cover hedge accounting on transition as follows:

- **Hedging relationship existing at date of transition** May adopt hedge accounting if hedge criteria are met on the date of transition.
- **Hedging relationship ceased to exist before date of transition as instrument was sold, expired, terminated or exercised** Can elect not to adjust for the effects of a hedging relationship that no longer exists.
- **Hedging relationship commenced post date of transition** Can elect to adopt hedge accounting from date criteria are met provided no later than date of authorization of first statements under FRS 102.
- **Entities opting for IAS 9/IFRS 9 under Section 12** Cannot adopt the transitional provisions above.

If it is **impracticable** to restate the opening balance sheet at the date of transition for one or more of the adjustments required by the FRS, an entity must apply the adjustments in the earliest period for which it is practicable to do so, and identify the data presented for prior periods that are not comparable with data for the period in which it prepares its first financial statements that conform to the FRS.

If it is impracticable for an entity to provide any disclosures required by this FRS for any period before the period in which it prepares its first financial statements that conform to the FRS, that omission must be disclosed.

The exemptions can continue to be applied until the assets and liabilities are derecognised.

However, if subsequently there is a significant change in circumstances to events existing at the date of transition, an entity must reassess whether it is still appropriate to use those exemptions to maintain a fair presentation of the financial statements.

15.4 DISCLOSURES

Explanation of Transition to the FRS 102

An entity should explain how the transition from previous GAAP to FRS 102 has affected the reporting of the financial position and performance of the entity.

Example 15.11: Disclosure of Transition to FRS 102

These financial statements for the year ended 31 December 2019 are Curragh Ltd's first financial statements that comply with FRS 102. The date of transition to FRS 102 is 1 January 2018.

The transition to FRS 102 has resulted in a small number of changes in accounting policies compared to those used previously.

The following notes to the financial statements describe the differences between the capital and reserves and profit or loss presented previously, and the amounts as restated to comply with the accounting policies selected in accordance with FRS 102 for the reporting period ended at 31 December 2018 (i.e. comparative information), as well as the capital and reserves presented in the opening balance sheet (i.e. at 1 January 2018). It also describes all the required changes in accounting policies made on first-time adoption of FRS 102.

If an entity previously applied FRS 102 but **not** in its most recent financial statements, it must disclose:

(a) the reason why the application of FRS 102 was stopped;
(b) the reason why the application of FRS 102 is being resumed; and
(c) if it has applied Section 35, i.e. the section on transition to FRS 102, or FRS 102 retrospectively regarding a change in policy under Section 10 *Accounting Policies, Estimates and Errors*.

15.5 RECONCILIATIONS

The first financial statements using FRS 102 should include:

(a) a description of the nature of each change in accounting policy;

(b) a reconciliation of its equity reported under previous GAAP to equity reported under FRS 102 for both:
  (i) the date of transition, and
  (ii) the end of the latest period presented in the entity's most recent annual financial statements under the previous framework; and
(c) a reconciliation of the profit or loss reported under previous GAAP for the latest period to the profit or loss under FRS for the same period.

If an entity becomes aware of errors made under previous GAAP, the reconciliations must distinguish those errors from any changes made in accounting policy.

If the entity did not previously present financial statements, it must disclose that fact in its first FRS 102 financial statements.

Example 15.12: Reconciliations

Required Amendments For a 1 January 2018 transition date, an entity is required to restate its 31 December 2017 balance sheet to a transition date balance sheet of 1 January 2018 by making the adjustments that are necessary to recognise all assets and liabilities in accordance with FRS 102. This may, for example, require an entity to:

1. recognise assets and/or liabilities previously not recognised, e.g. forward exchange contracts;
2. not recognise items as assets or liabilities if FRS 102 does not permit their recognition;
3. restate certain assets and liabilities at a different value, e.g. financial instruments measured at amortised cost using the effective interest rate, which may vary from a previously used historical cost; and
4. reclassify items, e.g. into different groupings within equity.

Adjustments on transition are usually recognised in retained profit (or loss) or, where appropriate, another category within capital and reserves.

15.6 HOW TO APPLY FRS 102 FOR THE FIRST TIME

It should be emphasised that in many cases FRS 102 is very similar to UK and Irish GAAP as many local accounting standards have been more or less aligned to their international counterparts. There are unlikely therefore to be many adjustments on first-time application of FRS 102.

15.7 FIRST-TIME ADOPTION

Under FRS 102, a first-time adopter must make an **explicit and unreserved** statement that the first annual financial statements conform to the standard. However, entities cannot make this explicit and unreserved statement if the financial statements do not **fully** comply with the standard.

EXAMPLE 15.13: TRANSITION

Strangford Ltd has a year-end of 31 December 2018. On 1 January 2019 it decided to report under FRS 102. Strangford Ltd manufactures iron railings and has a policy of including its stocks under the last in, first out (LIFO) method. It has continued to do so under FRS 102.

Strangford Ltd cannot make an explicit and unreserved statement that its first annual financial statements conform to FRS 102 because they do not. Under FRS 102, an entity cannot adopt the LIFO methodology – it must adopt either the first in, first out (FIFO) or weighted average method.

FRS 102 states that an entity's **first** set of financial statements under FRS are those, for example:

- which did not present financial statements for previous periods;
- which presented its most recent previous financial statements under national requirements that are not consistent with FRS 102 in all respects; or
- which presented its most recent previous financial statements in conformity with full IFRSs (i.e. adopted full IFRS voluntarily in the past).

Step-by-step approach

Paragraph 35.7 of FRS 102 details the procedures which should be applied when adopting FRS 102 for the first time. These procedures are fairly general. The steps required are as follows:

1. ***Recognise all assets and liabilities whose recognition is required by FRS 102***

As UK/Irish GAAP has been more or less aligned to IFRS (and FRS 102), it is likely to be rare that such assets and liabilities will be recognised where UK GAAP previously did not permit. However, an illustration of this could be in a country that adopts the FRS 102 equivalent (*IFRS for SMEs*) and whose GAAP did not allow provisions to be recognised in any circumstances. If this particular country adopted the *IFRS for SMEs*, then an entity in that country would be required to recognise a provision if circumstances met the recognition criteria of a provision (legal/constructive obligation, probable outflow of economic benefits, and the amount can be reliably estimated).

2. *Derecognise items as assets or liabilities if FRS 102 does not permit such recognition*
In contrast to (1) above, UK/Irish GAAP might have previously permitted recognition of some transactions as assets or liabilities, but such recognition may be prohibited under FRS 102. Though, again, as UK/Irish GAAP has been more or less aligned to the IFRS regime, derecognition of assets and liabilities is likely to be rare.

3. *Reclassify items that it recognised under its previous financial reporting framework as one type of asset, liability or component of equity, but are different types of asset, liability or component of equity under FRS 102*
Such instances are likely to be rare in the UK/Ireland. A typical example could be in jurisdictions where preference shares are shown in equity, with no consideration given as to the substance of the shares. Under FRS 102, if preference shares contain any sort of redemption feature, or entitle the holder of the preference shares to receive cash (e.g. dividends), all (or part) of the debt element of the preference shares would have to be reclassified as liabilities.

4. *Applying FRS 102 in measuring all recognised assets and liabilities*
This means that all assets and liabilities, going forward, will be measured in accordance with FRS 102. For example, entities will not be permitted to discount their deferred tax balances.

In practice, this is the approach that should be adopted to follow these steps:

Step 1 First, identify the date of transition to FRS 102.

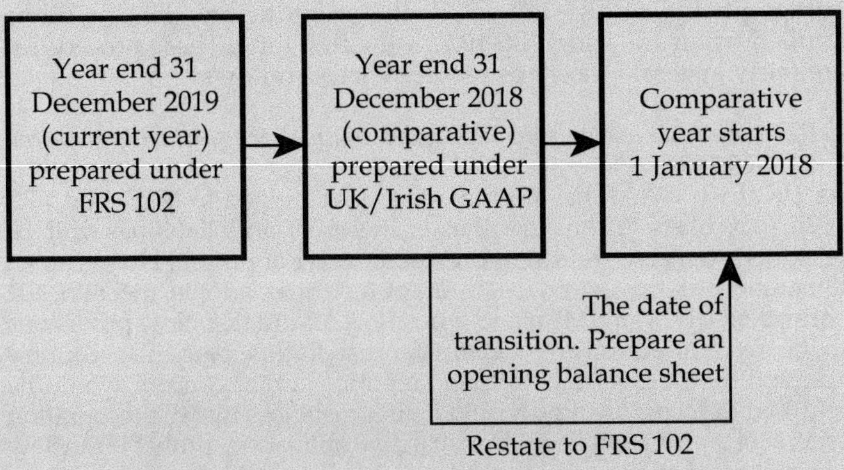

From the above diagram it can be seen that entities need to go back to the **earliest** period reported in the financial statements (the 2018 comparative year) and restate those, so the date of transition (and thus the balance sheet) that will need restating is 1 January 2018 (effectively, the 2017 closing balance sheet).

Step 2 Look at the accounting policies of the entity which have been applied under UK/Irish GAAP and consider any which FRS 102 requires (e.g. the exclusive use of the 'purchase method' if a company acquires a subsidiary), and also consider any which are not compliant with FRS 102 (e.g. the discounting of deferred tax balances or the valuation of stock under LIFO).

Strangford Ltd is preparing its FRS 102 financial statements as at 31 December 2019, but must produce an opening balance sheet as at the date of transition to FRS 102 (1 January 2018). In the 2018 financial statements, stock (inventory) was valued at €180,000 using the LIFO method. FRS 102 prohibits this method and so the entity has adopted weighted average (AVCO), which has produced a revised inventory valuation as at 31 December 2018 amounting to €150,000. The reduction in the revised inventory figure of €30,000 will be recognised directly in retained earnings:

Dr	Retained earnings	€30,000	
	Cr Inventory		€30,000

Step 3 Consider whether the entity is affected by any of the following:

Financial assets and financial liabilities Such assets and liabilities that were derecognised under UK/Irish GAAP before the date of transition to FRS 102, cannot be recognised at the date of transition to FRS 102. Additionally, such assets and liabilities that would be derecognised under FRS 102 in a transaction that took place prior to the date of transition to, but that were not previously derecognised under, UK/Irish GAAP will result in the entity having an option to:

- derecognise the financial assets and liabilities on adoption of FRS 102; or
- continue to recognise the financial assets and liabilities until they are disposed of or settled.

Accounting estimates Accounting estimates are never changed retrospectively, they are always changed prospectively (e.g. a change in depreciation method or useful life). A first-time adopter of FRS 102 should not, therefore, make any changes to accounting estimates retrospectively.

Non-controlling interests FRS 102 requires the allocation of profit or loss and total comprehensive income between the owners of the parent and non-controlling interests to be applied prospectively (going forward) from the date of transition to FRS. Similarly, accounting for changes in a parent company's interest in a subsidiary that does not result in a loss of control is only applied prospectively.

Step 4 When preparing the first FRS 102 financial statements, consider the exemptions contained at Section 35.10:

Business combinations Section 19 of FRS 102 deals with business combinations (i.e. where a company acquires a subsidiary). Merger accounting is not permitted (apart from PBEs) in FRS 102. However, in respect of business combinations that took place prior to the date of transition to FRS 102, a first-time adopter need not apply Section 19. However, in respect of all business combinations after the date of transition to FRS 102, the acquiring entity will apply the provisions in Section 19.

Share-based payments For equity instruments that were granted prior to the date of transition to FRS 102, a first-time adopter need not apply Section 26 of the FRS. This also applies to liabilities that arose as a result of share-based payment transactions that were settled prior to the date of transition to FRS 102.

Fair amounts as deemed cost for property, plant and equipment At the date of transition to FRS 102, a first-time adopter can use fair value as the deemed cost to measure items of property, plant and equipment, including investment property and intangible assets.

Revaluation as deemed cost Revaluation of fixed assets is permitted under FRS 102, but a first-time adopter of FRS 102 can use the revalued amount as the item of tangible, intangible or investment property's deemed cost at, or before, the date of transition to FRS 102.

Compound financial instruments These very rarely occur in medium-sized entities, but a first-time adopter need not use 'split accounting', i.e. split a compound financial instrument into its debt and equity components, where the liability element of the instrument is not outstanding at the date of transition to FRS 102.

Service concession arrangements – operators First-time adopters do not have to comply with the requirements in paragraphs 34.12–34.16 of FRS 102 in relation to service concession arrangements entered into prior to the date of transition to FRS 102.

Extractive industries Again, these are extremely uncommon for entities in the medium-sized sector, but essentially a first-time adopter using full cost accounting can elect to measure oil and gas assets at the amount determined under UK/Irish GAAP, but the entity must test those assets for impairment at the date of transition to FRS 102.

Arrangements containing a lease First-time adopters may elect to determine whether arrangements which exist at the date of transition to FRS 102 do, in fact, contain a lease having regard to the facts and circumstances at the date of transition, as opposed to when the arrangement was entered into.

Decommissioning liabilities included in the cost of property, plant and equipment Decommissioning liabilities are usually found in onerous contracts, and a first-time adopter can elect to measure the cost of such liabilities at the date of transition to FRS 102 as opposed to the date the obligation initially arose.

Dormant companies This part of FRS 102 is UK-specific. A company which is dormant in accordance with the Companies Act 2006 can elect to retain its accounting policies for measurement of reported assets, liabilities and equity at the date of transition to FRS 102 until such a time as any changes to those balances takes place, or the company undertakes new transactions.

Case Study 15.1: First-time Adoption

Assume Strangford Ltd has a reporting date of 31 December 2019 and has decided from 1 January 2019 to report under FRS 102. For the purposes of this case study it is important to understand the exact date of transition to FRS 102. The company has decided that its financial year ended 31 December 2019 will be reported under FRS 102; however, the comparative year would have been reported under UK/Irish GAAP, hence we need to go back to the **start** of the comparative year, i.e. 1 January 2018, to begin the restatement process. The balance sheet for Strangford Ltd as at 1 January 2018, together with supporting information, is as follows:

Strangford Ltd
BALANCE SHEET
(prepared under previous GAAP)
as at 1 January 2018

		€	€
Non-current Assets			
Goodwill	Note 1		390,000
Tangible fixed assets	Note 2		386,000
			776,000
Current Assets			
Stocks	Note 3	14,500	
Trade and other debtors		600,000	
Cash and bank		290,000	
		904,500	
Current Liabilities			
Trade and other creditors		425,000	
Net current assets			479,500
Total assets less current liabilities			1,255,500
Non-current Liabilities			
Loans		116,000	
Deferred taxation	Note 4	20,000	
			136,000
Net Assets			**1,119,500**
Capital and Reserves			
Called-up share capital			1,000
Retained earnings			1,118,500
			1,119,500

Notes:

1 Goodwill was recognised in accordance with FRS 10 *Goodwill and Intangible Assets* and, at the time of recognition, the directors felt the useful economic life of this goodwill was 20 years. The goodwill currently has 15 years left to run. However, at the date of transition to FRS 102, the directors feel this time period is excessive. In the annual general meeting the directors could not agree on the best estimate of the goodwill's remaining useful economic life.

2 Property, plant and equipment includes a building that was revalued on 1 January 2018. The valuation of the building amounted to €200,000 and the directors wish to use this valuation as the building's deemed cost at the date of transition to FRS 102.
3 The company has always valued its stock using the last in, first out (LIFO) method of valuation. As this method is not permissible under FRS 102, the directors have decided to use the average cost method of valuation. Such a method produces a stock valuation as at 1 January 2018 of €10,370.
4 The company's accounting policy in respect of deferred tax is to discount the deferred tax balance to present-day values.

If discounting had not been used, the deferred tax liability as at 1 January 2018 would have been €24,000.

Solution

Part of the process of the transition from previous GAAP to FRS 102 would involve looking at the entity's accounting policies and determining those which are permissible under the FRS and those which are not. In respect of Strangford Ltd, the points 1–4 above would be dealt with as follows:

1. The directors cannot place a reliable estimate as to the remaining useful economic life of the goodwill and, as such, will be required to conform with paragraph 19.23(a) of the FRS and amortise the remainder of the goodwill over 10 years. The calculation is as follows:

Initial recognition = €390,000 × 20 years/15 years

= €520,000

Annual amortisation rate = €520,000/20 years

= €26,000

Remaining useful life under previous GAAP 15 years

Goodwill write-down to conform with FRS 102 = €26,000 × 5 years

= €130,000

Therefore, the journal entry is:

Dr	Reserves		€130,000	
	Cr	Goodwill		€130,000

2. In accordance with FRS 102, a first-time adopter is permitted to use the revalued amount as deemed cost, so the building would be included in the opening balance sheet at €200,000.

3. As LIFO is not permitted as a valuation method under FRS 102, the directors must write down the stock (inventory) as follows:

	€
Stock valuation under LIFO per previous GAAP balance sheet	14,500
Revised stock valuation under FRS 102 (AVCO)	10,370
Write down	4,130

Dr	Reserves	€4,130	
Cr	Stock		€4,130

4. Under the provisions of FRS 102, specifically at paragraph 29.17, the discounting of deferred tax balances is prohibited, so an adjustment to the deferred tax liability, a non-current liability in the previous GAAP balance sheet is required, calculated as follows:

	€
Deferred tax per previous GAAP balance sheet	20,000
Add back the effects of discounting (prohibited under FRS 102)	4,000
Revised deferred tax balance	24,000

Having revised the accounting policies to conform to FRS 102, on transition to FRS 102 the opening balance sheet of Strangford Ltd as at 1 January 2018 (the date of transition) would be as follows.

Strangford Ltd
RECONCILIATION OF CAPITAL AND RESERVES
as at 1 January 2018

	As previously stated under previous GAAP	**Effect of transition**	**FRS 102 (as restated)**
	€	**€**	**€**
Fixed Assets			
Goodwill	390,000	(130,000)	260,000
Property, plant and equipment	386,000		386,000
	776,000	(130,000)	646,000
Current Assets			
Inventory	14,500	(4,130)	10,370
Trade and other receivables	600,000		600,000
Cash and cash equivalents	290,000		290,000
	904,500	(4,130)	900,370

Creditors: amounts falling due within one year			
Trade and other payables	425,000		425,000
Net current assets	479,500	(4,130)	475,370
Total assets less current liabilities	1,255,500	(134,130)	1,121,370
Creditors: amounts falling due after more than one year			
Loans	116,000		116,000
Deferred taxation	20,000	(4,000)	24,000
	136,000	(4,000)	140,000
Net assets	**1,119,500**	**(138,130)**	**981,370**
Capital and Reserves			
Called-up share capital	1,000		1,000
Retained earnings	1,118,500	(138,130)	980,370
	1,119,500	**(138,130)**	**981,370**

A similar reconciliation would take place at the end of the reporting period for the balance sheet (at 31 December 2018).

Case Study 15.2: First-time Adoption

Portaferry Ltd started its operations on 1 January 2010 and elected a reporting date of 31 December. The entity has been preparing its financial statements under previous GAAP since January 2010.

In 2019 the entity's management decided to adopt FRS 102. The financial statements for the year ended 31 December 2019 are the first set of financial statements presented by Portaferry Ltd that comply with FRS 102, including an explicit and unreserved statement of compliance with the FRS. Those financial statements include only one year of comparative information (i.e. the year 2018). The entity's date of transition to FRS 102 is 1 January 2018.

Portaferry Ltd adopted some accounting policies that differ from the accounting policies required or allowed by FRS 102. The material differences from FRS 102 are:

(a) Depreciation of the entity's sales office in accordance with the previous financial reporting framework was calculated without reference to its residual value. Consequently, at 1 January 2018 the carrying amount of fixed assets was €5,000 lower than it would have been had the entity applied

FRS 102. Profit for 2018 was €1,200 lower than if FRS 102 was used.

(b) In accordance with previous GAAP at 1 January 2018, intangible assets included €3,000 for home-grown brands that, in accordance with the FRS 102, would have been recognised in goodwill because they do not qualify for recognition as separate intangible assets. The effect on profit for 2018 is not material.

(c) Financial assets that Section 11 *Basic Financial Instruments* and Section 12 *Other Financial Instruments Issues* require to be accounted for at fair value through profit or loss were, in accordance with previous GAAP, carried at cost. As a consequence, at 1 January 2018 the carrying amount is €1,100 lower than if the FRS 102 had been used. In 2018 the increase in fair value of these financial assets was €900.

(d) In accordance with previous GAAP, a number of overheads were excluded from the cost of inventory, as a result the carrying amount of inventories at 1 January 2018 is €3,000 lower than if FRS 102 had been used. For the same reason, the cost of sales for 2018 is €1,100 lower than if FRS 102 had been used.

(e) A hedge relationship that hedges the foreign exchange risk of a particular forecast sale (i.e. forward foreign exchange contract) exists at the date of transition. In accordance with the previous GAAP, the hedging instrument was carried at cost (nil) and €900 of unrealised foreign exchange gains on the unmatured hedging instrument was not recorded in equity. Under FRS 102, paragraph 12.16, the hedging instrument qualifies for hedge accounting. In 2018 the decrease in fair value of such financial assets was €200.

(f) In accordance with previous GAAP, the cash basis was used to account for a particular pension liability as it was treated as a defined contribution scheme. Subsequently, at 1 January 2018, it was redefined as a defined benefit scheme and an employee benefits liability of €1,300 needs to be created on the entity's balance sheet.

(g) At 1 January 2018, a restructuring provision of €3,100 relating to head office activities was recognised under FRS 12 *Provisions, Contingent Liabilities and Contingent Assets*, but does not qualify for recognition as a liability in accordance with FRS 102. In 2018 (after the date of transition to the FRS) the €3,100 restructuring provision qualified for recognition in accordance with the FRS.

The following information was extracted from the balance sheet of Portaferry Ltd as at 31 December 2017 (i.e. at 1 January 2018, the date of transition):

Portaferry Ltd
BALANCE SHEET (EXTRACT)
(prepared under previous GAAP)
as at 31 December 2017

	€	€
Fixed assets		
Property, plant and equipment	81,400	
Goodwill	15,300	
Intangible assets	6,200	
Financial assets	4,100	
Total non-current assets		107,000
Current assets		
Inventories	6,300	
Trade and other receivables	5,100	
Other receivables	1,100	
Cash and cash equivalents	2,300	
Total current assets	14,800	
Creditors: amounts falling due within one year		
Trade and other payables	7,800	
Net current assets		7,000
Total assets less current liabilities		114,000
Creditors: amounts falling due after more than one year		
Interest-bearing loans	19,600	
Restructuring provision	3,100	
Other liabilities	1,200	
Non-current liabilities		23,900
Net assets		90,100
Issued capital	15,000	
Retained earnings	75,100	
Total equity		90,100

The following information was extracted from the statement of comprehensive income of Portaferry Ltd for the year ended 31 December 2018:

Portaferry Ltd

STATEMENT OF COMPREHENSIVE INCOME (EXTRACT)
(prepared under previous GAAP)
as at 31 December 2018

	€
Revenue	65,300
Cost of sales	(31,800)
Gross profit	33,500
Distribution costs	(3,400)
Administrative expenses	(3,000)
Finance income	2,000
Finance costs	(4,000)
Profit for the year	25,100
Loss on translating of foreign operation	(1,200)
Total comprehensive income for the year	23,900

Solution

The following is the reconciliation of equity at 1 January 2018, i.e. the date of transition to the FRS:

RECONCILIATION OF EQUITY FROM PREVIOUS GAAP TO FRS 102
as at 1 January 2018 (date of transition to FRS 102)

Note		Previous GAAP	Effect of transition to FRS 102	FRS 102
		€	€	€
	Fixed assets			
1	Property, plant and equipment	81,400	5,000	86,400
2	Goodwill	15,300	3,000	18,300
2	Intangible assets	6,200	(3,000)	3,200
3	Financial assets	4,100	1,100	5,200
	Total non-current assets	107,000	6,100	113,100
	Current assets			
	Inventories	6,300	3,000	9,300
4	Trade and other receivables	5,100	-	5,100
5	Other receivables	1,100	900	2,000
	Cash and cash equivalents	2,300	–	2,300
	Total current assets	14,800	3,900	18,700

	Creditors: amounts falling due within one year			
	Trade and other payables	7,800	–	7,800
	Net current assets	7,000		10,900
	Total assets less current liabilities	114,000		124,000
	Creditors: amounts falling due after more than one year			
	Interest-bearing loans	19,600	–	19,600
6	Employee benefits	–	1,300	1,300
7	Restructuring provision	3,100	(3,100)	–
	Other liabilities	1,200	–	1,200
	Non-current liabilities	23,900	(1,800)	22,100
	Total assets less total liabilities	90,100	11,800	101,900
	Capital and reserves			
	Issued capital	15,000	–	15,000
5	Hedging reserve	–	900	900
8	Retained earnings	75,100	10,900	86,000
	Total equity	90,100	11,800	101,900

Notes to the reconciliation of equity at 1 January 2018:

1 Depreciation, in accordance with the previous financial reporting framework, ignored an asset's residual value, but in accordance with FRS 102 an asset's depreciable amount is net of its residual value. The cumulative adjustment increased the carrying amount of property, plant and equipment by €5,000.

2 Intangible assets in accordance with the previous financial reporting framework included €3,000 for items that are transferred to goodwill under FRS 102 because they do not qualify for recognition as intangible assets as only purchases of intangibles or intangibles acquired in a business combination are permitted on the balance sheet.

3 Particular financial assets are, in accordance with FRS 102, measured at fair value, with changes in fair value recognised in profit or loss. In accordance with the previous financial reporting framework, those financial assets were measured at cost. As a consequence, at 1 January 2018 the carrying amount is €1,100 lower than if FRS 102 had been used. The resulting gains are included in retained earnings.

4 Inventories include overheads of €3,000 in accordance with FRS 102, but which were excluded in accordance with the previous financial reporting framework.

5 Unrealised gains of €900 on unmatured forward foreign exchange contracts are recognised in accordance with FRS 102, but were not recognised in accordance with the previous financial reporting framework. The resulting gains of €900 are included in the hedging reserve because the contracts hedge forecast sales.
6 A pension liability of €1,300 is recognised in accordance with FRS 102, but was not recognised in accordance with the previous financial reporting framework, which used a cash basis as it was classified as a defined contribution scheme.
7 A restructuring provision of €3,100 relating to head office activities was recognised in accordance with the previous financial reporting framework, but does not qualify for recognition as a liability in accordance with FRS 102.
8 The adjustments to retained earnings are as follows:

	€
Depreciation (note 1)	5,000
Financial assets (note 3)	1,100
Overheads (note 4)	3,000
Pension liability (note 6)	(1,300)
Restructuring provision (note 7)	3,100
Total adjustment to retained earnings	10,900

The following is the reconciliation of total comprehensive income for 2018:

RECONCILIATION OF TOTAL COMPREHENSIVE INCOME
FROM PREVIOUS GAAP TO FRS 102
for the year to 31 December 2018

Note		Previous GAAP	Effect of transition to FRS 102	FRS 102
		€	€	€
	Revenue	65,300	–	65,300
1, 2	Cost of sales	(31,800)	(1,100)	(32,900)
	Gross profit	33,500	(1,100)	32,400
4	Other income	–	900	900
2	Distribution costs	(3,400)	1,200	(2,200)
3	Administrative expenses	(3,000)	(3,100)	(6,100)
	Finance income	2,000	–	2,000
	Finance costs	(4,000)	–	(4,000)
	Profit for the year	25,100	(2,100)	23,000

5	Cash flow hedges	–	(200)	(200)
	Loss of translating of foreign operation	(1,200)	–	(1,200)
	Other comprehensive income	(1,200)	(200)	(1,400)
	Total comprehensive income	23,900	(2,300)	21,600

Notes to the reconciliation of total comprehensive income for 2018:

1 Cost of sales is higher by €1,100 in accordance with FRS 102 because inventories include fixed and variable production overheads in accordance with the FRS that were not included under the previous financial reporting framework.

2 Depreciation of property, plant and equipment decreased by €1,200 during 2018 due to buildings depreciation taking account of the building's residual value in accordance with FRS 102, unlike the previous financial reporting framework.

3 A restructuring provision of €3,100 was recognised in accordance with the previous financial reporting framework at 1 January 2018, but did not qualify for recognition in accordance with IFRSs until the year ended 31 December 2018. This increases administrative expenses for 2018 in accordance with FRS 102.

4 Financial assets at fair value through profit or loss increased in value by €900 during 2018. They were carried at cost in accordance with the previous financial reporting framework. Fair value changes have been included in 'Other income'.

5 The fair value of forward foreign exchange contracts that are effective hedges of forecast transactions decreased by €200 during 2018.

A good example of an Irish company transitioning to FRS 102 was provided by Musgrave Group Plc in 2014. Relevant extracts from their financial statements are provided below.

Musgrave Group Plc

ANNUAL REPORT 2014 – NOTES TO THE FINANCIAL STATEMENTS (EXTRACTS)

Year ended 31 December 2014

38 Transition to FRS 102

This is the first year that the Group and Company has presented its results under FRS 102. The last financial statements prepared under the previous Irish GAAP were for the year ended 31 December 2013. The date of transition to FRS 102 was 1 January 2013. The transition to FRS 102 has resulted in a number of changes in accounting policies compared to those used previously. Set out below are the critical judgements on transition to FRS 102 and the impact from the changes in accounting policies which reconcile the total equity shareholders' funds as at 1 January 2013 and 31 December 2013 and loss for the financial year ended 31 December 2013 between Irish GAAP as previously reported and FRS 102.

The critical judgements in applying the entity's accounting policies are as follows:

a) Exemptions on transition to FRS 102 – Business combinations
The Group has elected not to avail of an exemption in FRS 102 which would have enabled it to avoid re-opening certain business combinations undertaken before the transition date for FRS 102. On that basis, the Group elected to apply FRS 102 rules retrospectively to the accounting for the acquisition of Superquinn Limited in 2011 in the transition sheet.

b) Exemptions on transition to FRS 102 – valuation of land and buildings
The Group has elected to use the valuation of certain land and buildings at 31 December 2012 as the deemed cost on transition to FRS 102 at the transition date of 1 January 2013. Furthermore, the Group has elected not to revalue land and buildings thereafter in the future. The assets are being depreciated from the date of transition (1 January 2013) in accordance with the Group's accounting policies.

c) Useful economic life of Superquinn brand
The Group took the decision to replace the Superquinn brand with SuperValu in December 2012 and this was effected in the relevant stores in February 2014. The Group decided that the useful economic life of the Superquinn brand on the balance sheet should be written off over this accelerated period of 14 months.

Equity reconciliation	Notes	At 1 January 2013 €m	At 31 December 2013 €m
Equity shareholders' funds – as previously reported		461.6	313.6
Restatement of previous business combination	i)	(17.5)	(33.0)
Deferred taxation on revaluation reserve	ii)	(8.5)	(8.5)

Tangible assets revaluation	iii)	-	3.0
Loans and advances to third parties	iv)	(1.9)	(1.7)
Complex financial instruments	v)	(0.2)	-
Defined benefit pension schemes (net of deferred tax)	vi)	0.8	1.4
Equity shareholders' funds – FRS 102		434.3	274.8

Reconciliation of loss for the financial year	Notes	Year ended 31 December 2013 €m
Loss for the financial year – as previously reported		(94.9)
Restatement of previous business combination	i)	(15.5)
Tangible assets revaluation	iii)	(3.7)
Loans and advances to third parties	iv)	0.2
Defined benefit pension schemes	vi)	0.6
		(18.4)
Loss for the financial year – FRS 102		(113.3)

Reconciliation of other comprehensive income	Notes	Year ended 31 December 2013 €m
Comprehensive loss for the financial year – as previously reported		(126.9)
Adjustments to loss for the financial year		(18.4)
Reversal of deficit on revaluation of land and buildings	iii)	5.8
Deficit on investment properties now brought to the profit and loss account	iii)	0.8
Fair value of derivatives	v)	0.2
Comprehensive loss for the financial year – FRS 102		(138.5)

The following notes are applicable to the reconciliations set out above and reflect changes in accounting policies arising from the transition to FRS 102.

i) Restatement of previous business combination
FRS 102 enables preparers of financial statements to avail of an exemption in respect of legacy business combinations and these can be accounted for based on previous GAAP at the transition date. The Group has chosen not to avail of this exemption. The Group has retrospectively applied FRS 102 accounting rules to the Superquinn business acquired in October 2011. As a result, the Group was required to value the intangible assets arising on the acquisition. The directors, advised by independent experts, valued the Superquinn brand at €43.0 million and Superquinn customer relationships at €6.0 million. A deferred tax liability of €6.1 million was recognised on the intangible assets and a further €4.2 million on the difference between the fair value and taxation value of the tangible assets acquired under FRS 102 rules. The combination of these adjustments resulted in a net decrease of €38.7 million in goodwill at the date of acquisition.

The impacts arising on the restatement of the acquisition of Superquinn are as follows:

	Equity reconciliation		**Profit and loss account reconciliation**
	At 1 January 2013 €m	At 31 December 2013 €m	Year-ended 31 December 2013 €m
Amortisation of brand	(21.4)	(40.6)	(19.2)
Amortisation of customer relationships	(1.4)	(2.3)	(0.9)
Reduction in goodwill amortisation	3.1	5.6	2.5
Movement in deferred taxation on amortisation of brands	2.8	5.3	2.5
and customer relationships			
Net other	(0.6)	(1.0)	(0.4)
Total	(17.5)	(33.0)	(15.5)

The directors made the decision to change the name of Superquinn to SuperValu during 2012 and this was announced in 2013 and put into effect in 2014. An accelerated write down of the Superquinn brand was recognised over this period based on the shortened expected useful life of the asset.

ii) Deferred taxation on the revaluation reserve
On transition to FRS 102, the Group recognised a deferred taxation liability of €8.5 million on the revaluation reserve for land and buildings at the transition date, as required by FRS 102. This was unchanged at 31 December 2013.

iii) Tangible assets revaluation
On transition to FRS 102, the Group has elected to use the previous valuation of certain land and buildings at 31 December 2012 as the deemed cost for those assets and to discontinue its policy of revaluing land and buildings. There is no effect on the balance sheet on the transition date of 1 January 2013. The revaluation loss of €5.8 million previously booked in 2013 was reversed along with €0.1 million of other adjustments, and this was offset by a €2.9 million charge to the profit and loss account for additional impairments required, resulting in a net €3.0 million increase in tangible assets and equity as at 31 December 2013.

Under FRS 102, movements in the value of investment properties are taken to the profit and loss account rather than the revaluation reserve. A €0.8 million revaluation loss arose in 2013 and combined with the €2.9 million adjustment above, this resulted in €3.7 million total charge to the profit and loss account in 2013.

iv) Loans and advances to third parties
Under FRS 102, debtors are classified as basic financial instruments which must be carried at amortised cost. Long terms loans advanced to third parties have been assessed under the requirements of Chapter 11 of FRS 102 and a number of these arrangements constitute financing transactions and, consequently, need to be measured at the present value of the future payments discounted at the market rate of interest for a similar debt instrument at the inception of the arrangement. This has resulted in a measurement difference on certain debtors, particularly any loans and advances that are long term and not subject to market rates of interest. The impact of this was to decrease the carrying value of debtors by €1.9 million at 1 January 2013 and by €1.7 million at 31 December 2013 being the future interest to be earned over the life of the loans. This also resulted in additional interest income of €0.2 million in the profit and loss account in 2013.

v) Complex financial instruments
The Group uses financial instruments to hedge the Group's currency and fuel exposures. FRS 102 requires that any such instruments are fair valued and recorded on the balance sheet. As these derivatives meet the requirements to be treated as a cash flow hedge under FRS 102, the movement in the fair value of the hedge is accounted for through reserves. The fair value adjustment was a €0.2 million loss at 1 January 2013 and €Nil million at 31 December 2013. The movement of €0.2 million in 2013 is shown in the statement of comprehensive income.

vi) Defined benefit pension schemes
FRS 102 has less prescriptive rules in relation to the recognition of a pension surplus, compared to previous GAAP. As a result, an additional pension surplus has been recognised of €0.8 million at the transition date of 1 January 2013 and €1.4 million at 31 December 2013 on certain of the Group's pension schemes with a corresponding reduction in the net pension liability.

FRS 102 also has different rules for the calculation of the pension interest expense compared to previous GAAP. Previously, interest on defined benefit pension schemes was based on the difference between the expected return on assets and the interest cost on liabilities. FRS 102 requires that interest must be calculated based on the net pension deficit or surplus.

The effect of this and certain other smaller adjustments was to reduce the interest charge by €1.0 million, increase operating costs by €0.2 million and increase deferred taxation by €0 2 million. The net impact was a €0.6 million charge to the profit and loss account and this was offset in other comprehensive income. Other comprehensive income also includes a gain of €0.6 million for the increase in the previously unrecognised surplus in 2013. These two items then net to €Nil million in the consolidated statement of comprehensive income in 2013.

Other changes
Based on a more prescriptive definition of turnover in FRS 102, retailer rebates previously included as a charge in cost of sales have now been deducted from turnover. Lotto commission and other revenue previously included as a credit within cost of sales has now been added to turnover. Retailer rebates were €166.0 million and lotto commission and other income was €1.5 million and therefore the net impact on turnover was a reduction of €164.5 million.

In addition, certain other reclassification adjustments were made along with a number of other immaterial adjustments.

Company
There were no adjustments to the Company's balance sheet at 1 January 2013 or 31 December 2013, or to the Company's profit and loss account for the year ended 31 December 2013, on transition FRS 102.

15.8 SMALL ENTITIES

For small entities, the transitional rules are the same with the following exceptions:

- **Fair value measurement of financial instruments** Small entities need not restate comparatives to comply with Sections 11 and 12 of FRS 102 unless fair valued under previous UK and Irish GAAP.
- **Financing transactions involving related parties** Small entities need not restate comparatives to comply with Section 11 insofar as they relate to related parties.

15.9 MICRO-ENTITIES

FRS 105 transitional rules are largely the same as FRS 102 with the exception set out below.

Investment Properties

There is no requirement to retrospectively apply paragraph 12.15 of FRS 105 to determine the depreciated cost of each of the major components of an investment property at the date of transition.

However, if FRS 105 is adopted, a micro-entity must:

"(i) Determine the total cost of the investment property including all of its components. Where no depreciation had been charged previously, this can be calculated by reversing any revaluation gains or losses previously recognised in equity reserves.
(ii) The cost of land, if any, must be separated from buildings.
(iii) Estimate the total depreciated cost of the investment property (excluding land) at the date of transition by recognising accumulated depreciation since the date of initial acquisition calculated on the basis of the useful life of the most significant component of the item of investment property (e.g. the main structural elements of the building).
(iv) A portion of the estimated total depreciated cost calculated in paragraph (iii) is then be allocated to each of the other major com-

ponents (i.e. excluding the most significant component identified above) to determine their depreciated cost. The allocation should be made on a reasonable and consistent basis e.g. possibly multiply the current cost to replace the component by the ratio of its remaining useful life to the expected useful life of a replacement component.

(v) Any amount of the total depreciated cost not allocated under paragraph (iv) is then allocated to the most significant component of the investment property."

Example 15.14: Investment Property Under FRS 105 Transition Rules

Micro Ltd is applying FRS 105 for the first time for the year ended 31 December 2019. The opening balance sheet as at 1 January 2018 has an investment property carried at open market value of €150,000 and a revaluation surplus of €30,000. The investment property was purchased on 1 January 2015 and the value of the land was €37,000.

Step 1
The transitional provision in Section 28 of FRS 105 can be applied. The revaluation surplus of €30,000 can be reversed against the cost of the investment property and hence at the date of transition the investment property will have a cost for FRS 105 purposes of €120,000 (€150,000 less €30,000).

Step 2
Once the cost has been established, the value of the land is taken into consideration and accounted for separately because land does not depreciate. This will then allow the depreciable amount of the asset to be calculated as follows:

Cost	€120,000
Less land	(€ 37,000)
Buildings	€ 83,000

Step 3
Once the depreciable amount has been calculated, depreciation must be calculated since the date of initial acquisition on the basis of the property's useful life of the most significant component of the property (i.e. the main structural element). If this is considered to be

50 years from the acquisition date, the depreciation charge since the date of acquisition is calculated as follows:

Date of purchase:	1 January 2015
Depreciable amount:	€83,000
Depreciation:	(€83,000 x 2%) x 3 years (i.e. to 1 January 2018) = €4,980

At the date of transition (1 January 2018) an adjustment will be required as follows:

Dr	Retained earnings (accumulated profit and loss)	€4,980
Cr	Accumulated depreciation (investment property)	€4,980

Step 4
On the date of transition, the investment property has a total depreciated cost of €78,020 (€83,000 less €4,980). This depreciated cost then needs to be allocated to each of the other major components (i.e. excluding the most significant component) to determine their depreciated cost.

The director has identified that the central heating system will need replacing in three years' time from 1 January 2018. The current cost to replace the central heating system is €15,000.

The central heating system has a considerably shorter life than the main structure of the investment property and hence should be depreciated separately from the remainder of the property. The depreciation charge in the 2018 comparative year is as follows:

	Investment Property €	Central Heating €	Total €
Depreciable amount	53,020	15,000	78,020
Depreciation charge	*1,060	**5,000	6,060

* €53,020 × 2%
** €15,000/3 years

Disclosure Checklist: Transitional Arrangements to Implementing – FRS 102

(References are to the relevant Section of FRS 102)

	Para.
Explanation of transition to this FRS	
An entity shall explain how the transition from its previous financial reporting framework to this FRS affected its reported financial position and financial performance.	35.12
Reconciliations	
An entity that has applied FRS 102 in a previous reporting period but not in its most recent annual financial statements, as described in paragraph 35.2, shall disclose: (a) the reason it stopped applying FRS 102; (b) the reason it is resuming the application of FRS 102; and (c) whether it has applied this section or has applied FRS 102 retrospectively in accordance with Section 10.	35.12A
To comply with paragraph 35.12, an entity's first financial statements prepared using this FRS shall include: (a) a description of the nature of each change in accounting policy; (b) reconciliations of its equity determined in accordance with its previous financial reporting framework to its equity determined in accordance with this FRS for both of the following dates: (i) the date of transition to this FRS, and (ii) the end of the latest period presented in the entity's most recent annual financial statements determined in accordance with its previous financial reporting framework; (c) a reconciliation of the profit or loss determined in accordance with its previous financial reporting framework for the latest period in the entity's most recent annual financial statements to its profit or loss determined in accordance with this FRS for the same period.	35.13
If an entity becomes aware of errors made under its previous financial reporting framework, the reconciliations required by paragraph 35.13(b) and (c) shall, to the extent practicable, distinguish the correction of those errors from changes in accounting policies.	35.14
If an entity did not present financial statements for previous periods, it shall disclose that fact in its first financial statements that conform to this FRS.	35.15

Disclosure Checklist: Transition to FRS 102 – Small Entities

The disclosures are the same in Section 1A as for FRS 102.

Disclosure Checklist: Transition to FRS 105

There are no specific disclosures required.

Index